Educational Media and Technology Yearbook

More information about this series at http://www.springer.com/series/8617

Robert Maribe Branch • Hyewon Lee
Sheng-Shiang Tseng
Editors

Educational Media and Technology Yearbook

Volume 43 (2020)

Editors
Robert Maribe Branch
Learning, Design, and Technology
University of Georgia
Athens, GA, USA

Hyewon Lee
Learning, Design, and Technology
University of Georgia
Athens, GA, USA

Sheng-Shiang Tseng
Graduate Institute of Curriculum
and Instruction
Tamkang University
New Taipei City, Taiwan

ISSN 8755-2094
Educational Media and Technology Yearbook
ISBN 978-3-030-71773-5   ISBN 978-3-030-71774-2   (eBook)
https://doi.org/10.1007/978-3-030-71774-2

© Association for Educational Communications and Technology (AECT) 2021
This work is subject to copyright. All rights are reserved by the Publisher, whether the whole or part of the material is concerned, specifically the rights of translation, reprinting, reuse of illustrations, recitation, broadcasting, reproduction on microfilms or in any other physical way, and transmission or information storage and retrieval, electronic adaptation, computer software, or by similar or dissimilar methodology now known or hereafter developed.
The use of general descriptive names, registered names, trademarks, service marks, etc. in this publication does not imply, even in the absence of a specific statement, that such names are exempt from the relevant protective laws and regulations and therefore free for general use.
The publisher, the authors, and the editors are safe to assume that the advice and information in this book are believed to be true and accurate at the date of publication. Neither the publisher nor the authors or the editors give a warranty, expressed or implied, with respect to the material contained herein or for any errors or omissions that may have been made. The publisher remains neutral with regard to jurisdictional claims in published maps and institutional affiliations.

This Springer imprint is published by the registered company Springer Nature Switzerland AG
The registered company address is: Gewerbestrasse 11, 6330 Cham, Switzerland

Preface

Welcome to Volume 43 of the *Educational Media and Technology Yearbook*. The audience for the *Yearbook* typically consists of media and technology professionals in K-12 schools, higher education, and business contexts. The *Yearbook* editors have dedicated themselves to providing a record of contemporary trends related to educational communications and technology. They also strive to highlight special movements that have clearly influenced the educational technology field.

This volume also continues the tradition of offering topics of interest to professionals practicing in other areas of educational media and technology, as the Table of Contents demonstrates. All papers submitted to the *Yearbook* are subject to rigorous editorial review, and each set of authors is provided with multiple rounds of feedback on the quality of their work and manuscripts. As in prior volumes, the assumptions underlying the chapters are as follows:

1. Technology represents tools that act as extensions of the educator.
2. Media serve as delivery systems for educational communications.
3. Technology can be interpreted as machines and hardware, but technology also includes techniques and procedures derived from scientific research into ways to promote change in human performance.
4. That educational media and technology should be used to:

    (a) Achieve authentic learning outcomes
    (b) Situate learning tasks
    (c) Negotiate the complexities of guided learning
    (d) Facilitate the construction of knowledge
    (e) Aid in the assessment of learning
    (f) Support skill acquisition
    (g) Facilitate diversity

The *Educational Media and Technology Yearbook* has become a standard reference in many libraries and professional collections. Examined in relation to its companion volumes of the past, it provides a valuable historical record of current ideas and developments in the field of information and communication technology. Feel free to share your perspectives about the *Educational Media and Technology Yearbook* with the editor at rbranch@uga.edu.

Athens, GA, USA   Robert Maribe Branch
Athens, GA, USA   Hyewon Lee
New Taipei City, Taiwan   Sheng-Shiang Tseng

Acknowledgments

This book presents trends and issues in instructional technology and has been supported and encouraged in different ways by many to whom we owe a debt of gratitude. We would like to acknowledge their support and contributions to this book. We greatly appreciate the work of the book editors for their outstanding contributions. We are also thankful for the authors who submitted their manuscripts to the *Educational Media and Technology Yearbook* (Vol. 43): Senenge T. Andzenge, Abbie Brown, Kuo Hsiao Chien, Philena DeVaughn, Robert G. Doyle, Timothy Green, Brad Hokanson, Hyewon Lee, John Mativo, Isaac Pfleger, Jill Stefaniak, Sheng-Shiang Tseng, Rick West, and Xigui Yang. This book would not have been possible without their generosity in sharing their research.

Contents

Part I Trends and Issues in Learning, Design, and Technology

**Issues and Trends in Instructional Technology:
Increased Engagement with Distance Learning Informs
Live Instruction and Classroom Design** 3
Abbie Brown and Tim Green

Synchronous Distance Education and Being Live Online 13
Brad Hokanson and Senenge T. Andzenge

**The Preparation of Instructional Designers: An Exploration
of Design Pedagogy and Praxis** 17
Jill Stefaniak, Xigui Yang, and Philena DeVaughn

Robotics Education as an Integrator Tool 33
John Mativo

The 2020 Scholarship Rankings 43
Richard E. West and Isaac Pfleger

Part II Leadership Profiles

Introduction 59
Robert G. Doyle

Phil Harris 63
Robert G. Doyle

Barbara Lockee 67
Robert G. Doyle

Part III Organizations and Associations in North America

Introduction 75
Robert Maribe Branch

Organizations and Associations in the USA and Canada 77
Robert Maribe Branch

Part IV Graduate Programs

Introduction 151
Kuo Hsiao Chien, Hyewon Lee, and Sheng-Shiang Tseng

**Graduate Programs in Learning, Design, Technology,
Information, or Libraries** 153
Kuo Hsiao Chien, Hyewon Lee, and Sheng-Shiang Tseng

Part V Mediagraphy

Introduction 281
Sheng-Shiang Tseng

Mediagraphy 285
Sheng-Shiang Tseng

Index 305

Contributors

Senenge T. Andzenge University of Minnesota, Minneapolis, MN, USA

Robert Maribe Branch Learning, Design, and Technology, University of Georgia, Athens, GA, USA

Abbie Brown Department of Mathematics, Science, & Instructional Technology Education, East Carolina University, Greenville, NC, USA

Kuo Hsiao Chien Graduate Institute of Curriculum and Instruction, Tamkang University, New Taipei City, Taiwan

Philena DeVaughn Predestinated Image Consulting, Waldorf, MA, USA

Robert G. Doyle Harvard University, Cambridge, MA, USA

Tim Green Department of Elementary and Bilingual Education, California State University, Fullerton, CA, USA

Brad Hokanson College of Design, University of Minnesota, St. Paul, MN, USA

Hyewon Lee Learning, Design, and Technology, University of Georgia, Athens, GA, USA

John Mativo Department of Career and Information Studies (Workforce Education), University of Georgia, Athens, GA, USA

Isaac Pfleger IPT Department, Brigham Young University, Provo, UT, USA

Jill Stefaniak Learning, Design, and Technology, University of Georgia, Athens, GA, USA

Sheng-Shiang Tseng Graduate Institute of Curriculum and Instruction, Tamkang University, New Taipei City, Taiwan

Richard E. West IPT Department, Brigham Young University, Provo, UT, USA

Xigui Yang Learning, Design, and Technology, University of Georgia, Athens, GA, USA

Part I
Trends and Issues in Learning, Design, and Technology

Issues and Trends in Instructional Technology: Increased Engagement with Distance Learning Informs Live Instruction and Classroom Design

Abbie Brown and Tim Green

We continue the tradition of reporting the past year's issues and trends that shape attitudes and approaches to instructional technology. This chapter is comprised of four sections: Overall Developments, Corporate Training and Development, Higher Education, and K-12 Settings. The trends and issues described are based on major annual reports sponsored and/or conducted by organizations including the Association for Talent Development (ATD), EDUCAUSE, The eLearning Guild, Gartner Incorporated, Inside Higher Ed and Gallup, the Babson Survey Research Group, Education Week, and Project Tomorrow. These reports require time in terms of data collection, interpretation, and publication, the shortest of which take a year to complete, and therefore reflect the issues and trends of large groups over long periods of time. For a more immediate review of trending topics in instructional technology, please refer to the authors' biweekly podcast, *Trends & Issues in Instructional Design, Educational Technology, & Learning Sciences* (Brown & Green, 2020).

A. Brown (✉)
Department of Mathematics, Science, & Instructional Technology Education, East Carolina University, Greenville, NC, USA
e-mail: brownab@ecu.edu

T. Green
Department of Elementary and Bilingual Education, California State University, Fullerton, CA, USA

© The Author(s), under exclusive license to Springer Nature Switzerland AG 2021
R. M. Branch et al. (eds.), *Educational Media and Technology Yearbook*,
Educational Media and Technology Yearbook 43,
https://doi.org/10.1007/978-3-030-71774-2_1

1 Overall Developments

The reports reviewed indicate that the integration of instructional technology remains a priority in all three sectors. This is a similar theme of the past two reviews (Brown & Green, 2018, 2019). Spending on instructional technology in the three sectors increased over the previous year. The estimated spending for the year was slightly over $13 billion in K-12 with $8.4 billion of this amount spent on software (Davis, 2019; J-Pal North America, 2019). The total spending on state and local education instructional technology was estimated at $28 billion (GovTech Navigator, 2019). During the year under review, the use of instructional technology supported innovative design and delivery of teaching and learning with continued emphasis on the use of mobile devices and access to digital content (including open educational resources). Evident across all three sectors was the continued use of online delivery methods for instruction and training.

2 Corporate Training and Development

As with previous issues and trends chapters of this yearbook (e.g., Brown & Green, 2018, 2019), we continue to track corporate application of instructional technologies primarily by referring to the *State of the Industry* (Ho, 2019) report published by the Association for Talent Development (ATD). The report is based on data collected from organizations regularly submitting annual data, BEST award winners (organizations recognized by ATD for their exceptional efforts in support of learning within the enterprise), and a consolidated group of organizations that submitted their data via an online survey. This represents data collected in 2018 from 318 business organizations, 59 of which are ATD Best Award winners; the average number of employees is 14,406 (Ho, 2019). Additional sources used in this section are The eLearning Guild's *2018 Global eLearning Salary & Compensation Report* (Smolen, 2018), the U.S. Bureau of Statistics' *Occupational Outlook Handbook* (2019), and Gartner Incorporated's strategic technology trends report (Cearley & Burke, 2019).

2.1 Learning Expenditures

Among business organizations responding to ATD's *State of the Industry Report* survey, the average learning expenditure in 2018 was $1299 per employee (Ho, 2019). This represents a slight increase over the previous year and continues the upward trend from previous years. On average, this amount represents just under 4% of the organization's payroll and a little over 1% of its annual revenue (Ho, 2019). Expenditures for instructional development, delivery, and administration were divided among direct learning expenditures (62%), outsource learning suppliers (27%), and tuition reimbursement (11%) (Ho, 2019). This is similar to previous years' expenditures (Brown & Green, 2019).

When examining learning costs per person, company size is an important consideration. Large companies with 10,000 employees or more had an average direct learning expenditure of $707, while companies with fewer than 500 employees paid $2412. Larger companies reported workers engaged in considerably more hours of learning; the economies of scale work in favor of the larger organizations that can spread development and delivery costs (Ho, 2019).

2.2 Instructional Content

According to ATD's *State of the Industry Report*, the three most common instructional content areas developed and delivered in 2018 were related to management and supervision instruction (14%), mandatory and compliance training (13%), and interpersonal skill instruction (10%) (Ho, 2019); this is similar to previous years (Brown & Green, 2019). In 2018, ATD and LinkedIn both noted the need for interpersonal skill instruction in particular (Ho, 2019).

In their *Gartner Trend Insight Report*, Cearley and Burke (2019) describe the impact of artificial intelligence (AI), the Internet of Things (IoT), immersive digital experiences (such as virtual reality and augmented reality), and the increasingly seamless blending of digital and "real-world" activities on businesses. The authors note from a review of articles collected for their podcast series (Brown & Green, 2020) that a significant portion of instruction was devoted to each of these areas to prepare organizations and their constituents for their integration into general business practice.

2.3 Methods of Instructional Delivery

Instructor-led, face-to-face classroom instruction was the delivery method for 54% of the instructions documented in ATD's most recent *State of the Industry* report. This is consistent with the past few years (Brown & Green, 2019; Ho, 2019). Live and asynchronous, virtual classrooms were used for 11% of the documented instruction. About 22% of documented instruction was delivered as self-paced, online learning or eLearning (Ho, 2019). Overall, this indicates that the vast majority of instruction was delivered by a live facilitator, though a smaller but significant amount of instruction was delivered as eLearning. Ho's commentary (2019) emphasizes the importance of the live facilitator as a constant element in corporate instructional delivery.

2.4   Instructional Designers' Professional Prospects

According to The eLearning Guild's latest salary and compensation report, the average eLearning salary increased approximately 2% in 2018 from the previous year (Smolen, 2018). Globally, annual salaries range widely, between $84,421 in the United States (the highest ever reported) and $38,534 in India (Smolen, 2018).

In its *Occupational Outlook Handbook* (2019), the United States Office of Occupational Statistics and Employment Projections lists Instructional Coordinators and Training and Development Specialists as occupation categories encompassing instructional design in school and corporate settings, respectively. School positions typically require a master's degree and the median salary is $64,450; corporate positions typically require a bachelor's degree and the median salary is $60,870. According to Recruiter.com (2020), the instructional design/technology position vacancies in the United States have increased over 20% since 2004 and are expected to continue going up. Following the trend of recent years (Brown & Green, 2019), instructional design/technology positions have continued to be an attractive and lucrative career choice in the corporate sector.

3   Higher Education

We review higher education's instructional technology application by referring primarily to the *EDUCAUSE Horizon Report: 2019 Higher Education Edition* (Alexander et al., 2019); the Babson Survey Research Group's *Grade Increase: Tracking Distance Education in the United States* (Seaman, Allen, & Seaman, 2018); the EDUCAUSE Center for Analysis and Research (ECAR) studies, *ECAR Study of Undergraduate Students and Information Technology, 2019* (Gierdowski, 2019), and *Higher Education's 2019 Trend Watch and Top 10 Strategic Technologies* (Brooks & McCormack, 2019); and the *2019 Survey of Faculty Attitudes on Technology: A Study by Inside Higher Ed and Gallup* (Jaschik & Lederman, 2019). The EDUCAUSE and ECAR data, the Inside Higher Ed and Gallup study, and the Babson Research Group's report are based on large-scale survey results. *The Horizon Report* is a synthesis of responses from an international panel of experts.

3.1   Technology on Campus, in Classrooms, and Online

The *Horizon Report: Higher Education Edition* (Alexander et al., 2019), *Higher Education's Trend Watch and Top 10 Strategic Strategies* (Brooks & McCormack, 2019), and the *ECAR Study of Undergraduate Students and Information Technology* (Gierdowski, 2019) identify on-campus learning spaces as both critically important and an opportunity to incorporate technology in innovative ways. The ECAR undergraduate study found a large majority of students (70%) to prefer face-to-face learning environments (Gierdowski, 2019). The Horizon Report describes redesigning learning spaces as a short-term trend accelerating technology adoption (Alexander et al., 2019), while Brooks and McCormack (2019) report that private and public doctoral institutions are engaged in creating "active learning classrooms" (ACLs) which make use of movable furniture, large monitor displays, and other tools to support innovative instructional practice.

The past year's discussions regarding redesigning learning spaces were not limited to physical classrooms on campus. Virtual reality (VR), augmented reality (AR), and the umbrella term for both extended reality (XR) received a great deal of attention from digital learning leaders. The Horizon Report (Alexander et al., 2019) notes VR, AR, and XR as a short-term trend accelerating technology adoption similar to that of physical ACLs.

The ECAR study of undergraduates indicates that students continue to bring a variety of their own devices to campus. Over 60% of the students responding reported that their instructors use technology in their teaching, though it is not always with students' own devices (Gierdowski, 2019).

The increasing complexity and diversity of digital security threats are noted by Brooks and McCormack (2019) and it was a trend regularly reported by the authors over the past year (Brown & Green, 2020). Security concerns influence who is provided access to institutional networks and what devices are allowed to operate within those networks. These concerns therefore guided how technologies were employed for instructional purposes.

It must also be noted that the credentialing initiatives, referred to within the Horizon Report as "modularized and disaggregated degrees," were a topic of interest over the past year (Alexander et al., 2019; Brooks & McCormack, 2019; Brown & Green, 2020). The discussion and initiatives are focused on providing shorter, more flexible learning experiences that are credit bearing or otherwise validated.

3.2 Faculty Use of Technology for Instruction

The 2019 Survey of Faculty Attitudes on Technology (Jaschik & Lederman, 2019) found 35% of responding faculty to be identified as "early adopters" of new educational technologies. The study also reports a significant increase in faculty support for increased use of educational technologies (up 7% from the previous year). There was a significant increase in the number of faculty teaching blended, hybrid, or completely online courses as reported by Jaschik and Lederman (2019) as well as Seaman et al. (2018), though the vast majority of faculty make use of their institution's learning management system (LMS) primarily to share syllabus information and record grades (Jaschik & Lederman, 2019).

3.3 Teaching and Learning Online

Seaman et al. (2018) reported continued distance education enrollment increases in spite of general enrollment declines at higher education institutions and the issues surrounding the largest for-profit distance education institutions. More students studying in traditional campus settings have enrolled in online courses and the majority of online students are local; more than half took distance courses in combination with on-campus courses (Seaman et al., 2018).

Faculty are increasingly engaged in teaching online (Jaschik & Lederman, 2019) and the vast majority report that the experience has improved their teaching overall. Thirty-nine percent of faculty responding to the *Faculty Attitudes on Technology* survey reported working with an instructional designer and over 90% reported the experience as a good one (Jaschik & Lederman, 2019).

3.4 Student Use of Technology for Learning

As noted earlier in this section, students are bringing to campus a variety of networked computing devices (Gierdowski, 2019). Students also report finding online tools provided by their institutions that help with things like degree planning and auditing, as well as self-service referral systems for social and community resources to be increasingly useful (Gierdowski, 2019).

While undergraduate students generally prefer live activities such as lectures, labs, and conferences, they view technology as a means to extend their engagement with instructors and classmates. Blended learning designs are considered a trend driving technology adoption in higher education settings (Alexander et al., 2019) and the majority of students surveyed prefer forms of blended learning in which networked technologies facilitate collaboration, assignment submission, peer review, and question and answer (Gierdowski, 2019).

4 K-12 Education

We predominantly consult annual reports published by the Digital Learning Collaborative, Education Week, National Education Policy Center, and Project Tomorrow. The major reports we accessed were by the Digital Learning Collaborative, Education Week, National Education Policy Center, and Project Tomorrow. The major reports we accessed were *Keeping Pace with Digital Learning Report* (Digital Learning Collaborative, 2019); *Technology Counts 2019: Educators Tear Through the Hype* (Education Week, 2019); and *Digital Learning: Peril or Promise for Our K-12 Students* (Evans, 2019). *Technology Counts 2019* is the 20th edition of the report published by *Education Week*. This annual report focuses on the use of educational technology in K-12 schools. *Digital Learning: Peril or Promise for Our K-12 Students* is the most recent report published from the annual Speak Up Survey conducted by Project Tomorrow. This report focuses on students, parents, teachers, and administrator perceptions about and use of educational technology. The report was an analysis of data collected from 343,500 K-12 educators, students, parents, and administrators in the United States. *Keeping Pace with Digital Learning Report* is an annual report (except for 2017 and 2018) on the state of digital learning in K-12 in the United States.

4.1 Technology Availability and Use in Classrooms

The estimated spending for the year was slightly over $13 billion in K-12 with $8.4 billion of this amount spent on software (Davis, 2019; J-Pal North America, 2019). This is an increase from what was reported in our last review when we reported that approximately $12 billion was spent on instructional technology in K-12 (Brown & Green, 2019). Spending on instructional technology has continued to increase and the use of instructional technology continues to remain prevalent in K-12 classrooms.

According to the *State of the States Report* by Education Superhighway (2019), 99% of school districts have Internet access at the minimum of 100 kpbs. They reported that 46.3 million students have access at this speed. This is an increase of 1.6 million from 2018 to 2019 (p. 4). In addition to the students, there were 2.8 million teachers connected. The report also indicated that the median cost of Internet access has significantly decreased since 2013 from $22 per Mpbs to $2.24 per Mpbs in 2019 (p. 8).

The *State of the States Report* (2019) indicated, "Since 2015, students with access to digital learning in every classroom every day has grown" (p. 13). This has resulted in currently 94% of school districts with at least half of their classrooms using digital learning every week. According to the report, "90% of school districts are providing software, digital curriculum and devices specifically to encourage personalized learning and more than two-thirds of schools have dedicated instructional technologists" (p. 14). The report also indicates that about half of the teachers surveyed indicated that they were incorporating coding and over 50% were using video-based content (p. 14). This data is similar to the data reported by Gallup (2019) in the *Educational Technology Use in Schools Report*, which indicated that 65% of K-12 teachers surveyed (3210) indicated using digital learning tools every day to teach while 22% indicated using them a few days a week and 13% used these tools one or fewer times per week (p. 9).

Students have access to a variety of digital learning tools using various computing devices. The *Educational Technology Use in Schools Report* (Gallup, Inc, 2019) indicated that the 2696 US students surveyed indicated, "they use devices in a library or other room (41%), are given their own device to use (41%) or access devices on carts that are shared across classrooms (38%). About one-third say their classrooms are equipped with devices and 23% say they use their own personal device" (p. 9). The use of personal devices in K-12 schools by students surveyed was reported as 32% of high school students indicated that they are allowed to use personal devices "often or always to learn at school, compared with 15% of middle school students and 7% of elementary school students surveyed" (p. 9).

According to the Project Tomorrow's Speak Up Report, *Digital Learning: Peril or Promise for Our K-12 Students* (Evans, 2019), "students are likely to use multiple devices to support class-based learning" (para. 9). The report indicated, "The type of computing device varies by grade level with the youngest students more likely to use a tablet while their older siblings use a Chromebook type appliance" (para. 8). Sixty-four percent of students surveyed indicated having access to a Chromebook—an increase of 138% in student access to Chromebooks over the past 4 years (para. 7). Despite the use of digital technologies in K-12 classrooms, emerging technologies may not be used as widely as would be expected. The report indicated, "Other emerging technologies that are popular in media or at education technology conferences such as augmented reality, virtual reality environments or artificial intelligence have been implemented to date by less than 10% of schools" (para. 7).

In addition to instructional technology use in physical classrooms, the use of technology to support online schools increased. The *Keeping Pace with Digital Learning Report: Snapshot 2019 – A Review of K-12 Online, Blended, and Digital Learning Report* (Digital Learning Collaborative, 2019) indicates, "Enrollments in online schools that serve students across entire states are growing slowly but steadily, at a rate of about 6% per year" (p.). The report estimated that 310,000 students are enrolled in these schools across 32 states. Additionally, "State virtual schools (generally, supplemental online course programs that are state-supported) operate in 23 states, and serve about 420,000 students with almost a million online course enrollments" (Digital Learning Collaborative, 2019, p. 5).

4.2 Trends to Watch in K-12

We indicated in last year's review (Brown & Green, 2019) that data from reports we reviewed indicated that trends to watch were makerspaces, computer science (e.g., programming and coding), robotics, augmented reality, virtual reality, artificial intelligence and deep learning, and the Internet of Things. These trends were in addition to the continued trends of online learning and personalized learning that we discussed in our 2018 review (Brown & Green, 2018). For our current review, reports we reviewed along with our observations made on our biweekly podcast on trends and issues in instructional design, educational technology, and learning sciences (Brown & Green, 2020) indicate that online learning, mobile devices, mixed reality, open educational resources, cybersecurity, student data privacy, and digital citizenship are trends to watch.

5 Conclusion

The use of instructional technology remained pervasive in corporate training, higher education, and K-12 settings during the review period comprising this chapter. There remains a positive outlook for job prospects for instructional designers, training and development specialists, and eLearning practitioners in the upcoming year. The use of online learning remained a strong approach used in higher education and in K-12. An increase in corporate settings was observed. Continued use of online learning is predicted with the increase in fidelity and availability of different delivery tools (e.g., mixed reality, mobile devices, open educational resources). Access to and use of mobile devices and digital content continued to be used in all three sectors. Spending on instructional technology in all three sectors saw a slight increase from the previous review. Predictions are for continued spending on IT for the near future.

References

Alexander, B., Ashford-Rowe, K., Barajas-Murphy, N., Dobbin, G., Knott, J., McCormack, M., … Weber, N. (2019). *EDUCAUSE horizon report: 2019 higher education edition*. Louisville, CO: EDUCAUSE.

Brooks, D. C., & McCormack, M. (2019). *Higher education's 2019 trend watch and top 10 strategic technologies*. Louisville, CO: ECAR.

Brown, A., & Green, T. (2018). Issues and trends in instructional technology: Consistent growth in online learning, digital content, and the use of Mobile technologies. In R. M. Branch (Ed.), *Educational media and technology yearbook* (Vol. 41, pp. 61–71). New York: Springer.

Brown, A., & Green, T. (2019). Issues and trends in instructional technology: Access to Mobile technologies, digital content, and online learning opportunities continues as spending on IT remains steady. In R. M. Branch, H. Lee, & S. S. Tseng (Eds.), *Educational media and technology yearbook* (Vol. 42, pp. 3–12). New York: Springer.

Brown, A., & Green, T. (2020). *Trends and issues in instructional design, educational technology, and learning sciences* [Audio Podcast Series]. http://trendsandissues.com/

Cearley, D., & Burke, B. (2019). *Top 10 strategic technology trends for 2019: A Gartner trend insight report*. Stamford, CT: Gartner.

Davis, M. R. (2019). K-12 districts wasting millions by not using purchased software, new analysis finds. EDWEEK Market Brief. https://marketbrief.edweek.org/marketplace-k-12/unused-educational-software-major-source-wasted-k-12-spending-new-analysis-finds/

Digital Learning Collaborative. (2019). *Snapshot 2019: A review of K-12 online, blended, and digital learning*. https://www.digitallearningcollab.com

Education Superhighway. (2019). *State of the states*. https://stateofthestates.educationsuperhighway.org/#national

Education Week. (2019). *Technology counts 2019: Educators tear through the hype*. https://www.edweek.org/ew/collections/technology-counts-2019/index.html

Evans, J. (2019). *Digital learning: Peril or promise for uur k-12 students*. https://tomorrow.org/Speakup/downloads/2018_19-Speak-Up-National-Congressional-Briefing-Paper.pdf

Gallup, Inc. (2019). *Education technology use in schools: Student and educator perspectives*. http://www.newschools.org/wp-content/uploads/2019/09/Gallup-Ed-Tech-Use-in-Schools-2.pdf

Gierdowski, D. C. (2019). *ECAR study of undergraduate students and information technology, 2019*. Louisville, CO: EDUCAUSE.

GovTech Navigator. (2019). *2019 state and local education IT spend*. https://www.govtech.com/navigator/numbers/2019-state-and-local-government-ed_218.html

Ho, M. (2019). *2019 state of the industry: Talent development benchmarks and trends*. Alexandria, VA: ATD Research.

Jaschik, S., & Lederman, D. (2019). *2019 survey of faculty attitudes on technology: A study by inside higher Ed and Gallup*. Washington, DC: Inside Higher Ed.

J-Pal North America. (2019). What 126 studies say about educational technology. MIT News. http://news.mit.edu/2019/mit-jpal-what-126-studies-tell-us-about-education-technology-impact-0226

Recruiter.com. (2020). *Career outlook for instructional designers and technologists*. https://www.recruiter.com/careers/instructional-designers-and-technologists/outlook/

Seaman, J. E., Allen, I. E., & Seaman, J. (2018). *Grade increase: Tracking distance education in the United States*. Babson Park, MA: Babson Survey Research Group.

Smolen, T. (2018). *2018 global eLearning salary & compensation report*. Santa Rosa, CA: The eLearning Guild.

United States Bureau of Statistics Office of Occupational Statistics and Employment Projections. (2019). *Occupational outlook handbook*. Washington, DC: U.S. Bureau of Labor Statistics. https://www.bls.gov/ooh/

Synchronous Distance Education and Being Live Online

Brad Hokanson and Senenge T. Andzenge

How much has been lost in pursuit of convenience with the "learning anytime, anywhere" model? This aphorism stresses delivery and access as central goals of its broad application. Distance or technology-enhanced learning is an important step forward for education in general, but the learning effectiveness is low. Much of the challenge has come from a lack of learner engagement caused at least in part due to a lack of regular meeting times and personal connections. Education has surrendered to expediency in seeking learner access for an increasing heavy use of online education.

Compared to a face-to-face class experience, success in online learning is hindered by choices organized around an anytime learning model. Educators are not able to use many of the social elements of synchronous or face-to-face education to support learners. These include immediate feedback and interaction, high-fidelity communication, timely response to questions, and personal attention from faculty.

At the same time (pun intended), a developing technology trend available for higher education to use is synchronous video communication. Bolstered by technological improvements for video meetings, bandwidth, and interaction, some areas of education already make significant use of synchronous educational practice. For example, online high schools often make heavy use of online audio and video technologies. These have the potential to communicate with greater fidelity and immediacy than the inherent delay of asynchronous communication. As online classes

---

B. Hokanson (✉)
College of Design, University of Minnesota, St. Paul, MN, USA
e-mail: brad@umn.edu

S. T. Andzenge
University of Minnesota, Minneapolis, MN, USA
e-mail: senenge@umn.edu

© The Author(s), under exclusive license to Springer Nature Switzerland AG 2021
R. M. Branch et al. (eds.), *Educational Media and Technology Yearbook*,
Educational Media and Technology Yearbook 43,
https://doi.org/10.1007/978-3-030-71774-2_2

rely on student self-motivation, synchronous activities can also increase participation and engagement.

In addition to online tutoring by audio and video connection, some high schools offer a broad use of video meeting technology for student group meetings, study groups, and team projects. An example of the bricolage-form applications of video meeting technology is described by Elisha Raffa of the Minnesota Online High School:

> We wanted a system that could support active learning. We chose Elluminate, now Blackboard Collaborate, for the collision potential—especially the interactive whiteboard and breakout rooms. We planned to use it for online office hours, counseling and tutoring sessions, class meetings, open houses, back-to-school nights, and student council (StuCo) meetings. We never imagined how creative collisions like party games and talent shows could also knit together an online learning community (Raffa, n.d.).

Synchronous, set time events have a richness and immediacy that are more compelling and engaging than asynchronous events. As proof, we can view the example of our own practice in other areas. Most sports fans would eagerly view a live television broadcast, while few prefer to record a sports event for later viewing. Tickets to live concerts are often sold out even though studio-quality recording is readily available. And museums often tout the value of the live, viewing experience. These events are immediate, personal, and not offered at "anytime." They are also designed to be shared, authentic, and more like experiences learners will have in real-world contexts.

An early precursor of the technology, remote, coax television-based classrooms are also common in K-12 education, and are currently being upgraded to Internet-based systems. While some higher educational systems utilize the technologies, their use is still at the nascent level and is generally limited to meetings and not educational purposes.

Away from curricular uses, there are a number of available tools in use that provide synchronous communication and interaction inside and outside of education. For example, BestBuy Corporation uses synchronous technology to coordinate between offices in Minnesota, India, and Washington. Organizations such as AECT use it to support meetings across time zones and countries. Synchronous video meetings are now offered by a range of providers, including Zoom, Webex, Adobe, Skype, and Saba Meeting. These are commonly used in a variety of ways such as candidate interviews, planning sessions, and brainstorming sessions. It is now common for educational searches to have "Skype" interviews for a first round. While the technology is widely used, it is not currently widely utilized for supporting learners. It is also beginning to be integrated into major course management systems such as Canvas, Moodle, and Brightpoint/D2L.

Besides uses of video for synchronous online communications, live web chat is widely used by companies such as Internet service providers for tutorials and technical support. Although these experiences happen randomly and sporadically, instructors have used web chat to facilitate tutorials and hold office hours for camera-shy students or for students who require texts and transcripts to better accommodate their learning.

Like regularly scheduled face-to-face classes, regular synchronous events can be added into learner's schedules, as they would do in a regular class. The authors have experienced some pushback during online courses in scheduling set-time group meetings, but it is not uncommon for individuals to schedule personal distant connections. For example, we all set times for a special FaceTime call.

Synchronous events can also help provide the learner with a cognitive scaffolding in developing a regular habit for addressing online classwork. When not provided with a scheduled class session, online students may forget their needed participation in class. Physical, scheduled classes provide a regular, habitual commitment to the learning activity. Regular times for online courses may also alleviate some of the "virtual" yet less real aspect of an online class.

Despite some resistance across some delivery modes, online synchronous webinars have increased in popularity and availability in recent years, demonstrating the capability to present educational material to a broad audience. Although they can be used synchronously or asynchronously, attendance is generally higher at the initial event. This is perhaps because of the ability for interaction with presenters and other participants. While webinars can be recorded and made available for review at a different time, this may not be as effective and best practices would argue for different designs of presenting material if the audience is time delayed or not immediate.

Potential applications of synchronous technology that could be easily applied in higher education include online office hours, remote tutoring sessions, live webinars, selected classes, and student-to-student live discussions. An online video tutoring session can be very effective with small groups of students meeting a professor where it is intended to be highly interactive, with work done live by participants. Remote tutoring sessions can provide the intense, personal interaction with individual students or a group and have been found to be effective (Park & Bonk, 2007). There is a great difference between online tutorials such as those from YouTube and live, online tutoring sessions, where feedback, engagement, and interaction provide more than timely information.

Based on the experience of the authors, synchronous video and web chat communications may improve the efficacy of office hours. Currently, office hours are seldom used by students, but can provide the capability to resolve student problems, privately address student concerns, and discuss ideas in greater depth. Synchronous online learning activities can provide greater access and privacy as well as immediacy of interaction, but clearly new models are needed for this form of educational activity.

As with online classes there are skills that need to be developed for both instructors and learners. Synchronous events may be more like small seminars, which could hinder the development of introverted learners; management of live discussions online would require more skill from the instructor as well. Students often need to be trained to properly participate in online classes, and this form requires a considerably different set of interaction and learning skills.

Based on the authors' experiences, there are a number of implications for increased synchronous learning activities for online courses. Students often are irregular with their schedules, and online courses, even when times are pre-listed.

"Anytime" remains the expectation, but often results in "no time." Use of institutional resources for regular broadcast sessions may not be available as most resources are focused on generating stable, reusable elements such as video clips. This may shift online tutoring sessions or office hours to faculty offices. There will be more bandwidth pressure due to the wide range of technology access solutions. And there will be an increased pressure on audio quality as this appears to be a strong challenge for live, online sessions.

Learning and class engagement is increased when educational activities occur at a common time, increasing the potential for direct interaction with others. This is one of the potential areas for improvement in the field of educational technology, and one which will see increased use and development in the near future.

References

Park, Y. J., & Bonk, C. J. (2007). Is online life a breeze? A case study for promoting synchronous learning in a blended graduate course. *Journal of Online Learning and Teaching, 3*(3), 307–323.

Raffa, E. (n.d.). Retrieved 11.22.18 from https://mnohs.org/blog/209-traffic-cop-my-love-affair-with-webinar

The Preparation of Instructional Designers: An Exploration of Design Pedagogy and Praxis

Jill Stefaniak, Xigui Yang, and Philena DeVaughn

Instructional design is the process of creating detailed specifications of instructional solutions to support a situation warranting improvement. Instructional designers are responsible for assessing situations, identifying project needs, designing, developing, and implementing instructional solutions that are customized to address the needs of a project. The utility of instructional designers has become recognized across a variety of fields ranging across business and industry, healthcare, higher education, and K-12 education.

Throughout the past several decades, the instructional design field has identified a number of competencies required to support the systematic process and steps involved in instructional design. Competency is "a knowledge, skill, or attitude that enables one to effectively perform the activities of a given occupation or function to the standards expected in employment" (Sims & Koszalka, 2008, p. 569). The International Board of Standards for Training, Performance and Instruction (IBSTPI) developed a set of core competencies required of instructional designers in 1986. These competencies have continued to be revised, as needed, with the most recent revisions occurring in 2012. The current IBSTPI (2012) standards cover a number of performance-related tasks across five domains including professional foundations, planning and analysis, design and development, evaluation and implementation, and management (Koszalka, Russ-Eft, & Reiser, 2013).

The Association for Educational Communications and Technology (AECT) developed their own performance indicators to support the National Council for Accreditation of Teacher Education (NCATE) standards in 1982. These standards

---

J. Stefaniak (✉) · X. Yang
Learning, Design, and Technology, University of Georgia, Athens, GA, USA
e-mail: Jill.stefaniak@uga.edu

P. DeVaughn
Predestinated Image Consulting, Waldorf, MA, USA

© The Author(s), under exclusive license to Springer Nature Switzerland AG 2021
R. M. Branch et al. (eds.), *Educational Media and Technology Yearbook*,
Educational Media and Technology Yearbook 43,
https://doi.org/10.1007/978-3-030-71774-2_3

and performance indicators have been updated a number of times to accommodate advancements in technological innovations. The most recent standards and performance indicators were revised in 2012 to address content knowledge, content pedagogy, learning environments, professional knowledge and skills, and research (AECT, 2012).

A number of studies have been conducted exploring competencies expected of instructional designers (Dooley et al., 2007; Ritzhaupt & Kumar, 2015; Ritzhaupt & Martin, 2014; Sugar & Moore, 2015; York & Ertmer, 2016). These studies have consisted of surveying instructional designers in the field and reporting on performance standards required of them on a regular basis. Additional studies have been conducted examining instructional design job postings (Ritzhaupt, Martin, & Daniels, 2010; Sugar, Hoard, Brown, & Daniels, 2012).

In addition to recognizing the value that instructional designers may offer an organization, a number of organizations have increased their expectations regarding instructional design-related tasks. To date, a number of studies have been conducted to gather data on managing organizations' expectations of the instructional design role (Klein & Kelly, 2018; Larson, 2005; Larson & Lockee, 2004; Thompson-Sellers & Calandra, 2012; Villachica, Marker, & Taylor, 2010). These studies have indicated that discrepancies exist between employers' expectations and competencies promoted and valued among the instructional design field.

The results of these studies that have explored competencies and the alignment and discrepancies between instructional designers and their clients' and employers' expectations demonstrate the need for instructional designers to be prepared to serve in a number of expanded roles as instructional designers. As instructional design becomes more valued in different industries and settings, the need for instructional designers to be prepared to design in a number of different environments and along different career paths is further illuminated (Larson & Lockee, 2009).

Studies that have explored instructional design practices in the field have confirmed the need for instructional designers to be trained in designing decision-making practices (Bannan-Ritland, 2001; Jonassen, 2012; York & Ertmer, 2011), project management (Schwier & Wilson, 2010; van Rooij, 2010), and interpersonal skills (Visscher-Voerman, 2017). To accommodate the growing landscape of fields valuing instructional design work, instructional designers need to be prepared to be resilient and able to design among uncertainty and project constraints (Boling et al., 2017; Tracey & Boling, 2014).

An analysis of ID studies examining professional instructional designer practices revealed common practices in writing objectives, selecting instructional strategies, developing test items, and selecting media formats (Sugar, 2014a, 2014b). The analysis showed mixed results or no consensus, among ID practitioners in reference to evaluation activities, such as pilot testing. ID models were not represented in ID practice, rather instructional design events were supported by learning theories and context. ID competencies were a common thread.

Real-world projects, peer review process, case studies, and instructional support were determined as the most effective teaching methods in response to the question of how to best teach critical ID competencies. Although models were considered

The Preparation of Instructional Designers: An Exploration of Design Pedagogy... 19

supportive in teaching design skills and provided a springboard for instructional design work, the review failed to suggest a standard instructional system design model used by practitioners (Sugar, 2014b). The study reported that no decisive view of ID practice could be ascertained from the research; however, a significant difference between expert and novice instructional designers was disclosed. ID experts approached design projects from a systemic view that allowed for faster problem-solving and more efficient use of time.

In order to prepare instructional designers for what will be expected of them upon entering the instructional design workforce, graduate programs need to look at which competencies are being emphasized through their respective curricula. While a number of case studies have been conducted examining individual instructional design programs (Dabbagh & English, 2015; Larson & Lockee, 2009), additional studies are needed examining how instructional design programs are responding to the competencies and performance indicators identified by professional organizations such as AECT and IBSTPI as well as the expectations of organizations hiring graduates.

It is important that instructional design programs are preparing their graduates to effectively emulate and demonstrate competencies expected of the field as well as the ability to adapt to increasing technological demands that are inevitable for the future. The purpose of this chapter is to explore instructional design course offerings among programs across the United States as they relate to design pedagogy and praxis. We also offer discussion on the types of instructional exposure needed to prepare aspiring instructional designers for the field.

1 Overview of Instructional Design Programs and Offerings

We searched for higher education institutes that offer master's degrees in instructional design and analyzed their plan of study as shared on their website. A total number of 30 instructional design programs from 29 institutes were included in the analysis (see Appendix A). Despite the fact that the two ID programs offered by Boise State University have very distinct concentrations, they share quite a few courses, which were counted twice in our calculation because we treated each and every program as an individual unit. This way, the analysis of the programs of study included 458 courses.

The purpose of the analysis was to see which courses were most frequently offered across these programs. Courses with similar names and similar descriptions were grouped together under the typical course names and the frequency was recorded. Table 1 provides a list of courses that appeared at least three times in the list of all courses. Alternative names are also provided to clarify the variations of the courses in each category. The top ten courses are related to multimedia design, e-learning design, program evaluation, instructional design, research methods in education, foundations of instructional design, teaching and learning with technology, advanced instructional design, instructional game design, and educational technology integration.

Table 1 Frequency of course offerings by instructional design programs

#	Typical course names	Frequency	Alternative course names
1	Multimedia Design	39	Visual Design, Graphic Design, Visual Literacy, Message Design, Video Production
2	E-Learning Design	29	Online Learning, Online Teaching, Distance Education
3	Program Evaluation	28	Analysis of Performance, Evaluation and Assessment, Instrument Development, Evaluation of Needs and Performance, Measurement
4	Instructional Design	28	Instructional Design and Development, Instructional Design Process, Instructional Systems Design, Introduction to Instructional Design, Design and Development of Instruction
5	Research Methods in Education	24	Educational Research, Research in Educational Technology, Design Research in Practice
6	Foundations of Instructional Design	23	Instructional Design Foundations, Theoretical Foundations of Instructional Technology
7	Teaching and Learning with Technology	13	Technology for Teachers, Technology-Enhanced Teaching
8	Advanced Instructional Design	12	Instructional Design II, Advanced Instructional Systems Design, Application of Instructional Design Process
9	Instructional Game Design	10	Games and Learning, Games and Simulations, Gaming to Learning
10	Educational Technology Integration	9	Innovative Integration of Technology in Teaching, Integration of Technology into the Learning Environments
11	Seminar in Instructional Design and Technology	9	Readings Seminar in Learning Technologies
12	Trends and Issues in Instructional Design and Technology	9	Current Trends in Instructional Technology, Issues and Trends in Instructional Design and Technology
13	Educational Psychology	8	Learning and Cognition, Motivation
14	Educational Technology Leadership	8	Technology and Leadership, Leadership and Education
15	Special Topics	8	Selected Topics
16	Learning Environments Design	6	Designing Interactive Learning Environments, Designing Constructivist Learning Environments
17	Quantitative Research	6	Analysis of Quantitative Data, Statistics
18	Technical and Grant Writing	6	Grant Writing, Editing Professional Writing
19	Web Design for Instruction	6	Web Design and Development, Creating Educational Website
20	Adult Learning	5	Adult Learners, Adult Education
21	Learning Theory	5	Sociocultural Learning Theory
22	Blended Learning Environments	4	Blended Teaching

(continued)

Table 1 (continued)

#	Typical course names	Frequency	Alternative course names
23	Computers as Learning Tools	4	Computers as Cognitive Tools, Computers, Critical Thinking and Problem-Solving
24	Management of Instructional Technology	4	Managing Computer Applications, Management of Distance Education
25	Qualitative Research	4	Ethnographic Research
26	Design and Development Tools	3	Instructional Development Tools
27	Design Thinking	3	Design Thinking and Knowledge
28	Needs Assessment and Analysis	3	Instructional Needs Analysis
29	Project Management	3	Managing Educational Projects, Management of Instructional Projects

2 Discussion

Professional instructional design education programs that teach students practical knowledge for ill-structured and complex problems presented in the workplace, as well as technical knowledge and skills, were addressed through ID programs offering situated learning experiences. Learners perceived value in situated learning experiences when they could choose personally meaningful instructional topics and experience an eclectic problem-solving approach with a group. The research also found that learners ascribed value differently to various ID activities (Woolf & Quinn, 2009).

The knowledge and skills essential to the ill-structured problem-solving instructional design process are determined by environment, circumstances, and resources (Dabbagh & Blijd, 2010). The field of instructional design is tasked with mounting problem-solving responsibility (Jonassen & Hernandez-Serrano, 2002). Students without the opportunity for authentic experience may lack the depth of knowledge necessary for competent practice. Didactic models that encourage student understanding of expert instructional design practice through authentic experience, and foster a collaborative perspective to problem-solving, strengthen the preparation of ID students for various work experiences. ID students can be better served through immersion in problem-solving learning than focusing on a systems model approach (Dabbagh & Blijd, 2010).

Sugar (2014b) offered nine recommendations to consider for future research and education of instructional design professionals:

1. Replicate common studies of ID practices completed in the 1990s.
2. Consolidate data collection measures.
3. Conduct studies of ID practices that are all-inclusive.
4. Complete longitudinal studies.
5. Establish interrelated ID competencies.
6. Understand ID relationships and roles.

7. Provide support for developing ID expertise.
8. Explore interrelationships between ID decision-making and ID best practices.
9. Consider innovative methods to collect and represent ID development and ID practices.

In accordance with Sugar's recommendations, ongoing research concerning the difference in approach to design, by experts and novices, could continue to support the selection of appropriate competencies for educating and preparing design students to meet employer expectations (Ertmer et al., 2009; Gray et al., 2015).

In addition to the competencies inherent in most instructional design practices related to the design and implementation of instructional solutions, it is necessary for instructional design programs to prepare their graduates to be able to adapt to the complexities often associated with instructional design projects. The majority of instructional design projects are touted as being ill structured, requiring instructional designers to engage in problem-solving, manage constraints, and demonstrate resilience. As evidenced in the course offerings by instructional design programs around the country, graduate programs are placing emphasis on the promotion of design thinking, user experience design, and performance improvement through real-world experiences.

2.1 Design Thinking

Design thinking is a philosophy that promotes an iterative approach to problem-solving through empathy, ideation, prototyping, and evaluation (Dorst, 2011; Razzouk & Shute, 2012). This iterative process assists designers with understanding the needs of their audience and the types of solutions required to improve the situation (Köppen & Meinel, 2015; Roberts, Fisher, Trowbridge, & Bent, 2016).

Students should be provided with opportunities to learn and apply a variety of design skills and strategies. Design thinking is a philosophy that assists them with stretching themselves as a designer as they become more comfortable promoting creativity and embracing uncertainty, ambiguity, and other design constraints. Design thinking, as a mindset, enables the instructional designer to empathize with their learning audience, and customize and prioritize solutions that go through a number of design iterations to achieve long-term effects. This mindset ultimately provides instructional designers with the necessary skills to embrace the uncertainties prevalent in ill-structured problems (Stefaniak, 2020).

2.2 User Experience Design

With continued technological advances and affordances, instructional designers have the unique challenge of determining optimal training platforms for delivering their learning solutions. With a growth in online and distance education, instructional designers' designs must address any disconnects that may occur between the learners and the instructional materials. As the technological tools available to instructional designers continue to evolve at what seems like an exponential rate, the field of instructional design is paying closer attention to other disciplines such as human factor psychology and human-computer interactions that have been employing user design tactics to gain a clear understanding of the learner's interactions with technology from training to application (Earnshaw, Tawfik, & Schmidt, 2018; Gray, 2016).

Researchers in instructional design have begun re-examining tasks often associated with learner analysis. This has resulted in the promotion of the use of learner personas to better understand the learning needs of individual learners; the knowledge, skills, and attitudes they bring with them to an instructional experience; as well as what they need for transferring their acquisition of knowledge to a real-world setting. By placing more attention to information gathered during the learner analysis phase, instructional designers can better engage in design thinking by ideating and prototyping potential solutions that are better aligned with the project needs. As a result, our field is beginning to conduct research on empathetic design practices that support user experience design and other instructional design tasks by employing strategies that promote empathy throughout the instructional design process (Matthews, Williams, Yanchar, & McDonald, 2017; Tracey & Hutchinson, 2019; Van Rooij, 2012; Vann, 2017).

2.3   Performance Improvement

The purpose of instructional design is to facilitate learning and improve performance. Upon completion of the program, students should have an understanding of the tools needed to implement change in their organization. Not only should students be equipped to design instructional solutions, but they should also be trained in recognizing the noninstructional solutions needed to support the diffusion of change. Examples of topics that should be addressed in the curriculum would be general systems theory, human performance technology, and communicating and identifying instructional and noninstructional solutions.

An increased number of universities are identifying the importance of threading employability skills into program curricula to address employers' needs and to increase the likelihood of students' workplace success. The U.S. Department of Education (2020) has identified nine skill areas that enhance the success of employees in the workforce: applied academic skills, systems thinking, technology skills, critical thinking skills, resource management, information use, communication skills, personal qualities, and interpersonal skills. Instructional designers report the critical nature of each of these skills in the workplace. Employers identify the lack of technical and interpersonal skills, such as evaluation and collaboration, as deficits in the training of instructional designers.

Ensuring that instructional designers are competent to identify and create solutions to underlying causes for gaps, between current and desired performance outcomes, increases their organizational value. The preparedness to evaluate instruction effectiveness allows instructional designers to verify that the correct intervention was implemented. Evaluation provides the opportunity to confirm the cost-effectiveness of performance gap solutions.

A systemic and systematic approach to an organizational challenge begins with the needs assessment and analysis (Hays & Singh, 2012). Effective evaluation is contingent upon credible needs assessment conclusions and analysis. The process of diffusion communicates a change solution through formal and informal channels to organization members (Rogers, 2003, p. 198). Competency-based curricula for instructional designs should emphasize the acquisition of communication, interpersonal skills, systems thinking, and theory to create viable performance solutions for adoption in the organization.

2.4 Project Management

Project management models focus on project planning and timely and efficient delivery. Strong leadership, communication, and interpersonal skills are key competencies of effective project management (Williams van Rooij, 2010). The advantage of developing the project manager competencies for instructional designers is the ability to conceptualize a performance gap solution from needs assessment to implementation and to evaluation, with a systematic and holistic approach. Achieving buy-in for resources, from managers and other stakeholders, is more likely when the instructional designer effectively presents a solution with the use of project management tools.

This strand will promote leadership skills necessary to manage, coordinate, and communicate in a professional capacity. Greer (1992) and Gentry (1994) initially identified the importance of intertwining instructional design and project management skills for successful deployment of instruction projects in organizations. Job postings for instructional designers more frequently list project management skills as a qualification (Klein & Kelly, 2018; Ritzhaupt & Martin, 2014). While instructional design leaders have expressed the need for instructional designers to embody project management attributes, criticisms have emerged that project management is not effectively conveyed in existing instructional design models (Brill, Bishop, & Walker, 2006; van Rooij, 2010, 2011).

2.5 Promoting a Reflective Instructional Designer

Reflective practice is a skill set promoted and taught by multiple design disciplines. Research has shown the benefits of developing a reflective practitioner in instructional design settings (Schon, 2010). Students should be able to reflect and articulate their design decisions. Incorporating meaningful reflective activities will assist students in their ability to articulate and communicate their rationale for instructional design practices among their peers, design teams, and clients (Tracey, Hutchinson, & Grzebyk, 2014). It also demonstrates their ability to make design decisions that are informed by sound instructional design theoretical and foundational perspectives.

2.6 Supporting Design Pedagogy by Providing Authentic Instructional Design Experiences

Clark (1978) proposed that graduate programs prepare students through authentic practice and experienced role models, who provide strategiesv and procedures to navigate the nuances of their chosen professions. Novice instructional design students are expected to graduate from ID programs with the ability to identify and employ suitable ID models for their workplace context (Koszalka et al., 2013; Slagter van Tryon, McDonald, & Hirumi, 2018). Project-based learning and authentic learning experiences motivate students through the integration of realistic problem-solving that promotes cognitive realism (Herrington & Herrington, 2008; Herrington, Oliver, & Reeves, 2003). Authentic learning experiences have provided practice, in the application of theory, and development of important professional skills that are critical to postgraduate employment (Wakeham, 2016).

When students have the opportunity to engage in a PBL experience that mimics the professional process through authentic decision-making with the option for multiple outcomes, there is buy-in (Roach, Tilley, & Mitchell, 2018). Interestingly, "real" client experience and business context were unnecessary for professional novices to experience cognitive realism. The application of professional practices requiring realistic outcomes served to create successful authentic learning activities (Roach et al., 2018). Studies have demonstrated that tasks perceived to be of personal value to the students, and to the industry community of practice, motivate students to take ownership of their learning (Herrington, 2015; Roach et al., 2018; Slagter van Tryon et al., 2018).

3 Conclusion

While certain foundational skills associated with instructional design practices are most likely to remain relevant, it is important that instructional design programs and higher education institutes continue to adapt their program and course offerings to reflect the current trends in the field and employer expectations in order to maintain instructional design as a viable contribution to organizational development. A goal of this chapter was to take a look at current instructional design offerings in 2020 to help instructional designers and instructors reflect on the extent that alignment exists between curricula and real-world praxis.

Appendix A

A list of instructional design master's programs

#	School	Program	Plan of study
1	Arizona State University	M.A.Ed. in Instructional Technology (Online)	https://education.asu.edu/sites/default/files/med-educational-technology-handbook.2018-2019.pdf
2	Boise State University (College of Education)	M.Ed. in Curriculum and Instruction (Educational Technology)	https://edtech.boisestate.edu/course-schedule-2/
3	Boise State University (College of Engineering)	MS in Organizational Performance and Workplace Learning	http://opwl.boisestate.edu/courses/course-descriptions/
4	East Carolina University	MS.Ed. in Instructional Systems Technology	https://drive.google.com/file/d/1i9ajYhBRugKMuSl5Bdxv3RLgCWbHlyu8/view
5	Florida State University	MA in Instructional Design and Technology	https://distance.fsu.edu/students/instructional-systems-and-learning-technologies-ms
6	George Washington University	MS.Ed. in Learning Design and Technology	https://gsehd.gwu.edu/programs/masters-educational-technology-leadership
7	Georgia College	M.Ed. in Instructional Technology	http://gcsu.smartcatalogiq.com/2017-2018/Graduate-Catalog/John-H-Lounsbury-College-of-Education/Professional-Learning-and-Innovation/Instructional-Technology-MEd-Online
8	Georgia Southern University	M.Ed. in Instructional Technology	https://coe.georgiasouthern.edu/itec/courses/
9	Georgia State University	MS in Instructional Design and Technology	https://catalog.gsu.edu/graduate20182019/college-of-education-and-human-development/#instructional-design-and-technology-m-s
10	Indiana University	M.Ed. in Instructional Psychology and Technology	http://bulletins.iu.edu/iu/educ-grad/current/ist/msed-ist-online.shtml

#	School	Program	Plan of study
11	Michigan State University	M.Ed. in Learning, Design, and Technology	http://edutech.educ.msu.edu/programs/masters/courses/
12	Ohio State University	M.Ed. in Learning, Design, and Technology, Instructional Design and Development	https://ehe.osu.edu/sites/ehe.osu.edu/files/learning-technologies-mlt.pdf
13	Old Dominion University	M.Ed. in Learning, Design, and Technology	https://www.odu.edu/stemps/academics/idt/masters#tab194=0
14	Pennsylvania State University	MS in Instructional Technology	https://www.worldcampus.psu.edu/degrees-and-certificates/penn-state-online-masters-in-learning-design-technology/courses
15	Piedmont College	MA in Instructional Technology	http://piedmont.smartcatalogiq.com/en/2016-2017/Graduate-Catalog/School-of-Education/School-of-Education-Graduate-Programs/Teaching-and-Learning/Instructional-Technology/Instructional-Technology-Non-Certification-M-A
16	Purdue University	MS in Learning Technologies	https://online.purdue.edu/ldt/learning-design-technology/courses
17	Texas Tech University	Master's in Educational Technology	https://www.depts.ttu.edu/education/graduate/psychology-and-leadership/documents/EDIT_MasterHndbk_Rev_Sep2017_V9.pdf
18	University of Arkansas	MS in Instructional Systems and Learning Technologies	https://catalog.uark.edu/graduatecatalog/programsofstudy/educationaltechnologyetecmed/#medineducationtechnologytext
19	University of Central Florida	MA in Instructional Technology and Learning Sciences	http://catalog.ucf.edu/preview_program.php?catoid=4&poid=1303
20	University of Florida	M.Ed. in Instructional Systems Technology	https://education.ufl.edu/educational-technology/online-masters/
21	University of Georgia	M.Ed. in Educational Technology	http://gclinton.coe.uga.edu/idd/IDDonline_graduate_student_handbook.pdf
22	University of Hawaii, Manoa	MA in Educational Technology	http://www.catalog.hawaii.edu/courses/departments/ltec.htm
23	University of Memphis	M.Ed. in Instructional Technology	https://docs.google.com/document/d/1OsXAFXGsK-nDf-VxECBxXwPqtt-iCu045g6n4zNk17g/edit

#	School	Program	Plan of study
24	University of North Carolina, Charlotte	Master's in Learning Technologies	https://edld.uncc.edu/programs/instructional-systems-technology-program
25	University of North Texas	MA in Education and Human Development (Educational Technology Leadership)	http://lt.unt.edu/masters/lt_program_details#courses
26	University of Oklahoma	MS in Instructional Design and Technology	http://www.ou.edu/education/edpy/instructional-psychology-and-technology-degrees-and-programs/instructional-psychology-and-technology-masters/instructional-design
27	University of West Georgia	M.Ed. in Media (Instructional Technology Concentration)	https://www.westga.edu/academics/education/program_page.php?program_id=115
28	Utah State University	M.Ed. in Learning Design and Technology (Online)	http://itls.usu.edu/files/students/plan_sheets/ma.pdf
29	Virginia Polytechnic and State University	M.Ed. in Educational Technology	https://drive.google.com/file/d/1i9ajYhBRugKMuSl5Bdxv3RLgCWbHlyu8/view
30	Wayne State University	MS.Ed. in Secondary Education, Instructional Design, and Technology	http://coe.wayne.edu/aos/ldt/design-pow.php

References

AECT (Association for Educational Communications and Technology). (2012). AECT standards, 2012 version. Retrieved from http://ocw.metu.edu.tr/pluginfile.php/3298/course/section/1171/AECT_Standards_adopted7_16_2.pdf.

Bannan-Ritland, B. (2001). Teaching instructional design: An action learning approach. *Performance Improvement Quarterly, 14*(2), 37–52.

Boling, E., Alangari, H., Hajdu, I. M., Guo, M., Gyabak, K., Khlaif, Z., et al. (2017). Core judgments of instructional designers in practice. *Performance Improvement Quarterly, 30*(3), 199–219.

Brill, J. M., Bishop, M. J., & Walker, A. E. (2006). The competencies and characteristics required of an effective project manager: A web-based Delphi study. *Educational Technology Research and Development, 54*(2), 115–140.

Clark, R. E. (1978). Doctoral research training in educational technology. *Educational Communication and Technology Journal, 26*(2), 165–173.

Dabbagh, N., & Blijd, C. W. (2010). Students' perceptions of their learning experiences in an authentic instructional design context. *Interdisciplinary Journal of Problem-based Learning, 4*(1), 6–29.

Dabbagh, N., & English, M. (2015). Using student self-ratings to assess the alignment of instructional design competencies and courses in a graduate program. *TechTrends, 59*(4), 22–31.

Dooley, K. E., Lindner, J. R., Telg, R. W., Irani, T., Moore, L., & Lundy, L. (2007). Roadmap to measuring distance education instructional design competencies. *Quarterly Review of Distance Education, 8*(2).

Dorst, K. (2011). The core of "design thinking" and its application. *Design Studies, 32*(6), 521–532.

Earnshaw, Y., Tawfik, A. A., & Schmidt, M. (2018). User experience design. In R. E. West (Ed.), *Foundations of learning and instructional design technology: Historical roots and current trends.* Available from https://lidtfoundations.pressbooks.com/chapter/user-experience-design/

Ertmer, P. A., Stepich, D. A., Flanagan, S., Kocaman-Karoglu, A., Reiner, C., Reyes, L., et al. (2009). Impact of guidance on the problem-solving efforts of instructional design novices. *Performance Improvement Quarterly, 21*(4), 117–132.

Gentry, C. G. (1994). *Introduction to instructional development: Process and technique.* Belmont, CA: Wadsworth.

Gray, C. M. (2016). "It's more of a mindset than a method": UX practitioners' conception of design methods. In *Proceedings of the 2016 CHI conference on human factors in computing systems* (pp. 4044–4055). New York, NY: ACM.

Gray, C. M., Dagli, C., Demiral-Uzan, M., Ergulec, F., Tan, V., Altuwaijri, A. A., et al. (2015). Judgment and instructional design: How ID practitioners work in practice. *Performance Improvement Quarterly, 28*(3), 25–49.

Greer, M. (1992). *ID project management: Tools and techniques for instructional designers and developers.* Englewood Cliffs, NJ: Educational Technology Publications.

Hays, D., & Singh, A. (2012). Qualitative inquiry in clinical and educational settings. Guilford Press.

Herrington, J. (2015). Introduction to authentic learning. Inn V. Bozalek, D. Ng'ambi, D. Wood, J. Herrington, J. Hardman, & A. Amory (Eds.), Activity theory, authentic learning, and emerging technologies: Towards a transformative higher education pedagogy (pp. 61–67). Routledge.

Herrington, A., & Herrington, J. (2008). What is an authentic learning environment? In *Authentic learning environments in higher education* (pp. 68–77). London: Information Science Publishing.

Herrington, J., Oliver, R., & Reeves, T. C. (2003). Patterns of engagement in authentic online learning environments. *Australian Journal of Educational Technology, 19*(1), 59–71.

IBSTPI (International Board of Standards for Training, Performance and Instruction) (2012). *The 2012 instructional designer competencies.* Retrieved from http://www.ibstpi.org/introducing-the-2012-instructional-design-competencies/

Jonassen, D. H. (2012). Designing for decision making. *Educational Technology Research and Development, 60*(2), 341–359.

Jonassen, D. H., & Hernandez-Serrano, J. (2002). Case-based reasoning and instructional design: Using stories to support problem solving. *Educational Technology Research and Development, 50*(2), 65–77.

Klein, J. D., & Kelly, W. Q. (2018). Competencies for instructional designers: A view from employers. *Performance Improvement Quarterly, 31*(3), 225–247.

Köppen, E., & Meinel, C. (2015). Empathy via design thinking: Creation of sense and knowledge. In H. Plattner, C. Meinel, & L. Leifer (Eds.), *Design thinking research: Building innovators* (pp. 15–28). New York: Springer.

Koszalka, T. A., Russ-Eft, D. F., & Reiser, R. (2013). *Instructional designer competencies: The standards* (4th ed.). New York, NY: Information Age Publishing.

Larson, M. B. (2005). Instructional design career environments: Survey of the alignment of preparation and practice. *TechTrends, 49*(6), 22–32.

Larson, M. B., & Lockee, B. B. (2004). Instructional design practice: Career environments, job roles, and a climate of change. *Performance Improvement Quarterly, 17*(1), 22–40.

Larson, M. B., & Lockee, B. B. (2009). Preparing instructional designers for different career environments: A case study. *Educational Technology Research and Development, 57*(1), 1–24.

Matthews, M. T., Williams, G. S., Yanchar, S. C., & McDonald, J. K. (2017). Empathy in distance learning design practice. *TechTrends, 61*(5), 486–493.

Razzouk, R., & Shute, V. (2012). What is design thinking and why is it important? *Review of Educational Research, 82*(30), 330–348.

Ritzhaupt, A. D., & Kumar, S. (2015). Knowledge and skills needed by instructional designers in higher education. *Performance Improvement Quarterly, 28*(3), 51–69.

Ritzhaupt, A. D., & Martin, F. (2014). Development and validation of the educational technologist multimedia competency survey. *Educational Technology Research and Development, 62*(1), 13–33.

Ritzhaupt, A., Martin, F., & Daniels, K. (2010). Multimedia competencies for an educational technologist: A survey of professionals and job announcement analysis. *Journal of Educational Multimedia and Hypermedia, 19*(4), 421–449.

Roach, K., Tilley, E., & Mitchell, J. (2018). How authentic does authentic learning have to be? *Higher Education Pedagogies, 3*(1), 495–509.

Roberts, J. P., Fisher, T. R., Trowbridge, M. J., & Bent, C. (2016). A design thinking framework for healthcare management and innovation. *Healthcare, 4*(1), 11–14.

Rogers, E. M. (2003). *Diffusion of innovations* (5th ed.). New York: Free Press.

Schon, D. A. (2010). Educating the reflective practitioner: Toward a new design for teaching and learning in the professions. *Australian Journal of Adult Learning, 50*(2), 448–451.

Schwier, R. A., & Wilson, J. R. (2010). Unconventional roles and activities identified by instructional designers. *Contemporary Educational Technology, 1*(2), 134–147.

Sims, R., & Koszalka, T. A. (2008). Competencies for the new-age instructional designer. In J. M. Spector, M. D. Merrill, J. van Merriënboer, & M. P. Driscoll (Eds.), *Handbook of research on educational communications and technology* (3rd ed., pp. 569–575). New York: Taylor & Francis.

Slagter van Tryon, P. J., McDonald, J., & Hirumi, A. (2018). Preparing the next generation of instructional designers: A cross-institution faculty collaboration. *Journal of Computing in Higher Education, 30*(1), 125–153.

Stefaniak, J. (2020). The utility of design thinking to promote systemic instructional design practices in the workplace. *TechTrends, 64*(2), 202–210.

Sugar, W. (2014a). Development and formative evaluation of multimedia case studies for instructional design and technology students. *TechTrends, 58*(5), 36–52.

Sugar, W. (2014b). *Studies of ID practices: A review and synthesis of research on ID current practices.* New York, NY: Springer International Publishing.

Sugar, W., Hoard, B., Brown, A., & Daniels, L. (2012). Identifying multimedia production competencies and skills of instructional design and technology professionals: An analysis of recent job postings. *Journal of Educational Technology Systems, 40*(3), 227–249.

Sugar, W., & Moore, R. L. (2015). Documenting current instructional design practices: Towards a typology of instructional designer activities, roles, and collaboration. *The Journal of Applied Instructional Design, 5*(1).

Thompson-Sellers, I., & Calandra, B. (2012). Ask the instructional designers: A cursory glance at practice in the workplace. *Performance Improvement, 51*(7), 21–27.

Tracey, M. W., & Boling, E. (2014). Preparing instructional designers and educational technologists: Traditional and emerging perspectives. In M. Spector, D. Merrill, J. Elen, & M. J. Bishop (Eds.), *Handbook of research on educational communications and technology* (4th ed., pp. 653–660). New York: Springer.

Tracey, M. W., & Hutchinson, A. (2019). Empathic design: Imagining the cognitive and emotional learner experience. *Educational Technology Research and Development, 67*(5), 1259–1272.

Tracey, M. W., Hutchinson, A., & Grzebyk, T. Q. (2014). Instructional designers as reflective practitioners: Developing professional identity through reflection. *Educational Technology Research and Development, 62*(3), 315–334.

van Rooij, S. W. (2010). Project management in instructional design: ADDIE is not enough. *British Journal of Educational Technology, 41*(5), 852–864.

van Rooij, S. W. (2011). Instructional design and project management: Complementary or divergent? *Educational Technology Research and Development, 59*(1), 139–158.

van Rooij, S. W. (2012). Research-based personas: Teaching empathy in professional education. *Journal of Effective Teaching, 12*(3), 77–86.

Vann, L. S. (2017). Demonstrating empathy: A phenomenological study of instructional designers making instructional strategy decisions for adult learners. *International Journal of Teaching and Learning in Higher Education, 29*(2), 233–244.

Villachica, S. W., Marker, A., & Taylor, K. (2010). But what do they really expect? Employer perceptions of the skills of entry-level instructional designers. *Performance Improvement Quarterly, 22*(4), 33–51.

Visscher-Voerman, I. (2017). Necessary ingredients for the education of designers. In A.A. Carr-Chellman & G. Rowland (Eds.), Issues in technology, learning, and instructional design: Classic and contemporary dialogues (pp. 73–80). Routledge.

Wakeham, W. (2016). Wakeham review of STEM degree provision and graduate employability. Retrieved February 27, 2017, from https://assets.publishing.service.gov.uk/government/uploads/system/uploads/attachment_data/file/518582/ind-16-6-wakeham-review-stem-graduateemployability.pdf

Woolf, N., & Quinn, J. (2009). Learners' perceptions of instructional design practice in a situated learning activity. *Educational Technology Research and Development, 57*(1), 25–43.

York, C. S., & Ertmer, P. A. (2011). Towards an understanding of instructional design heuristics: An exploratory Delphi study. *Educational Technology Research and Development, 59*(6), 841–863.

York, C. S., & Ertmer, P. A. (2016). Examining instructional design principles applied by experienced designers in practice. *Performance Improvement Quarterly, 29*(2), 169–192.

Robotics Education as an Integrator Tool

John Mativo

1 Introduction

The prevalence of robots, across the globe for both autonomous and radio controlled, is amazingly high. Examples of extracurricular events such as FIRST Robotics and First Lego League Robotics depict the technology and device acceptability and attraction to students of all levels across the globe. Robots and related technology lend to be used as tools in the study of mathematics, science, and engineering. In mathematics, the study can be a simple search for an optimized operation from moving from one site to another, or to solve a transport problem in the most efficient way. The science part of robots is use of scientific concepts and exploration. What laws of physics govern motion? Where can robots go? What are the conditions to access such locations? What tools can be placed on the robot to ensure that the objectives are met? The engineering components of robots include clearly defining the problem, identifying the criteria used to ensure satisfactory solution, and generating methods of solving the problem. The use of robots to aforementioned activities creates interest and maintains motivation of the students as they explore solutions to problems.

J. Mativo (✉)
Department of Career and Information Studies (Workforce Education), University of Georgia, Athens, GA, USA
e-mail: jmativo@uga.edu

© The Author(s), under exclusive license to Springer Nature Switzerland AG 2021
R. M. Branch et al. (eds.), *Educational Media and Technology Yearbook*,
Educational Media and Technology Yearbook 43,
https://doi.org/10.1007/978-3-030-71774-2_4

2 Method

A description of the development of a curriculum is given, followed by its application in the three case studies.

2.1 Development of Robotics Education Curriculum

Industry and academia joined hands to develop a science lesson using robots as part of learning strategy for 5th- and 6th-grade students. The first step in the development of the curriculum was to identify a lesson required by a state in the southeast region of the United States. The lesson had to be challenging to teach and the robots would be used to intervene in reaching the students and make learning interesting. A "team" of school district teachers, administrators, graduate students, and university faculty designed a 5th-grade lesson titled "Danger Zone" to study volcanos using robots. The curriculum resulted in the use of the engineering design process, mathematics, and science. The students were required to apply all three subject matter areas.

2.2 Danger Zone: The Lesson

Danger zone referred to a place that caution is of utmost importance. This is a lesson about volcanos that is required for 5th-grade students in a state in southeast United States (Choi et al., 2015). The lesson was developed as a form of a question. It stated: If a person cannot explore an active volcano safely, what can he or she do to

Table 1 An overview of eight robotic lessons for 5th grade

Lesson	Name	Driving question
1	Danger Zone	How can scientists study dangerous environments?
2	Build a Bot	How do engineers build robots to accomplish specific tasks?
3	Primary Programming	How can the basic movements of a robot be controlled using simple programming commands?
4	Purposeful Programming	How can sequential movements of a robot be controlled using sequential programming commands?
5	Terrain Task	How can a robot be programmed to perform a specific task?
6	Prime Optimization	How can math be used to efficiently program a robot to perform a specific task?
7	Making Sense	How can sensors be used to program a robot to efficiently perform a specific task?
8	Share	How does the engineering design process help with problem-solving?

actively learn about it (Mativo, Hill, Choi, Kopcha, & McGregor, 2017). Several discussions led to the proposal of using a robot that can be sent to the volcano sites and collect samples needed. The overview of the eight robotic lessons is presented in Table 1.

3 Case Study I: United States

The problem posed to students stated: use a robot to safely visit the five sites that have been created on a 6 × 6 grid that simulate a volcano landscape (Fig. 1). The sites included the mud flow, lava, side vent, volcanic bomb, and ash. Once they understood the problem and designed their path to solving it, they embarked on building robots from kits, supplied by industry. This activity was part of their engineering design. Students used tools from the kits and built robots using assembly directions. In the next step, students programed the robot to administer the given tasks. Finally, they deployed the robot to complete all tasks and return to the starting point. In performing these tasks, students worked within their constraints and optimized their solutions.

3.1 Mathematical Concepts

Calculating distance, speed of the robot, and time the robot would complete its tasks were part of the mathematical concepts engaged in the process. Table 2 shows both the domain and clusters in this effort.

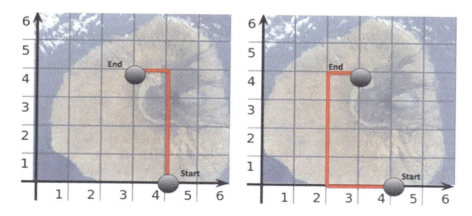

Fig. 1 Sample grid

Table 2 Mathematical curriculum from CCGPS for 5th grade

Domain	Cluster
Operations and algebraic thinking	• Write and interpret numerical expressions. • Analyze patterns and relationships.
Number and operations in base ten	• Understand the place value system. • Perform operations with multi-digit whole numbers and with decimals to hundredths.
Number and operations—fractions	• Use equivalent fractions as a strategy to add and subtract fractions. • Apply and extend previous understandings of multiplication and division to multiply and divide fractions.
Measurement and data	• Convert like measurement units within a given measurement system. • Represent and interpret data. • Geometric measurement: understand concepts of volume and relate volume to multiplication and to addition.
Geometry	• Graph points on the coordinate plane to solve real-world and mathematical problems. • Classify two-dimensional figures into categories based on their properties.

Fig. 2 Testing robot on movement on grid

3.2 Data Collection and Analysis

Faculty and graduate students videotaped 5th-grade students ($n = 257$) as they worked through the learning exercise as shown in Fig. 2. Interest for this case study was centered in lessons 4, 5, and 6. Two primary codes developed were engagement in the engineering design process and displaying computational thinking.

The code engagement in the engineering design process was applied to video segments in which students were observed to be actively engaged in the prototyping, testing, and revising of their programming solution (Mativo et al., 2017).

Throughout the three-lesson video, the engagement in the engineering design process was applied to 27 unique video segments with 13 instances occurring in Lesson 4, 8 instances occurring in Lesson 5, and 6 instances occurring in Lesson 6. Further analysis found that while the number of occurrences of engaging in the engineering design process decreased as students progressed through the curriculum the amount of time spent in planning the programming moves incrementally increased from Lesson 4 to Lesson 6. One potential reason for the decrease in the number of instances of engagement in the engineering design process and the simultaneous increase in the amount of time spent engaging in each cycle of the engineering design process is that students' progress through the curriculum followed an intentional design.

The code of displaying computational thinking was broken down into the subcodes of abstraction, elaboration, reasoning, and automation (Mativo et al., 2017). Throughout the three lessons, students showed multiple instances of displays of computational thinking with increased instances in Lesson 5 and Lesson 6 after mathematics was introduced through the curriculum design. For example, in Lesson 4 student displays of computational thinking were coded for reasoning only for the fact that displays were focused on generating new ideas for how to program the robot. In Lesson 5 and Lesson 6, as the curriculum and students' thinking evolved, their displays of computational thinking began to include abstract thinking, automation, reasoning, and elaboration. Abstract thinking came in the form of displays such as students being able to look at the code on the screen, rather than at the robot's actual movements, and understanding where to make changes in their code. Instances of displays of elaboration and abstraction combined were observed in the form of students being able to create their own algorithm for chips needed to program the robots' movement from one point on the grid to the next and being able to apply that algorithm to future movements throughout Lesson 5 and Lesson 6 leading to automation of the programming.

3.3 Reflection

Students worked in teams to find solutions to the problems presented. The activities allowed students to build, program, and actuate robots using them as vehicles to access locations of interest, retrieve information, and return to their headquarters in a given time frame. Results demonstrated increased student engagement in learning mathematics and science and a positive impact on learning climate (Mativo et al., 2017).

4 Case Study II: Honduras

Researchers used the "Danger Zone" curriculum to promote robot education as an integrator in STEM education for students in Honduras. Students living in rural areas of Honduras lack educational opportunities (Sekiya & Ashida, 2017). Exposing students to hands-on learning experiences with science, technology, engineering, and math (STEM) is essential not only for their future success but also for the nation's economic growth (Kuenzi, 2008; National Research Council, 2010). In the same effort as case study 1, industry and academia joined hands to provide Honduran students the opportunity to immerse in the robotics education experience.

The objective in the intervention experience to the 5th- and 6th-grade students in Honduras was to determine the impact of the curriculum on them and impart a long-term interest in STEM-related fields. Students ($n = 29$) were divided into two classrooms, and each was led by four trained teachers. Learning outcomes were assessed with pre- and posttest survey, while overall learning experience was assessed with a survey at the end of the implementation (Walters et al., 2019) (Fig. 3). An example of learning activity during our workshop in Honduras is shown in Fig. 3. Here, one one of the teachers we trained is transfering his knowledge to the 5th and 6 th grade students.

4.1 Results

A paired t-test between pre- and posttest overall scores showed that the 5th graders' overall problem-solving scores did not significantly change ($t(15) = -1.42$, $p = 0.177$). Similarly, a paired t-test between pre- and posttest overall scores showed

Fig. 3 Honduras students

Robotics Education as an Integrator Tool

Table 3 Pre- and posttest results on problem-solving for 6th graders ($N = 15$)

Main problem theme	Possible points	Pretest M (SD)	Posttest M (SD)	t	df	p
Engineering design	30	3.33 (4.08)	4.33 (4.58)	−0.716	14	0.49
Coordinate grid	15	0.00 (0.00)	1.00 (3.87)	−1.000	14	0.34
Distance and time	20	3.33 (3.62)	3.00 (4.14)	0.269	14	0.79
Flowchart	20	2.00 (5.61)	4.67 (5.16)	−1.740	14	0.10
Velocity	10	0.20 (0.77)	2.20 (3.84)	−2.197	14	0.05*
Total score	95	15.80 (11.97)	19.87 (15.43)	−1.421	14	0.18

*$p \leq 0.05$

Table 4 Pre- and post-math and engineering attitude survey results for 5th and 6th graders

	Pretest and posttest					
	n	M (SD)	M (SD)	t	df	p
5th Grade						
Knowing how to use math and science together will allow me to invent useful things	14	4.86 (0.36)	4.29 (0.83)	2.28	13	0.040*
I am good at building and fixing things	15	3.60 (1.55)	4.13 (0.99)	−2.78	14	0.015*
I can handle most subjects well, but I cannot do a good job with math	20	4.00 (1.29)	4.35 (1.18)	−2.64	12	0.022*
6th Grade						
Knowing how to use math and science together will allow me to invent useful things	14	4.79 (0.43)	4.21 (0.70)	4.163	13	0.001***
Designing products or structures will be important for my future work	14	4.14 (0.77)	4.43 (0.76)	−2.280	13	0.040*
I am the type of student to do well in math	12	4.58 (0.67)	3.83 (1.11)	2.283	11	0.043*
I am good at math	12	4.50 (1.00)	4.00 (1.13)	3.317	11	0.007**

*$p < 0.05$
**$p < 0.01$
***$p < 0.001$

that the 6th graders' overall problem-solving scores did not significantly change ($t(14) = −1.97$, $p = 0.069$). However, further ad hoc analysis revealed that the 6th graders demonstrated a statistically significant improvement in the velocity question. See Table 3 for the paired t-test results for each question.

Students also completed a survey on mathematics and engineering attitudes. A paired t-test showed that the 5th-grade students indicated a significant attitude change on three items. Additionally, the 6th-grade students indicated a significant attitude change on four items. Students attitude change reflects the influence of robotics to showing relevance to learning. See Table 4 for details.

4.2 Reflection

Overall, the students enjoyed the STEM robotics curriculum. Students were engaged in building the robots, brainstorming on the best way to solve the problem of collecting goods from sites given, and bringing them back to the starting point. The local application they said they could use the lesson for was to collect sugarcane from different sites and take them to the processing plant.

Table 5 Themes of what students valued most: Qualitative study

What did you like most about this activity?	Building a robot because it teaches many things
	I would like to become a medical doctor and use robots to treat people
	I am glad to have been taught and now I know how to make a robot
	Making a robot
	How to program robots and make them actuate
	I enjoyed developing a robot and I like how it helps people in performing different tasks
	To make robots and play with a computer—I was very pleased
What meaningful thing did you learn from this activity?	To program a robot
	To discover how to make a robot and understand procedures in creating a robot and many things about robots
	Creating a robot with the help of teachers and visitors
	How a robot works and drives
	It made my brain think; helped me think deeper
	A robot can do many things
	A robot can go forward, backward, right, left, like a human being
	To command a robot and it obeys
What can make this activity better	To listen to our teachers and use the equipment well
	To be courageous and lots of brain when designing things
	To operate such robots in industry, such as to fetch sand
	To spread the technology to the entire world
	You have to be better than a robot to make an impact
	To teach others to make robots
	Study hard
	Help people climb the mountain
	To elaborate so that people can understand better

Fig. 4 Tanzanian students and teachers

5 Case Study III: Tanzania

The "Danger Zone" curriculum was adapted to the local Tanzanian economy and setting. The scenario was composed of everyday chores of collecting firewood and fetching water. The question was to find the best path possible that minimized the time spent in those activities. Two middle schools composing of 5th- and 6th-grade students ($n = 44$) participated in the study. Interviews were conducted to determine how much students valued most from a 1-day experience. Themes that emerged from the responses to the three questions asked are presented in Table 5.

The themes emerging from the three questions indicate that students enjoyed the challenge and they saw lots of potential to use robots in various spheres of work, such as hospitals, industry, and home. They also proposed to spread the technology to all regions of the world. Figure 4 shows students proud of their accomplishment.

6 Conclusion

Robotics education is an integrator in STEM and can be adapted to local settings and economy. The technology, as a tool to teach computing and programing, has a versatile reach and should be promoted in all aspects of education. From all three case studies, with different research methods employed, it is evident that a positive impact is achieved and learning is enhanced using the robot as a tool.

References

Choi, I., Hill, R., Kopcha, T., Mativo, J., Bae, Y., Hodge, E., et al. (2015). *Danger zone: A STEM-integrated robotics unit – My design journal*. Seoul, Korea: RoboRobo, Ltd..

Kuenzi, J. J. (2008). Science, technology, engineering, and mathematics (STEM) education: Background, federal policy and legislative action. *Congressional Research Service*. https://digitalcommons.unl.edu/crsdocs/35/

Mativo, J. M., Hill, R. B., Choi, I., Kopcha, T.J., McGregor, J. (2017). Lessons learned in teaching science using an integrative approach that used engineering design process. *ASEE – PC…* Columbus Ohio, June 25-28.

National Research Council. (2010). Successful K-12 STEM education: Identifying effective approaches in science, technology, engineering, and mathematics. *Committee of Highly Successful Schools or Programs for K-12 STEM Education*.

Sekiya, T., & Ashida, A. (2017). An analysis of primary school dropout patterns in Honduras. *Journal of Latinos and Education, 16*(1), 65–73. https://doi.org/10.1080/15348431.2016.1179185.

Walters, K., Choi, I., Ocak, C., Mativo, J., Kwon, S., & Truong, E. (2019, October). A case study for train-the-trainer and teacher-empowerment in Honduras: 6th grade STEM-integrated robotics curriculum implementation. In *Poster presented at the annual conference of the Association for Educational Communications and Technology*. Las Vegas, NV.

The 2020 Scholarship Rankings

Richard E. West and Isaac Pfleger

The field of educational technology has a rich history of scholarly research incorporating a wide variety of methods, spanning both qualitative and quantitative paradigms, that has been published in an even wider collection of journals. Because our discipline integrates with other disciplines as a "meta" field, publication data is difficult to collect and interpret. However, there have been frequent studies seeking to understand what is being published, by whom and where, and what implications will be resulting. These meta-syntheses are useful because they help us understand the reach and boundaries of our discipline and what topics are being discussed, and which ones are not. They also help us become aware of new scholars, including internationally.

In this chapter, we report our analysis of the last 5 years of educational technology scholarship indexed in the Scopus scholarship database. In doing so, we follow similar methods we utilized in a previous study, published in *British Journal of Educational Technology* (Bodily, Leary, & West, 2019) and then revised for the 2019 version of the *Educational Technology Media Yearbook* (West & Bodily, 2019).

In reporting this data, we reiterate a caution we have offered before: the field of educational technology is unique in that faculty and departments have a dual purpose of not only researching and developing theory about technology and its utility and effects in education, but also focusing on affecting practice through design, development, and collaboration with school partners. Thus, the measure of a strong department, scholar, or university in the field of educational technology should consider the effect on practice, equally as much as the effect on research. Unfortunately, there is not good data on the effect we are having on practice, or on the quality of design education that a program provides, which makes it difficult to understand

---

R. E. West (✉) · I. Pfleger
IPT Department, Brigham Young University, Provo, UT, USA
e-mail: rickwest@byu.edu

© The Author(s), under exclusive license to Springer Nature Switzerland AG 2021
R. M. Branch et al. (eds.), *Educational Media and Technology Yearbook*,
Educational Media and Technology Yearbook 43,
https://doi.org/10.1007/978-3-030-71774-2_5

how we are doing as a field, department, or individuals. However, even though we cannot easily measure our impact on practice, we should never forget that improving outcomes for learners is why we do our research, and that sometimes design interventions can be equally or even more impactful than a published article.

With that caution, we will explain briefly our methods for collecting this data, and then share our results.

1 Methods

In this section we will explain our methodology, which follows closely and replicates our previous methodologies, except that we limited it to the five most recent years, in order to showcase recent trends, and to allow for the emergence of new scholars doing significant work. In addition, we emphasize domestic scholars because the *Educational Technology Media Yearbook* focuses on domestic programs in the field. However, we do provide data on international authors/programs as well as useful information. In our analysis, we were guided by the following question:

What trends exist in the Scopus database related to authorship, citations, and article topics for IDT journals from 2015 to 2019?

1.1 Database Selection

In this study we utilized an automated method to retrieve, organize, and compile results using Scopus. Scopus (https://www.elsevier.com/solutions/scopus), owned by Elsevier, indexes peer-reviewed literature and claims to be the "largest abstract and citation database of peer-reviewed literature" ("About Scopus," 2017). In our previous article (Bodily et al., 2019), we compared citation patterns in Scopus with Google Scholar, and found them to be comparable in regard to which journals and individuals were cited the most. Thus, while Scopus is not as expansive as Google Scholar in what scholarship it indexes, the overall patterns should be similar. Note also that because Google Scholar is more expansive, an individual scholar will see higher citation counts for their articles in Google Scholar, as would be the case for all scholars.

1.2 Journal Inclusion Criteria

Bodily et al. (2019) searched in Scopus for all journals that included the keywords technology AND (learning OR education OR school OR instruction), computer AND (learning OR education OR school OR instruction), online AND (learning OR education OR school OR instruction), distance AND (learning OR education OR school OR instruction), media AND (learning OR education OR school OR instruction), learning, instruction, and e-learning. They then included any additional journals listed in Ritzhaupt, Sessums, and Johnson's (2012) study of the most important journals in the field. After scanning the journal titles, they excluded any journals that were not a good fit for the field of instructional design and technology, for example if they focused on computer science or elementary education. We utilized this same list of journals, excluding any that ceased to operate during our time period. The final number of active journals included in our analysis was 62 (see https://bit.ly/ETMYdata). To access article metadata for a particular journal in the Scopus API, we used the International Standard Serial Number (ISSN) for the journal that must be used in the request.

1.3 Data Retrieval

We used an R script that was very similar to the Python script from our 2019 article to access the Scopus API. The script pulled journal metrics and article metadata. There were 13,258 articles retrieved from the 62 journals included in our analysis—3586 were included in the domestic-only data set. When calculating domestic data, we included any article in our data set that had at least one author affiliated with a university from the United States.

1.4 Data Analysis

Once we retrieved the data for 2015–2019, we determined the top authors, cited works, originating institutions, and countries. We excluded generic author keywords (e.g., learning, student, technology, education). The top authors were identified by counting the number of publications for each author. Points for a medal count analysis were calculated as follows: three points for first author, two points for second author, and one point for any remaining authors.

2 Findings

The field of educational technology is very international, which is represented in the Scopus authorship data. However, because the Educational Technology Media Yearbook focuses primarily on programs located in the United States, we first share domestic data, followed by international data. In Table 1 we present the top US authors with the most publications, along with their medal count score (e.g., results weighted by authorship order). This medal count score shows a different ranking, indicating that some authors excelled in co-authoring many papers, while others excelled in more lead authorship roles. Table 2 reports the top global authors.

Table 1 Top US published authors in the Scopus database of educational technology journals, 2015–2019. This data is sorted by number of publications

Author	# of publications	Medal count	Citations
Henriksen D.	25	57	97
Mishra P.	22	33	188
Watson S.	18	41	214
Kimmons R.	18	49	134
Xing W.	17	42	121
Watson W.	16	32	207
Stefaniak J.	16	38	34
Ke F.	14	36	191
Ching Y.	13	28	72
Schunn C.	13	21	66
Graham C.R.	12	20	361
Tawfik A.	12	32	98
Ritzhaupt A.	12	28	82
Kim C.	11	28	160
Akcaoglu M.	11	24	111
Baldwin S.	11	25	72
West R.	11	25	69
Craig S.D.	11	21	68
Adesope O.	10	22	168
Trust T.	10	28	148
Xie K.	10	26	141
Hsu Y.	10	21	106
Kopcha T.	10	23	73
Poitras E.	10	27	70
Schroeder N.L.	10	28	61
Gao F.	10	19	55
Bers M.	9	16	191
Richardson J.	9	20	173
Crompton H.	9	23	141
Carpenter J.	9	19	131
Lowenthal P.	9	24	92
Liu M.	9	27	90
Reigeluth C.	9	15	85
Martin F.	9	24	61
Baker R.S.	9	18	49
Luo T.	9	24	36
Kim D.	8	20	146
Bodily R.	8	16	123
Chen B.	8	23	117
Bonk C.J.	8	16	93

Table 2 Top published authors (global) in the Scopus database of educational technology journals, 2015–2019, sorted by total number of publications

Author	# of publications	Medal count	Citations
Hwang G.	66	125	1179
Huang Y.	39	67	590
Tsai C.	35	50	387
Zhu C.	35	61	278
Teo T.	29	71	369
Hwang W.	29	62	319
Voogt J.	28	48	534
Tondeur J.	25	50	580
Kirschner P.	25	35	348
Henriksen D.	25	57	97
Gaševic D.	23	34	935
Shadiev R.	23	55	356
Mishra P.	22	32	188
Doleck T.	22	49	127
Chai C.	21	37	249
Chen N.	20	20	187
Gu X.	20	40	87
Veletsianos G.	19	47	338
Watson S.	18	41	214
Rienties B.	18	34	163
Kimmons R.	18	46	134
Lajoie S.	18	29	107
Hong J.C.	18	51	86
Hew K.	17	37	427
Paas F.	17	20	271
Xing W.	17	40	121
Dawson S.	16	19	707
Watson W.	16	32	207
Chen C.	16	40	161
Costley J.	16	41	82
Stefaniak J.	16	38	34
Godwin-Jones R.	15	45	156
Fraser B.	15	29	108
Bazelais P.	15	24	84
Tai K.H.	15	17	73
Hwang M.	15	29	51
Gibson D.	14	26	380
Lan Y.J.	14	36	255
Sun J.	14	37	209
Ke F.	14	34	191

Table 3 presents the topmost cited US authors, which represents citations by other Scopus-indexed publications. Table 4 presents the topmost cited global authors. A few interesting findings are that Danah Henriksen was the top US scholar both in total publications and in the medal count, indicating a large amount of lead authorship roles. Sunnie Watson, Royce Kimmons, and Wanli Xing, similarly, were in the top five on both lists. In addition, Henriksen, Punya Mishra, Watson, Kimmons, Xing, William Watson, Jill Stefaniak, and Fengfeng Ke are the only US scholars to also be represented in the top 40 of global scholars. Globally, Gwan-Hwan Hwang had an impressive 5-year pattern of scholarship, as he was the top published scholar, and the top cited scholar by large amounts in both categories. In terms of the most cited scholars, the two topmost highly cited scholars in the United States (Michael D. Hanus and Jesse Fox) produced only one Scopus-indexed article on educational technology during the 5-year period—but this article ("Assessing the effects of gamification in the classroom: A longitudinal study on intrinsic motivation, social comparison, satisfaction, effort, and academic performance") accrued 442 citations in these 5 years to place these scholars at the top of the domestic table. Also interesting to note is that these scholars only show up at #13 in the global list of most cited authors, confirming that there is a substantial amount of significant scholarship in the field being contributed from outside the United States.

An important note to accompany this analysis is that many scholars have similar names, and may conflate Scopus results. We have attempted to identify and correct any errors by using the database-given author IDs. However, there is always the chance that an author has two or more IDs in Scopus, or that some other error has occurred in compiling the data from the database.

When looking at where the top scholarship is being produced, the United States was the dominant country in the data set, over four times higher than any other country (see Table 5). Of course, this likely represents in part the dominance of the English language in the Scopus data, the population size of the United States, and the high number of US universities. The United Kingdom was the second top country, followed by Taiwan, Turkey, and Australia (Table 5).

In considering the top-publishing universities in the Scopus database for educational technology publications, we similarly report global leaders as well as the data from the United States specifically. As shown in Table 6, there are strong Asian influences in our field, as two Taiwanese universities led all other institutions, along with Purdue, the Open University, and the University of Hong Kong. The top publishing universities in the United States were Purdue, Michigan State, Pennsylvania State, Indiana University, and University of Georgia (see Table 7 for the top US universities).

We also sorted the data by article citation, to understand which articles were the most significant, at least in terms of citations, in the last 5 years. The limitation, of course, is that this is a relatively small window of time for citations to accrue, and other publications (especially the more recent ones) may prove more significant over time. Table 8 shows the top 20 cited articles. The citation average for all articles in the global data set is 7 citations/article, or 6.6 for articles in the domestic data set.

Table 3 Top US cited authors in the Scopus database of educational technology journals, 2013–2018, sorted by citations

Author	Medal count	Articles	Citations
Fox J.	2	1	442
Hanus M.	3	1	442
Graham C.R.	20	12	361
Siemens G.	14	5	338
Greenhow C.	14	5	222
Watson S.	41	18	214
Wang M.	12	5	209
Watson W.	32	16	207
Henrie C.R.	10	4	197
Yadav A.	10	5	196
Ke F.	36	14	191
Bers M.	16	9	191
Mishra P.	33	22	188
Hofkens T.	3	3	187
Kizilcec R.	3	1	177
Maldonado J.	2	1	177
Hilton J.	16	7	174
Richardson J.	20	9	173
Adesope O.	22	10	168
Halverson L.R.	3	2	161
Lim J.	8	5	160
Kim C.	28	11	160
Trust T.	28	10	148
Kim D.	20	8	146
Crompton H.	9	23	141
Xie K.	10	26	141
Jurow A.	4	11	135
Kimmons R.	18	49	134
Salmela-Aro K.	4	6	133
Carpenter J.	9	19	131
Grant S.	1	3	129
Knight E.	1	2	129
Bodily R.	8	16	123
Azevedo R.	5	11	122
Fredricks J.	2	5	122
Xing W.	17	42	121
Burke D.	3	5	120
Ottenbreit-Leftwich A.	6	16	119
Krutka D.	6	11	119
Karabulut-Ilgu A.	3	9	119

Table 4 Top global authors in the Scopus database of educational technology journals, 2015–2019, sorted by citations

Author	Medal count	Articles	Citations
Hwang G.	125	66	1179
Gaševic D.	34	23	935
Dawson S.	19	16	707
Huang Y.	67	39	590
Tondeur J.	50	25	580
Phillips C.	2	1	568
O'Flaherty J.	3	1	568
Chang K.	18	12	558
Lim T.	4	3	534
Voogt J.	48	28	534
Sung Y.	19	11	532
Fox J.	3	1	442
Hanus M.	2	1	442
Hew K.	37	17	427
Lai C.	24	11	425
Agre G.	1	1	418
Angelova G.	1	1	418
Dichev C.	2	1	418
Dicheva D.	3	1	418
De Freitas S.	9	4	414
Boyle E.A.	11	6	393
Tsai C.	50	35	387
Gibson D.	26	14	380
Connolly T.	3	2	378
Hainey T.	5	2	378
Arnab S.	15	7	378
Liu T.	11	7	371
Teo T.	29	71	369
Graham C.	12	20	361
Littlejohn A.	9	20	361
Shadiev R.	23	55	356
Kirschner P.	25	35	348
Veletsianos G.	19	47	338
Siemens G.	5	7	338
Milligan C.	4	8	327
Hwang W.	29	62	319
Hone K.	3	7	313
Ninaus M.	3	5	302
Scherer R.	11	25	292
Ott M.	2	3	289

Table 5 Countries producing the most scholarship in educational technology in 2015–2019

Country	# of publications
United States	3310
United Kingdom	872
Taiwan	868
Turkey	767
Australia	727
China	618
Canada	496
Spain	473
Germany	456
Netherlands	401
Malaysia	330
India	309
Indonesia	271
South Korea	248
Italy	234
Greece	212
Israel	197
Hong Kong	193
Finland	187

Table 6 Universities producing the most scholarship in educational technology in 2015–2019

University	# of publications
National Taiwan Normal University	194
National Taiwan University of Science and Technology	131
Open University	110
Purdue University	110
The University of Hong Kong	109
National Central University Taiwan	94
Open University of the Netherlands	94
Pennsylvania State University	90
Michigan State University	89
Anadolu Üniversitesi	87
Beijing Normal University	86
Curtin University	86
Indiana University Bloomington	82
The Education University of Hong Kong	78
The University of Georgia	78
National Cheng Kung University	76
University of Malaya	73
Brigham Young University	70
University of South Africa	69
Boise State University	68

Table 7 Universities in the United States producing the most scholarship in educational technology (2015–2018)

University	# of publications
Purdue University	112
Michigan State University	90
Pennsylvania State University	90
Indiana University Bloomington	82
The University of Georgia	80
Brigham Young University	70
Boise State University	68
Arizona State University	62
Old Dominion University	58
University of North Texas	56
University of Illinois at Urbana-Champaign	55
Florida State University	48
Northern Illinois University	46
University of Florida	46
University of Pittsburgh	45
The University of Texas at Austin	44
Utah State University	41
University of California, Irvine	40
Iowa State University	37
Kent State University	37

Table 8 Top-cited articles in educational technology from 2015 to 2019

Article	Authors	Journal	Citations
Assessing the effects of gamification in the classroom: A longitudinal study on intrinsic motivation, social comparison, satisfaction, effort, and academic performance	Hanus M.; Fox J.	Computers and Education	442
Gamification in education: A systematic mapping study	Dicheva D.; Dichev C.; Agre G.; Angelova G.	Educational Technology and Society	418
Let's not forget: Learning analytics are about learning	Gaševic D.; Dawson S.; Siemens G.	TechTrends	265
Self-regulated learning strategies predict learner behavior and goal attainment in Massive Open Online Courses	Kizilcec R.; Pérez-Sanagustín M.; Maldonado J.	Computers and Education	177
Measuring student engagement in technology-mediated learning: A review	Henrie C.R.; Halverson L.R.; Graham C.R.	Computers and Education	136
Digital badges in education	Gibson D.; Ostashewski N.; Flintoff K.;Grant S.; Knight E.	Education and Information Technologies	129

The 2020 Scholarship Rankings

Table 8 (continued)

Article	Authors	Journal	Citations
Social media and education: reconceptualizing the boundaries of formal and informal learning	Greenhow C.; Lewin C.	Learning, Media and Technology	121
Mobile apps for science learning: Review of research	Zydney J.; Warner Z.	Computers and Education	109
Enhancing learning and engagement through embodied interaction within a mixed reality simulation	Lindgren R.; Tscholl M.; Wang S.; Johnson E.	Computers and Education	106
Understanding the relationship between teachers' pedagogical beliefs and technology use in education: a systematic review of qualitative evidence	Tondeur J.; van Braak J.; Ertmer P.A.; Ottenbreit-Leftwich A.	Educational Technology Research and Development	99
A systematic review of research on the flipped learning method in engineering education	Karabulut-Ilgu A.; Jaramillo Cherrez N.; Jahren C.	British Journal of Educational Technology	98
Computational thinking in compulsory education: Towards an agenda for research and practice	Voogt J.; Fisser P.; Good J.; Mishra P.; Yadav A.	Education and Information Technologies	97
"Together we are better": Professional learning networks for teachers	Trust T.; Krutka D.; Carpenter J.	Computers and Education	87
Using the flipped classroom to enhance EFL learning	Chen Hsieh J.S.; Wu W.C.V.; Marek M.W.	Computer Assisted Language Learning	86
Impact of mobile technology on student attitudes, engagement, and learning	Heflin H.; Shewmaker J.; Nguyen J.	Computers and Education	86
How teacher emotional support motivates students: The mediating roles of perceived peer relatedness, autonomy support, and competence	Ruzek E.; Hafen C.; Allen J.; Gregory A.; Mikami A.; Pianta R.	Learning and Instruction	86
Open educational resources and college textbook choices: a review of research on efficacy and perceptions	Hilton J.	Educational Technology Research and Development	81
Examining the moderating effect of individual-level cultural values on users' acceptance of e-learning in developing countries: a structural equation modeling of an extended technology acceptance model	Tarhini A.; Hone K.; Liu X.; Tarhini T.	Interactive Learning Environments	81
A meta-analysis of the effects of audience response systems (clicker-based technologies) on cognition and affect	Hunsu N.J.; Adesope O.; Bayly D.J.	Computers and Education	78
Understanding the massive open online course (MOOC) student experience: An examination of attitudes, motivations, and barriers	Shapiro H.B.; Lee C.H.; Wyman Roth N.E.; Li K.; Çetinkaya-Rundel M.; Canelas, D.A.	Computers and Education	75

This analysis showed the valuable contribution that literature syntheses and theoretical scholarship can provide to the discipline, as 8 of the top 20 papers were literature reviews, syntheses, or theoretical papers. Second, the scholarship in our discipline is fed by a wide variety of journals, as 10 different journals contributed to this list of top-cited articles. This is significant, as it means that a scholar can publish in many different locations and still be well cited. However, *Computers and Education* (9 articles) was a dominant publication venue. Unfortunately, there remains a strong need for open-access publication options, as only one open-access journal published a significant (top 20) paper: *Educational Technology and Society*. However, this journal has ceased to publish new articles. Finally, a few trends were readily apparent in this corpus of top-cited articles, as the top 2 articles focused on gamification, 3 articles in the top 20 discussed mobile learning and/or social media, 3 discussed some aspect of open education (open badges, open educational resources, or MOOCs), 2 discussed flipped learning, and 2 were at least partially related to student engagement.

Our final analysis considered the keywords and topics that are most common over the past 3 years, according to author-provided keywords. As seen in Table 9, clearly the most important topic in the discipline is that of online learning (or alternatively called distance education, online education, or e-learning), with one of these terms being listed as a keyword 392 times. The most common name for this category of education was "online learning" with 188 occurrences. Higher education was much more common than K-12 environments for this scholarship, and even when K-12 contexts were studied, it was often for preservice education. While specific technologies were frequently mentioned, such as MOOCs and Twitter, there was a high focus on instructional design and pedagogy, which is a positive trend. Problem-solving and collaborative learning approaches were also commonly studied.

Table 9 Most frequent author keywords in articles published in educational technology journals from 2015 to 2019

Words	Occurrences
Online/distance/e-learning	392
Higher education	112
Instructional design	101
Technology	77
Social media	72
Professional development	68
Technology integration	66
Mobile learning	64
Learning analytics	62
Educational technology	57
Learning	56
Assessment	55
Motivation	55
Teacher education	55
Collaborative learning	52

Table 9 (continued)

Words	Occurrences
Computer-mediated communication	49
Education	48
Collaboration	47
Mathematics	45
Blended learning	43
Improving classroom teaching	41
Memory	41
Interactive learning environments	40
Student engagement	40
Feedback	37
Problem-solving	37
Engagement	36
Self-regulated learning	36
Teaching learning strategies	35
OPEN educational resources	34
Information literacy	33
Game-based learning	32
MOOC	32
Self-efficacy	32
VIRTUAL reality	32
Pedagogical issues	31
COMPUTATIONAL thinking	30
SCIENCE education	30
Social presence	30
Working memory	30
Design-based research	29
Pedagogy	29
Tpack	29
Twitter	29
Cognitive load	28
Stem	28

3 Conclusion

Similarly to our analysis in last year's yearbook, we found that recent scholarship continues to be very international, with impressive contributions from universities around the globe. Many of the key scholars remain the same from that analysis, with newer additions to the top list representing some of the emerging leaders in the field. The field continues to be technology centric, with a focus on online and distance learning, which is not surprising given the titles of the journals selected for analysis. However, instructional design and various instructional strategies such as problem-solving, blended learning, and collaborative learning were frequently mentioned.

The field also continues to emphasize research in higher education environments over younger age levels, and review and theoretical scholarship continue to dominate within the list of the most highly cited articles.

References

Bodily, R., Leary, H., & West, R. E. (2019). Research trends in instructional design and technology journals. *British Journal of Educational Technology*. Available online https://onlinelibrary.wiley.com/doi/full/10.1111/bjet.12712

Ritzhaupt, A. D., Sessums, C. D., & Johnson, M. C. (2012). Where should educational technologists publish their research? An examination of peer-reviewed journals within the field of educational technology and factors influencing publication choice. *Educational Technology, 52*, 47.

West, R. E., & Bodily, B. (2019). Scholarship and program rankings. In R. M. Branch, H. Lee, & S. S. Tseng (Eds.), *Educational media and technology yearbook* (Vol. 42). https://doi.org/10.1007/978-3-030-27986-8.

Part II
Leadership Profiles

Introduction

Robert G. Doyle

In this section, two distinguished individuals who have made significant contributions to the field of educational media and communication technology are profiled. In each volume of *Educational Media and Technology Yearbook*, leaders are highlighted who have typically held prominent offices, composed seminal works, and made significant contributions that influence the contemporary vision of the field. The people profiled in this section have mentored individuals, who have become recognized for their own contributions to learning, design, and technology.

You are encouraged to nominate individuals to be featured in this section of the Yearbook. The editors of this Yearbook will carefully consider your nomination. Please direct comments, questions, and suggestions about the selection process to Robert G. Doyle <rgdoyle12@gmail.com> or Rob Branch <rbranch@uga.edu>.

This volume of the *Educational Media and Technology Yearbook* remembers two outstanding members of the community who continue to positively impact leadership and scholarship. The leaders profiled this year are:

Phillip Harris
Barbara B. Lockee

The following people [listed alphabetically] were profiled in earlier volumes of the *Educational Media and Technology Yearbook*:

John C. Belland
Robert K. Branson
James W. Brown
Edward Caffarella
Bob Casey
Betty Collis

R. G. Doyle (✉)
Harvard University, Cambridge, MA, USA

© The Author(s), under exclusive license to Springer Nature Switzerland AG 2021
R. M. Branch et al. (eds.), *Educational Media and Technology Yearbook*,
Educational Media and Technology Yearbook 43,
https://doi.org/10.1007/978-3-030-71774-2_6

Richard Cornell (Volume 42)
Robert E. De Kieffer
Robert M. Diamond
Walter Dick
J. Ana Donaldson (Volume 42)
Philip L. Doughty
Frank Dwyer
Donald P. Ely
James D. Finn
Robert Mills Gagné
Castelle (Cass) G. Gentry
Thomas F. Gilbert
Kent Gustafson
John Hedberg
Robert Heinich
Jacquelyn (Jackie) Hill
Stanley A. Huffman
Harry Alleyn Johnson
David H. Jonassen
Roger Kaufman
Jerrold E. Kemp
Addie Kinsinger
David R. Krathwohl
Jean E. Lowrie
Wesley Joseph McJulien
M. David Merrill
Michael Molenda
David Michael Moore
Robert M. Morgan
Robert Morris
James Okey
Ronald Oliver
Tjeerd Plomp
Tillman (Tim) James Ragan
W. Michael Reed
Thomas C. Reeves
Rita C. Richey
Paul Saettler
Wilbur Schramm
Charles Francis Schuller
Sharon Smaldino
Don Carl Smellie
Glenn Snelbecker
Howard Sullivan
William Travers

Introduction

Constance Dorothea Weinman
Paul Welliver
Paul Robert Wendt
Ronald Zemke

Phil Harris

Robert G. Doyle

1 Engagement, Connectivity, and Interest

Many members of the Association for Educational Communications and Technology (AECT) have known just one executive director, Dr. Phil Harris. They might assume that he has spent his entire professional career with the organization. The many lives that Harris has led, however, might encourage us to wonder if he has more lives than a cat.

A native of Louisville, Kentucky, Harris has lived most of his life in that area of the nation. Although he has spent his professional life in education, he has focused on various aspects of it.

Harris began his higher education work with a Bachelor of Science degree in elementary education from Indiana University. During his undergraduate years, he

R. G. Doyle (✉)
Harvard University, Cambridge, MA, USA

© The Author(s), under exclusive license to Springer Nature Switzerland AG 2021
R. M. Branch et al. (eds.), *Educational Media and Technology Yearbook*,
Educational Media and Technology Yearbook 43,
https://doi.org/10.1007/978-3-030-71774-2_7

married Joan, who often attends AECT conferences and helps out. They have four children including one son and three daughters: Steven, a faculty member at Queens College; Victoria, an adjunct faculty member at Indiana University; Janine, who is with the Institute for Restorative Justice at Ohio State University; and Katherine, who teaches sociology at Miami University of Ohio.

Initially, Dr. Harris planned to be a lifelong educator. After earning his undergraduate degree, he taught 5th and 6th grades in the Bloomington Metropolitan School System in Bloomington. Several years later, one of his former professors encouraged him to attend graduate school. He discovered that his graduate school stipend would be larger than his teaching salary, so he discussed the proposal with Joan and made the leap. In addition to the aforementioned B.S., Harris earned a Master of Science degree in elementary education with studies in reading, psychology, and research at Indiana University. Without taking a breath, he continued studies at the same institution and earned an Ed.D. in elementary education with a focus on reading, research, and instructional design. During his graduate studies, Harris worked in multiple roles as a graduate assistant at the university's Center for Child Study, as a research assistant, and as a lecturer.

After completing his dissertation, he received a postdoc offer from Indiana University's psychology department and accepted it.

Upon completion of that work, he became a lecturer at the Indiana University School of Education. He taught clinical methods for teaching reading. Harris was a visiting lecturer at Louisiana Tech University, Marquette University, and Nazareth College of Rochester, NY. Early in his career, Harris developed a philosophy on teaching. He believes that one cannot teach without an interest in teaching and the subject. Moreover, one must be fully focused on educating students. Having these attributes helps educators to connect with the students.

As true today as it was in graduate school, Harris has frequently sought various methods to feed his range of academic interests. After teaching assignments, Harris became the director of the Programmed Teaching Research and Development Center. He oversaw the professional and support personnel, developed and managed the budget, secured funding by contacting publishers and public school systems, and wrote proposals. The work also required him to present the Center's findings and work to school administrators, reading supervisors, classroom teachers, and community groups nationwide. Moreover, he organized and established Programmed Tutoring projects in 40 states and established over 300 projects in public and private schools.

Following 13 years in that role, Harris became the director of the Center for Reading and Language Studies in the Smith Research Center at Indiana University. His duties ranged from supervising the professional staff, securing funding, and administrative responsibilities to writing proposals, collaborating with school systems, and preparing evaluation reports. In using the data from those sources, Harris presented at professional meetings, taught graduate and undergraduate courses, and chaired numerous university and department committees.

In stepping out of a higher education institution for the first time since beginning his undergraduate studies in the field, Harris accepted an offer to become the director of the Center for Professional Development and Services with Phi Delta Kappa International. His new role included a combination of some familiar responsibilities and some new and challenging tasks. He collaborated with the National Curriculum Audit Center, National Center for Effective Schools, and Gabbard Institutes. Harris presented at state and national conferences, developed marketing and promotional plans, performed needs assessments to identify major educational issues, and, of course, prepared and managed budgets.

Harris further posits that educators must monitor the brain because that is where learning takes place and learning and performance must be separated. Learning is a multidimensional process. Cognitive psychologists judge learning other than through learning. One does not have to take a test to measure what you have learned because not everyone is skilled at test taking. In the next decade, there will be more access to what is going on in the brain to tailor individual learning plans. Technology will help to explore learning, but what are the properties of learning and units of measure? To help every human to become what they want to be needs to be our vision.

Before the beginning of Harris's tenure as Executive Director, AECT was a partner with the International Communications and Industries Association (ICIA) in InfoComm. During its 1992 annual convention in Washington, DC, the AECT board announced its separation from ICIA, and membership quickly decreased. Membership at that time included many practitioners, and a large number of them left for associations that were better aligned with their careers. The members who remained included professors, librarians, teachers, and some remaining practitioners. When membership's decline finally ceased, the organization was a fraction of its past. A few years later and in a cost-saving measure, the decision was made to move out of Washington, DC, with its high office leasing prices and to relocate to Bloomington, Indiana (AIT) Agency for Instructional Technology offered space and staff support.

Although we will not list the extensive range of Harris's publications, grants, articles, and conference presentations in this writing, several deserve mention. Harris's most recent book was published by Rowman & Littlefield Publishers, Inc. and is entitled *The Myths of Standardized Tests*. A sampling of his grants was obtained from the National Science Foundation, Briggs Institute of Medical Technology, the Psychological Corporation, the U.S. Department of Defense, and the U.S. Department of Education.

Now, we reach the point when Dr. Harris began the challenging work for which all of us know him well. AECT's aforementioned move out of Washington meant that the association would seek a new Executive Director. He received this unusual offer in 1999. The description of AECT led Harris to believe that the organization and its finances were in good condition, its future was robust, and the next issue of *TechTrends* was ready to be published.

Harris resigned from his position as director of Phi Delta Kappa's Professional Development Center, and he accepted AECT's job offer. He delved deeply into the association's financial books, its recent history, the condition of its publications, and its membership. Every page he turned, every call he answered, and every envelope he opened revealed another sign of near-rigor mortis throughout AECT. The phone in his office rang regularly, and the caller was most often a debt collector or vendor unhappy about a lack of payment. Harris soon feared the constant ringing, as rarely did it bring good news. Harris soon discovered that membership was decreasing, that the bank accounts were empty, that the debt was enormous, and that the next issue of *TechTrends* was not ready for publication or anything; only the cover had been prepared.

The unavoidable question in 1999 and 2000 was not would AECT pass, but when. A Chicago lawyer's office called, and Harris logically assumed that he would hear more bad news and possibly a lawsuit. Reluctantly and with fear that the caller could mean the end of a long-standing association established in 1923, he accepted the call. The lawyer mentioned the name, Louise Benton Wagner, but Harris did not know her. He called Kyle Peck, but he did not know her. Next, he called Robert Harrell but he lacked information as well. Finally, Harris reached Addie Kissinger and she knew Ms. Wagner. The Chicago lawyer was calling to inform Harris that Ms. Wagner had left more than $375,000 in her estate for AECT. After months of wondering if AECT would survive, the organization was solvent. Clearly, it was not rich but it was finally above water.

With the combination of Harris, AECT presidents, the AECT board, and careful fiscal management, AECT began its successful return trip to reach life. AECT, however, had to reinvent itself. Just as Harris believes that educators have to focus on learning to succeed in their classrooms, AECT had to focus on its mission and develop a strategic plan, a growth plan, and new goals.

Under Dr. Harris's careful and purposeful direction, not only has AECT morphed from a near-death status in 1999 to its current strong and highly respected position, but it is also on a trend to even greater success. Moreover, in a few short years it will celebrate its 100th birthday.

During the 2018 AECT conference in Kansas City, MO, and with the support from a large number of AECT board members and past presidents, an award was established to honor and recognize Dr. Harris's significant dedication to and accomplishments for AECT. The name of the award is the Phil Harris Leadership Internship fund.

Dr. Phil Harris, the *man behind the curtain*, was the indomitable and central figure in revitalizing the Association for Educational Communications and Technology. For this accomplishment and many others, we are forever grateful.

Barbara Lockee

Robert G. Doyle

1 I Can't Think of a Project I Haven't Loved

The title of this writing, a remark made by our subject, best describes the positive attitude, philosophy, and motivation of the former president of the Association for Educational Communications and Technology (AECT), Dr. Barbara Lockee of Virginia Polytechnic Institute and State University.

Dr. Lockee was born in McMinnville, Tennessee, which is a small town serving as the seat in Warren County and located about 75 miles southeast of Nashville. At the time, her father was a student at Middle Tennessee State University while working on the Apollo 11 rocket system. Upon completion of school, he was hired as a technical writer for AT&T in Winston-Salem, NC, and so the family ventured east to North Carolina.

Her father, being a technical writer/designer, instigated Dr. Lockee's interest in technology. He told her that if she could learn Linux, she could do anything. She started with a Commodore 64 and a cassette tape to learn how to develop programs

R. G. Doyle (✉)
Harvard University, Cambridge, MA, USA

on a computer. Her high school English teacher, also her debate team coach, encouraged her to pursue writing as a career path. This encouragement played a significant role in Lockee's developing interest in journalism, research, and communications. These two interests—computing and writing—would converge and find their way into her story at a later point in time.

After graduating from Davie High School in Mocksville, North Carolina, Lockee attended Appalachian State University in Boone, NC, where she earned a degree in communications media. Although Lockee hoped to work in advertising upon graduation, she accepted a position with the Winston-Salem, NC, property of Hyatt Hotels in a management-training role. Management training meant working in all areas of the hotel to gain knowledge of each facet of hoteling and management. When she worked as a bartender, some of her customers included Refrigerator Perry, Michael Jordan, Tony Bennett (yes—he ordered Frosted Flakes), and Natalie Cole. She had an opportunity to meet many celebrities because golf tournaments were frequently held in the area. With an interest in communications and technology, Lockee moved into her last position at Hyatt as a systems administrator, managing the computers used for the hotel sales and catering operations.

Deciding to leave the corporate world and attend graduate school in pursuit of becoming a documentary filmmaker, Lockee enrolled in an educational media master's degree program at Appalachian State University. The institution instantly discovered Lockee's significant skills and abilities to teach and motivate students and asked her to teach a course; she loved it! Approaching graduation, she acquired a Mac and began to learn about videodiscs and how to use them with photography and film to create educational programs.

With a newly found passion for teaching, Lockee decided to seek a Ph.D. at Virginia Tech and work towards a career in teaching. As part of her dissertation research, she developed an interest in using technology for Native American language preservation. Lockee's father was of Cherokee descent, and she wanted to learn more about his ancestry. Her indomitable curiosity led her to begin work on preserving the Cherokee language. While performing doctoral work, she created a computer program to demonstrate how technology could be used to teach Cherokee. She used culturally relevant materials in multimedia formats so that students could see and hear language in a cultural context. Lockee worked with people on the Cherokee reservation during the early stages of design and development, as well as pilot testing. This design and development study played a role in demonstrating how hypermedia and multimedia technologies could support language learning in locally meaningful ways.

While studying for her terminal degree, she served as a graduate assistant in the Office of Distance Learning, supporting faculty teaching on television. With the rapid growth of the Internet and the proliferation of online programing, she was hired upon graduation to help faculty members produce online courses.

Lockee's next adventure led her to a tenure track teaching position with the IDT program focused on distance education and instructional design. She continued to collaborate with practitioners in industry, the military, and K-12 education. Her roles, however, spanned a significant range. She obtained funding for distance education initiatives, as well as funding for instructional design and development projects in veterinary medicine. With her IDT colleagues, she began to offer an online M.A. program in 1998, and it continues to grow stronger more than 20 years after its beginning. She developed opportunities for international collaboration in Malawi through the United States Agency for International Development, and she and her colleagues worked with Mzuzu University to establish distance education capacity there and to develop the school's first distance education programming.

One of the most revealing remarks of Lockee's deep interests in research and pedagogy is her statement, "I can't think of a project I haven't loved." With a National Science Foundation grant, Lockee has enhanced girls' awareness of and interest in information technology careers in the Appalachian region. She worked within the cultural standards in Appalachia, where women are often expected to remain in the community. Collaborating with parents and teachers to inform them about IT jobs, she has mentored many of them and encouraged them to enroll in local community colleges to obtain IT skills, thus allowing them to obtain advanced positions without leaving their families and communities. Some IT companies have recently relocated to the region, providing significant job opportunities and serving as important collaborators in the building of local interest in IT careers. During her 7 years on this project, Lockee organized many workshops in an effort to create sustainable partnerships between industry and education, which included working within rural communities across five states in the Appalachian region.

In a more recent project, a new training administrator at the NASA Jet Propulsion Lab sought to enhance workplace learning approaches in his department, so he contacted the IDT program at Virginia Tech. Lockee offered to conduct a needs assessment and then later designed and led train-the-trainer workshops for the manufacturing training department. Following these initiatives, she directed a project in which a VT student team created the organization's first e-learning modules, focusing on safety issues for building spacecraft. Moreover, she collaborated on the Mars 2020 project. This a partnership that was especially meaningful to her, given her father's earlier work on the Apollo mission.

In her professional community, Lockee is extraordinarily active. In addition to being a past president of AECT, she served as Research & Theory Division president and board member representative, Executive Committee Member-At-Large, and President (2011). She is also involved in the Awards Committee and the History & Archives Committee. She developed AECT's HistoryMakers Project, which was later renamed the AECT Legends & Legacies Project. The grassroots origins of the project were a collaborative effort to capture the voices of our scholars and leaders through video interviews. Lockee formed a Virginia Tech student team that created an online, searchable archive of those interviews. More recently, she has conducted interviews, and has added audio interviews from the 1970s. The archive is used globally to support courses and research in the field.

At one of the International Academic Forum (IAFOR) conferences in Osaka, Japan, Lockee served as a keynote speaker. She spoke about using technology innovations in support of language learning, an interest she developed while working on the Cherokee language project. She enjoyed conversations with the organizers and attendees and their forum for interdisciplinary exchange. She stated, "I liked the interactive nature of the conferences and the opportunity to engage with a variety of different disciplines." She now serves as their Vice President for Education and recently directed the highly successful 2019 conference, IAFOR Conference on Educational Research & Innovation at Virginia Tech, which included professors and graduate students from 15 nations.

The number of tenured faculty members in Lockee's department has dropped from six to two, so she is currently managing the advising of 16 doctoral students. In addition to her research and publications, Professor Lockee is a faculty fellow in the Virginia Tech Office of the Provost, working in support of faculty professional development. She is still teaching and advising doctoral students—which she identifies as her favorite part of the position and, until recently, she directed the VT School of Education's Office of Educational Research and Outreach. This office supports pre-award and post-award sponsored research for faculty, services which include locating grant opportunities; supporting proposal development; faculty implementation of research and outreach programs; fiscal management; federal, state, and university compliance; and office operation functions. She has advised three dozen students on their successful completion of a doctoral dissertation. Her nearly 40-page-long CV reveals that Dr. Lockee has written several books and edited several others; she has authored approximately 20 book chapters; more than 40 Referred Journal Publications; 24 National Conference presentations; 15 Invited Columns; 16 Referred Conference Proceedings; 6 Evaluation Reports to Sponsors; 13 Invited and Commissioned Publications; 14 keynote addresses in the USA, Japan, and England; more than 30 Invited Presentations; 4 abstracts; and dozens of national presentations. Lockee has directed 14 externally funded research projects with over $8,500,000 in resources, as well as 18 internally funded projects. Moreover, she has been honored with multiple awards and recognition from AECT and Virginia Tech.

AECT has regularly acknowledged Lockee's contributions to the field of Educational Technology. In 2011, she was honored with the International Contributions Award; in 2013 with the Special Service Award; and in 2017 with the Distinguished Service Award. These awards were earned through Lockee's long commitment to AECT by serving as President and additional positions in the Research and Development Division; AECT Conference Planner in 2009; President-Elect and Conference Planner in 2010; AECT President in 2010–2011; Past President in 2011–2012; and ECT Foundation Liaison in 2011–2012.

In addition to numerous honors received at Virginia Tech, Lockee's most recent award is the Zenobia Lawrence Hikes Award. In announcing the 2019 recipient, the University stated during the Faculty Women of Color in the Academy conference, "Throughout her career, Lockee has been dedicated to fusing her academic work with knowledge empowerment for people of color." Dr. Menah Pratt-Clarke, Virginia Tech's Vice President for Diversity and Inclusion, describes Lockee as a "powerful, calm, humble presence and force in the academy."

With Dr. Barbara Lockee completing her first quarter century of membership with AECT, she has earned the respect of the membership through unending involvement, counsel, and dedication. We will close this writing, which is too brief to explain all of Lockee's accomplishments, projects, publications, and research, with the hope that she gives us another quarter century of AECT colleagueship and membership.

Part III
Organizations and Associations in North America

Introduction

Robert Maribe Branch

Part III includes annotated entries for associations and organizations, most of which are headquartered in the USA and Canada, whose interests are in some manner significant to the fields of learning, design, and technology or library and information science. For the most part, these organizations consist of professionals in the field or agencies that offer services to the educational media community. In an effort to only list active organizations, I deleted all organizations that have not updated their information since 2007. Readers are encouraged to contact the editors with names of unlisted media-related organizations for investigation and possible inclusion in the 2021 edition.

Information for this section was obtained through e-mails directing each organization to an individual web form through which the updated information could be submitted electronically into a database created by Michael Orey. Although the section editor made every effort to contact and follow up with organization representatives, responding to the annual request for an update was the responsibility of the organization representatives. The editorial team would like to thank those respondents who helped assure the currency and accuracy of this section by responding to the request for an update. Figures quoted as dues refer to annual amounts unless stated otherwise. Where dues, membership, and meeting information are not applicable, such information is omitted.

R. M. Branch (✉)
Learning, Design, and Technology, University of Georgia, Athens, GA, USA
e-mail: rbranch@uga.edu

© The Author(s), under exclusive license to Springer Nature Switzerland AG 2021
R. M. Branch et al. (eds.), *Educational Media and Technology Yearbook*,
Educational Media and Technology Yearbook 43,
https://doi.org/10.1007/978-3-030-71774-2_9

Organizations and Associations in the USA and Canada

Robert Maribe Branch

This information will be used solely to construct a directory of relevant organizations and associations within the *Educational Media & Technology Yearbook*. The data supplied here will **not** be intentionally shared or publicized in any other form. Thank you for your assistance.

Name of Organization or Association—Adaptech Research Network
Acronym—n/a
Address:
Dawson College, 3040 Sherbrooke St. West
Montreal, QC
H3Z 1A4
Canada
Phone Number—514-931-8731 #1546; **Fax Number**—514-931-3567 Attn: Catherine Fichten
Email Contact—catherine.fichten@mcgill.ca; **URL**—http://www.adaptech.org
Leaders—Catherine Fichten, Ph.D., Co-director; Jennison V. Asuncion, M.A., Co-Director; Maria Barile, M.S.W., co-director
Description—Based at Dawson College (Montreal), we are a Canada-wide, grant-funded team, conducting bilingual empirical research into the use of computer, learning, and adaptive technologies by postsecondary students with disabilities. One of our primary interests lies in issues around ensuring that newly emerging instructional technologies are accessible to learners with disabilities.
Membership—Our research team is composed of academics, practitioners, students, consumers, and others interested in the issues of access to technology by students with disabilities in higher education.

R. M. Branch (✉)
Learning, Design, and Technology, University of Georgia, Athens, GA, USA
e-mail: rbranch@uga.edu

© The Author(s), under exclusive license to Springer Nature Switzerland AG 2021
R. M. Branch et al. (eds.), *Educational Media and Technology Yearbook*,
Educational Media and Technology Yearbook 43,
https://doi.org/10.1007/978-3-030-71774-2_10

Dues—n/a

Meetings—n/a

Publications—Jorgensen, S., Fichten, C.S., & Havel, S. (2011). College satisfaction and academic success/Satisfaction et réussite académique au cégep. Final report presented to PAREA (206 pages). Montréal: Dawson College. Eric Document Reproduction Service (ED522996.); Asuncion, J.V., Fichten, C.S., Ferraro, V., Barile, M., Chwojka, C., Nguyen, M.N., & Wolforth, J. (2010). Multiple perspectives on the accessibility of e-learning in Canadian colleges and universities. Assistive Technology Journal, 22(4), 187-199. DOI: https://doi.org/10.1080/10400430903519944 2010; Fichten, C.S., Asuncion, J.V., Nguyen, M.N., Budd, J., & Amsel, R. (2010). The POSITIVES Scale: Development and validation of a measure of how well the ICT needs of students with disabilities are met. Journal of Postsecondary Education and Disability, 23(2), 137-154.; Fichten, C.S., Nguyen, M.N., Asuncion, J.V., Barile, M., Budd, J., Amsel, R. & Libman, E. (2010). Information and communication technology for French and English speaking postsecondary students with disabilities: What are their needs and how well are these being met? Exceptionality Education International, 20(1), 2-17.; Fichten, C.S., Asuncion, J.V., Nguyen, M.N., Budd, J., Barile, M., & Tibbs, A. (2010). The POSITIVES Scale: A method for assessing technology accessibility in postsecondary education. Proceedings of the CSUN (California State University, Northridge) Technology and Persons with Disabilities Conference, Los Angeles, California. Proceedings paper retrieved April 4, 2011, from http://www.letsgoexpo.com/utilities/File/viewfile.cfm?LCID=3861&eID=80000218; Asuncion, J.V., Fichten, C.S., Budd, J., Gaulin, C., Amsel, R., & Barile, M. (2010). Preliminary findings on social media use and accessibility: A Canadian perspective. Proceedings of the CSUN (California State University, Northridge) Technology and Persons with Disabilities Conference, Los Angeles, California. Proceedings paper retrieved April 4, 2011, from http://www.letsgoexpo.com/utilities/File/viewfile.cfm?LCID=4145&eID=80000218; Fichten, C.S., Ferraro, V., Asuncion, J.V., Chwojka, C., Barile, M., Nguyen, M.N., Klomp, R., & Wolforth, J. (2009). Disabilities and e-learning problems and solutions: An exploratory study. Educational Technology and Society, 12 (4), 241–256; Fichten, C.S., Asuncion, J.V., Barile, M., Ferraro, & Wolforth, J. (2009). Accessibility of eLearning, computer and information technologies to students with visual impairments in postsecondary education. Journal of Visual Impairment and Blindness, 103(9), 543-557; Jorgensen, S., Fichten, C.S., & Havel, A. (2009). Academic success of graduates with and without disabilities—A comparative study of university entrance scores. Pédagogie Collégiale, 22(5) Special Issue, 26-29.; Ferraro, V., Fichten, C.S., & Barile, M. (2009). Computer use by students with disabilities: Perceived advantages, problems and solutions. Pédagogie Collégiale, 22(5) Special Issue, 20-25.; Nguyen, M.N., Fichten, C.S., & Barile, M. (2009). Les besoins technologiques des élèves handicapés du postsecondaire sont-ils satisfaits ? Résultats de l'utilisation de l'Échelle d'accessibilité des technologies informatiques adaptatives pour les élèves handicapés au postsecondaire

Organizations and Associations in the USA and Canada

(SAITAPSD): version pour les élèves. Pédagogie Collégiale, 22(2), 6-11; Fichten, C.S., Asuncion, J.V., Nguyen, M.N., Wolforth, J., Budd, J., Barile, M., Gaulin, C., Martiniello, N., Tibbs, A., Ferraro, V., & Amsel, R. (2009). Development and validation of the Positives Scale (Postsecondary Information Technology Initiative Scale) (136 pages). Final report for the Canadian Council on Learning. ERIC (Education Resources Information Center) ED505763. Retrieved July 27, 2009, http://www.eric.ed.gov/ERICWebPortal/contentdelivery/servlet/ERICServlet?accno=ED505763 and Retrieved August 29, 2010, from http://www.ccl-cca.ca/pdfs/OtherReports/Fichten-Report.pdf Jorgensen, S., Fichten, C.S., & Havel, A. (2009). Prédire la situation de risque des étudiants au collège: Hommes et étudiants ayant des incapacités/Predicting the at risk status of college students: Males and students with disabilities. (257 pages). Final report to PAREA. ERIC (Education Resources Information Center) (ED505871). Retrieved July 30, 2009, from http://www.eric.ed.gov/ERICDocs/data/ericdocs2sql/content_storage_01/0000019b/80/44/a4/62.pdf; Jorgensen, S., Ferraro, V., Fichten, C.S., & Havel, A. (2009). Predicting college retention and dropout: Sex and disability. (10 pages). ERIC (Education Resources Information Center) (ED505873). Retrieved July 30, 2009, from http://www.eric.ed.gov/ERICDocs/data/ericdocs2sql/content_storage_01/0000019b/80/44/a4/65.pdf

Name of Organization or Association—Agency for Instructional Technology
Acronym—AIT
Address:
Box A
Bloomington, IN
47402-0120
USA
Phone Number—(812)339-2203; **Fax Number**—(812)333-4218
Email Contact—info@ait.net; **URL**—http://www.ait.net
Leaders—Charles E. Wilson, Executive Director
Description—The Agency for Instructional Technology has been a leader in educational technology since 1962. A nonprofit organization, AIT is one of the largest providers of instructional TV programs in North America. AIT is also a leading developer of other educational media, including online instruction, CDs, videodiscs, and instructional software. AIT learning resources are used on six continents and reach nearly 34 million students in North America each year. AIT products have received many national and international honors, including an Emmy and Peabody award. Since 1970, AIT has developed 39 major curriculum packages through the consortium process it pioneered. American state and Canadian provincial agencies have cooperatively funded and widely used these learning resources. Funding for other product development comes from state, provincial, and local departments of education; federal and private institutions; corporations and private sponsors; and AIT's own resources.
Membership—n/a
Dues—n/a

Meetings—No regular public meetings
Publications—n/a

Name of Organization or Association—American Association of Colleges for Teacher Education
Acronym—AACTE
Address:
1307 New York Ave., N.W., Suite 300
Washington, DC
20005-4701
USA
Phone Number—202/293-2450; **Fax Number**—202/457-8095
Email Contact—jmills@aacte.org; **URL**—http://www.aacte.org/
Leaders—Sharon P. Robinson, President and Chief Executive Officer
Description—The American Association of Colleges for Teacher Education is a national alliance of educator preparation programs dedicated to the highest quality professional development of teachers and school leaders in order to enhance PK-12 student learning. The 800 institutions holding AACTE membership represent public and private colleges and universities in every state, the District of Columbia, the Virgin Islands, Puerto Rico, and Guam. AACTE's reach and influence fuel its mission of serving learners by providing all school personnel with superior training and continuing education. AACTE employs three key strategies to achieve its goals: Advocacy: AACTE maintains a constant presence on Capitol Hill to expand its congressional network and provide members with up-to-the-minute analysis of education policy. Leadership: AACTE believes in consensus-building through open and free-flowing dialogue on education matters, consistent support for diverse learners, and serving as a principal authority on issues pertaining to teacher quality. Service: AACTE provides members with vital communication regarding policy issues and events, publications targeting various areas of interest, and unique professional development opportunities.
Membership—Membership in AACTE is institutional with over 5500 institutional representatives. There are two categories of membership: regular membership and affiliate membership. Regular membership is available to 4-year degree-granting colleges and universities with significant commitment to the preparation of education personnel and that meet all the criteria for regular membership. Affiliate membership is also available. For more information please contact the membership department at membership@aacte.org or 202/293-2450.
Dues—n/a
Meetings—Annual Members Meeting, New Leadership Academy. State Leaders Institute, and more
Publications—n/a

Name of Organization or Association—American Association of Community Colleges
Acronym—AACC
Address:

One Dupont Circle, NW, Suite 410
Washington, DC
20036-1176
USA

Phone Number—(202)728-0200; **Fax Number**—(202)833-9390
Email Contact—twhissemore@aacc.nche.edu; **URL**—http://www.aacc.nche.edu
Leaders—Walter G. Bumphus, President and CEO
Description—AACC is a national organization representing the nations more than 1195 community, junior, and technical colleges. Headquartered in Washington, DC, AACC serves as a national voice for the colleges and provides key services in the areas of advocacy, research, information, and leadership development. The nation's community colleges serve more than 11 million students annually, almost half (46%) of all US undergraduates.
Membership—1167 institutions, 31 corporations, 15 international associates, 79 educational associates, 4 foundations
Dues—Vary by category
Meetings—Annual Convention, April of each year; 2012: April 21–24 Orlando, FL
Publications—Community College Journal (bi-mo.); Community College Times (biweekly online); Community College Press (books, research and program briefs, and monographs)
Name of Organization or Association—American Association of School Librarians
Acronym—AASL
Address:
50 East Huron Street
Chicago, IL
60611-2795
USA

Phone Number—(312) 280-4382 or (800) 545-2433, ext. 4382; **Fax Number**—(312) 280-5276
Email Contact—aasl@ala.org; **URL**—http://www.ala.org/aasl
Leaders—Julie A. Walker, Executive Director
Description—A division of the American Library Association, the mission of the American Association of School Librarians is to advocate excellence, facilitate change, and develop leaders in the school library media field.
Membership—9500
Dues—Personal membership in ALA (beginning FY 2009, first year, $65; second year, $98; third and subsequent years, $130) plus $50 for personal membership in AASL. Student, retired, organizational, and corporate memberships are available.
Meetings—National conference every 2 years; next national conference to be held in 2009.
Publications—School Library Media Research (electronic research journal at http://www.ala.org/aasl/SLMR); Knowledge Quest (print journal and online companion at http://www.ala.org/aasl/kqweb); AASL Hotlinks (e-mail

newsletter); non-serial publications (http://www.ala.org/ala/aasl/aaslpubsand-journals/aaslpublications.cfm)

Name of Organization or Association—American Educational Research Association

Acronym—AERA

Address:

1430 K Street, NW, Suite 1200

Washington, DC

20005

USA

Phone Number—(202) 238-3200; **Fax Number**—(202) 238-3250

Email Contact—outreach@aera.net; **URL**—http://www.aera.net

Leaders—Arnetha Ball, President of the Council, 2011–2012

Description—The American Educational Research Association (AERA) is the national interdisciplinary research association for approximately 25,000 scholars who undertake research in education. Founded in 1916, AERA aims to advance knowledge about education, to encourage scholarly inquiry related to education, and to promote the use of research to improve education and serve the public good. AERA members include educators and administrators; directors of research, testing, or evaluation in federal, state, and local agencies; counselors; evaluators; graduate students; and behavioral scientists. The broad range of disciplines represented include education, psychology, statistics, sociology, history, economics, philosophy, anthropology, and political science. AERA has more than 160 Special Interest Groups, including Advanced Technologies for Learning, NAEP Studies, Classroom Assessment, and Fiscal Issues, Policy, and Education Finance.

Membership—25,000 regular members: Eligibility requires satisfactory evidence of active interest in educational research as well as professional training to at least the master's degree level or equivalent. Graduate student members: Any graduate student may be granted graduate student member status with the endorsement of a voting member who is a faculty member at the student's university. Graduate students who are employed full time are not eligible. Graduate student membership is limited to 5 years.

Dues—Vary by category, ranging from $40 for graduate students to $150 for voting members, for 1 year. See AERA website for complete details: www.aera.net

Meetings—2009 Annual Meeting, April 13–17, San Diego, California

Publications—Educational Researcher; American Educational Research Journal; Journal of Educational and Behavioral Statistics; Educational Evaluation and Policy Analysis; Review of Research in Education; Review of Educational Research. Books: Handbook of Research on Teaching, (revised, 4th edition) Ethical Standards of AERA, Cases and Commentary; Black Education: A Transformative Research and Action Agenda for the New Century; Studying Teacher Education: The Report of the AERA Panel on Research and Teacher Education, 2006 Handbook of Education Policy Research; Studying Diversity in

Teacher Education, 2011 Standards for Educational and Psychological Testing (revised and expanded, 1999). Co-published by AERA, American Psychological Association, and the National Council on Measurement in Education

Name of Organization or Association—American Foundation for the Blind
Acronym—AFB
Address:
11 Penn Plaza, Suite 300
New York, NY
10001
USA
Phone Number—(212)502-7600, (800)AFB-LINE (232-5463); **Fax Number**—(212)502-7777
Email Contact—afbinfo@afb.net; **URL**—http://www.afb.org
Leaders—Carl R. Augusto, Pres.; Kelly Parisi, Vice Pres. of Communications
Description—The American Foundation for the Blind (AFB) is a national nonprofit that expands possibilities for people with vision loss. AFB's priorities include broadening access to technology; elevating the quality of information and tools for the professionals who serve people with vision loss; and promoting independent and healthy living for people with vision loss by providing them and their families with relevant and timely resources. In addition, AFB's website serves as a gateway to a wealth of vision loss information and services. AFB is also proud to house the Helen Keller Archives and honor the over 40 years that Helen Keller worked tirelessly with AFB. For more information visit us online at www.afb.org.
Membership—n/a
Dues—n/a
Meetings—n/a
Publications—AFB News (free); Journal of Visual Impairment & Blindness; AFB Press Catalog of Publications (free). AccessWorld™; Subscriptions Tel: (800) 232-3044 or (412) 741-1398

Name of Organization or Association—American Library Association
Acronym—ALA
Address:
50 E. Huron St.
Chicago, IL
60611
USA
Phone Number—(800) 545-2433; **Fax Number**—(312) 440-9374
Email Contact—library@ala.org; **URL**—http://www.ala.org
Leaders—Keith Michael Fiels, Exec. Dir.
Description—The ALA is the oldest and largest national library association. Its 62,000 members represent all types of libraries: state, public, school, and academic, as well as special libraries serving persons in government, commerce, armed services, hospitals, prisons, and other institutions. The ALA is the chief advocate of achievement and maintenance of high-quality library information

services through protection of the right to read, educating librarians, improving services, and making information widely accessible. See separate entries for the following affiliated and subordinate organizations: American Association of School Librarians; Association of Library Trustees, Advocates, Friends and Foundations; Association for Library Collections and Technical Services; Association for Library Service to Children; Association of College and Research Libraries; Association of Specialized and Cooperative Library Agencies; Library Leadership and Management Association; Library and Information Technology Association; Public Library Association; Reference and User Services Association; Young Adult Library Services Association; and the Learning Round Table of ALA (formerly the Continuing Library Education Network and Exchange Round Table).

Membership—62,000 members at present; everyone who cares about libraries is allowed to join the American Library Association.

Dues—Professional rate: $65, first year; $98, second year; third year and renewing: $130. Library support staff: $46; student members: $33; retirees: $46; international librarians: $78; trustees: $59; associate members (those not in the library field): $59.

Meetings—June 21–26, 2012-Anaheim, CA; June 27–July 2, 2013-Chicago, IL// Midwinter Meeting: January 20–24, 2012-Dallas, TX; January 25–29, 2013-Seattle, WA

Publications—American Libraries; Booklist; BooklistOnline.com; Choice; Choice Reviews Online

Name of Organization or Association—American Society for Training & Development

Acronym—ASTD

Address:
1640 King St., Box 1443
Alexandria, VA
22313-2043
USA

Phone Number—(703)683-8100; **Fax Number**—(703)683-8103

Email Contact—customercare@astd.org; **URL**—http://www.astd.org

Leaders—Tony Bingham, President and CEO

Description—ASTD (American Society for Training & Development) is the world's largest professional association dedicated to the training and development field. In more than 100 countries, ASTD's members work in organizations of all sizes, in the private and public sectors, as independent consultants, and as suppliers. Members connect locally in 125 US chapters and with 20 international partners. ASTD started in 1943 and in recent years has widened the profession's focus to align learning and performance to organizational results, and is a sought-after voice on critical public policy issues. For more information, visit www. astd.org.

Membership—37,000 members in 100 countries

Organizations and Associations in the USA and Canada

Dues—The Classic Membership ($199.00) is the foundation of ASTD member benefits. Publications, newsletters, research reports, discounts, services, and much more are all designed to help you do your job better. There are also student memberships, joint chapter memberships, and a special rate for international members. Here is what you have to look forward to when you join: T+D magazine—Monthly publication of ASTD. Stay informed on trends, successful practices, case studies, and more. ASTD LINKS—bimonthly newsletter for and about members. The Buzz—a weekly compilation of news about the training profession. Learning Circuits—Monthly Webzine feature articles, departments, and columns that examine learning technologies and how they are being applied to workplace learning. Special Reports and Research—Research reports are published on topics that reflect important issues and trends in the industry. The State of the Industry report is published annually and analyzes spending, practices, and other important data related to learning and development. Do Your Own Research—Members can access the Online Library to research thousands of publications. Career Navigator Tool—find out where you are in your career and what you need to do to develop professionally. Membership Directory—Online directory and searchable by a variety of criteria. Access to the Membership Directory is for members only. EXPO 365 Buyers Guide—A one-stop resource for information on hundreds of training suppliers and consultants.

Meetings—TechKnowledge Conference: January 25–27, 2012, Las Vegas, NV; International Conference & Exposition, May 6–9, 2012, Denver, CO

Publications—T+D (Training & Development) Magazine; Infoline; Learning Circuits; Training and Development Handbook; State of the Industry Report; ASTD Press books; Research reports

Name of Organization or Association—Association for Childhood Education International

Acronym—ACEI

Address:
17904 Georgia Ave., Suite 215
Olney, MD
20832
USA

Phone Number—(301)570-2111; **Fax Number**—(301)570-2212

Email Contact—headquarters@acei.org; **URL**—http://www.acei.org

Leaders—Diane P. Whitehead, Acting Executive Director

Description—ACEI publications reflect careful research, broad-based views, and consideration of a wide range of issues affecting children from infancy through early adolescence. Many are media related in nature. The journal (Childhood Education) is essential for teachers, teachers-in-training, teacher educators, day care workers, administrators, and parents. Articles focus on child development and emphasize practical application. Regular departments include book reviews (child and adult), film reviews, pamphlets, software, research, and classroom idea sparkers. Six issues are published yearly, including a theme issue devoted to critical concerns.

Membership—10,000

Dues—$45, professional; $29, student; $23, retired; $85, institutional

Meetings—2009 Annual Conference, March 18–21, Chicago, IL, USA

Publications—Childhood Education (official journal) with ACEI Exchange (insert newsletter); Journal of Research in Childhood Education; professional focus newsletters (Focus on Infants and Toddlers, Focus on Pre-K and K, Focus on Elementary, Focus on Middle School, Focus on Teacher Education, and Focus on Inclusive Education); various books

Name of Organization or Association—Association for Computers and the Humanities

Acronym—ACH

Address:

771 Commonwealth Ave

Boston

02215

USA

Phone Number—617-358-6379; **Fax Number**—n/a

Email Contact—kretzsh@uga.edu; **URL**—http://www.ach.org/

Leaders—Executive Secretary, ACH

Description—The Association for Computers and the Humanities is an international professional organization. Since its establishment, it has been the major professional society for people working in computer-aided research in literature and language studies, history, philosophy, and other humanities disciplines, and especially research involving the manipulation and analysis of textual materials. The ACH is devoted to disseminating information among its members about work in the field of humanities computing, as well as encouraging the development and dissemination of significant textual and linguistic resources and software for scholarly research.

Membership—300

Dues—Individual regular member, US$65; student or emeritus faculty member, US$55; joint membership (for couples), add US$7.

Meetings—Annual meetings held with the Association for Literary and Linguistic Computing

Publications—ACH Publications: Literary & Linguistic Computing—Humanist

Name of Organization or Association—Association for Continuing Higher Education

Acronym—ACHE

Address:

OCCE Admin Bldg Rm 233, 1700 Asp Ave

Norman, OK

73072

USA

Organizations and Associations in the USA and Canada

Phone Number—800-807-2243; **Fax Number**—405-325-4888
Email Contact—admin@acheinc.org; **URL**—http://www.acheinc.org/
Leaders—James P. Pappas, Ph.D., Executive Vice President
Description—ACHE is an institution-based organization of colleges, universities, and individuals dedicated to the promotion of lifelong learning and excellence in continuing higher education. ACHE encourages professional networks, research, and exchange of information for its members and advocates continuing higher education as a means of enhancing and improving society.
Membership—Approximately 1600 individuals in approximately 650 institutions. Membership is open to institutions of higher learning, professionals, and organizations whose major commitment is in the area of continuing education.
Dues—$85, professional; $510, institutional
Meetings—For a list of annual and regional meetings, see http://www.acheinc.org.
Publications—Journal of Continuing Higher Education (3/year); 5 min with ACHE (newsletter, 9/year); proceedings (annual)

Name of Organization or Association—Association for Educational Communications and Technology
Acronym—AECT
Address:
1800 N Stonelake Dr., Suite 2 P.O. Box 2447
Bloomington, IN
47404-2447
USA
Phone Number—(812) 335-7675; **Fax Number**—(812) 335-7678
Email Contact—pharris@aect.org; **URL**—http://www.aect.org
Leaders—Phillip Harris, Executive Director; Ana Donaldson, Board President
Description—AECT is an international professional association concerned with the improvement of learning and instruction through media and technology. It serves as a central clearinghouse and communications center for its members, who include instructional technologists, library media specialists, religious educators, government media personnel, school administrators and specialists, and training media producers. AECT members also work in the armed forces, public libraries, museums, and other information agencies of many different kinds, including those related to the emerging fields of computer technology. Affiliated organizations include the International Visual Literacy Association (IVLA), Minorities in Media (MIM), New England Educational Media Association (NEEMA), SICET (the Society of International Chinese in Educational Technology), and KSET (the Korean Society for Educational Technology). The ECT Foundation is also related to AECT. Each of these affiliated organizations has its own listing in the Yearbook. AECT Divisions include Instructional Design & Development, Information, Training & Performance, Research & Theory, Systemic Change, Distance Learning, Media & Technology, Teacher Education, International, and Multimedia Productions.

Membership—2500 members in good standing from K-12, college, and university and private sector/government training. Anyone interested can join. There are different memberships available for students, retirees, corporations, and international parties. We also have a new option for electronic membership for international affiliates.

Dues—1,250,000 standard membership discounts are available for students and retirees. Additional fees apply to corporate memberships or international memberships.

Meetings—Summer Leadership Institute held each July. In 2007 it was in Chicago, IL. AECT holds an annual conference each year in October. In 2007, it was held in Anaheim, CA.

Publications—TechTrends (6/year, free with AECT membership available by subscription through Springer at www.springeronline.com); Educational Technology Research and Development (6/year $46 members; available by subscription through Springer at www.springeronline.com); Quarterly Review of Distance Education (q., $55 to AECT members)

Name of Organization or Association—Association for Experiential Education

Acronym—AEE

Address:
3775 Iris Avenue, Ste 4
Boulder, CO
80301-2043
USA

Phone Number—(303)440-8844; **Fax Number**—(303)440-9581

Email Contact—executive@aee.org; **URL**—http://www.aee.org

Leaders—Paul Limoges, Executive Director

Description—AEE is a nonprofit, international, professional organization committed to the development, practice, and evaluation of experiential education in all settings. AEE's vision is to be a leading international organization for the development and application of experiential education principles and methodologies with the intent to create a just and compassionate world by transforming education.

Membership—Nearly 1500 members in over 30 countries including individuals and organizations with affiliations in education, recreation, outdoor adventure programming, mental health, youth service, physical education, management development training, corrections, programming for people with disabilities, and environmental education

Dues—$55–$115, individual; $145, family; $275–$500, organizational

Meetings—AEE annual conference in November. Regional conferences in the spring.

Publications—The Journal of Experiential Education (3/year); Experience and the Curriculum; Adventure Education; Adventure Therapy; Therapeutic Applications of Adventure Programming; Manual of Accreditation Standards for Adventure Programs; The Theory of Experiential Education, Third Edition; Experiential Learning in Schools and Higher Education; Ethical Issues in Experiential

Education, Second Edition; The K.E.Y. (Keep Exploring Yourself) Group: An Experiential Personal Growth Group Manual; Book of Metaphors, Volume II; Women's Voices in Experiential Education; Bibliographies, directories of programs, and membership directory. New publications since last year: Exploring the Boundaries of Adventure Therapy; A Guide to Women's Studies in the Outdoors; Administrative Practices of Accredited Adventure Programs; Fundamentals of Experience-Based Training; Wild Adventures: A Guidebook of Activities for Building Connections with Others and the Earth; Truth Zone: An Experimental Approach to Organizational Development; Exploring the Power of Solo, Silence, and Solitude

Name of Organization or Association—Association for Library and Information Science Education

Acronym—ALISE

Address:

65 E. Wacker Place Suite 1900

Chicago, IL

60601

USA

Phone Number—312-795-0996; **Fax Number**—312-419-8950

Email Contact—contact@alise.org; **URL**—http://www.alise.org

Leaders—Kathleen Combs, Executive Director

Description—Seeks to advance education for library and information science and produces annual Library and Information Science Education Statistical Report. Open to professional schools offering graduate programs in library and information science; personal memberships open to educators employed in such institutions; other memberships available to interested individuals.

Membership—201 individuals, 71 institutions

Dues—Institutional, sliding scale, $350–2500; international $145.00; full-time personal, $125.00; part time/retired $75.00; student $60.00

Meetings—January 4–7, 2011, San Diego, CA

Publications—Journal of Education for Library and Information Science; ALISE Directory; Library and Information Science Education Statistical Report

Name of Organization or Association—Association for Library Collections & Technical Services

Acronym—ALCTS

Address:

50 E. Huron St.

Chicago, IL

60611

USA

Phone Number—(312)280-5037; **Fax Number**—(312)280-5033

Email Contact—alcts@ala.org; **URL**—www.ala.org/alcts

Leaders—Charles Wilt, Executive Director

Description—A division of the American Library Association, ALCTS is dedicated to acquisition, identification, cataloging, classification, and preservation of library materials; development and coordination of the country's library resources; and aspects of selection and evaluation involved in acquiring and developing library materials and resources. Sections include Acquisitions, Cataloging and Classification, Collection Management and Development, Preservation and Reformatting, and Serials.

Membership—4300 membership is open to anyone who has an interest in areas covered by ALCTS.

Dues—$65 plus membership in ALA

Meetings—Annual Conference; Anaheim, June 21–26, 2012; Chicago, June 27–July 2, 2013; Las Vegas, June 26–July 1; 2014, San Francisco, June 25–30, 2015

Publications—Library Resources & Technical Services (q.); ALCTS Newsletter Online (q.)

Name of Organization or Association—Association for Library Service to Children

Acronym—ALSC

Address:

50 E. Huron St.

Chicago, IL

60611

USA

Phone Number—(312)280-2163; **Fax Number**—(312)944-7671

Email Contact—alsc@ala.org; **URL**—http://www.ala.org/alsc

Leaders—Diane Foote

Description—Information about ALSC can be found at http://www.ala.org/alsc/aboutalsc. Information on ALSCs various awards, including the nationally known Newbery Medal for authors and the Caldecott Medal for illustrators can be found at http://www.ala.org/alsc/awardsgrants/bookmedia/caldecott. The Association for Library Service to Children develops and supports the profession of children's librarianship by enabling and encouraging its practitioners to provide the best library service to our nation's children. The Association for Library Service to Children is interested in the improvement and extension of library services to children in all types of libraries. It is responsible for the evaluation and selection of book and nonbook library materials and for the improvement of techniques of library service to children from preschool through the eighth grade or junior high school age, when such materials and techniques are intended for use in more than one type of library. Committee membership is open to ALSC members. Full list of ALSC boards and committees can be found at http://www.ala.org/alsc/aboutalsc/coms.

Membership—Over 4000 members

Dues—$45 plus membership in ALA; $18 plus membership in ALA for library school students; $25 plus membership in ALA for retirees

Meetings—National Institute, fall

Publications—Children and Libraries: The Journal of the Association for Library Service to Children (3x per year); ALSConnect (quarterly newsletter). ALSC Blog

Name of Organization or Association—Association of American Publishers
Acronym—AAP
Address:
50 F Street, NW, Suite 400
Washington, DC
20001
USA
Phone Number—(202)347-3375; **Fax Number**—(202)347-3690
Email Contact—aoconnor@publishers.org; **URL**—http://www.publishers.org
Leaders—Tom Allen, Pres. and CEO (DC); Judith Platt, Dir. of Communications/ Public Affairs.
Description—The Association of American Publishers is the national trade association of the US book publishing industry. AAP was created in 1970 through the merger of the American Book Publishers Council, a trade publishing group, and the American Textbook Publishers Institute, a group of educational publishers. AAP's more than 300 members include most of the major commercial book publishers in the USA, as well as smaller and nonprofit publishers, university presses, and scholarly societies. AAP members publish hardcover and paperback books in every field and a range of educational materials for the elementary, secondary, postsecondary, and professional markets. Members of the Association also produce computer software and electronic products and services, such as online databases and CD-ROMs. AAP's primary concerns are the protection of intellectual property rights in all media, the defense of free expression and freedom to publish at home and abroad, the management of new technologies, the development of education markets and funding for instructional materials, and the development of national and global markets for its member products.
Membership—Regular membership in the Association is open to all US companies actively engaged in the publication of books, journals, looseleaf services, computer software, audiovisual materials, databases, and other electronic products such as CD-ROM and CD-I, and similar products for educational, business, and personal use. This includes producers, packagers, and co-publishers who coordinate or manage most of the publishing process involved in creating copyrightable educational materials for distribution by another organization. "Actively engaged" means that the candidate must give evidence of conducting an ongoing publishing business with a significant investment in the business. Each regular member firm has one vote, which is cast by an official representative or alternate designated by the member company. Associate membership (nonvoting) is available to US not-for-profit organizations that otherwise meet the qualifications for regular membership. A special category of associate membership is open to non-profit university presses. Affiliate membership is a nonvoting membership open to paper manufacturers, suppliers, consultants, and other non-publishers directly involved in the industry.

Dues—Dues are assessed on the basis of annual sales revenue from the print and electronic products listed above (under regular membership), but not from services or equipment. To maintain confidentiality, data is reported to an independent agent.

Meetings—Annual meeting (February), small and independent publishers' meeting (February)

Publications—AAP Monthly Report

Name of Organization or Association—Association of College and Research Libraries

Acronym—ACRL

Address:
50 E. Huron St.
Chicago, IL
60611-2795
USA

Phone Number—(312)280-2523; **Fax Number**—(312)280-2520

Email Contact—acrl@ala.org; **URL**—http://www.ala.org/acrl

Leaders—Mary Ellen Davis, Executive Director

Description—The Association of College and Research Libraries (ACRL), the largest division of the American Library Association, is a professional association of academic librarians and other interested individuals. It is dedicated to enhancing the ability of academic library and information professionals to serve the information needs of the higher education community and to improve learning, teaching, and research. ACRL is the only individual membership organization in North America that develops programs, products, and services to meet the unique needs of academic and research librarians. Information on ACRL's various committees, task forces, discussion groups, and sections can be found at http://www.ala.org/aboutala/committees. Information on ACRL's various awards can be found at http://www.ala.org/awardsgrants/node/30789.

Membership—With over 13,000 members, it is a national organization of academic and research libraries and librarians working with all types of academic libraries—community and junior college, college, and university—as well as comprehensive and specialized research libraries and their professional staffs.

Dues—$55 plus membership in ALA; $35 plus membership in ALA for library school students and for retirees. Sections (two at no charge, additional sections $5 each): African American Studies Librarians (AFAS); Anthropology and Sociology Section (ANSS); Arts Section; Asian, African, and Middle Eastern Section (AAMES); College Libraries Section (CLS); Community and Junior College Libraries Section (CJCLS); Distance Learning Section (DLS); Education and Behavioral Sciences Section (EBSS); Instruction Section (IS); Law and Political Science Section (LPSS); Literatures in English (LES); Rare Books and Manuscripts Section (RBMS); Science and Technology Section (STS); Slavic and East European Section (SEES); University Libraries Section (ULS); Western European Studies Section (WESS); Women's Studies Section (WSS).

Organizations and Associations in the USA and Canada 93

Meetings—ACRL 14th National Conference—March 12–15, 2009, Seattle, WA, Theme: Pushing the Edge: Explore, Engage, Extend

Publications—List of all print and electronic publications at ACRLog: Blogging for and by academic and research librarians—ACRL Insider—The mission of the ACRL Insider Weblog is to keep the world current and informed on the activities, services, and programs of the Association of College & Research Libraries, including publications, events, conferences, and eLearning opportunities. ACRL Podcasts—Academic Library Trends & Statistics (annually). Statistics data for all academic libraries reporting throughout the USA and Canada. Trends data examines a different subject each year. Available from ALA Order Fulfillment, P.O. Box 932501, Atlanta, GA 31193–2501 and from the ALA Online Store. Choice: Editor and Publisher, Irving E. Rockwood. ISSN 0009–4978. Published monthly. Only available by subscription: $315 per year for North America; $365 outside North America. CHOICE Reviews on Cards: $390 per year for North America—USA, Canada, and Mexico); $440 outside North America. ChoiceReviews.org: See pricing for site licenses at https://www.choice360.org/products/choice-reviews/subscribe/. College & Research Libraries (6 bimonthly journal issues). Sent to all ACRL members. Subscriptions, $70—USA. $75—Canada and other PUAS countries. $80—Other foreign countries. College & Research Libraries News (11 monthly issues, July–Aug, combined). Sent to all ACRL members. Subscriptions: $46—USA. $52—Canada and other PUAS countries. $57—Other foreign countries. RBM: A Journal of Rare Books, Manuscripts, and Cultural Heritage (two issues). Subscriptions, $42—USA. $47—Canada and other PUAS countries. $58—Other foreign countries

Name of Organization or Association—Association of Specialized and Cooperative Library Agencies

Acronym—ASCLA

Address:

50 E. Huron St.

Chicago, IL

60611

USA

Phone Number—(800)545-2433, ext. 4398.; **Fax Number**—(312)944-8085

Email Contact—ascla@ala.org; **URL**—http://www.ala.org/ascla

Leaders—Susan Hornung, Executive Director

Description—A division of the American Library Association, the Association of Specialized and Cooperative Library Agencies (ASCLA) enhances the effectiveness of library service by providing networking, enrichment, and educational opportunities for its diverse members, who represent state library agencies, libraries serving special populations, library organizations, and independent librarians.

Membership—800

Dues—You must be a member of ALA to join ASCLA. See www.ala.org/membership for most current ALA due rates. ASCLA individual membership: $50; organization membership: $50; State Library Agency dues: $500.

Meetings—ASCLA meets in conjunction with the American Library Association.

Publications—Interface, quarterly online newsletter; see website http://www.ala.org/ascla for the list of other publications.

Name of Organization or Association—Canadian Library Association/Association canadienne des bibliothèques

Acronym—CLA/ACB

Address:

1150 Morrison Drive, Suite 400

Ottawa, ON

K2H 8S9

Canada

Phone Number—(613)232-9625; **Fax Number**—(613)563-9895

Email Contact—info@cla.ca; **URL**—http://www.cla.ca

Leaders—Linda Sawden Harris, Manager of Financial Services; Judy Green, Manager, Marketing & Communications; Kelly Moore, Executive Director

Description—Our Mission CLA/ACB is my advocate and public voice, educator, and network. We build the Canadian library and information community and advance its information professionals. Our values: We believe that libraries and the principles of intellectual freedom and free universal access to information are key components of an open and democratic society. Diversity is a major strength of our Association. An informed and knowledgeable membership is central in achieving library and information policy goals. Effective advocacy is based upon understanding the social, cultural, political, and historical contexts in which libraries and information services function. Our operating principles: A large and active membership is crucial to our success. Our Association will have a governance structure that is reviewed regularly and ensures that all sectors of the membership are represented. Our Association will be efficiently run, fiscally responsible, and financially independent. Technology will be used in efficient and effective ways to further our goals. Our Association places a high value on each of our members. Our Association will ensure that its staff are provided with tools and training necessary for them to excel at their jobs. Our Association's strategic plan will be continually reviewed and updated.

Membership—The CLA/ACB membership consists of a diverse group of individuals and organizations involved or interested in library or information sciences. A large proportion of CLA/ACB members work in college, university, public, special (corporate, nonprofit, and government), and school libraries. Others sit on the boards of public libraries, work for companies that provide goods and services to libraries, or are students in graduate level or community college programs. Membership categories of the Canadian Library Association/Association canadienne des bibliothèques include Personal, Institutional, Associate, and Trustee. Total membership fees on October 10, 2011, was 4200.

Dues—$25–$1000
Meetings—2012—Ottawa, Ontario, Wednesday May 30—Saturday, June 2
Publications—Feliciter (membership and subscription magazine, 6/year)

Name of Organization or Association—Canadian Museums Association/ Association des musées canadiens
Acronym—CMA/AMC
Address:
280 Metcalfe St., Suite 400
Ottawa, ON
K2P 1R7
Canada
Phone Number—(613)567-0099; **Fax Number**—(613)233-5438
Email Contact—info@museums.ca; **URL**—http://www.museums.ca
Leaders—John G. McAvity, Exec. Dir.
Description—The Canadian Museums Association is a nonprofit corporation and registered charity dedicated to advancing public museums and museum works in Canada, promoting the welfare and better administration of museums, and fostering a continuing improvement in the qualifications and practices of museum professionals.
Membership—2000 museums and individuals, including art galleries, zoos, aquariums, historic parks, etc.
Dues—Voting categories: Individual: For those who are, or have been, associated with a recognized museum in Canada. A $10 discount applies if you are associated with a CMA institutional member or if you are a member of a provincial museum association. $85 a year. Senior: For those who are retired and have been associated with a recognized museum in Canada. $50 a year. Institutional association: For all recognized Canadian museums that are nonprofit, have a collection, and are open to the public. The fee is 0.001 (one-tenth of 1%) of your operating budget (i.e., if your budget is $150,000, you would pay $150). The minimum fee payable is $100, and the maximum $2750. Nonvoting categories: Affiliate: For those outside of the museum community who wish to support the aims and programs of the CMA. $100 a year. International: For individuals and institutions outside of Canada. $100 a year. Corporate: For corporations wishing to support the aims and programs of the CMA while developing opportunities within the museum community. $250 a year. Student: For students in Canada. Please enclose a photocopy of your student ID. $50 a year. *Membership fees may be tax deductible. Check with your financial advisor for details.
Meetings—CMA Annual Conference, spring
Publications—Muse (bimonthly magazine, color, Canada's only national, bilingual, magazine devoted to museums, it contains museum-based photography, feature articles, commentary, and practical information); the Official Directory of Canadian Museums and Related Institutions (online directory) lists all museums in Canada plus information on government departments, agencies, and provincial and regional museum associations.

Name of Organization or Association—Centre for Educational Technology, University of Cape Town

Acronym—CET

Address:

Hlanganani Building, Upper Campus University of Cape Town, Rondebosch

Cape Town

7700

South Africa

Phone Number—27 21 650 3841; **Fax Number**—27 21 650 5045

Email Contact—Laura.Czerniewicz@uct.ac.za; **URL**—http://www.cet.uct.ac.za

Leaders—Director Laura Czerniewicz

Description—The Centre for Educational Technology (CET) enables, promotes, and investigates the integration of learning technologies in teaching and learning at the University of Cape Town and in higher education. CET's areas of work are curriculum development, learning technologies, staff development, and research.

Membership—We employ educational technology researchers, developers, staff developers, and learning designers with strong educational interests in diversity, redress, and access.

Dues—n/a

Meetings—n/a

Publications—See our website at http://www.cet.uct.ac.za. Recent research publications are listed at http://www.cet.uct.ac.za/ResearchOut.

Name of Organization or Association—Close Up Foundation

Acronym—CUF

Address:

44 Canal Center Plaza

Alexandria, VA

22314

USA

Phone Number—(703)706-3300; **Fax Number**—(703)706-3329

Email Contact—cutv@closeup.org; **URL**—http://www.closeup.org

Leaders—Timothy S. Davis, President and CEO

Description—A nonprofit, nonpartisan civic engagement organization dedicated to providing individuals of all backgrounds with the knowledge, skills, and confidence to actively participate in democracy. Each year, Close Up brings 15,000 secondary and middle school students and teachers to Washington, DC, for weeklong government study programs. In addition, Close Up produces an array of multimedia civic education resources for use in classrooms and households nationwide, including Close Up at the Newseum, a weekly youth-focused current affairs program C-SPAN.

Membership—Any motivated middle or high school student who wants to learn about government and American history is eligible to come on our programs. No dues or membership fees.

Dues—Tuition is required to participate in Close Up educational travel programs. A limited amount of tuition assistance is available to qualified students through the Close Up Fellowship program. With a designated number of students, teachers receive a fellowship that covers the adult tuition and transportation price. Please contact 1-800-CLOSE UP for more information.

Meetings—Meetings take place during weeklong educational programs in Washington, DC.

Publications—Current Issues (new edition produced annually); The Bill of Rights: A Users Guide; Perspectives; International Relations; The American Economy; Face the Music: Copyright, Art & the Digital Age; documentaries on domestic and foreign policy issues

Name of Organization or Association—Computer Assisted Language Instruction Consortium

Acronym—CALICO

Address:
214 Centennial Hall, Texas State University, 601 University Dr.
San Marcos, TX
78666
USA

Phone Number—(512)245-1417; **Fax Number**—(512)245-9089

Email Contact—info@calico.org; **URL**—http://calico.org

Leaders—Esther Horn, Manager

Description—CALICO is devoted to the dissemination of information on the application of technology to language teaching and language learning.

Membership—1000 members from the USA and 20 foreign countries. Anyone interested in the development and use of technology in the teaching/learning of foreign languages is invited to join.

Dues—$65 annual/individual

Meetings—2012, University of Notre Dame; 2013, University of Hawaii; 2014, University of Ohio; 2015, University of Colorado; 2016, Michigan State University

Publications—CALICO Journal Online (three issues per year), CALICO Monograph Series (Monograph IX, 2010: Web 2.0 topics; Monograph V, second edition 2011: teaching languages with technology topics; Monograph X, 2012: teaching writing with technology topics)

Name of Organization or Association—Consortium of College and University Media Centers

Acronym—CCUMC

Address:
601 E. Kirkwood Ave. Franklin Hall 0009
Bloomington, IN
47405
USA

Phone Number—(812)855-6049; **Fax Number**—(812)855-2103

Email Contact—ccumc@ccumc.org; **URL**—www.ccumc.org

Leaders—Aileen Scales, Executive Director

Description—CCUMC is a professional group whose mission is to provide leadership and a forum for information exchange to the providers of media content, academic technology, and support for quality teaching and learning at institutions of higher education. It fosters cooperative media/instructional technology-related support in higher education institutions and companies providing related products. It also gathers and disseminates information on improved procedures and new developments in instructional technology and media center management.

Membership—750 individuals at 325 institutions/corporations: Institutional memberships—Individuals within an institution of higher education who are associated with the support to instruction and presentation technologies in a media center and/or technology support service. Corporate memberships—Individuals within a corporation, firm, foundation, or other commercial or philanthropic enterprise whose business or activity is in support of the purposes and objectives of CCUMC. Associate memberships—Individuals not eligible for an institutional or corporate membership; from a public library, religious, governmental, or other organizations not otherwise eligible for other categories of membership. Student memberships—Any student in an institution of higher education who is not eligible for an institutional membership.

Dues—Institutional or corporate membership: $325 for 1–2 persons, $545 for 3–4 persons, $795 for 5–6 persons, $130 for each additional person beyond six, associate membership $325 per person, student membership $55 per person.

Meetings—2010 Conference, Buffalo New York (October 6–10, 2010); 2011 Conference South Padre Island Texas (October 5–9, 2011)

Publications—College & University Media Review (journal—annual), Leader (newsletter, three issues annually)

Name of Organization or Association—Council for Exceptional Children

Acronym—CEC

Address:

1110 N. Glebe Rd. #300

Arlington, VA

22201

USA

Phone Number—(703)620-3660. TTY: (703)264-9446; **Fax Number**—(703)264-9494

Email Contact—cec@cec.sped.org.; **URL**—http://www.cec.sped.org

Leaders—Bruce Ramirez, Exec. Dir.

Description—CEC is the largest international organization dedicated to improving the educational success of students with disabilities and/or gifts and talents. CEC advocates for governmental policies supporting special education, sets professional standards, provides professional development, and helps professionals obtain conditions and resources necessary for high-quality educational services for their students.

Organizations and Associations in the USA and Canada 99

Membership—Teachers, administrators, professors, related service providers (occupational therapists, school psychologists…), and parents. CEC has approximately 50,000 members.

Dues—$111 a year

Meetings—Annual convention and expo attracting approximately 6000 special educators

Publications—Journals, newsletters, books, and videos with information on new research findings, classroom practices that work, and special education publications (see also the ERIC Clearinghouse on Disabilities and Gifted Education)

Name of Organization or Association—East-West Center

Acronym—n/a

Address:

1601 East-West Rd.
Honolulu, HI
96848-1601
USA

Phone Number—(808)944-7111; **Fax Number**—(808)944-7376

Email Contact—ewcinfo@EastWestCenter.org; **URL**—http://www.eastwest-center.org/

Leaders—Dr. Charles E. Morrison, Pres.

Description—The U.S. Congress established the East-West Center in 1960 with a mandate to foster mutual understanding and cooperation among the governments and peoples of Asia, the Pacific, and the USA. Officially known as the Center for Cultural and Technical Interchange Between East and West, it is a public, non-profit institution with an international board of governors. Funding for the Center comes from the U.S. Government, with additional support provided by private agencies, individuals, and corporations, and several Asian and Pacific governments. The Center, through research, education, dialog, and outreach, provides a neutral meeting ground where people with a wide range of perspectives exchange views on topics of regional concern. Scholars, government and business leaders, educators, journalists, and other professionals from throughout the region annually work with Center staff to address issues of contemporary significance in such areas as international economics and politics, environment, population, energy, media, and Pacific islands' development.

Membership—The East-West Center is not a membership-based institution. However, our alumni organization, the East-West Center Association (EWCA), is an international network of professionals who have a past affiliation with the East-West Center. Regardless of the length of stay or type of participation, all are automatically members (associates) of the EWCA. There are no membership fees or other requirements to participate in the EWCA.

Dues—n/a

Meetings—Events are listed on our website, eastwestcenter.org/events.

Publications—East-West Center expertise and research findings are published by the East-West Center and by presses and collaborating organizations throughout the region and the world. Publications address a range of critical issues in the Asia Pacific region. The East-West Center sponsors or publishes several series, from short papers to books (see below). For more information about EWC publications, visit http://www.eastwestcenter.org/publications/. The Asia Pacific Bulletin (APB), produced by the East-West Center in Washington, publishes summaries of Congressional Study Groups, conferences, seminars, and visitor roundtables, as well as short articles and opinion pieces. APB summaries are always two pages or less, designed for the busy professional or policymaker to capture the essence of dialogue and debate on issues of concern in US-Asia relations. The East-West Dialogue, an online publication, is an interactive forum for discussion and debate of key issues in Asia-US economic relations. The East-West Dialogue seeks to develop and promote innovative policy, business, and civic initiatives to enhance this critical partnership. Contemporary Issues in Asia and the Pacific is a book series that focuses on issues of contemporary significance in the Asia Pacific region, most notably political, social, cultural, and economic change. The series seeks books that focus on topics of regional importance, on problems that cross disciplinary boundaries, and that have the capacity to reach academic and other interested audience. The Contemporary Issues in Asia and the Pacific book series is published by Stanford University Press. The Studies in Asian Security book series, published by Stanford University Press and sponsored by the East-West Center, promotes analysis, understanding, and explanation of the dynamics of domestic, transnational, and international security challenges in Asia. The peer-reviewed publications in the Series analyze contemporary security issues and problems to clarify debates in the scholarly community, provide new insights and perspectives, and identify new research and policy directions. With a Series committee comprising individuals from diverse theoretical persuasions who have undertaken extensive work on Asian security, books in the Studies in Asian Security series are designed to encourage original and rigorous scholarship, and seek to engage scholars, educators, and practitioners. Policy Studies presents scholarly analysis of key contemporary domestic and international political, economic, and strategic issues affecting Asia in a policy-relevant manner. Written for the policy community, academics, journalists, and informed public, the peer-reviewed publications in this series provide new policy insights and perspectives based on extensive fieldwork and rigorous scholarship. Pacific Islands Policy examines critical issues, problems, and opportunities that are relevant to the Pacific Islands region. The series is intended to influence the policy process, affect how people understand a range of contemporary Pacific issues, and help fashion solutions. A central aim of the series is to encourage scholarly analysis of economic, political, social, and cultural issues in a manner that will advance common understanding of current challenges and policy responses. East-West Center Special Reports present in-depth analysis and exposition that offer insights into specialists yet are accessible to readers outside the author's discipline. These peer-reviewed publications address diverse topics relevant to current and emerging policy debates in the Asia Pacific region and the USA. Papers in the AsiaPacific Issues series address topics of broad interest and significant impact relevant to current and emerging policy debates. These eight-page, peer-reviewed papers are accessible to readers outside the author's discipline.

Name of Organization or Association—Education Development Center, Inc.
Acronym—EDC
Address:
55 Chapel Street
Newton, MA
02458-1060
USA
Phone Number—(617)969-7100; **Fax Number**—(617)969-5979
Email Contact—emarshall@edc.org; **URL**—http://www.edc.org
Leaders—Dr. Luther S. Luedtke, President and CEO
Description—EDC is a global nonprofit organization that designs, delivers, and evaluates innovative programs to address some of the world's most urgent challenges in education, health, and economic opportunity. Working with public sector and private partners, we harness the power of people and systems to improve education, health promotion and care, workforce preparation, communications technologies, and civic engagement. EDC conducts 350 projects in 35 countries around the world.
Membership—Not applicable
Dues—Not applicable
Meetings—Not applicable
Publications—(1) Annual Report; (2) EDC Update, quarterly magazine; (3) EDC Online Report, quarterly newsletter; (4) detailed website with vast archive of publications, technical reports, and evaluation studies

Name of Organization or Association—Education Northwest (formerly Northwest Regional Educational Laboratory)
Acronym—n/a
Address:
101 SW Main St., Suite 500
Portland, OR
97204
USA
Phone Number—(503)275-9500; **Fax Number**—503-275-0448
Email Contact—info@educationnorthwest.org; **URL**—http://education-northwest.org
Leaders—Dr. Carol Thomas, Exec. Dir.
Description—Chartered in the Pacific Northwest in 1966 as Northwest Regional Educational Laboratory, Education Northwest now conducts more than 200 projects annually, working with schools, districts, and communities across the country on comprehensive, research-based solutions to the challenges they face. At Education Northwest, we are dedicated to and passionate about learning. Through our work, we strive to create vibrant learning environments where all youth and

adults can succeed. Everything we do is evidence based, giving us a solid foundation upon which we stand with confidence. We work with teachers, administrators, policymakers, and communities to identify needs, evaluate programs, and develop new solutions. The breadth of our work—ranging from training teachers to developing curriculum, to restructuring schools, and to evaluating programs—allows us to take a comprehensive look at education and to bring wide-ranging expertise and creativity to our clients' challenges. Our approach is highly customized to meet the needs of our clients, and our staff members take great pride in working closely with customers in the field to design the right approach for each situation. We are proud of our 40-year track record, but we do not rest on our laurels—instead, we strive constantly to identify and address emerging needs and trends in teaching and learning.

Membership—856 organizations

Dues—n/a

Meetings—n/a

Publications—Education Northwest Magazine (quarterly journal)

Name of Organization or Association—Educational Communications

Acronym—EC

Address:

P.O. Box 351419

Los Angeles, CA

90035

USA

Phone Number—(310)559-9160; **Fax Number**—(310)559-9160

Email Contact—ECNP@aol.com; **URL**—www.ecoprojects.org

Leaders—Nancy Pearlman, Executive Director and Executive Producer

Description—Educational Communications is dedicated to enhancing the quality of life on this planet and provides radio and television programs about the environment and cultural documentaries. It serves as a clearinghouse on ecological issues through the Ecology Center of Southern California. Programming is available on 50 stations in 25 states and the Internet. These include ECONEWS television series and ENVIRONMENTAL DIRECTIONS radio series. It provides ethnic folk dance performances through Earth Cultures. It also assists groups in third-world countries through Humanity and the Planet, especially "Wells for Burkina Faso" and "Environmental Education in Kenya." Services provided include a speakers bureau, award-winning public service announcements, radio and television documentaries, volunteer and intern opportunities, and input into the decision-making process. Its mission is to educate the public about both the problems and the solutions in the environment. Other projects include Project Ecotourism, Environmental Resources Library, and more.

Membership—$20.00 for yearly subscription to the Compendium Newsletter

Dues—$20 for regular. All donations accepted

Meetings—As needed

Publications—Compendium Newsletter (bimonthly newsletter); Environmental Directions radio audio cassettes (1750 produced to date); ECONEWS and ECO-TRAVEL television series (over 550 shows in the catalog available on 3/4″, VHS, and DVD)

Name of Organization or Association—Edvantia, Inc. (formerly AEL, Inc.)
Acronym—Edvantia
Address:
P.O. Box 1348
Charleston, WV
25325-1348
USA

Phone Number—(304)347-0400, (800)624-9120; **Fax Number**—(304)347-0487
Email Contact—carla.mcclure@edvantia.org; **URL**—http://www.edvantia.org
Leaders—Dr. Doris L. Redfield, President and CEO
Description—Edvantia is a nonprofit education research and development corporation, founded in 1966, that partners with practitioners, education agencies, publishers, and service providers to improve learning and advance student success. Edvantia provides clients with a range of services, including research, evaluation, professional development, and consulting.
Membership—n/a
Dues—n/a
Meetings—n/a
Publications—The Edvantia Electronic Library contains links to free online tools and information created by staff on a wide array of education-related topics. Visitors to the Edvantia website can also access archived webcasts and webinars and sign up for a free monthly newsletter.

Name of Organization or Association—ENC Learning Inc.
Acronym—ENC
Address:
1275 Kinnear Rd.
Columbus, OH
43212
USA

Phone Number—800-471-1045; **Fax Number**—877-656-0315
Email Contact—info@goenc.com; **URL**—www.goenc.com
Leaders—Dr. Len Simutis, Director
Description—ENC provides K-12 teachers and other educators with a central source of information on mathematics and science curriculum materials, particularly those that support education reform. Among ENC's products and services is ENC Focus, a free online magazine on topics of interest to math and science educators. Users include K-12 teachers, other educators, policymakers, and parents.
Membership—ENC is a subscription-based online resource for K-12 educators. Subscriptions are available for schools, school districts, college and universities,

and individuals. Information for subscribers is available at www.goenc.com/subscribe.

Dues—n/a

Meetings—n/a

Publications—ENC Focus is available as an online publication in two formats: ENC Focus on K-12 Mathematics and ENC Focus on K-12 Science. Each is accessible via www.goenc.com/focus.

Name of Organization or Association—Film Arts Foundation

Acronym—Film Arts

Address:

145 9th St. #101

San Francisco, CA

94103

USA

Phone Number—(415)552-8760; **Fax Number**—(415)552-0882

Email Contact—info@filmarts.org; **URL**—http://www.filmarts.org

Leaders—K.C. Price, Interim Executive Director

Description—Service organization that supports the success of independent film and video makers. Some services are for members only and some open to the public. These include low-cost classes in all aspects of filmmaking; affordable equipment rental (including digital video, 16 mm, Super-8, Final Cut Pro editing, ProTools mix room, optical printer, etc.); resource library; free legal consultation; bimonthly magazine Release Print; grants program; year-round events and exhibitions; nonprofit sponsorship; regional and national advocacy on media issues; and significant discounts on film- and video-related products and services.

Membership—nearly 3000

Dues—$45 for "Subscriber"-level benefits including bimonthly magazine, discounts, and access to libraries and online databases. $65 for full "Filmmaker" benefits including the abovementioned plus significant discounts on classes and equipment rentals, eligibility for nonprofit fiscal sponsorship, free legal consultation, and filmmaking consultation

Meetings—Annual membership meeting and regular networking events

Publications—The award-winning bimonthly magazine Release Print

Name of Organization or Association—Great Plains National ITV Library

Acronym—GPN

Address:

P.O. Box 80669

Lincoln, NE

68501-0669

USA

Phone Number—(402)472-2007, (800)228-4630; **Fax Number**—(800)306-2330

Email Contact—npba@umd.edu; **URL**—http://shopgpn.com/

Leaders—Stephen C. Lenzen, Executive Director

Organizations and Associations in the USA and Canada

Description—It produces and distributes educational media, video, CD-ROMs and DVDs, prints, and Internet courses. It is also available for purchase for audiovisual or lease for broadcast use.

Membership—Membership not required

Dues—There are no dues required.

Meetings—There are no meetings. We do attend subject-specific conventions to promote our products.

Publications—GPN Educational Video Catalogs by curriculum areas; periodic brochures. Complete listing of GPN's product line is available via the Internet along with online purchasing. Free previews are available.

Name of Organization or Association—Health Sciences Communications Association

Acronym—HeSCA

Address:

One Wedgewood Dr., Suite 27

Jewett City, CT

06351-2428

USA

Phone Number—(203)376-5915; **Fax Number**—(203)376-6621

Email Contact—hesca@hesca.org; **URL**—http://www.hesca.org/

Leaders—Ronald Sokolowski, Exec. Dir.

Description—An affiliate of AECT, HeSCA is a nonprofit organization dedicated to the sharing of ideas, skills, resources, and techniques to enhance communications and educational technology in the health sciences. It seeks to nurture the professional growth of its members; serve as a professional focal point for those engaged in health science communications; and convey the concerns, issues, and concepts of health science communications to other organizations which influence and are affected by the profession. International in scope and diverse in membership, HeSCA is supported by medical and veterinary schools, hospitals, medical associations, and businesses where media are used to create and disseminate health information.

Membership—150

Dues—$150, indiv.; $195, institutional ($150 additional institutional dues); $60, retiree; $75, student; $1000, sustaining. All include subscriptions to the journal and newsletter.

Meetings—Annual meetings, May–June

Publications—Journal of Biocommunications; Feedback (newsletter)

Name of Organization or Association—Institute for the Future

Acronym—IFTF

Address:

124 University Avenue, 2nd Floor

Palo Alto, CA

94301

USA

Phone Number—(650)854-6322; **Fax Number**—(650)854-7850
Email Contact—info@iftf.org; **URL**—http://www.iftf.org
Leaders—Dale Eldredge, COO
Description—The Institute for the Future (IFTF) is an independent nonprofit research group. We work with organizations of all kinds to help them make better, more informed decisions about the future. We provide the foresight to create insights that lead to action. We bring a combination of tools, methodologies, and a deep understanding of emerging trends and discontinuities to our work with companies, foundations, and government agencies. We take an explicitly global approach to strategic planning, linking macro trends to local issues in such areas as * Work and daily life * Technology and society * Health and health care * Global business trends * Changing consumer society. The Institute is based in California's Silicon Valley, in a community at the crossroads of technological innovation, social experimentation, and global interchange. Founded in 1968 by a group of former RAND Corporation researchers with a grant from the Ford Foundation to take leading-edge research methodologies into the public and business sectors, the IFTF is committed to building the future by understanding it deeply.
Membership—To become a member of IFTF, companies and organizations can join one or more of its membership programs or contract the IFTF for private work. Each membership program offers a distinct set of deliverables at different membership prices and enrollment terms. Please visit the individual program sites for more detailed information on a particular program. For more information on membership contact Sean Ness at sness@iftf.org or 650-854-6322. * Ten-Year Forecast Program * Technology Horizons Program * Health Horizons Program * Custom Private Work.
Dues—Corporate-wide memberships are for 1-year periods: * Ten-Year Forecast—$15,000/year * Technology Horizons—$65,000/year * Health Horizons—$65,000/year. At present, we do not have university, individual, or small-company programs set up. For those companies that support our research programs, we will often conduct custom research.
Meetings—Several a year, for supporting members
Publications—IFTF blogs * Future Now—http://future.iftf.org—emerging technologies and their social implications * Virtual China—http://www.virtual-china.org—an exploration of virtual experiences and environments in and about China * Future of Marketing—http://fom.iftf.org—emerging technology, global change, and future of consumers and marketing * Ten-Year Forecast (members only)—http://blogger.iftf.org/tyf—a broad scan of the leading edge of change in business, government, and global community * Technology Horizons (members only).

Name of Organization or Association—Instructional Technology Council
Acronym—ITC
Address:
One Dupont Cir., NW, Suite 360

Washington, DC
20036-1130
USA
Phone Number—(202)293-3110; **Fax Number**—(202)822-5014
Email Contact—cmullins@itcnetwork.org; **URL**—http://www.itcnetwork.org
Leaders—Christine Mullins, Executive Director
Description—An affiliated council of the American Association of Community Colleges established in 1977, the Instructional Technology Council (ITC) provides leadership, information, and resources to expand access to, and enhance learning through, the effective use of technology. ITC represents higher education institutions in the USA and Canada that use distance learning technologies. ITC members receive a subscription to the ITC News and ITC LISTSERV with information on what is happening in distance education, participation in ITC's professional development audioconference series, distance learning grant information, updates on distance learning legislation, and discounts to attend the annual e-learning conference which features more than 80 workshops and seminars.
Membership—Members include single institutions and multicampus districts; regional and statewide systems of community, technical, and 2-year colleges; for-profit organizations; 4-year institutions; and nonprofit organizations that are interested or involved in instructional telecommunications. Members use a vast array of ever-changing technologies for distance learning. They often combine different systems according to students' needs. The technologies they use and methods of teaching include audio and video conferences, cable television, compressed and full-motion video, computer networks, fiber optics, interactive videodisc, ITFS, microwave, multimedia, public television, satellites, teleclasses, and telecourses.
Dues—$450, institutional; $750, corporate
Meetings—Annual e-learning conference
Publications—ITC Newsletter—Quarterly Quality Enhancing Practices in Distance Education: Vol. 2 Student Services; Quality Enhancing Practices in Distance Education: Vol. 1 Teaching and Learning; New Connections: A Guide to Distance Education (2nd ed.); New Connections: A College President's Guide to Distance Education; Digital Video: A Handbook for Educators; Faculty Compensation and Support Issues in Distance Education; ITC News (monthly publication/ newsletter); ITC LISTSERV

Name of Organization or Association—International Association for Language Learning Technology
Acronym—IALLT
Address:
Information Technology Services, Concordia College
Moorhead, MN
56562
USA

Phone Number—(218) 299-3464; **Fax Number**—(218) 299-3246
Email Contact—business@iallt.org; **URL**—http://iallt.org
Leaders—Mikle Ledgerwood, President; Ron Balko, Treasurer
Description—IALLT is a professional organization whose members provide leadership in the development, integration, evaluation, and management of instructional technology for the teaching and learning of language, literature, and culture.
Membership—400 members; Membership/Subscription Categories * Educational member: for people working in an academic setting such as a school, college, or university. These members have voting rights. * Full-time student member: for full-time students interested in membership. Requires a signature of a voting member to verify student status. These members have voting rights. * Commercial member: for those working for corporations interested in language learning and technology. This category includes for example language laboratory vendors, software, and textbook companies. * Library subscriber: receives our journals for placement in libraries.
Dues—1 year: $50, voting member; $25, student; $200 commercial, 2 years: $90, voting member; $380 commercial
Meetings—Biennial IALLT conferences treat the entire range of topics related to technology in language learning as well as management and planning. IALLT also sponsors sessions at conferences of organizations with related interests, including CALICO and ACTFL.
Publications—IALLT Journal of Language Learning Technologies (two times annually); materials for language lab management and design, language teaching, and technology. Visit our website for details, http://iallt.org.

Name of Organization or Association—International Association of School Librarianship
Acronym—IASL
Address:
PO Box 83
Zillmere, QLD
4034
Australia
Phone Number—61-7-3216-5785; **Fax Number**—61-7-3633-0570
Email Contact—iasl@kb.com.au; **URL**—www.iasl-slo.org/
Leaders—Peter Genco-President; Karen Bonanno-Executive Secretary
Description—Seeks to encourage development of school libraries and library programs throughout the world; promote professional preparation and continuing education of school librarians; achieve collaboration among school libraries of the world; foster relationships between school librarians and other professionals connected with children and youth; and coordinate activities, conferences, and other projects in the field of school librarianship.
Membership—550 plus

Organizations and Associations in the USA and Canada

Dues—$50 Zone A (e.g., the USA, Canada, Western Europe, Japan); $35 Zone B (e.g., Eastern Europe, Latin America, the Middle East); $20 Zone C (e.g., Angola, India, Bulgaria, China). Based on GNP

Meetings—Annual Conference, Lisbon, Portugal, July 2006

Publications—IASL Newsletter (3/year); School Libraries Worldwide (semiannual); Conference Professionals and Research Papers (annual)

Name of Organization or Association—International Center of Photography
Acronym—ICP
Address:
1114 Avenue of the Americas at 43rd Street
New York, NY
10036
USA
Phone Number—(212)857-0045; **Fax Number**—(212)857-0090
Email Contact—info@icp.org; **URL**—http://www.icp.org
Leaders—Willis Hartshorn, Dir.; Phil Block, Deputy Dir. for Programs and Dir. of Education; Kelly Heisler, Dir. of Marketing Communications
Description—The International Center of Photography (ICP) was founded in 1974 by Cornell Capa (1918–2008) as an institution dedicated to photography that occupies a vital and central place in contemporary culture as it reflects and influences social change. Through our museum, school, and community programs, we embrace photography's ability to open new opportunities for personal and aesthetic expression, transform popular culture, and continually evolve to incorporate new technologies. ICP has presented more than 500 exhibitions, bringing the work of more than 3000 photographers and other artists to the public in one-person and group exhibitions, and provided thousands of classes and workshops that have enriched tens of thousands of students. Visit www.icp.org for more information.
Membership—4000
Dues—Current levels available on request
Meetings—xxxx
Publications—Hiroshima: Ground Zero 1945; The Mexican Suitcase; Jasper, Texas: The Community Photographs of Alonzo Jordan; Miroslav Tichý; Dress Codes: The Third ICP Triennial of Photography and Video; Martin Munkacsi; Ecotopia; Atta Kim: ON-AIR; Snap Judgments: New Positions in Contemporary African Photography; African American Vernacular Photography: Selections from the Daniel Cowin Collection; Modernist Photography: Selections from the Daniel Cowin Collection; Young America: The Daguerreotypes of Southworth and Hawes; and others!

Name of Organization or Association—International Council for Educational Media
Acronym—ICEM
Address:
Postfach 114
Vienna, n/a

A-1011
Austria
Phone Number—+43 660 5113241; **Fax Number**—n/a
Email Contact—lylt@a1.net; **URL**—www.icem-cime.org
Leaders—John Hedberg, President; Ray Laverty, Secretary General
Description—Welcome to ICEM. Our purposes are: * To provide a channel for the international exchange and evaluation of information, experience, and materials in the field of educational media as they apply to preschool, primary and secondary education, technical and vocational, industrial and commercial training, teacher training, and continuing and distance education. * To foster international liaison among individuals and organizations with professional responsibility in the field of educational media. * To cooperate with other international organizations in the development and application of educational technology for practice, research, production, and distribution in this field.
Membership—What are the main advantages of ICEM membership? ICEM membership enables those professionally involved in the production, distribution, and use of media in teaching and learning to establish a broad network of contacts with educators, researchers, managers, producers, and distributors of educational media from around the world. It also provides opportunities to discuss topics of mutual concern in an atmosphere of friendship and trust, to plan and carry out co-productions, to compare and exchange ideas and experiences, to keep abreast of the latest developments, and to work together toward the improvement of education on an international level. Membership in ICEM includes a subscription to the ICEM quarterly journal, Educational Media International, an entry in the Who's who on the ICEM webpage, registration at ICEM events and activities either free of charge or at reduced rates, eligibility to engage in working groups or become a member of the Executive Committee, participate at the General Assembly, and numerous other advantages. Our purposes are: * To provide a channel for the international exchange and evaluation of information, experience, and materials in the field of educational media as they apply to preschool, primary and secondary education, technical and vocational, industrial and commercial training, teacher training, and continuing and distance education. * To foster international liaison among individuals and organizations with professional responsibility in the field of educational media. * To cooperate with other international organizations in the development and application of educational technology for practice, research, production, and distribution in this field. Who can be a member of ICEM? Members are organizations and individuals who are involved in educational technology in any one of a variety of ways. There are several different types and categories of ICEM members: individual members, national representatives, deputy representatives, and coordinators. Individual members may join ICEM by paying individual membership fees. National representatives are appointed by their Ministry of Education. National coordinators are elected by other ICEM members in their country. Regional representatives and coordinators represent a group of several countries. ICEM Secretariat, c/o Ray Laverty SG Pf 114 1011 WIEN AUSTRIA, email: lylt-at-a1.net.

Dues—n/a

Meetings—Annual General Assembly in autumn; Executive Committee meeting in spring; Locations vary.

Publications—Educational Media International (quarterly journal), http://www. icem-cime.org/emi/issues.asp. Aims & Scope Educational media has made a considerable impact on schools, colleges, and providers of open and distance education. This journal provides an international forum for the exchange of information and views on new developments in educational and mass media. Contributions are drawn from academics and professionals whose ideas and experiences come from a number of countries and contexts. Abstracting & Indexing Educational Media International is covered by the British Education Index; Contents Pages in Education; Educational Research Abstracts online (ERA); Research into Higher Education Abstracts; ERIC; EBSCOhost; and ProQuest Information and Learning.

Name of Organization or Association—International Recording Media Association

Acronym—IRMA

Address:

182 Nassau St., Suite 204

Princeton, NJ

08542-7005

USA

Phone Number—(609)279-1700; **Fax Number**—(609)279-1999

Email Contact—info@recordingmedia.org; **URL**—http://www.recording-media.org

Leaders—Charles Van Horn, President; Guy Finley, Associate Exec. Director

Description—IRMA, the content delivery and storage association, is the worldwide forum on trends and innovation for the delivery and storage of entertainment and information. Founded in 1970, this global trade association encompasses organizations involved in every facet of content delivery. Beginning with the introduction of the audiocassette, through the home video revolution, and right up to today's digital delivery era, IRMA has always been the organization companies have turned to for news, networking, market research, information services, and leadership.

Membership—With over 400 corporations, IRMA's membership includes raw material providers, manufacturers, replicators, duplicators, packagers, copyright holders, logistics providers, and companies from many other related industries. Corporate membership includes benefits to all employees.

Dues—Corporate membership dues based on gross dollar volume in our industry.

Meetings—Annual Recording Media Forum (Palm Springs, CA); December Summit (New York, NY)

Publications—9X annual Mediaware Magazine; Annual International Source Directory, Quarterly Market Intelligence

Name of Organization or Association—International Society for Performance Improvement

Acronym—ISPI

Address:

1400 Spring Street, Suite 260

Silver Spring, MD

20910

USA

Phone Number—301-587-8570; **Fax Number**—301-587-8573

Email Contact—emember@ispi.org; **URL**—http://www.ispi.org

Leaders—Richard D. Battaglia, Exec. Dir.

Description—The International Society for Performance Improvement (ISPI) is dedicated to improving individual, organizational, and societal performance. Founded in 1962, ISPI is the leading international association dedicated to improving productivity and performance in the workplace. ISPI represents more than 10,000 international and chapter members throughout the USA, Canada, and 40 other countries. ISPI's mission is to develop and recognize the proficiency of our members and advocate the use of human performance technology. This systematic approach to improving productivity and competence uses a set of methods and procedures and a strategy for solving problems for realizing opportunities related to the performance of people. It is a systematic combination of performance analysis, cause analysis, intervention design and development, implementation, and evaluation that can be applied to individuals, small groups, and large organizations.

Membership—10,000 Performance technologists, training directors, human resource managers, instructional technologists, human factor practitioners, and organizational consultants are members of ISPI. They work in a variety of settings including business, academia, government, health services, banking, and armed forces.

Dues—Membership categories: Active membership ($145 annually): This is an individual membership receiving full benefits and voting rights in the society. Student membership ($60 annually): This is a discounted individual full membership for full-time students. Proof of full-time enrollment must accompany the application. Retired membership ($60 annually): This is a discounted individual full membership for individuals who are retired from full-time employment. Special organizational membership categories: These groups support the society at the top level. Sustaining membership ($950 annually): This is an organizational membership and includes five active memberships and several additional value-added services and discounts. Details are available upon request. Patron membership ($1400 annually): This is an organizational membership and includes five active memberships and several additional value-added services and discounts. Details are available upon request.

Meetings—Annual International Performance Improvement Conference, Fall Symposiums, Professional Series Workshops, Human Performance Technology Institutes.

Organizations and Associations in the USA and Canada 113

Publications—Performance Improvement Journal (10/year): The common theme is performance improvement practice or technique that is supported by research or germane theory. PerformanceXpress (12/year): Monthly newsletter published online. Performance Improvement Quarterly, PIQ, is a peer-reviewed journal created to stimulate professional discussion in the field and to advance the discipline of HPT through publishing scholarly works. ISPI Bookstore: The ISPI online bookstore is hosted in partnership with John Wiley & Sons.

Name of Organization or Association—International Visual Literacy Association
Acronym—IVLA
Address:
Dr. Karen Kaminski, IVLA Treasurer, Colorado State University, School of Education—1588
Fort Collins, CO
80523
USA
Phone Number—970-491-3713; **Fax Number**—970-491-1317
Email Contact—IVLA_Treasurer@netzero.com; **URL**—www.ivla.org
Leaders—IVLA Treasurer, Karen Kaminski
Description—IVLA provides a multidisciplinary forum for the exploration, presentation, and discussion of all aspects of visual learning, thinking, communication, and expression. It also serves as a communication link bonding professionals from many disciplines who are creating and sustaining the study of the nature of visual experiences and literacy. It promotes and evaluates research, programs, and projects intended to increase the effective use of visual communication in education, business, arts, and commerce. IVLA was founded in 1968 to promote the concept of visual literacy and is an affiliate of AECT.
Membership—Membership of 500 people, mostly from academia and many disciplines. We are an international organization and have conferences abroad once every third year. Anyone interested in any visual-verbal area should try our organization: architecture, engineering, dance, arts, computers, video, design, graphics, photography, visual languages, mathematics, acoustics, physics, chemistry, optometry, sciences, literature, library, training, education, etc.
Dues—$60 regular; $30 student and retired; $60 outside USA; $500 lifetime membership
Meetings—Yearly conference usually Oct./Nov. in selected locations
Publications—The Journal of Visual Literacy (biannual—juried research papers) and Selected Readings from the Annual Conference

Name of Organization or Association—Knowledge Alliance
Acronym—n/a
Address:
815 Connecticut Avenue, NW, Suite 220
Washington, DC
20006
USA

Phone Number—202-518-0847; **Fax Number**—n/a
Email Contact—waters@KnowledgeAll.net; **URL**—http://www.knowledgeall.net
Leaders—James W. Kohlmoos, Pres.

Description—Knowledge Alliance (formerly known as NEKIA) was founded in 1997 as a nonprofit, nonpartisan strategic alliance to address the increasingly urgent need to apply rigorous research to persistent educational challenges faced by the country's schools. Composed of leading education organizations, Alliance members are involved in high-quality education research, development, dissemination, technical assistance, and evaluation at the federal, regional, state, tribal, and local levels. The Alliance works closely with the US Congress, US Department of Education, and other federal agencies in advocating knowledge-based policy for innovation and improvement in education. Its Mission Knowledge Alliances mission is to improve K-12 education by widely expanding the development and use of research-based knowledge in policy and practice. It also believes that the effective use of research-based knowledge is essential to increasing student achievement and closing achievement gaps and should be a central organizing concept for the education reform efforts at all levels. It envisions a new knowledge era in education policy and practice that focuses on the effective use of research-based knowledge to achieve successful and sustainable school improvement.

Membership—28

Dues—Not available

Meetings—Board Meetings and Retreats; Invitational R&D Summit (2009); Hill Days; Communicators Institute

Publications—n/a

Name of Organization or Association—Learning Point Associates
Acronym—(n/a)
Address:
1120 E. Diehl Road Suite 200
Naperville, IL
60563-1486
USA
Phone Number—(630)649-6500, (800)356-2735; **Fax Number**—(630)649-6700
Email Contact—info@learningpt.org; **URL**—www.learningpt.org
Leaders—Gina Burkhardt, Chief Executive Officer

Description—Learning Point Associates, with offices in Naperville, Illinois; Chicago; New York; and Washington, DC, is a nonprofit educational organization with more than 20 years of direct experience working with and for educators and policymakers to transform educational systems and student learning. The national and international reputation of Learning Point Associates is built on a solid foundation of conducting rigorous and relevant education research and evaluation; analyzing and synthesizing education policy trends and practices; designing and conducting client-centered evaluations; delivering high-quality professional services; and developing and delivering tools, services, and

Organizations and Associations in the USA and Canada

resources targeted at pressing education issues. Learning Point Associates manages a diversified portfolio of work ranging from direct consulting assignments to major federal contracts and grants, including REL Midwest, the National Comprehensive Center for Teacher Quality, Great Lakes East Comprehensive Assistance Center, Great Lakes West Comprehensive Assistance Center, the Center for Comprehensive School Reform and Improvement, and the NCLB Implementation Center.

Membership—Not applicable

Dues—n/a

Meetings—n/a

Publications—Visit the Publications section of our website.

Name of Organization or Association—Library Administration and Management Association

Acronym—LAMA

Address:

50 E. Huron St.

Chicago, IL

60611

USA

Phone Number—(312)280-5032; **Fax Number**—(312)280-5033

Email Contact—lama@ala.org; **URL**—http://www.ala.org/lama

Leaders—Lorraine Olley, Executive Director; Catherine Murray-Rust, President

Description—MISSION: The Library Administration and Management Association encourages and nurtures current and future library leaders, and develops and promotes outstanding leadership and management practices. VISION: LAMA will be the foremost organization developing present and future leaders in library and information services. IMAGE: LAMA is a welcoming community where aspiring and experienced leaders from all types of libraries, as well as those who support libraries, come together to gain skills in a quest for excellence in library management, administration, and leadership. Sections include Buildings and Equipment Section (BES); Fundraising and Financial Development Section (FRFDS); Library Organization and Management Section (LOMS); Human Resources Section (HRS); Public Relation and Marketing Section (PRMS); Systems and Services Section (SASS); and Measurement, Assessment, and Evaluation Section (MAES).

Membership—4800

Dues—$50, regular (in addition to ALA membership); $65, organizations and corporations; $15, library school students

Meetings—ALA Annual Conference 2006, New Orleans, June 22–27; Midwinter Meeting 2007, San Diego, Jan 9–14

Publications—Library Administration & Management (q); LEADS from LAMA (electronic newsletter, irregular)

Name of Organization or Association—Library and Information Technology Association

Acronym—LITA

Address:

50 E. Huron St.

Chicago, IL

60611

USA

Phone Number—(312)280-4270, (800)545-2433, ext. 4270; **Fax Number**—(312)280-3257

Email Contact—lita@ala.org; **URL**—http://www.lita.org

Leaders—Mary C. Taylor, Exec. Dir., mtaylor@ala.org

Description—A division of the American Library Association, LITA is concerned with library automation; the information sciences; and the design, development, and implementation of automated systems in those fields, including system development, electronic data processing, mechanized information retrieval, operation research, standard development, telecommunications, video communications, networks and collaborative efforts, management techniques, information technology, optical technology, artificial intelligence and expert systems, and other related aspects of audiovisual activities and hardware applications.

Membership—LITA members come from all types of libraries and institutions focusing on information technology in libraries. They include library decision makers, practitioners, information professionals, and vendors. Approximately 4300 members.

Dues—$60 plus membership in ALA; $25 plus membership in ALA for library school students

Meetings—National Forum, fall

Publications—LITA Blog—Information Technology and Libraries. ITAL: This contains the table of contents, abstracts, and some full text of ITAL, a refereed journal published quarterly by the Library and Information Technology Association. Technology Electronic Reviews (TER): TER is an irregular electronic serial publication that provides reviews and pointers to a variety of print and electronic resources about information technology. LITA Publications List: Check for information on LITA Guides and Monographs.

Name of Organization or Association—Lister Hill National Center for Biomedical Communications

Acronym—LHNCBC

Address:

US National Library of Medicine, 8600 Rockville Pike

Bethesda, MD

20894

USA

Phone Number—(301)496-4441; **Fax Number**—(301)402-0118

Email Contact—lhcques@lhc.nlm.nih.gov; **URL**—http://lhncbc.nlm.nih.gov/

Leaders—Clement J. McDonald, MD, Director, ClemMcDonald@mail.nih.gov

Description—The Lister Hill National Center for Biomedical Communications is an intramural research and development division of the US National Library of Medicine (NLM). The Center conducts and supports research and development in the dissemination of high-quality imagery, medical language processing, high-speed access to biomedical information, intelligent database system development, multimedia visualization, knowledge management, data mining, and machine-assisted indexing. The Center also conducts and supports research and development projects focusing on educational applications of state-of-the-art technologies including the use of microcomputer technology incorporating stereoscopic imagery and haptics, the Internet, and videoconferencing technologies for training healthcare professionals and disseminating consumer health information. The Center's Collaboratory for High Performance Computing and Communication serves as a focus for collaborative research and development in those areas, cooperating with faculties and staff of health science educational institutions. Health profession educators are assisted in the use and application of these technologies through periodic training, demonstrations, and consultations. High-definition (HD) video is a technology area that has been explored and developed within the Center, and is now used as the NLM standard for all motion imaging projects considered to be of archival value. Advanced three-dimensional animation and photorealistic rendering techniques have also become required tools for use in visual projects within the Center.

Membership—n/a

Dues—n/a

Meetings—n/a

Publications—Fact sheet (and helpful links to other publications) at http://www.nlm.nih.gov/pubs/factsheets/lister_hill.html. Fellowship and postdoctoral opportunities are ongoing: http://lhncbc.nlm.nih.gov/lhc/servlet/Turbine/template/training%2CTrainingoppor.vm.

Name of Organization or Association—Media Communications Association-International

Acronym—MCA-I

Address:

PO Box 5135

Madison WI 53705-0135, WI

53705-0135

USA

Phone Number—Use Contact Form; **Fax Number**—Please Ask.

Email Contact—info@mca-i.org; **URL**—http://www.mca-i.org

Leaders—Lois Weiland and Connie Terwilliger, Co-executive Director

Description—Formerly the International Television Association. Founded in 1968, MCA-I's mission is to provide media communications professionals opportunities for networking, forums for education, and resources for information. MCA-I also offers business services, such as low-cost insurance and buying programs, to reduce operating costs. MCA-I also confers the highly acclaimed MCA-I Media Festival awarding the Golden Reel. Visit MCA-I's website for full details.

Membership—Individual, student, and corporate members. Membership programs are also available to vendors for relationship and business development.

Dues—$80, individual. See the website for complete dues schedule.

Meetings—Various partnerships with association conferences

Publications—MCA-I eNews (monthly), LeaderLinks (monthly), CONNECT (quarterly), Find a Pro Directory (online)

Name of Organization or Association—Medical Library Association
Acronym—MLA
Address:
65 E. Wacker Pl., Ste. 1900
Chicago, IL
60601-7246
USA
Phone Number—(312)419-9094; **Fax Number**—(312)419-8950
Email Contact—info@mlahq.org; **URL**—http://www.mlanet.org
Leaders—Carla J. Funk, MLS, MBA, CAE, Executive Director

Description—MLA, a nonprofit, educational organization, comprises health science information professionals with more than 4500 members worldwide. Through its programs and services, MLA provides lifelong educational opportunities, supports a knowledgebase of health information research, and works with a global network of partners to promote the importance of quality information for improved health to the healthcare community and the public.

Membership—MLA, a nonprofit, educational organization, comprises health science information professionals with more than 4500 members worldwide. Through its programs and services, MLA provides lifelong educational opportunities, supports a knowledgebase of health information research, and works with a global network of partners to promote the importance of quality information for improved health to the healthcare community and the public. Membership categories: regular membership, institutional membership, international membership, affiliate membership, and student membership.

Dues—$165, regular; $110, introductory; $255–600, institutional, based on total library expenditures, including salaries, but excluding grants and contracts; $110, international; $100, affiliate; $40, student

Meetings—National annual meeting held every May; most chapter meetings are held in the fall.

Publications—MLA News (newsletter, 10/year); Journal of the Medical Library Association (quarterly scholarly publication); MLA DocKit series, collections of representative, unedited library documents from a variety of institutions that illustrate the range of approaches to health science library management topics); MLA BibKits, selective, annotated bibliographies of discrete subject areas in the health science literature; standards; surveys; and copublished monographs.

Organizations and Associations in the USA and Canada 119

Name of Organization or Association—Mid-continent Research for Education and Learning
Acronym—McREL
Address:
4601 DTC Blvd., Suite 500
Denver, CO
80237
USA
Phone Number—(303)337-0990; **Fax Number**—(303)337-3005
Email Contact—info@mcrel.org; **URL**—http://www.mcrel.org
Leaders—J. Timothy Waters, Exec. Dir.
Description—McREL is a private, nonprofit organization whose purpose is to improve education through applied research and development. McREL provides products and services, primarily for K-12 educators, to promote the best instructional practices in the classroom. McREL houses one of the ten regional educational laboratories funded by the U.S. Department of Education, Institute for Educational Science. The regional laboratory helps educators and policymakers work toward excellence in education for all students. It also serves at the North Central Comprehensive Center, providing school improvement support to the states of Iowa, Minnesota, Nebraska, North Dakota, and South Dakota. McREL has particular expertise in standards-based education systems, leadership for school improvement, effective instructional practices, teacher quality, mathematics and science education improvement, early literacy development, and education outreach programs.
Membership—not a membership organization
Dues—no dues
Meetings—n/a
Publications—Changing Schools (q. newsletter); Noteworthy (irregular monograph on topics of current interest in education reform). Numerous technical reports and other publications. Check website for current listings.

Name of Organization or Association—Minorities in Media (an affiliate of the Association for Educational Communications & Technology)
Acronym—MIM
Address:
P.O. Box 439147
Chicago, IL
60643-9147
USA
Phone Number—(773) 841-3732; **Fax Number**—(773) 409-8583
Email Contact—pyoung@umbc.edu; **URL**—http://aectmim.ning.com/
Leaders—Patricia A. Young, President (2009–2011); Brandon C. Taylor, President Elect (2011–2013)
Description—Mission statement: Minorities in Media's purpose is to encourage the effective utilization of educational media in the teaching learning process;

provide leadership opportunities in advancing the use of technology as an integral part of the learning process; provide a vehicle through which minorities might influence the utilization of media in institutions; develop an information exchange network common to minorities in media; study, evaluate, and refine the educational technology process as it relates to the education of minorities; and encourage and improve the production of effective materials for the education of minorities.

Membership—Dr. Wesley Joseph McJulien founded Minorities in Media (MIM) around the late 1970s. In the April 1987 issue of TechTrends, the article Black Contributors to Educational Technology chronicled the history of MIM. John W. Green & Wesley J. McJulien wrote: "In 1975, a group of Black technologists met in Dallas in an effort to band together and provide more opportunities for Blacks in the Association for Educational Communications and Technology. One of the assignments was to find the Black person who was the outstanding author in the field of educational technology and invite him to speak at the 1977 meeting of BUDDIES (an organization now called Minorities In Media). Dr. Greene was selected and his presentation, 'The Role of Blacks in Instructional Technology,' stressed that Black must participate in all areas of AECT and especially in research (p. 18)." This history is the foundation of who we are today as an organization. We celebrate our past and continue to spearhead our future. Membership is open to professionals and academics whose interests align with MIM's mission.

Dues—$10, student; $30, professional

Meetings—Annual meetings held during the Association for Educational Communications & Technology conference—www.aect.org

Publications—MIM NING is free to sign up—http://aectmim.ning.com/

Name of Organization or Association—National Aeronautics and Space Administration

Acronym—NASA

Address:

NASA Headquarters, 300 E Street SW

Washington, DC

20546

USA

Phone Number—(202)358-0103; **Fax Number**—(202)358-3032

Email Contact—education@nasa.gov; **URL**—http://education.nasa.gov

Leaders—Angela Phillips Diaz, Assistant Administrator for Education

Description—From elementary through postgraduate school, NASA's educational programs are designed to inspire the next generation of explorers by capturing students interested in science, mathematics, and technology at an early age; to channel more students into science, engineering, and technology career paths; and to enhance the knowledge, skills, and experiences of teachers and university faculty. NASA's educational programs include NASA Spacelink (an electronic information system); videoconferences (60-min interactive staff development

Organizations and Associations in the USA and Canada 121

videoconferences to be delivered to schools via satellite); and NASA Television (informational and educational television programming). Additional information is available from the Office of Education at NASA Headquarters and counterpart offices at the nine NASA field centers. Further information may be obtained from the NASA Education Homepage and also accessible from the NASA Public Portal at See learning in a whole new light!

Membership—n/a

Dues—n/a

Meetings—n/a

Publications—Publications and products can be searched and downloaded from the following URL—http://www.nasa.gov/audience/foreducators/5-8/learning/index.html.

Name of Organization or Association—National Alliance for Media Arts and Culture

Acronym—NAMAC

Address:
145 Ninth Street, Suite 250
San Francisco, C
94103
USA

Phone Number—(415)431-1391; **Fax Number**—(415)431-1392

Email Contact—namac@namac.org; **URL**—http://www.namac.org

Leaders—Helen DeMichel, Co-director

Description—NAMAC is a nonprofit organization dedicated to increasing public understanding of and support for the field of media arts in the USA. Members include media centers, cable access centers, universities, and media artists, as well as other individuals and organizations providing services for production, education, exhibition, distribution, and preservation of video, film, audio, and intermedia. NAMAC's information services are available to the general public, arts and non-arts organizations, businesses, corporations, foundations, government agencies, schools, and universities.

Membership—300 organizations, 75 individuals

Dues—$75–$450, institutional (depending on the annual budget); $75, indiv.

Meetings—Biennial conference

Publications—Media Arts Information Network; The National Media Education Directory, annual anthology of case studies "A Closer Look," periodic White Paper reports, Digital Directions: Convergence Planning for the Media Arts

Name of Organization or Association—National Association for Visually Handicapped

Acronym—NAVH

Address:
22 West 21st St., 6th Floor
New York, NY
10010

USA
Phone Number—(212) 889-3141; **Fax Number**—(212) 727-2931
Email Contact—navh@navh.org; **URL**—http://www.navh.org
Leaders—Dr. Lorraine H. Marchi, Founder/CEO; Cesar Gomez, Executive Director
Description—NAVH ensures that those with limited vision do not lead limited lives. We offer emotional support; training in the use of visual aids and special lighting; access to a wide variety of optical aids, electronic equipment, and lighting; a large print, nationwide, free-by-mail loan library; large print educational materials; free quarterly newsletter; referrals to eye care specialists and local low-vision resources; self-help groups for seniors and working adults; and educational outreach to the public and professionals.
Membership—It is not mandatory to become a member in order to receive our services. However, your membership helps others retain their independence by allowing NAVH to provide low-vision services to those who cannot afford to make a donation. In addition, members receive discounts on visual aids, educational materials, and our catalogs. Corporations and publishers may also join to help sponsor our services. Please contact us for more information.
Dues—Membership is $50 a year for individuals. Publishers and corporations interested in membership should contact NAVH.
Meetings—Seniors' support group two times in a month; seminar on low vision for ophthalmology residents; yearly showcase of the latest in low-vision technology, literature, and services
Publications—Free quarterly newsletter distributed free throughout the English-speaking world; Visual Aids Catalog; Large Print Loan Library Catalog; informational pamphlets on vision, common eye diseases, and living with limited vision; booklets for professionals who work with adults and children with limited vision

Name of Organization or Association—National Association of Media and Technology Centers
Acronym—NAMTC
Address:
NAMTC, 7105 First Ave. SW
Cedar Rapids, IA
52405
USA
Phone Number—319-654-0608; **Fax Number**—319-654-0609
Email Contact—bettyge@mchsi.com; **URL**—www.namtc.org
Leaders—Betty Gorsegner Ehlinger, Executive Director
Description—NAMTC is committed to promoting leadership among its membership through networking, advocacy, and support activities that will enhance the equitable access to media, technology, and information services to educational communities. Membership is open to regional, K-12, and higher education media centers.
Membership—Institutional and corporate members numbering approximately 200

Organizations and Associations in the USA and Canada

Dues—$125, institutions; $335, corporations

Meetings—A national leadership summit is held in the winter.

Publications—Electronic NAMTC Newsletter is published five times per academic year.

Name of Organization or Association—National Commission on Libraries and Information Science

Acronym—NCLIS

Address:

1800 M Street, NW; Suite 350 North Tower

Washington, DC

20036-5841

USA

Phone Number—(202)606-9200; **Fax Number**—(202)606-9203

Email Contact—info@nclis.gov.; **URL**—http://www.nclis.gov

Leaders—C. Beth Fitzsimmons, Chairman

Description—A permanent independent agency of the U.S. Government charged with advising the executive and legislative branches on national library and information policies and plans. The Commission reports directly to the president and Congress on the implementation of national policy; conducts studies, surveys, and analyses of the nation's library and information needs; appraises the inadequacies of current resources and services; promotes research and development activities; conducts hearings and issues publications as appropriate; and develops overall plans for meeting national library and information needs and for coordinating activities at the federal, state, and local levels. The Commission provides general policy advice to the Institute of Museum and Library Services (IMLS) director relating to library services included in the Library Services and Technology Act (LSTA).

Membership—16 commissioners (14 appointed by the president and confirmed by the Senate, the Librarian of Congress, and the Director of the IMLS)

Dues—n/a

Meetings—Average 2–3 meetings a year

Publications—n/a

Name of Organization or Association—National Communication Association

Acronym—NCA

Address:

1765 N Street, NW

Washington, DC

22003

USA

Phone Number—202-464-4622; **Fax Number**—202-464-4600

Email Contact—dwallick@natcom.org; **URL**—http://www.natcom.org

Leaders—Roger Smitter, Exec. Dir.

Description—A voluntary society organized to promote study, criticism, research, teaching, and application of principles of communication, particularly of speech communication. Founded in 1914, NCA is a nonprofit organization of researchers, educators, students, and practitioners, whose academic interests span all forms of human communication. NCA is the oldest and largest national organization serving the academic discipline of communication. Through its services, scholarly publications, resources, conferences, and conventions, NCA works with its members to strengthen the profession and contribute to the greater good of the educational enterprise and society. Research and instruction in the discipline focus on the study of how messages in various media are produced, used, and interpreted within and across different contexts, channels, and cultures.

Membership—7700

Dues—From $60 (student) to $300 (patron). Life membership also available

Meetings—Four regional conferences (ECA, ESCA SSCA, WSCA) and one annual national conference

Publications—Spectra Newsletter (mo.); Quarterly Journal of Speech; Communication Monographs; Communication Education; Critical Studies in Mass Communication; Journal of Applied Communication Research; Text and Performance Quarterly; Communication Teacher; Index to Journals in Communication Studies through 1995; National Communication Directory of NCA and the Regional Speech Communication Organizations (CSSA, ECA, SSCA, WSCA). For additional publications, request brochure

Name of Organization or Association—National Council of Teachers of English

Acronym—NCTE

Address:

1111 W. Kenyon Rd.

Urbana, IL

61801-1096

USA

Phone Number—(217)328-3870; **Fax Number**—(217)328-0977

Email Contact—public_info@ncte.org; **URL**—http://www.ncte.org

Leaders—Kent Williamson, NCTE Executive Director

Description—The National Council of Teachers of English, with 35,000 individual and institutional members worldwide, is dedicated to improving the teaching and learning of English and the language arts at all levels of education. Among its position statements and publications related to educational media and technology are "Code of Best Practices in Fair Use for Media Literacy Education," "The NCTE Definition of 21st Century Literacies," and "Position Statement on Teaching, Learning, and Assessing Writing in Digital Environments."

Membership—NCTE members include elementary, middle, and high school teachers; supervisors of English programs; college and university faculty; teacher educators; local and state agency English specialists; and professionals in related fields.

Dues—Membership in NCTE is $50 a year; subscription to its journals is in addition to the membership fee.

Organizations and Associations in the USA and Canada 125

Meetings—http://www.ncte.org/annual/ 101st NCTE Annual Convention, Nov. 17–20, 2011, Chicago, IL; 102nd NCTE Annual Convention, Nov. 15–20, 2012, Las Vegas, NV; 103rd NCTE Annual Convention, Nov. 21–26, 2013, Boston, MA

Publications—NCTE publishes about 10 books a year. Visit http://www.ncte.org/books and http://www.ncte.org/store. NCTE's journals include Language Arts Voices from the Middle English Journal College English College Composition and Communication English Education Research in the Teaching of English Teaching English in the Two-Year College Talking Points English Leadership Quarterly The Council Chronicle (included in NCTE membership). Journal information is available at http://www.ncte.org/journals/.

Name of Organization or Association—National EBS Association
Acronym—NEBSA
Address:
PO Box 121475
Clermont, FL
34712-1475
USA
Phone Number—(407) 401-4630; **Fax Number**—(321) 406-0520
Email Contact—execdirector@nebsa.org; **URL**—http://nebsa.org
Leaders—Lynn Rejniak, Chair, Bd. of Dirs.; Don MacCullough, Exec. Dir.
Description—Established in 1978, NEBSA is a nonprofit, professional organization of Educational Broadband Service (EBS) licensees, applicants, and others interested in EBS broadcasting. EBS is a very-high-frequency television broadcast service that is used to broadcast distance learning classes, two-way Internet service, and wireless and data services to schools and other locations where education can take place. The goals of the association are to gather and exchange information about EBS, gather data on utilization of EBS, act as a conduit for those seeking EBS information, and assist migration from video broadcast to wireless, broadband Internet services using EBS channels. The NEBSA represents EBS interests to the FCC, technical consultants, and equipment manufacturers. The association uses its website and LISTSERV list to provide information to its members in areas such as technology, programming content, FCC regulations, excess capacity leasing, and license and application data.
Membership—The current membership consists of educational institutions and nonprofit organizations that hold licenses issued by the Federal Communications Commission for Educational Broadband Service (EBS). We also have members that have an interest in EBS and members such as manufacturers of EBS-related equipment and law firms that represent licensees.
Dues—We have two main types of memberships: voting memberships for EBS licensees only and nonvoting memberships for other educational institutions and sponsors. See the website http://www.nebsa.org for details.
Meetings—Annual Member Conference, February 20–23, 2012, Newport Beach Marriott, Newport Beach, CA
Publications—http://www.nebsa.org

Name of Organization or Association—National Endowment for the Humanities
Acronym—NEH
Address:
Division of Public Programs, Americas Media Makers Program, 1100 Pennsylvania
   Ave., NW, Room 426
Washington, DC
20506
USA
Phone Number—(202)606-8269; **Fax Number**—(202)606-8557
Email Contact—publicpgms@neh.gov; **URL**—http://www.neh.gov
Leaders—Karen Mittelman, Deputy Director, Division of Public Programs
Description—The NEH is an independent federal grant-making agency that sup-
   ports research, educational, and public programs grounded in the disciplines of
   the humanities. The Division of Public Programs Media Program supports film
   and radio programs in the humanities for public audiences, including children
   and adults. All programs in the Division of Public Programs support various
   technologies, specifically websites both as stand-alone projects and as extensions of larger projects such as museum exhibitions.
Membership—Nonprofit institutions and organizations including public television
   and radio stations
Dues—not applicable
Meetings—not applicable
Publications—Visit the website (http://www.neh.gov) for application forms and
   guidelines as well as the Media Log, a cumulative listing of projects funded
   through the Media Program.

Name of Organization or Association—National Federation of Community
   Broadcasters
Acronym—NFCB
Address:
1970 Broadway, Ste. 1000
Oakland, CA
94612
USA
Phone Number—510 451-8200; **Fax Number**—510 451-8208
Email Contact—ginnyz@nfcb.org; **URL**—http://www.nfcb.org
Leaders—Maxie C Jackson III, President and CEO
Description—NFCB represents noncommercial, community-based radio stations
   in public policy development at the national level.
Membership—250 Noncommercial community radio stations, related organiza-
   tions, and individuals
Dues—range from $200 to $4000 for participant and associate members
Meetings—Annual Community Radio Conference; 2010 St. Paul; 2011 San
   Francisco; 2012 Houston

Publications—Public Radio Legal Handbook; Digital AudioCraft; Guide to Underwriting

Name of Organization or Association—National Film Board of Canada
Acronym—NFBC
Address:
1123 Broadway, STE 307
New York, NY
10010
USA
Phone Number—(212)629-8890; **Fax Number**—(212)629-8502
Email Contact—NewYork@nfb.ca; **URL**—www.nfb.ca
Leaders—Dylan McGinty, US Sales Manager; Laure Parsons, US Sales and Marketing Associate
Description—Established in 1939, the NFBC's main objective is to produce and distribute high-quality audiovisual materials for educational, cultural, and social purposes.
Membership—n/a
Dues—n/a
Meetings—n/a
Publications—n/a

Name of Organization or Association—National Freedom of Information Coalition
Acronym—NFOIC
Address:
133 Neff Annex, University of Missouri
Columbia, MO
65211-0012
USA
Phone Number—(573)882-4856; **Fax Number**—(573)884-6204
Email Contact—daviscn@missouri.edu; **URL**—http://www.nfoic.org
Leaders—Dr. Charles N. Davis, Executive Director
Description—The National Freedom of Information Coalition is a national membership organization devoted to protecting the public's right to oversee its government. NFOIC's goals include helping start-up FOI organizations; strengthening existing FOI organizations; and developing FOI programs and publications appropriate to the membership.
Membership—The NFOIC offers active memberships to freestanding nonprofit state or regional Freedom of Information Coalitions, academic centers and First Amendment Centers, and associated memberships to individuals and entities supporting NFOIC's mission. Membership information is available on the NFOIC web page. Achieving and maintaining active membership in all 50 states is the primary goal of NFOIC.
Dues—Membership categories and levels of support are described on the NFOIC website.

Meetings—The National Freedom of Information Coalition hosts an annual meeting and a spring conference.

Publications—The FOI Advocate, an electronic newsletter available for free through email subscription. The FOI Report, a periodic White Paper, published electronically

Name of Organization or Association—National Gallery of Art
Acronym—NGA
Address:
Department of Education Resources, 2000B South Club Drive
Landover, MD
20785
USA
Phone Number—(202)842-6269; **Fax Number**—(202)842-6935
Email Contact—EdResources@nga.gov; **URL**—http://www.nga.gov/education/classroom/loanfinder/
Leaders—Leo J. Kasun, Head, Department of Education Resources
Description—This department of NGA is responsible for the production and distribution of 120+ educational audiovisual programs, including interactive technologies. Materials available (all loaned free to individuals, schools, colleges and universities, community organizations, and noncommercial television stations) range across DVDs, CD-ROMs, videocassettes, and teaching packets with either image CD-ROMs or color slides. All DVD and videocassette programs are closed captioned. A free catalog describing all programs is available upon request. Many of these programs are available for long-term loan.
Membership—Our free-loan lending program resembles that of a library and because we are a federally funded institution we do not have a membership system. Last year we lent programs directly to over one million borrowers. Our programs are available to anyone who requests them which ranges from individuals to institutions.
Dues—n/a
Meetings—n/a
Publications—Extension Programs Catalogue

Name of Organization or Association—National PTA
Acronym—National PTA
Address:
541 North Fairbanks Ct, Ste. 1300
Chicago, IL
60611
USA
Phone Number—(312)670-6782; **Fax Number**—(312)670-6783
Email Contact—info@pta.org; **URL**—http://www.pta.org
Leaders—Warlene Gary, Chief Executive Officer
Description—Advocates the education, health, safety, and well-being of children and teens. Provides parenting education and leadership training to PTA volun-

teers. National PTA partners with the National Cable & Telecommunications Association on the "Taking Charge of Your TV" project by training PTA and cable representatives to present media literacy workshops. The workshops teach parents and educators how to evaluate programming so they can make informed decisions about what to allow their children to see. The National PTA in 1997 convinced the television industry to add content information to the TV rating system.

Membership—6.2 million memberships open to all interested in the health, welfare, and education of children and support the PTA mission—http://www.pta.org/aboutpta/mission_en.asp

Dues—vary by local unit—national dues portion is $1.75 per member annually.

Meetings—National convention, held annually in June in different regions of the country, is open to PTA members; convention information is available on the website.

Publications—Our Children (magazine) plus electronic newsletters and other Web-based information for members and general public

Name of Organization or Association—National Public Broadcasting Archives
Acronym—NPBA
Address:
Hornbake Library, University of Maryland
College Park, MD
20742
USA
Phone Number—(301)405-9160; **Fax Number**—(301)314-2634
Email Contact—npba@umd.edu; **URL**—http://www.lib.umd.edu/NPBA
Leaders—Karen King, Acting Curator
Description—NPBA brings together the archival record of the major entities of noncommercial broadcasting in the USA. NPBA's collections include the archives of the Corporation for Public Broadcasting (CPB), the Public Broadcasting Service (PBS), and the National Public Radio (NPR). Other organizations represented include the Midwest Program for Airborne Television Instruction (MPATI), the Public Service Satellite Consortium (PSSC), Americas Public Television Stations (APTS), Children's Television Workshop (CTW), and the Joint Council for Educational Telecommunications (JCET). NPBA also makes available the personal papers of many individuals who have made significant contributions to public broadcasting, and its reference library contains basic studies of the broadcasting industry, rare pamphlets, and journals on relevant topics. NPBA also collects and maintains a selected audio and video program record of public broadcastings' national production and support centers and of local stations. Oral history tapes and transcripts from the NPR Oral History Project and the Televisionaries Nal History Project are also available in the archives. The archives are open to the public from 9 A.M. to 5 P.M., Monday through Friday. Research in NPBA collections should be arranged by prior appointment. For further information, call (301)405-9988.

Membership—n/a
Dues—n/a
Meetings—n/a
Publications—n/a

Name of Organization or Association—National Telemedia Council Inc.
Acronym—NTC
Address:
1922 University Ave.
Madison, WI
53726
USA
Phone Number—(608)218-1182; **Fax Number**—n/a
Email Contact—NTelemedia@aol.com; **URL**—http://www.nationaltelemedia-council.org, and www.journalofmedialiteracy.org
Leaders—Karen Ambrosh, President; Marieli Rowe, Exec. Dir.
Description—The National Telemedia Council is a national, nonprofit professional organization that has been promoting a media-wise society for nearly six decades. Embracing a positive, nonjudgmental philosophy that values education, evaluation, and reflective judgment, NTC has a long history of a broad array of initiatives that have included annual conferences; workshops; major and innovative interactive forums; local, national, and international events for diverse participants (including children); and its major ongoing award, the "Jessie McCanse Award for Individual, Long-Term Contribution to the Field of Media Literacy." NTC's ongoing current activities continue to include its major publication, The Journal of Media Literacy, published up to three times per year (and a part of the organization since its inception in 1953 and earlier); the development of its archival website; and interactive collaborations to advance the field such as the "media literacy cafes" in connection with issues of the Journal of Media Literacy.
Membership—Member/subscribers to the Journal of Media Literacy, currently over 500, including individuals, organizations, schools, and university libraries across the globe including Asia, Australia, Europe, and North and South America. Our membership is open to all those are interested in media literacy.
Dues—Individuals: $35, basic; $50, contributing; $100, patron. Organizations/library: $60. Corporate sponsorship: $500 (additional postage for overseas: Canada or Mexico, add $18.00; all other outside North America, add $23.00)
Meetings—No major meetings scheduled this year
Publications—The Journal of Media Literacy

Name of Organization or Association—Native American Public Telecommunications, Inc.
Acronym—NAPT
Address:
1800 North 33rd St.
Lincoln, NE
68503

Organizations and Associations in the USA and Canada 131

USA
Phone Number—(402) 472-3522; **Fax Number**—(402) 472-8675
Email Contact—native@unl.edu; **URL**—http://www.nativetelecom.org
Leaders—Shirley K. Sneve, Executive Director
Description—Native American Public Telecommunications, Inc. (NAPT), a non-profit 501(c)(3) which receives major funding from the Corporation for Public Broadcasting, shares Native stories with the world through support of the creation, promotion, and distribution of Native media. Founded in 1977, through various media—Public Television, Public Radio, and the Internet—NAPT brings awareness of Indian and Alaska Native issues. NAPT operates AIROS Audio, offering downloadable podcasts with Native filmmakers, musicians, and tribal leaders. VisionMaker is the premier source for quality Native American educational and home videos. All aspects of our programs encourage the involvement of young people to learn more about careers in the media—to be the next generation of storytellers. NAPT is located at the University of Nebraska-Lincoln. NAPT offers student employment, internships, and fellowships. Reaching the general public and the global market is the ultimate goal for the dissemination of Native-produced media.
Membership—No membership
Dues—n/a
Meetings—n/a
Publications—VisionMaker E-Newsletter, NAPT General E-Newsletter, Producer E-Newsletter, AIROS E-Newsletter, Educational Catalog Annual Report, Post Viewer Discussion Guides, Educational Guides.

Name of Organization or Association—Natural Science Collections Alliance
Acronym—NSC Alliance
Address:
P.O. Box 44095
Washington, DC
20026-4095
USA
Phone Number—(202)633-2772; **Fax Number**—(202)633-2821
Email Contact—ddrupa@burkine.com; **URL**—http://www.nscalliance.org
Leaders—Executive Director
Description—Fosters the care, management, and improvement of biological collections and promotes their utilization. Institutional members include free-standing museums, botanical gardens, college and university museums, and public institutions, including state biological surveys and agricultural research centers. The NSC Alliance also represents affiliate societies, and keeps members informed about funding and legislative issues.
Membership—80 institutions, 30 affiliates, 120 individual and patron members
Dues—Depend on the size of collections
Meetings—Annual Meeting (May or June).

Publications—Guidelines for Institutional Policies and Planning in Natural History Collections; Global Genetic Resources; A Guide to Museum Pest Control

Name of Organization or Association—New England School Library Association (formerly New England Educational Media Association)
Acronym—NESLA (formerly NEEMA)
Address:
c/o Merlyn Miller, President Burr & Burton Academy, 57 Seminary Avenue
Manchester, VT
05254
USA
Phone Number—802-362-1775; **Fax Number**—802-362-0574
Email Contact—mmiller@burrburton.org; **URL**—www.neschoolibraries.org
Leaders—Merlyn Miller, President
Description—An affiliate of AECT, NESLA is a regional professional association dedicated to the improvement of instruction through the effective utilization of school library media services, media, and technology applications. For over 90 years, it has represented school library media professionals through activities and networking efforts to develop and polish the leadership skills, professional representation, and informational awareness of the membership. The Board of Directors consists of representatives from local affiliates within all six of the New England states, as well as professional leaders of the region. An annual leadership conference is offered.
Membership—NESLA focuses on school library media issues among the six New England states; consequently, membership is encouraged for school library media specialists in this region.
Dues—Regular membership $30. Student/retired membership $15
Meetings—Annual Leadership Conference and Business Meeting
Publications—NESLA Views

Name of Organization or Association—New York Festivals
Acronym—NYF
Address:
260 West 39th Street, 10th Floor
New York, NY
10018
USA
Phone Number—212-643-4800; **Fax Number**—212-643-0170
Email Contact—info@newyorkfestivals.com; **URL**—http://www.newyorkfestivals.com
Leaders—Rose Anderson, Executive Director
Description—The New York Festivals® World's Best Television & Films™ recognizes the "World's Best Work™" in news, sports, documentary, information, and entertainment program as well as in music videos, infomercials, promotion spots, openings, and IDs. Now entering its 55th year, the total number of entries continues to grow, now representing over 35 different countries, making the

Organizations and Associations in the USA and Canada

NYF™ Television & Film Awards one of the most well-known and widely respected competitions on the globe. In 2010, NYF™ combined both the Television Program Awards and the Film & Video Awards, thus creating one of the world's largest international competitions dedicated to both the TV and film industries. New categories mirror today's trends in worldwide program and encourage the next generation of storytellers. The 2012 TV & Film Awards ceremony for the World's Best TV & Films was held in conjunction with the NAB Show in Las Vegas in April. The ceremony was held on Tuesday, April 17th. The Grand Award winners were screened in the Content Theater on April 18th. DEADLINE EXTENDED TO: NOVEMBER 7TH, 2011. For more information and fees, plus a full list of categories and the rules and regulations, please visit www.newyorkfestivals.com.

Membership—No membership feature. The competition is open to any broadcast and nonbroadcast including online media production.

Dues—n/a.

Meetings—n/a

Publications—Winners are posted on our website at www.newyorkfestivals.com.

Name of Organization or Association—Northwest College and University Council for the Management of Educational Technology

Acronym—NW/MET

Address:

c/o WITS, Willamette University, 900 State St.

Salem, OR

97301

USA

Phone Number—(503)370-6650; **Fax Number**—(503)375-5456

Email Contact—mmorandi@willamette.edu; **URL**—http://www.nwmet.org

Leaders—Doug McCartney, Director (effective April 14, 2007); Marti Morandi, Membership Chair

Description—NW/MET is a group of media professionals responsible for campus-wide media services. Founded in 1976, NW/MET is comprised of members from two provinces of Canada and four northwestern states.

Membership—The membership of NW/MET is composed of individuals who participate by giving time, energy, and resources to the support and advancement of the organization. Full membership may be awarded to individuals whose primary professional role involves the facilitation of educational technology, who are employed by an institution of higher education located in the NW/MET membership region, and who submit a membership application in which they list their professional qualifications and responsibilities.

Dues—$35

Meetings—An annual conference and business meeting are held each year, rotating through the region.

Publications—An annual directory and website

Name of Organization or Association—OCLC Online Computer Library Center, Inc.

Acronym—OCLC

Address:
6565 Kilgour Place
Dublin, OH
43017-3395
USA

Phone Number—(614)764-6000; **Fax Number**—(614)764-6096

Email Contact—oclc@oclc.org; **URL**—http://www.oclc.org

Leaders—Jay Jordan, President and CEO

Description—Founded in 1967, OCLC is a nonprofit, membership, computer library service, and research organization dedicated to the public purposes of furthering access to the world's information and reducing information costs. More than 60,000 libraries in 112 countries and territories around the world use OCLC services to locate, acquire, catalog, lend, and preserve library materials. Researchers, students, faculty, scholars, professional librarians, and other information seekers use OCLC services to obtain bibliographic, abstract, and full-text information. OCLC and its member libraries cooperatively produce and maintain WorldCat, the world's largest database for discovery of library materials. OCLC publishes the Dewey Decimal Classification. OCLC Digital Collection and Preservation Services provide digitization and archiving services worldwide. OCLC's NetLibrary provides libraries with eContent solutions that support web-based research, reference, and learning.

Membership—OCLC welcomes information organizations around the world to be a part of its unique cooperative. A variety of participation levels are available to libraries, museums, archives, historical societies, other cultural heritage organizations, and professional associations. OCLC membership represents more than 60,000 libraries in 112 countries and territories around the world.

Dues—n/a

Meetings—OCLC Members Council (3/year) Held in Dublin, Ohio

Publications—Annual Report (1/year; print and electronic); OCLC Newsletter (4/year; print and electronic); OCLC Abstracts (1/week, electronic only)

Name of Organization or Association—Ontario Film Association, Inc. (also known as the Association for the Advancement of Visual Media/Lassociation pour lavancement des médias visuels)

Acronym—OLA

Address:
50 Wellington St East Suite 201
Toronto, ON
M5E 1C8
Canada

Phone Number—(416)363-3388; **Fax Number**—1-800-387-1181

Email Contact—info@accessola.com; **URL**—www.accessola.com

Organizations and Associations in the USA and Canada

Leaders—Lawrence A. Moore, Exec. Dir.
Description—A membership organization of buyers and users of media whose objectives are to promote the sharing of ideas about visual media through education, publications, and advocacy
Membership—112
Dues—$120, personal membership; $215, associate membership
Meetings—OFA Media Showcase, spring
Publications—Access

Name of Organization or Association—Pacific Film Archive
Acronym—PFA
Address:
University of California, Berkeley Art Museum, 2625 Durant Ave.
Berkeley, CA
94720-2250
USA
Phone Number—(510)642-1437 (library); (510)642-1412 (general).; **Fax Number**—(510)642-4889
Email Contact—NLG@berkeley.edu; **URL**—http://www.bampfa.berkeley.edu
Leaders—Susan Oxtoby, Senior Curator of Film; Nancy Goldman, Head, PFA Library and Film Study Center
Description—Sponsors the exhibition, study, and preservation of classic, international, documentary, animated, and avant-garde films. Provides on-site research screenings of films in its collection of over 10,000 titles. Provides access to its collections of books, periodicals, stills, and posters (all materials are noncirculating). Offers BAM/PFA members and University of California, Berkeley, affiliates reference and research services to locate film and video distributors, credits, stock footage, etc. Library hours are 1 P.M.–5 P.M., Mon.–Thurs. Research screenings are by appointment only and must be scheduled at least 2 weeks in advance; other collections are available for consultation on a drop-in basis during library hours.
Membership—Membership is through its parent organization, the UC Berkeley Art Museum and Pacific Film Archive, and is open to anyone. The BAM/PFA currently has over 3000 members. Members receive free admission to the museum; reduced-price tickets to films showing at PFA; access to the PFA Library & Film Study Center; and many other benefits. Applications and more information are available at http://www.bampfa.berkeley.edu/join/.
Dues—$50, individuals and nonprofit departments of institutions
Meetings—n/a
Publications—BAM/PFA Calendar (6/year)

Name of Organization or Association—Pacific Resources for Education and Learning
Acronym—PREL
Address:
900 Fort Street Mall, Suite 1300

Honolulu, HI
96813
USA
Phone Number—(808) 441-1300; **Fax Number**—(808) 441-1385
Email Contact—askprel@prel.org; **URL**—http://www.prel.org/
Leaders—Thomas W. Barlow, Ed.D., President and Chief Executive Officer
Description—Pacific Resources for Education and Learning (PREL) is an independent, nonprofit 501(c)(3) corporation that serves the educational community in the US-affiliated Pacific islands, the continental USA, and countries throughout the world. PREL bridges the gap between research, theory, and practice in education and works collaboratively to provide services that range from curriculum development to assessment and evaluation. PREL serves the Pacific educational community with quality programs and products developed to promote educational excellence. We work throughout school systems, from classroom to administration, and collaborate routinely with governments, communities, and businesses. Above all, we specialize in multicultural and multilingual environments. From direct instruction to professional development to creation of quality educational materials, PREL is committed to ensuring that all students, regardless of circumstance or geographic location, have an equal opportunity to develop a strong academic foundation. PREL brings together in the Center for Information, Communications, and Technology (CICT) an experienced cadre of specialists in website development and design, educational technology, distance and online learning, multimedia production, interactive software development, writing and editing, graphics, and print production. By combining tested pedagogy with leading-edge technology, PREL can create learning materials encompassing a wide variety of subject matter and delivery methods. PREL partners with researchers, schools, evaluators, publishers, and leaders in the learning technology industry to develop state-of-the-art learning tools and technology solutions. There are vast disparities across the Pacific when it comes to school resources, technology access, and bandwidth. PREL's goal is to work effectively in any type of setting in which an application is needed. With routine travel and a staff presence throughout the northern Pacific, PREL has resolved to reach underserved communities, determine their needs, and meet their requirements with the appropriate delivery and dissemination methods. Multimedia, software, and website conception, design, and delivery have become critical components of many learning programs. Our projects include development of teacher and student resources and resource kits, learning games, software solutions, and complex interactive database design. Distance learning content and delivery extend educational resources to audiences and individuals outside the classroom setting. Distance options both enhance and exponentially increase learning opportunities. The CICT is a premier provider of distance education, integrating curriculum and technology. High-quality publications are a PREL hallmark. PREL produces and distributes numerous high-quality publications for educators, including its research compendium, Research into Practice; Pacific Educator

Organizations and Associations in the USA and Canada 137

magazine; educational books and videos; and briefs and reports on research findings and current topics of interest.

Membership—We serve teachers and departments and ministries of education in American Samoa, Commonwealth of the Northern Mariana Islands, Federated States of Micronesia (Chuuk, Kosrae, Pohnpei, and Yap), Guam, Hawaii, the Republic of the Marshall Islands, and the Republic of Palau. In addition we work with the educational community on the continental USA and countries throughout the world. We are not a membership organization. We are grant funded with grants from the United States Departments of Education, Labor, Health, and Human Services, and other federal funding agencies such as the Institute of Museum and Library Services and the National Endowment for the Arts. In addition we have projects in partnership with regional educational institutions. Internationally we have worked with the International Labor Organization and the World Health Organization and are currently working with Save the Children on a US AID project in the Philippines.

Dues—n/a

Meetings—PREL supports the annual Pacific Educational Conference (PEC), held each July.

Publications—Publications are listed on the PREL website at http://ppo.prel.org/. Most are available in both PDF and HTML formats. Some recent publications are described below: Focus on Professional Development, (Research Based Practices in Early Reading Series) A Focus on Professional Development is the fourth in the Research-Based Practices in Early Reading Series published by the Regional Educational Laboratory (REL) at Pacific Resources for Education and Learning (PREL). Because reading proficiency is fundamental to student achievement across all subjects and grades, the preparation of the teachers and administrators who are responsible for providing early reading instruction is of special importance. This booklet examines what research tells us about professional development and about the role that effective professional development plays in improving both teacher performance and student achievement. http://www.prel.org/products/re_/prodevelopment.pdf (902 K), Look and See: Using the Visual Environment as Access to Literacy (Research Brief). This paper describes how the visual environment—what we see when we look—can be used to develop both visual and verbal literacy, including aesthetic appreciation, comprehension, and vocabulary. http://www.prel.org/products/re_/look_see.pdf (1 M), Measuring the Effectiveness of Professional Development in Early Literacy: Lessons Learned (Research Brief). This research brief focuses on the methodology used to measure professional development (PD) effectiveness. It examines the needs that generated this research, what PREL did to meet those needs, and lessons that have been learned as a result. In particular, it discusses the development of a new instrument designed to measure the quality of PD as it is being delivered. http://www.prel.org/products/re_/effect_of_pd.pdf (730 K), Pacific Early Literacy Resource Kit CD-ROM (Early Literacy Learning Resources): The Pacific Early Literacy Resource Kit was developed from PREL's research-based work performed with early literacy teachers in US-affiliated

Pacific islands. The contents of the Resource Kit represent information, products, and processes we found beneficial as we worked to support literacy teachers in their efforts to improve student literacy achievement. http://www.prel.org/toolkit/index.htm, Research Into Practice 2006 (PREL Compendium): This 86-page volume of PREL's annual research compendium brings together articles detailing research conducted during 2005 by PREL. The six articles in this issue focus on putting research findings to work to improve education. http://www.prel.org/products/pr_/compendium06/tableofcontents.asp

Name of Organization or Association—Reference and User Services Association, a division of the American Library Association
Acronym—RUSA
Address:
50 E. Huron St.
Chicago, IL
60611
USA
Phone Number—(800)545-2433, ext. 4398.; **Fax Number**—Fax (312)280-5273
Email Contact—rusa@ala.org; **URL**—http://rusa.ala.org
Leaders—Susan Hornung, Executive Director
Description—A division of the American Library Association, the Reference and User Services Division (RUSA) is responsible for stimulating and supporting the delivery of general library services and materials, and the provision of reference and information services, collection development, readers' advisory, and resource sharing for all ages, in every type of library.
Membership—4200
Dues—Join ALA and RUSA $120; RUSA membership $60 (added to ALA membership); student member $55 ($30 for ALA and $25 for RUSA); retired, support staff, or nonsalaried $72 ($42 for ALA and $30 for RUSA)
Meetings—Meetings are held in conjunction with the American Library Association.
Publications—RUSQ (q.), information provided on RUSA website at www.ala.org/rusa; RUSA Update, online membership newsletter, select publications

Name of Organization or Association—Research for Better Schools, Inc.
Acronym—RBS
Address:
112 North Broad Street
Philadelphia, PA
19102-1510
USA
Phone Number—(215)568-6150; **Fax Number**—(215)568-7260
Email Contact—info@rbs.org; **URL**—http://www.rbs.org/
Leaders—Keith M. Kershner Executive Director
Description—Research for Better Schools is a nonprofit education organization that has been providing services to teachers, administrators, and policymakers since 1966. Our mission is to help students achieve high learning standards by

Organizations and Associations in the USA and Canada 139

supporting improvement efforts in schools and other education environments. The staff are dedicated to and well experienced in providing the array of services that schools, districts, and states need to help their students reach proficient or higher learning standards: (1) technical assistance in improvement efforts; (2) professional development that is required for the successful implementation of more effective curricula, technologies, or instruction; (3) application of research in the design of specific improvement efforts; (4) evaluation of improvement efforts; (5) curriculum implementation and assessment; and (6) effective communication with all members of the school community. RBS has worked with a wide range of clients over the years, representing all levels of the education system, as well as business and community groups.

Membership—There is no membership in Research for Better Schools.

Dues—n/a

Meetings—n/a

Publications—RBS publishes a variety of books and other products designed for educators to use for school's improvement. The catalog for RBS Publications is online (visit our homepage at http://www.rbs.org).

Name of Organization or Association—SERVE Center @ UNCG

Acronym—We no longer use the acronym.

Address:
5900 Summit Avenue, Dixon Building
Browns Summit, FL
27214
USA

Phone Number—800-755-3277, 336-315-7457; **Fax Number**—336-315-7457

Email Contact—info@serve.org; **URL**—http://www.serve.org/

Leaders—Ludy van Broekhuizen, Executive Director

Description—The SERVE Center at the University of North Carolina at Greensboro, under the leadership of Dr. Ludwig David van Broekhuizen, is a university-based education organization with the mission to promote and support the continuous improvement of educational opportunities for all learners in the Southeast. The organization's commitment to continuous improvement is manifest in an applied research-to-practice model that drives all of its work. Building on research, professional wisdom, and craft knowledge, SERVE staff members develop tools, processes, and interventions designed to assist practitioners and policymakers with their work. SERVE's ultimate goal is to raise the level of student achievement in the region. Evaluation of the impact of these activities combined with input from stakeholders expands SERVE's knowledge base and informs future research. This rigorous and practical approach to research and development is supported by an experienced staff strategically located throughout the region. This staff is highly skilled in providing needs assessment services, conducting applied research in schools, and developing processes, products, and programs that support educational improvement and increase student achievement. In the last 3 years, in addition to its basic research and development work with over 170 southeastern schools, SERVE staff provided technical assistance and training to more than 18,000 teachers and administrators across the region. The SERVE Center is governed by a board of directors that includes the governors, chief state school officers, educators, legislators, and private sector leaders from Alabama, Florida, Georgia, Mississippi, North Carolina, and South Carolina. SERVE's operational core is the Regional Educational Laboratory. Funded by the U.S. Department of Education's Institute of Education Sciences, the Regional Educational Laboratory for the Southeast is one of the ten laboratories providing research-based information and services to all 50 states and territories. These laboratories form a nationwide education knowledge network, building a bank of information and resources shared and disseminated nationally and regionally to improve student achievement. SERVE's National Leadership Area, Expanded Learning Opportunities, focuses on improving student outcomes through the use of exemplary pre-K and extended-day programs.

Membership—n/a

Dues—n/a

Meetings—n/a

Publications—Three titles available in the highlighted products' area of website: A Review of Methods and Instruments Used in State and Local School Readiness Evaluations Abstract: This report provides detailed information about the methods and instruments used to evaluate school readiness initiatives, discusses important considerations in selecting instruments, and provides resources and recommendations that may be helpful to those who are designing and implementing school readiness evaluations. Levers for Change: Southeast Region State Initiatives to Improve High Schools Abstract: This descriptive report aims to stimulate discussion about high school reform among Southeast Region states. The report groups recent state activities in high school reform into six "levers for change." To encourage critical reflection, the report places the reform discussion in the context of an evidence-based decision-making process and provides sample research on reform activities. Evidence-Based Decision making: Assessing Reading Across the Curriculum Intervention Abstract: When selecting reading across the curriculum interventions, educators should consider the extent of the evidence base on intervention effectiveness and the fit with the school or district context, whether they are purchasing a product from vendors or developing it internally. This report provides guidance in the decision-making.

Name of Organization or Association—Society for Photographic Education

Acronym—SPE

Address:

126 Peabody Hall, The School of Interdisciplinary Studies, Miami University

Oxford, OH

45056

USA

Phone Number—(513) 529-8328; **Fax Number**—(513) 529-9301

Email Contact—speoffice@spenational.org; **URL**—www.spenational.org

Organizations and Associations in the USA and Canada 141

Leaders—Richard Gray, Chairperson of SPE Board of Directors
Description—An association of college and university teachers of photography, museum photographic curators, writers, publishers, and students. **Membership**—1800 membership dues are for the calendar year, January through December.
Dues—Membership dues: $90, regular membership; $50, student membership; $600, corporate member; $380, collector member (with print); $150, sustaining member; $65, senior member
Meetings—Denver, CO, March 13–16, 2008
Publications—Exposure (photographic journal), biannual, Quarterly Newsletter, Membership Directory, Conference Program Guide

Name of Organization or Association—Society of Cable Telecommunications Engineers
Acronym—SCTE
Address:
140 Philips Rd.
Exton, PA
19341-1318
USA
Phone Number—(610)363-6888; **Fax Number**—(610)363-5898
Email Contact—scte@scte.org; **URL**—http://www.scte.org
Leaders—Mark L, Dzuban, Pres. and CEO
Description—The Society of Cable Telecommunications Engineers (SCTE) is a nonprofit professional association that provides technical leadership for the telecommunications industry and serves its members through professional development, standards, certification, and information. SCTE currently has more than 14,000 members from the USA and 70 countries worldwide and offers a variety of programs and services for the industry's educational benefit. SCTE has 68 chapters and meeting groups and more than 3000 employees of the cable telecommunications industry hold SCTE technical certifications. SCTE is an ANSI-accredited standard development organization. Visit SCTE online at www. scte.org.
Membership—SCTE is comprised of a global network of more than 14,000 broadband engineers, technology experts, industry analysts, technicians, corporate managers, and CEOs who work within the cable telecommunications industry. SCTE offers industry professionals a multitude of learning opportunities on the latest technological advances, industry news, and targeted resources to help keep members better informed, outperform their peers, and advance in their careers at a pace that works best for them.
Dues—$68 individual, $350 expo partner, $34 full-time student, unemployed, or retired (1 year)
Meetings—SCTE Cable-Tec Expo®, Denver, CO, Oct. 28–30, 2009; SCTE Conference on Broadband Learning & Development, Denver, CO, Oct. 27, 2009; SCTE Conference on Emerging Technologies®

Publications—SCTE Interval SCTE Monthly SCTE NewsBreak Credentials Standards Bulletin

Name of Organization or Association—Society of Photo Technologists
Acronym—SPT
Address:
11112 S. Spotted Rd.
Cheney, WA
99004
USA
Phone Number—800-624-9621 or (509)624-9621; **Fax Number**—(509)624-5320
Email Contact—cc5@earthlink.net; **URL**—http://www.spt.info/
Leaders—Chuck Bertone, Executive Director
Description—An organization of photographic equipment repair technicians, which improves and maintains communications between manufacturers and repair shops and technicians. We publish repair journals, newsletters, parts and service directory, and industry newsletters. We also sponsor SPTNET (a technical email group), remanufactured parts, and residence workshops.
Membership—1000 shops and manufacturers worldwide, eligible people or businesses are any who are involved full or part time in the camera repair field.
Dues—$125.00–$370. Membership depends on the size/volume of the business. Most one-man shops are Class A/$195 dues. Those not involved full time in the field are $125.00/Associate Class.
Meetings—SPT Journal; SPT Parts and Services Directory; SPT Newsletter; SPT Manuals—Training and Manufacturer's Tours
Publications—Journals and newsletters

Name of Organization or Association—Southwest Educational Development Laboratory
Acronym—SEDL
Address:
211 East Seventh St.
Austin, TX
78701
USA
Phone Number—(512) 476-6861; **Fax Number**—(512) 476-2286
Email Contact—info@sedl.org; **URL**—http://www.sedl.org
Leaders—Dr. Wesley A. Hoover, Pres. and CEO
Description—The Southwest Educational Development Laboratory (SEDL) is a private, not-for-profit education research and development corporation based in Austin, Texas. SEDL has worked in schools to investigate the conditions under which teachers can provide student-centered instruction supported by technology, particularly computers alone with other software. From that field-based research with teachers, SEDL has developed a professional development model and modules, which resulted in the production of Active Learning with

Technology (ALT) portfolio. ALT is a multimedia training program for teachers to learn how to apply student-centered, problem-based learning theory to their instructional strategies that are supported by technologies. Copies of Active Learning with Technology Portfolio and other products used to integrate technology in the classroom can be viewed and ordered online at http://www.sedl.org/pubs/category_technology.html from SEDL's Office of Institutional Communications. SEDL operates the Southeast Comprehensive Center (SECC), funded by the U.S. Department of Education, which provides high-quality technical assistance in the states of Alabama, Georgia, Louisiana, Mississippi, and South Carolina. The goals of the SECC are to build the capacities of states in its region to implement the programs and goals of the No Child Left Behind Act of 2001 (NCLB) and to build state's capacity to provide sustained support of high-needs districts and schools. SECC works closely with each state in its region to provide access and use of information, models, and materials that facilitate implementation of and compliance with NCLB. SEDL's Texas Comprehensive Center provides technical assistance and support to the Texas Education Agency to assure that Texas has an education system with the capacity and commitment to eliminate achievement gaps and enable all students to achieve at high levels.

Membership—Not applicable

Dues—Not applicable

Meetings—Not applicable

Publications—SEDL LETTER and other newsletters and documents are available for free general distribution in print and online. Topic-specific publications related to educational change, education policy, mathematics, language arts, science, and disability research and a publications catalog are available at http://www.sedl.org/pubs on the SEDL website.

Name of Organization or Association—Special Libraries Association

Acronym—SLA

Address:

331 South Patrick St.

Alexandria, VA

22314

USA

Phone Number—703-647-4900; **Fax Number**—703-647-4901

Email Contact—sla@sla.org; **URL**—http://www.sla.org

Leaders—The Honorable Janice R. Lachance, CEO

Description—The Special Libraries Association (SLA) is a nonprofit global organization for innovative information professionals and their strategic partners. SLA serves more than 11,000 members in 75 countries in the information profession, including corporate, academic, and government information specialists. SLA promotes and strengthens its members through learning, advocacy, and networking initiatives. For more information, visit us on the Web at www.sla.org.

Membership—11,500

Dues—Full membership: USD 160.00 (members earning greater than USD 35,000 in annual salary); USD 99.00 (members earning USD 35,000 or less in annual salary). Student/retired membership: USD 35.00

Meetings—2006 Annual Conference and Exposition: 11–14 June, Baltimore; 2007 Annual Conference and Exposition: 3–6 June, Denver

Publications—Information Outlook (monthly glossy magazine that accepts advertising). SLA Connections (monthly electronic newsletter for members and stakeholders)

Name of Organization or Association—Teachers and Writers Collaborative
Acronym—T&W
Address:
520 Eighth Avenue, Suite 2020
New York, NY
10018
USA
Phone Number—(212)691-6590, Toll-free (888)266-5789; **Fax Number**—(212)675-0171

Email Contact—bmorrow@twc.org; **URL**—http://www.twc.org and http://www.writenet.org

Leaders—Amy Swauger, Dir.

Description—T&W brings the joys and pleasures of reading and writing directly to children. As an advocate for the literary arts and arts education, we support writers and teachers in developing and implementing new teaching strategies; disseminate models for literary arts education to local, national, and international audiences; and showcase both new and established writers via publications and literary events held in our Center for Imaginative Writing. T&W was founded in 1967 by a group of writers and educators who believed that professional writers could make a unique contribution to the teaching of writing and literature. Over the past 40 years, 1500 T&W writers have taught writing workshops in New York City's public schools. Approximately 700,000 New York City students have participated in our workshops, and we have worked with more than 25,000 teachers. Our wealth of experience, which is reflected in T&W's 80 books about teaching writing, led the National Endowment for the Arts to single out T&W as the arts-in-education group "most familiar with creative writing/literature in primary and secondary schools." The American Book Review has written that T&W "has created a whole new pedagogy in the teaching of English."

Membership—T&W has over 1000 members across the country. The basic membership is $35; patron membership is $75; and benefactor membership is $150 or more. Members receive a free book or T-shirt; discounts on publications; and a free 1-year subscription to Teachers & Writers magazine. (Please see http://www.twc.org/member.htm.)

Dues—T&W is seeking general operating support for all of our programs and program support for specific projects, including (1) T&W writing residencies in New York City area schools; (2) T&W publications, books, and a quarterly

Organizations and Associations in the USA and Canada   145

magazine, which we distribute across the country; (3) T&W events, including readings for emerging writers and small presses; and (4) T&W's Internet programs for teachers, writers, and students. Grants to T&W's Endowment support the stability of the organization and help to guarantee the continuation of specific programs.

Meetings—T&W offers year-round public events in our Center for Imaginative Writing in New York City. For a list of events, please see http://www.twc.org/events.htm.

Publications—T&W has published over 80 books on the teaching of imaginative writing, including the T&W Handbook of Poetic Forms; Luna, Luna: Creative Writing from Spanish and Latino Literature; The Nearness of You: Students and Teachers Writing On-Line. To request a free publications catalog, please send an email to info@twc.org or call 888-BOOKS-TW. (Please see http://www.twc.org/pubs.)

Name of Organization or Association—The George Lucas Educational Foundation
Acronym—GLEF
Address:
P.O. Box 3494
San Rafael, CA
94912
USA
Phone Number—(415)662-1600; **Fax Number**—(415)662-1619
Email Contact—edutopia@glef.org; **URL**—http://edutopia.org
Leaders—Milton Chen, PhD., Exec. Dir.
Description—Mission: The George Lucas Educational Foundation (GLEF) is a nonprofit operating foundation that documents and disseminates models of the most innovative practices in our nation's K-12 schools. We serve this mission through the creation of media—from films, books, and magazine to CD-ROMS and DVDs. GLEF works to provide its products as tools for discussion and action in conferences, workshops, and professional development settings. Audience: A successful educational system requires the collaborative efforts of many different stakeholders. Our audience includes teachers, administrators, school board members, parents, researchers, and business and community leaders who are actively working to improve teaching and learning. Vision: The Edutopian vision is thriving today in our country's best schools: places where students are engaged and achieving at the highest levels, where skillful educators are energized by the excitement of teaching, where technology brings outside resources and expertise into the classroom, and where parents and community members are partners in educating our youth.

Membership—All online content and the Edutopia magazine are offered free of charge to educators.

Dues—Free subscription to Edutopia magazine for those working in education.

Meetings—No public meetings; advisory council meets annually; board of directors meets quarterly.

Publications—Edutopia Online: The Foundation's website, Edutopia (www.edutopia.org) celebrates the unsung heroes who are making Edutopia a reality. All of GLEF's multimedia content dating back to 1997 is available on its website. A special feature, the Video Gallery, is an archive of short documentaries and expert interviews that allow visitors to see these innovations in action and hear about them from teachers and students. Detailed articles, research summaries, and links to hundreds of relevant websites, books, organizations, and publications are also available to help schools and communities build on successes in education. Edutopia: Success Stories for Learning in the Digital Age: This book and CD-ROM include numerous stories of innovative educators who are using technology to connect with students, colleagues, local community, and the world beyond. The CD-ROM contains more than an hour of video footage. Published by Jossey-Bass. Teaching in the Digital Age (TDA) Videocassettes: This video series explores elements of successful teaching in the Digital Age. The project grows out of GLEF's belief that an expanded view is needed of all our roles in educating children and supporting teachers. The series explores school leadership, emotional intelligence, teacher preparation, and project-based learning and assessment. Learn & Live: This documentary film and 300-page companion resource book showcases innovative schools across the country. The film, hosted by Robin Williams, aired on public television stations nationwide in 1999 and 2000. The Learn & Live CD-ROM includes digital versions of the film and book in a portable, easy-to-use format. Edutopia Magazine: A free magazine which shares powerful examples of innovative and exemplary learning and teaching. Edutopia Newsletter: This free, semiannual print newsletter includes school profiles, summaries of recent research, and resources and tips for getting involved in public education. Instructional Modules: Free teaching modules developed by education faculty and professional developers. They can be used as extension units in existing courses, or can be used independently in workshops. It includes presenter notes, video segments, and discussion questions. Topics include project-based learning, technology integration, and multiple intelligences.

Name of Organization or Association—The NETWORK, Inc.
Acronym—NETWORK
Address:
136 Fenno Drive
Rowley, MA
01969-1004
USA
Phone Number—800-877-5400, (978)948-7764; **Fax Number**—(978)948-7836
Email Contact—davidc@thenetworkinc.org; **URL**—www.thenetworkinc.org
Leaders—David Crandall, President
Description—A nonprofit research and service organization providing training, research and evaluation, technical assistance, and materials for a fee to schools, educational organizations, and private sector firms with educational interests. The NETWORK has been helping professionals manage and learn about change

Organizations and Associations in the USA and Canada 147

since 1969. Our Leadership Skills series of computer-based simulations extends the widely used board game versions of Making Change (tm) and Systems Thinking/Systems Changing(tm) with the addition of Improving Student Success: Teachers, Schools and Parents to offer educators a range of proven professional development tools. Now available, Networking for Learning, originally developed for the British Department for Education and Skills, offers a contemporary leadership development resource for educators exploring the challenges of complex collaborations involving multiple organizations.

Membership—n/a.

Dues—No dues, fee for service

Meetings—Call

Publications—Making Change: A Simulation Game [board and computer versions]; Systems Thinking/Systems Changing: A Simulation Game [board and computer versions]; Improving Student Success: Teachers, Schools and Parents [computer-based simulation]; Systemic Thinking: Solving Complex Problems; Benchmarking: A Guide for Educators; Networking for Learning; Check Yourself into College: A quick and easy guide for high school students

Name of Organization or Association—University Continuing Education Association

Acronym—UCEA

Address:

One Dupont Cir. NW, Suite 615
Washington, DC
20036
USA

Phone Number—(202)659-3130; **Fax Number**—(202)785-0374

Email Contact—kjkohl@ucea.edu; **URL**—http://www.ucea.edu/

Leaders—Kay J. Kohl, Executive Director, kjkohl@ucea.edu

Description—UCEA is an association of public and private higher education institutions concerned with making continuing education available to all population segments and promoting excellence in continuing higher education. Many institutional members offer university and college courses via electronic instruction.

Membership—425 institutions, 2000 professionals

Dues—Vary according to membership category; see http://www.ucea.edu/membership.htm.

Meetings—UCEA has an annual national conference and several professional development seminars throughout the year. See http://www.ucea.edu/page02.htm.

Publications—Monthly newsletter; quarterly; occasional papers; scholarly journal, Continuing Higher Education Review; Independent Study Catalog. With Peterson's, The Guide to Distance Learning; Guide to Certificate Programs at American Colleges and Universities; UCEA-ACE/Oryx Continuing Higher Education book series; Lifelong Learning Trends (a statistical factbook on continuing higher education); organizational issues series; membership directory

Name of Organization or Association—Young Adult Library Services Association

Acronym—YALSA
Address:
50 E. Huron St.
Chicago, IL
60611
USA
Phone Number—(312)280-4390; **Fax Number**—(312)280-5276
Email Contact—yalsa@ala.org; **URL**—http://www.ala.org/yalsa
Leaders—Beth Yoke, Executive Director; Judy T. Nelson, President
Description—A division of the American Library Association (ALA), the Young Adult Library Services Association (YALSA) seeks to advocate, promote, and strengthen service to young adults as part of the continuum of total library services. It is responsible within the ALA to evaluate and select books and media and to interpret and make recommendations regarding their use with young adults. Selected List Committees include Best Books for Young Adults, Popular Paperbacks for Young Adults, Quick Picks for Reluctant Young Adult Readers, Outstanding Books for the College Bound, Selected Audiobooks for Young Adults, Great Graphic Novels for Teens, and Selected Films for Young Adults. To learn more about our literary awards, such as the Odyssey Award for best audiobook production, and recommended reading, listening, and viewing lists go to www.ala.org/yalsa/booklists. YALSA celebrates Teen Tech Week the first full week of March each year. To learn more go to www.ala.org/teentechweek.
Membership—5500. YALSA members may be young adult librarians, school librarians, library directors, graduate students, educators, publishers, or anyone for whom library service to young adults is important.
Dues—$50; $20 students; $20 retirees (in addition to ALA membership)
Meetings—Two ALA conferences yearly, midwinter (January) and annual (June); one biennial Young Adult Literature Symposium (beginning in 2008)
Publications—Young Adult Library Services, a quarterly print journal Attitudes, a quarterly electronic newsletter for members only

Part IV
Graduate Programs

Introduction

Kuo Hsiao Chien, Hyewon Lee, and Sheng-Shiang Tseng

Part IV includes annotated entries for graduate programs that offer degrees in the fields of learning, design, and technology. All readers are encouraged to contact the institutions that are not listed for investigation and possible inclusion in the 2021 edition.

Information for this section was obtained through a questionnaire in collaboration with AECT directing each program to an individual web form through which the updated information could be submitted electronically. Although the section editors made every effort to contact and follow up with program representatives, responding to the annual request for an update was the responsibility of the program representatives. The editing team would like to thank those respondents who helped assure the currency and accuracy of this section by responding to the request for an update. In this year's edition, we asked for data on name of institution, name of department or program, program website, name of contact person, email address of contact person, program description, admission requirements, degree requirements, and number of full-time, part-time, and adjunct faculty. Readers should be aware that these data are only as accurate as the person who filled the form for their program.

Kuo Hsiao Chien, Hyewon Lee, and Sheng-Shiang Tseng contributed equally to Part IV.

K. H. Chien · S.-S. Tseng
Graduate Institute of Curriculum and Instruction, Tamkang University,
New Taipei City, Taiwan

H. Lee (✉)
Learning, Design, and Technology, University of Georgia, Athens, GA, USA
e-mail: ehyewon@uga.edu

© The Author(s), under exclusive license to Springer Nature Switzerland AG 2021
R. M. Branch et al. (eds.), *Educational Media and Technology Yearbook*,
Educational Media and Technology Yearbook 43,
https://doi.org/10.1007/978-3-030-71774-2_11

Graduate Programs in Learning, Design, Technology, Information, or Libraries

Kuo Hsiao Chien, Hyewon Lee, and Sheng-Shiang Tseng

This information will be used solely to construct a directory of relevant organizations and associations within the *2020 Educational Media and Technology Yearbook*. The data supplied here will **not** be intentionally shared or publicized in any other form. Thank you for your assistance.

Name of Institution—Western Illinois University
Name of Department or Program—Instructional Design and Technology
Program Website (URL)—http://www.wiu.edu/cbt/engineering_technology/idt.php
Name of Contact Person—Hoyet Hemphill
Email Address of Contact Person—HH-Hemphill@wiu.edu
Program Description—The Master of Science program in Instructional Design and Technology (IDT) prepares students to assess, design, develop, and evaluate instruction, instructional material, and information resources. The 30-credit degree program also allows students to design and implement technologies and to apply design thinking to support teaching and learning. Students are able to pursue their personal professional interests in a curriculum that integrates conceptual coursework with hands-on experience in real-world settings. The program provides students with knowledge and skills in the following areas: coursework and training program development; online instruction and e-learning applications in training and education; systematic instructional design and evaluation of instruction and training; multimedia applications in training and

---

K. H. Chien · S.-S. Tseng
Graduate Institute of Curriculum and Instruction, Tamkang University, New Taipei City, Taiwan

H. Lee (✉)
Learning, Design, and Technology, University of Georgia, Athens, GA, USA
e-mail: ehyewon@uga.edu

© The Author(s), under exclusive license to Springer Nature Switzerland AG 2021
R. M. Branch et al. (eds.), *Educational Media and Technology Yearbook*,
Educational Media and Technology Yearbook 43,
https://doi.org/10.1007/978-3-030-71774-2_12

education; technology integration for classrooms, building levels, and training sites; instructional software development and use; and instructional design and technology professionals working in a variety of business, industry, government, K-12 and higher education, health, and nonprofit settings. Coursework, projects, internships, and practice allow students to explore career paths and focus on a chosen field of work.

Admission Requirements—The IDT program welcomes and invites qualified applicants from diverse fields and interests. Applicants desiring admission into the IDT graduate program must formally apply to the School of Graduate Studies declaring Instructional Design and Technology as their area of study. Furthermore, applicants must indicate whether they are applying for the General Instructional Design and Technology Emphasis or the Technology Specialist Emphasis. Learn about the graduate application process. Applicants may qualify for admission to the General Instructional Design and Technology Emphasis under the following conditions: Applicants must meet the general admission requirements of the School of Graduate Studies. Currently, the School of Graduate Studies admits students with an overall undergraduate GPA of at least 2.75 (or a GPA of at least 3.0 for the final 2 years of undergraduate coursework). If undergraduate requirements are not met, the departmental admissions committee will consider for admission applicants who have completed at least 12 semester hours of graduate coursework with a cumulative graduate GPA of 3.2 or higher from a regionally accredited university. All others will be denied admission. No more than nine semester hours completed before being admitted to the program can be used to meet degree requirements, unless the hours were earned while in an IDT Postbaccalaureate Certificate program. Applicants must submit a 1000-word structured essay that describes their interests and career goals as they apply to the field of instructional design and technology. Download the structured essay questions (docx) (pdf). Applicants must submit three letters of recommendation from individuals who can attest to the applicant's academic potential at the graduate level. International students whose native language is not English must satisfy one of the following criteria: meet the minimum TOEFL admission score required by the School of Graduate Studies; complete the WESL program prior to taking IDT graduate courses; and hold a bachelor's degree (with 4 years in residence) from an accredited college/university within the USA and within 2 years of matriculation at WIU. Applicants who want to apply at completion of the M.S. with a Technology Specialist Emphasis program for an Illinois endorsement for Technology Specialist must have a valid Illinois teaching license. Completion of the Technology Specialist Emphasis does not automatically lead to an Illinois State Board of Education Technology Specialist endorsement. Questions concerning this licensure should be directed to the IDT Graduate Advisor.

Degree Requirements—Students seeking the Master of Science in Instructional Design and Technology will complete the required courses and an exit option: IDT 603 Portfolio, IDT 600 Applied Project, or IDT 605 Thesis. Students will defend their exit option work in person or virtually.

Graduate Programs in Learning, Design, Technology, Information, or Libraries 155

Number of Full-Time Faculty—4; **Number of Other Faculty** -.

Name of Institution—University of Northern Colorado
Name of Department or Program—Technology, Innovation, and Pedagogy
Program Website (URL)—https://www.unco.edu/programs/technology-innovation-pedagogy/
Name of Contact Person—Heng-Yu Ku
Email Address of Contact Person—hengyu.ku@unco.edu
Program Description—*Technology, Innovation, and Pedagogy M.A.*: The M.A. in Technology, Innovation, and Pedagogy provides an advanced degree in technology knowledge and pedagogical practices that culminates with a comprehensive exam and optional research-based project or thesis. Graduates work in a variety of learning contexts (K-12, higher education, online environments, military training, business/organizational, and international settings) as scholars, educators, professional developers, program developers, and consultants. Cooperative research and other scholarly projects are encouraged among students and faculty. Students are encouraged to publish research and present in scholarly venues. The program is designed to be rigorous but practical. *Technology, Innovation, and Pedagogy Ph.D.*: The Doctor of Philosophy in Technology, Innovation, and Pedagogy provides a terminal degree in educational technology that culminates in a dissertation of original research in the field. Graduates work in a variety of learning contexts (PK-12, higher education, online environments, military training, business/organizational, and international settings) as professors, researchers, consultants, innovation officers, and scholars. Cooperative research, design, teaching, and other scholarly projects are encouraged among students and faculty. The program is research focused and designed to be rigorous but practical. Students are expected to engage in theoretical and practical experiences throughout the program documented in the comprehensive exam process.
Admission Requirements—*Technology, Innovation, and Pedagogy M.A.*: https://www.unco.edu/graduate-school/degrees-and-programs/masters-specialist--programs/technology-innovation-pedagogy-ma.aspx; *Technology, Innovation, and Pedagogy Ph.D.*: https://www.unco.edu/graduate-school/degrees-and--programs/doctorate-programs/technology-innovation-pedagogy-phd.aspx
Degree Requirements—*Technology, Innovation, and Pedagogy M.A.* (30 credits): http://unco.smartcatalogiq.com/current/Graduate-Catalog/Graduate-Programs/Masters-Degrees/Technology-Innovation-and-Pedagogy-MA; *Technology, Innovation, and Pedagogy Ph.D.* (67 credits): http://unco.smartcatalogiq.com/current/Graduate-Catalog/Graduate-Programs/Doctoral-Degrees/Technology-Innovation-and-Pedagogy-PhD
Number of Full-Time Faculty—3; **Number of Other Faculty**—2

Name of Institution—Arizona State University
Name of Department or Program—Learning Design and Technologies
Program Website (URL)—https://webapp4.asu.edu/programs/t5/majorinfo/ASU00/EDTECHMED/graduate/false
Name of Contact Person—Leanna Archambault

Email Address of Contact Person—leanna.archambault@asu.edu

Program Description—The M.Ed. program in learning design and technologies emphasizes the design of learning environments, systems, applications, and instructional materials for multiple learning contexts. The program prepares learning design and technology professionals for a variety of formal and informal settings in business, industry, museums, nonprofits, government organizations, and education, such as K-12 schools and colleges or universities. Through projects that address real-world problems, students apply current research and learning theories, along with the use of existing and emergent technologies, to the practice of learning and instructional design. All courses are online and combine a range of resources and technologies to facilitate direct interaction between students, program faculty, and classmates. Program graduates are prepared with the knowledge and skills required to address real-world problems and emerging challenges through the process of learning design.

Admission Requirements—Applicants must fulfill the requirements of both the Graduate College and Mary Lou Fulton Teachers College. Applicants are eligible to apply to the program if they have earned a bachelor's or master's degree, in any field, from a regionally accredited institution. Applicants must have a minimum cumulative GPA of 3.00 (scale is 4.00 = "A") in the last 60 h of their first bachelor's degree program, or applicants must have a minimum cumulative GPA of 3.00 (scale is 4.00 = "A") in an applicable master's degree program. All applicants must submit graduate admission application and application fee, official transcripts, three letters of recommendation, personal statement, resume, and proof of English proficiency.

Degree Requirements—30 credit hours including the required applied project course (EDT 593), Required Core (24 credit hours), COE 501 Introduction to Research and Evaluation in Education (3), EDP 540 Learning Theories and Instructional Strategies (3), EDT 501 Foundations of Learning Design and Technologies (3), EDT 502 Design and Development of Instruction (3), EDT 503 Design of Effective Communications (3), EDT 504 Modalities of Learning (3), EDT 506 Evaluation of Learning Systems (3), EDT 523 Issues in Online and Distance Education (3), Elective (3 credit hours), Culminating Experience (3 credit hours), EDT 593 Applied Project (3).

Number of Full-Time Faculty—4; **Number of Other Faculty**—1

Name of Institution—Pennsylvania State University
Name of Department or Program—Learning, Design, and Technology
Program Website (URL)—https://ed.psu.edu/lps/ldt
Name of Contact Person—Priya Sharma
Email Address of Contact Person—pus3@psu.edu
Program Description—A common thread throughout all programs is that candidates have basic competencies in the understanding of human learning; instructional design, development, and evaluation; and research procedures. Practical experience is available in mediated independent learning, research, instructional development, computer-based education, and dissemination projects. There are

exceptional opportunities for collaboration with faculty (more than 30% of publications and presentations are collaborative between faculty and students).

Admission Requirements—D.Ed., Ph.D.: GRE (including written GRE), TOEFL, transcript, three letters of recommendation, writing sample, vita or resume, and letter of application detailing rationale for interest in the degree, match with interests of faculty

Degree Requirements—M.Ed.: 33 semester hours; M.S.: 36 h, including either a thesis or a project paper; doctoral: candidacy exam, courses, residency, comprehensives, dissertation

Number of Full-Time Faculty—11; **Number of Other Faculty** -.

Name of Institution—Fischler College of Education and School of Criminal Justice, Nova Southeastern University

Name of Department or Program—Instructional Technology and Distance Education

Program Website (URL)—https://education.nova.edu/doctoral/edd/itde.html

Name of Contact Person—Michael Simonson

Email Address of Contact Person—simsmich@nova.edu

Program Description—Our graduates have become instructional technologists, educational software consultants, and directors of educational technology, training and development, or distance learning. Now is your chance to follow their lead and, just like technology, continue to evolve. Who should apply: practicing professionals with backgrounds in teaching or administration, training and professional development, media technology, instructional technology, curriculum development, staff development, or distance education OR individuals with master's degrees or above who wish to obtain a doctoral degree and increase their knowledge and skills in instructional technology and distance education OR individuals considering a Ph.D. in instructional technology who would instead like to explore the benefits of an Ed.D. in instructional technology program Entrance Requirements Curriculum Course Equivalencies/Substitutions Convenient Delivery Options Summer Institute Certification/Licensure.

Admission Requirements—Master's Degree

Degree Requirements—50 Semester credits with 24 credits in instructional technology and distance education, and including a 12-credit applied dissertation

Number of Full-Time Faculty—30; **Number of Other Faculty**—30

Name of Institution—Sam Houston State University

Name of Department or Program—Department of Library Science and Technology

Program Website (URL)—https://www.shsu.edu/libraryscience

Name of Contact Person—Rebecca Lewis

Email Address of Contact Person—rebecca1@shsu.edu

Program Description—*The Master of Education in Instructional Systems Design and Technology* is designed for individuals who wish to learn more about the use of instructional technology in educational, learning, instructional, and training environments. This program blends coursework from faculty with expertise in education and technology to promote a strong working knowledge of technology--oriented learning environments. The degree requires 30 h of graduate credit. *The Doctorate in Instructional Systems Design and Technology (ISDT)* is a fully online professional practice and scholarly doctoral program designed to prepare individuals to lead the learning analysis in diverse contexts and the integration of technology into different types of learning environments. Primarily, this doctoral program prepares individuals as scholars of learning technologies who will lead learning analysis research and leaders of instructional technology who will guide their organizations toward achieving meaningful integration of technology.

Admission Requirements—*Master of Education in Instructional Systems Design and Technology*: graduate application, application fee, official transcript from the baccalaureate institution with a GPA of 3.0 or higher; *Doctorate in Instructional Systems Design and Technology*: graduate application, application fee, official transcript(s) showing receipt of a baccalaureate degree and a master's degree from an accredited institution, GRE scores, a sample of professional work (published article or example of experience in instructional technology or multimedia design), a current resume or vita, and three letters of recommendation from educational or direct service settings

Degree Requirements—*Master of Education in Instructional Systems Design and Technology*: 30 total hours (15 h of coursework in Curriculum and Instruction and 15 h of coursework in Computer Science); *Doctorate in Instructional Systems Design and Technology*: 60 total hours, successful passing of a comprehensive examination (dossier process), and completion of a dissertation

Number of Full-Time Faculty -; Number of Other Faculty -.

Name of Institution—Grand Valley State University

Name of Department or Program—Literacy and Technology/Educational Technology

Program Website (URL)—https://www.gvsu.edu/grad/edtech/

Name of Contact Person—Andrew Topper

Email Address of Contact Person—toppera@gvsu.edu

Program Description—Prepares educators at all levels to integrate technology into teaching and learning, coordinate technology, manage technological resources, work in local or regional media centers, or explore the benefits of technology for instruction. The program prepares teachers and leaders to enhance the potential of their students and to evaluate the social and ethical implications of educational policies and practices.

Admission Requirements—Graduate application, application fee, official transcripts from all previous colleges or universities attended, and copies of teaching/administrative certificates if required for program admission or approved waiver; one or more professional or academic recommendations on COE recommendation forms, addressing the candidate's potential for graduate study; grade point average of 3.0 or better for the last 60 credits of undergraduate work taken from a regionally accredited institution; or a prior master's degree from a

Graduate Programs in Learning, Design, Technology, Information, or Libraries   159

regionally accredited institution that will be accepted in lieu of the minimum grade point average

Degree Requirements—6 credits in educational foundations courses, 21 credits in educational technology courses, a field (3 credits), and capstone (3-credit project OR 6-credit thesis) experience (33 or 36 credits total)

Number of Full-Time Faculty—3; **Number of Other Faculty**—6

Name of Institution—The University of Texas at Austin

Name of Department or Program—Curriculum and Instruction, Learning Technologies

Program Website (URL)—https://education.utexas.edu/departments/curriculum--instruction/graduate-programs/learning-technologies

Name of Contact Person—Min Liu

Email Address of Contact Person—mliu@austin.utexas.edu

Program Description—Learning Technologies (LT) applies contemporary research and development from interdisciplinary fields such as education, psychology, communications, and technology. We use knowledge from these fields to design effective, efficient, interactive, and engaging learning environments. The LT Program offers graduate-level master's and doctoral degrees which prepare professionals for various positions in education as well as professional industries. Working closely with faculty, students can expect to be involved in contemporary research and design projects using state-of-the-art technologies. Courses in this program cover topics such as instructional design, foundations of LT, teaching and learning with technologies, multimedia design, analysis of emerging educational technologies, and future of online learning. Our graduates serve as university faculty, instructional designers, evaluators, trainers, and managers of instructional systems in public schools, business, government, higher education, military, and other settings.

Admission Requirements—A bachelor's degree from an accredited institution in the USA, or proof of equivalent training at a foreign institution. A minimum GPA of 3.0, particularly during the last 2 years of college and in any previous graduate study. The department will consider applications with lower GPAs. If you feel that your grade point averages or test scores are not valid indicators of your ability, please wait till you have submitted your application and upload a miscellaneous document explaining your concerns. We also consider teaching experience as a criterion during the admission process. EC-12 teaching experience, especially among underserved populations, is preferred by most program areas, https://education.utexas.edu/departments/curriculum-instruction/information/prospective-students/how-apply.

Degree Requirements—Masters: https://education.utexas.edu/departments/curriculum-instruction/graduate-programs/learning-technologies/master-arts--master-education-degree-programs; doctorate: https://education.utexas.edu/departments/curriculum-instruction/graduate-programs/learning-technologies/doctor-philosophy-degree-program

Number of Full-Time Faculty—3; **Number of Other Faculty**—1

Name of Institution—University of Delaware

Name of Department or Program—M.Ed. in Educational Technology

Program Website (URL)—http://www.education.udel.edu/masters/edtech/

Name of Contact Person—Fred T. Hofstetter

Email Address of Contact Person—fth@udel.edu

Program Description—The Master of Education in Educational Technology (EDTC) program is based on the assumption that new media and the Internet can have a positive effect on teaching and learning. The EDTC program provides the master's degree candidate with both a theoretical and a practical grounding in educational technology methods and techniques, emphasizing theories of teaching and learning that support these methods. To demonstrate mastery of the program's goals, all candidates complete the same series of seven program assessments. Depending on the candidate's career path, these assessments are evaluated by rubrics developed according to standards of the International Society for Technology in Education (ISTE) or the Association for Educational Communications and Technology (AECT). Candidates who hold a basic teaching license follow the ISTE standards, which are assessed via rubrics through which K-12 teachers exhibit the knowledge, skills, and dispositions needed to teach technology applications, support student learning, and prepare other teachers to use technology effectively across the curriculum. Candidates from higher education, government, and industry are assessed via rubrics based on the five AECT standards involving content knowledge, pedagogy, learning environments, professional skills, and research.

Admission Requirements—(1) A bachelor's degree in a field relevant to the applicant's proposed program. (2) An undergraduate grade point average of 3.0 or higher. (3) GRE scores are NOT required. (4) A minimum TOEFL score of 100 (iBT), 600 (paper-based test), or 250 (computer-based test) from applicants whose first language is not English, or a minimum IELTS score of 7.0. International candidates can request conditional admission if they do not meet these English language requirements. (5) Three letters of recommendation testifying to the applicant's academic abilities. (6) Written essay describing goals and objectives.

Degree Requirements—Students admitted to the program must maintain a 3.0 grade point average and make steady progress toward assembling the portfolio of items required for graduation. All students take required core courses (6 credits) in curriculum (EDUC 638) and technology and cognition (EDUC 650). All students enroll in three required educational technology courses (9 credits): EDUC 611, Introduction to Educational Technology; EDUC 685, Multimedia Literacy; and EDUC 621, Internet Technologies. Students complete the master's coursework by taking educational technology electives (12–18 credits) that cover a broad range of topics across K-12 education (ISTE) as well as higher education and industry (AECT). Students who write a master's thesis take 12 elective credits plus 6 thesis credits. Students who do a major project take 15 elective credits plus 3 credits of independent study with their major professor. All other students take 18 credits of electives. It is in consultation with their advisor that students

Graduate Programs in Learning, Design, Technology, Information, or Libraries 161

decide whether to write a thesis and which specific courses to elect in order to prepare appropriately for their intended workplace.

Number of Full-Time Faculty—3; **Number of Other Faculty**—3

Name of Institution—Concordia University

Name of Department or Program—Master of Arts in Educational Technology (internship option); Master of Arts in Educational Technology (thesis option); Graduate Diploma in Instructional Technology; Ph.D. in Education

Program Website (URL)—*M.A. in Educational Technology*: www.concordia.ca/ academics/graduate/educational-technology-ma.html; *Graduate Diploma in Instructional Technology*: http://www.concordia.ca/academics/graduate/ instructional-technology.html; *Ph.D. in Education*: http://www.concordia.ca/ academics/graduate/education-phd.html

Name of Contact Person—Mary Marciniak

Email Address of Contact Person—education.gpa@concordia.ca

Program Description—*M.A. in Educational Technology (internship option)*: The M.A. in Educational Technology prepares you for a career as a designer and developer of instructional and educational materials. Graduates work with technology in educational settings, and act as performance consultants for a variety of teaching organizations. Students will learn how to assess needs and identify the cause of performance gaps in educational technology. You will design and implement instructional programs and evaluate the outcomes of these programs. The objective of the discipline is to facilitate learning and improve performance by creating and managing appropriate technological resources. Course-related projects include partnerships with start-ups, NGOs, corporations, schools, and universities. An internship option is available. With a wide network of private, nonprofit, and government partners to choose from, you will be able to tailor your work environment to your specific interests. *M.A. in Educational Technology (thesis option)*: The M.A. in Educational Technology prepares you for a career as a designer and developer of instructional and educational materials. Graduates work with technology in educational settings, and act as performance consultants for a variety of teaching organizations. Students will learn how to assess needs and identify the cause of performance gaps in educational technology. You will design and implement instructional programs and evaluate the outcomes of these programs. The objective of the discipline is to facilitate learning and improve performance by creating and managing appropriate technological resources. Course-related projects include partnerships with start-ups, NGOs, corporations, schools, and universities. An internship option is available. With a wide network of private, nonprofit, and government partners to choose from, you will be able to tailor your work environment to your specific interests. *Graduate Diploma in Instructional Technology*: The Graduate Diploma in Instructional Technology prepares you for a career as a designer and developer of instructional materials and technology in educational settings. You will learn to evaluate learning materials and reorganize instructional systems to improve overall performance for individuals and organizations. You will learn to assess needs related to materials and technologies, apply sound learning theories, and design solutions for classrooms and other educational organizations. The course draws on partnerships with start-ups, NGOs, corporations, and universities to link classroom learning with real-world training. We offer a "field work" option that gives you the opportunity to apply the skills you have learned in a work situation. *Ph.D. in Education*: The Ph.D. in Education will give you advanced knowledge of the qualitative and quantitative methods used in educational research. You will examine the disciplinary links between childhood and adult education and strengthen your understanding of underlying educational philosophies. Our program provides a solid foundation from which to pursue research across disciplines and orientations. Our faculty members specialize in four major subfields: applied linguistics, child studies, educational studies, and educational technology. Graduate students have exclusive use of our state-of-the-art facilities, including personalized research spaces, computer workstations, and a media development lab. Along with a growing number of students and faculty you will be contributing to cutting-edge research in education and the civic life of the department.

Admission Requirements—*M.A. in Educational Technology (internship option)*: 3.0 undergraduate GPA 6.5 minimum score on each of the four component tests of the IELTS test or 24 minimum score on each of the component tests of TOEFL; *M.A. in Educational Technology (thesis option)*: 3.0 minimum GPA at the undergraduate-level English proficiency: Minimum score of 6.5 on each of the four component tests of IELTS or minimum score of 24 on each of the four component tests of TOEFL; *Graduate Diploma in Instructional Technology*: 2.7 GPA at the undergraduate-level English proficiency: Minimum score of 6.5 on each of the four component tests of IELTS or minimum score of 24 on each of the four component tests of TOEFL; *Ph.D. in Education*: Completed master's degree. Minimum GPA of 3.0 at both the undergraduate- and graduate-level English proficiency: Minimum score of 6.5 on each of the four component tests of IELTS or minimum score of 24 on each of the four component tests of TOEFL.

Degree Requirements—*M.A. in Educational Technology (internship option)*: 15 credits—Core Courses: ETEC 613—Learning Theories (3 credits). ETEC 640—Research Methods I (3 credits). ETEC 650—Fundamentals of Instructional Design (3 credits). ETEC 651—Fundamentals of Human Performance Technology (3 credits). ETEC 671—Administering Educational Technology Groups (3 credits). ETEC 672—Project Management (3 credits). ETEC 673—Consulting Skills for Educational Technologists (3 credits). 12 credits minimum—Elective Courses: ETEC 607—Philosophical Issues in Educational Research (3 credits). ETEC 621—Educational Cybernetics (3 credits). ETEC 635—Principles of Educational Message Design (3 credits). ETEC 636—Evaluation in Education and Training (3 credits). ETEC 637—Educational Gaming and Modelling (3 credits). ETEC 652—Knowledge Management (3 credits). ETEC 660—Introduction to Educational Computing (3 credits). ETEC 662—Social Technologies and the Sociocultural Aspects of Learning (3 credits). ETEC 665—Introduction to Digital Media in Education (3 credits). ETEC 666—Contemporary Use of Simulation in Training and Education (3 credits). ETEC

Graduate Programs in Learning, Design, Technology, Information, or Libraries   163

669—Designing and Developing Interactive Instruction (3 credits). ETEC 676—Human Resources Development (3 credits). ETEC 680—Global Perspectives in E-Learning (3 credits). ETEC 681—Fundamentals of Distance Education (3 credits). ETEC 690—Field Experience (for Option A-Thesis/Thesis-Equivalent only) (3 credits). ETEC 691—Advanced Readings and Research in Educational Technology I (3 credits). ETEC 692—Advanced Readings and Research in Educational Technology II (3 credits). ETEC 693—Special Issues in Educational Technology (3 credits). 18 credits—Internship and Internship Report: ETEC 791—Internship (15 credits). ETEC 792—Internship Report (3 credits). *M.A. in Educational Technology (thesis option)*: 12 credits—Core Courses: ETEC 613—Learning Theories (3 credits). ETEC 640—Research Methods I (3 credits). ETEC 641—Research Methods II (3 credits). ETEC 650—Fundamentals of Instructional Design (3 credits). 15 credits—Elective Courses: ETEC 607—Philosophical Issues in Educational Research (3 credits). ETEC 621—Educational Cybernetics (3 credits). ETEC 635—Principles of Educational Message Design (3 credits). ETEC 636—Evaluation in Education and Training (3 credits). ETEC 637—Educational Gaming and Modelling (3 credits). ETEC 652—Knowledge Management (3 credits). ETEC 660—Introduction to Educational Computing (3 credits). ETEC 662—Social Technologies and the Sociocultural Aspects of Learning (3 credits). ETEC 665—Introduction to Digital Media in Education (3 credits). ETEC 666—Contemporary Use of Simulation in Training and Education (3 credits). ETEC 669—Designing and Developing Interactive Instruction (3 credits). ETEC 676—Human Resources Development (3 credits). ETEC 680—Global Perspectives in E-Learning (3 credits). ETEC 681—Fundamentals of Distance Education (3 credits). ETEC 690—Field Experience (for Option A-Thesis/Thesis-Equivalent only) (3 credits). ETEC 691—Advanced Readings and Research in Educational Technology I (3 credits). ETEC 692—Advanced Readings and Research in Educational Technology II (3 credits). ETEC 693—Special Issues in Educational Technology (3 credits). 18 credits—Thesis (Area I) or Thesis-Equivalent (Area II): ETEC 795—Thesis Proposal (3 credits). ETEC 796—Thesis or Thesis-Equivalent (15 credits). *Graduate Diploma in Instructional Technology*: Fully qualified candidates are required to complete a minimum of 30 credits. 12 credits—Required Courses: ETEC 513—Learning Theories (3 credits). ETEC 550—Fundamentals of Instructional Design (3 credits). ETEC 551—Fundamentals of Human Performance Technology (3 credits). ETEC 571—Administering Educational Technology Groups (3 credits) or ETEC 572—Project Management (3 credits) or ETEC 573—Consulting Skills for Educational Technologists (3 credits). 18 credits—Elective Courses: ETEC 507—Philosophical Issues in Educational Research. ETEC 521—Educational Cybernetics. ETEC 535—Principles of Educational Message Design. ETEC 536—Evaluation in Education and Training. ETEC 537—Educational Gaming and Modelling. ETEC 540—Research Methods I. ETEC 541—Research Methods II. ETEC 552—Knowledge Management. ETEC 560—Introduction to Educational Computing. ETEC 562—Social Technologies and the Sociocultural Aspects of Learning. ETEC

565—Introduction to Digital Media in Education. ETEC 566—Contemporary Use of Simulation in Training and Education. ETEC 569—Designing and Developing Interactive Instruction. ETEC 576—Human Resources Development. ETEC 580—Global Perspectives in E-Learning. ETEC 581—Fundamentals of Distance Education. ETEC 590—Field Experience. ETEC 593—Special Issues in Educational Technology. *Ph.D. in Education*: Fully qualified candidates are required to complete a minimum of 90 credits. 12 credits—Required Courses: EDUC 806—Quantitative Methods (3 credits). EDUC 807—Qualitative Methods (3 credits). EDUC 808—Reporting Research (3 credits). EDUC 809—Advanced Issues in Education (3 credits). 9 credits—Elective Courses: 12 credits—Comprehensive Examination. EDUC 890—Comprehensive Examination (12 credits). 9 credits—Doctoral Proposal: EDUC 891—Doctoral Proposal (9 credits). 48 credits—Doctoral Dissertation: EDUC 895—Doctoral Dissertation (48 credits)

Number of Full-Time Faculty—Master of Arts in Educational Technology (internship option), Master of Arts in Educational Technology (thesis option), Graduate Diploma in Instructional Technology: 7; Ph.D. in Education: 30

Number of Other Faculty—Master of Arts in Educational Technology (internship option), Master of Arts in Educational Technology (thesis option), Graduate Diploma in Instructional Technology: 3; Ph.D. in Education: 5

Name of Institution—Kent State University

Name of Department or Program—Educational Technology

Program Website (URL)—https://www.kent.edu/ehhs/tlcs/etec

Name of Contact Person—Elena Novak

Email Address of Contact Person—enovak6@kent.edu

Program Description—The Educational Technology program at Kent State University offers a Master of Education degree with five possible specializations: Management of Educational Technologies, Computer Science, Designing Instructional and Performance Solutions, Immersive Technologies for Learning, and Online and Blended Learning and Teaching. Students with an existing teaching license may obtain two endorsements with the M.Ed. degree in Educational Technology: (1) the Computer/Technology endorsement by completing the Management of Educational Technologies concentration and (2) the Computer Science endorsement by completing the Computer Science concentration. The endorsements allow teachers to teach computer applications or computer science courses in the classroom or assume technology leadership positions in a school or at the district level. There is a 9-credit-hour certificate program in Online and Blended Learning and Teaching, as well as the opportunity to add the Computer Technology and Computer Science endorsements to a license by itself to students who already hold a Master of Education or other related degree. The program offers undergraduate-level courses to students to improve their technology knowledge and skills as they prepare as teachers and other professionals. In addition, the Educational Technology program offers the Ed.D. degree in Interprofessional Leadership with the Educational Technology cognate area for

Graduate Programs in Learning, Design, Technology, Information, or Libraries 165

people who want to assume leadership positions in the field of educational technology. Finally, the Educational Technology program is a concentration within the Curriculum and Instruction Ph.D. program for people who want to do research in the field.

Admission Requirements—Master's degree applicants must have completed a bachelor's degree. Admission requirements include a completed application form, a goal statement describing in detail the applicant's reasons for seeking a master's degree in Educational Technology, official transcripts for all prior coursework, an undergraduate grade point average of at least 3.0, and two professional letters of recommendation.

Degree Requirements—Master's: 34–39 semester hours, portfolio, practicum for licensure. Doctoral: minimum of 45 post-master's semester hours, comprehensive exam, dissertation

Number of Full-Time Faculty—5; **Number of Other Faculty**—0

Name of Institution—University of West Florida

Name of Department or Program—Department of Instructional Design and Technology (IDT); programs include BS in IDT, M.Ed. in IDT, and Ed.D. in IDT.

Program Website (URL)—*Department*: https://uwf.edu/ceps/departments/instructional-design-and-technology/. *BS*: https://onlinedegrees.uwf.edu/online--degrees/bs-instructional-design/. *M.Ed.*: https://uwf.edu/ceps/departments/instructional-design-and-technology/graduate-programs/instructional-design--and-technology-med/. *Ed.D.*: https://onlinedegrees.uwf.edu/online-degrees/edd-instructional-design-technology/.

Name of Contact Person—Nancy B. Hastings, Assistant Dean and Department Chair

Email Address of Contact Person—nhastings@uwf.edu

Program Description—BS: Provides students with a holistic perspective of human performance improvement based on foundations of instructional design, instructional technology, and human performance technology. Emphasizes collaborative and individualized projects, building skills, and engaging students in the application of classroom knowledge in real-world settings. *M.Ed.*: Emphasizes the systematic application of behavioral science and learning, communication, and instructional theories to resolve learning and/or performance-based problems. Curriculum encompasses the identification and analysis of problems and the design, development, implementation, evaluation, and management of the technology-based processes and resources that make up the solution. *Ed.D.*: Designed for professionals who want to effectively apply research and theory to achieve educational goals and improve performance in a variety of settings. This program prepares graduates to fulfill leadership roles related to organizational development, technology integration, and workplace learning across sectors. The program is aligned with the principles and framework of the Carnegie Project for the Education Doctorate (CPED) and focused on preparing students to identify and resolve complex problems of practice utilizing the principles of improvement science and action research.

Admission Requirements—*BS*: Open enrollment. *M.Ed.*: Undergraduate GPA of 3.00 or higher, competitive scores on GRE or MAT (may be waived with GPA of 3.25), and letter of intent communicating academic and professional background, experiences, and goals. *Ed.D.*: GPA of 3.5 or higher on most recent graduate degree, competitive scores on GRE or MAT (may be waived with GPA of 3.75 on most recent graduate degree), three letters of recommendation (at least two must speak to academic abilities), letter of intent communicating academic and professional background, experiences, and goals; and Web-based interview.

Degree Requirements—*BS*: Minimum major GPA of 2.50 (2.0 overall), minimum grade of C in all major courses, successful completion of capstone experience and exit interview. *M.Ed.*: Minimum GPA of 3.0, minimum grade of B in all courses, completion of 36 credit hours of coursework, successful completion of capstone experience, and exit interview. *Ed.D.*: Minimum GPA of 3.25, minimum grade of B in all courses, participation in three required residencies, successful completion and defense of a dissertation-in-practice focused on solving a compelling problem of practice, and exit interview

Number of Full-Time Faculty—6; **Number of Other Faculty**—10

Name of Institution—Georgia Southern University
Name of Department or Program—Instructional Technology
Program Website (URL)—https://coe.georgiasouthern.edu/itec/
Name of Contact Person—Mete Akcaoglu
Email Address of Contact Person—makcaoglu@georgiasouthern.edu
Program Description—Online M.Ed. and GA certification for School Library Media and Instructional Technology Specialists. An online Ed.S. is available in both concentrations as well. The Online Teaching and Learning Endorsement is offered at both levels. Completely online program. Strong emphasis on technology and use of Web 2.0 tools. Online portfolios as culminating program requirement for M.Ed. students.

Admission Requirements—BS (teacher certification NOT required), GRE, or MAT not required for applicants who are certified teachers with a 2.5 undergraduate grade point average. M.Ed. required for admission to the Ed.S. program

Degree Requirements—36 semester hours for the M.Ed. 30 semester hours for the Ed.S. 9 semester hours for Online Teaching and Learning Endorsement.

Number of Full-Time Faculty—5; **Number of Other Faculty**—5

Name of Institution—University of Toledo
Name of Department or Program—Curriculum and Instruction: Educational Technology (Doctoral Program)
Program Website (URL)—https://www.utoledo.edu/Programs/grad/Educational-Technology/
Name of Contact Person—Berhane Teclehaimanot
Email Address of Contact Person—Berhane.Teclehaimanot@utoledo.edu
Program Description—Advances in technology and educational media have transformed learning and teaching environments. The University of Toledo's graduate program in educational technology teaches how to integrate this constantly

Graduate Programs in Learning, Design, Technology, Information, or Libraries 167

evolving technology into new instructional strategies and curricula. The doctoral program is designed for individuals who wish to become professional educators or simply expand their knowledge and skill sets in teaching and learning. An educational technology graduate degree can benefit leaders in many fields, whether you are working in the private sector or the government or at a university. The programs emphasize instructional design and educational technology and include a solid foundation in research, curriculum, and teaching skills. About 70% of Ph.D. classes in educational technology are online.

Admission Requirements—What to submit with your application: Prospective students must apply online directly to the College of Graduate Studies. Students will need to submit these materials: • An online application for graduate school admission • Official copies of all undergraduate and graduate transcripts, including credits and degrees earned • A statement of purpose that describes the applicant's background and goals as well as the importance of the selected doctoral program in achieving these goals • Professional letters of reference describing the applicant's potential for successfully completing a doctoral program (2–3 letters as required by the program) • Samples of academic writing (e.g., report, thesis, project, or academic paper) • A current resume or curriculum vitae, when required by the program • GRE scores, when required by the program • A nonrefundable application fee.

Degree Requirements—61 Semester credit hours (51 credit hours of coursework and 9 credit hours of dissertation)

Number of Full-Time Faculty—2; **Number of Other Faculty**—0

Name of Institution—University of West Georgia

Name of Department or Program—M.Ed. in Instructional Technology, Media, and Design (Instructional Technology Concentration); Ed.S. in Instructional Technology, Media, and Design (Instructional Technology Concentration)

Program Website (URL)—https://www.westga.edu/academics/education/etf/

Name of Contact Person—Kim Huett

Email Address of Contact Person—khuett@westga.edu

Program Description—*The online Master of Education with a Major in Instructional Technology, Media, and Design (Instructional Technology Concentration) degree* is designed to prepare progressive, innovative, academically grounded instructional technologists. Graduates of the program apply their skills in P-12 schools, higher education, and corporate, healthcare, and government organizations. While learning in the program, students collaborate with various stakeholders through an array of technology-based tools and applications. Through professional field experiences and clinical practices, the learning experiences are performance based and problem based. Faculty teaching in the program is grounded in theoretical perspectives, instructional design strategies, and practical application of knowledge to ensure that candidates can immediately apply what they learn in diverse educational settings. The purpose of *the Ed.S. program in Instructional Technology, Media, and Design (Instructional Technology Concentration)* is to provide superior student-focused education that is personally relevant and intellectually challenging. The program is committed to the following areas of excellence: preparing progressive, innovative, academically grounded instructional technologists; building and enhancing skills in research and program evaluation to support instructional growth and improvement; developing innovative delivery options to maximize educational experiences; cultivating diversity of ideas, values, and persons responsive to changing needs and technologies; and promoting the advancement of learning through scholarship and service.

Admission Requirements—*M.Ed. Degree*: Students must hold a bachelor's degree from a regionally accredited institution to be admitted to the program. A teaching certificate is not required for this program, but teacher certification is required for students seeking a certificate upgrade for the Georgia Professional Standards Commission: GPA of 2.7 on most recent degree. International applicants are subject to additional requirements and application deadlines. See Procedures for International Students. Official transcripts from a regionally or nationally accredited institution are required and should be sent directly to the UWG Admissions Office. *Ed.S. Degree*: Students must hold a master's degree from a regionally accredited institution to be admitted to the program. A teaching certificate is not required for this program, but teacher certification is required for students seeking a certificate upgrade for the Georgia Professional Standards Commission: GPA of 3.0 on most recent degree. International applicants are subject to additional requirements and application deadlines. See Procedures for International Students. Official transcripts from a regionally or nationally accredited institution are required and should be sent directly to the UWG Admissions Office.

Degree Requirements — https://www.westga.edu/academics/education/etf/
Number of Full-Time Faculty—7; **Number of Other Faculty**—6

Name of Institution—Boise State University
Name of Department or Program—Educational Technology
Program Website (URL)—https://www.boisestate.edu/education-edtech/
Name of Contact Person—*Ed.D. in Educational Technology*. Co-coordinators: Ross Perkins and Patrick Lowenthal; *Ed.S. in Educational Technology*. Coordinator: Ross Perkins; *Master of Educational Technology*. Coordinator: Chareen Snelson
Email Address of Contact Person—Ross Perkins (rossperkins@boisestate.edu), Patrick Lowenthal (patricklowenthal@boisestate.edu), Chareen Snelson (csnelson@boisestate.edu)
Program Description—*The Master of Educational Technology* is our professional degree, focusing on skills for improved performance at all levels of education, in the classroom and beyond. This program is perfect for going onto our Ed.D. program and does not require GREs for admittance. The Master of Educational Technology degree is 100% online. Coursework focuses on theoretical foundations, hands-on technology skills, and integration strategies for today's learning environments. All MET students will complete a portfolio as their Culminating Activity. *The Education Specialist (Ed.S.) in Educational Technology* is an ideal

program of study for professionals in education and/or training who already have a master's degree, but who wish to improve technology leadership or faculty development roles or who want to use technology more effectively for improved student engagement and learning. The Ed.S. in Educational Technology program at Boise State University can be completed entirely online; there are no on-campus or in-person requirements. All courses and exams/defenses can be completed at a distance, though in some cases synchronous (same time) attendance is required. The Education Specialist in Educational Technology program is 100% online. *Doctor of Education in Educational Technology* (100% online program): The doctoral program in educational technology, leading to an Ed.D. degree, has as its goal the development of innovative leaders in the field. Students in this program explore the use of current and emerging technologies for effective and efficient teaching in a dynamic, global society. Areas of particular focus include online teaching and learning, technology integration, academic technology leadership, innovative teaching in K-12 and higher education, educational software development for the Web and mobile platforms, and educational games and simulations. The Ed.D. in Educational Technology program at Boise State University can be completed entirely online; there are no on-campus or in-person requirements. All courses and exams/defenses can be completed at a distance, though in some cases synchronous (same time) attendance is required.

Admission Requirements—*MET Admission Requirements*: Applicants are required to have earned at least a baccalaureate degree from a regionally accredited US college or university or a degree from a non-US institution of higher education that is judged equivalent to a US baccalaureate degree by the International Admissions office and have an undergraduate grade point average (GPA) of 3.00 (based on a 4-point scale) computed for all undergraduate credits from the applicant's most recent baccalaureate degree. Academic background must also be judged by the program coordinator as adequate for enrollment in graduate courses in education and educational technology. A prospective student may apply at any time and should follow the general graduate application procedure for degree-seeking students (see Graduate Admission Regulations). Admission to the program is based on official transcripts from all colleges attended. An essay describing educational and professional background, career goals, and how the coursework will help you to attain them. Also, tell us why you are choosing our program and why you will be a successful graduate student. Completion of the Program Development Form. Note: MET students can also earn a graduate certificate in one of the four specializations: Online Teaching, School Technology Coordination, Technology Integration, or Games and Simulations. In order to do so, please indicate the appropriate certificate on the Graduate Admissions application form. It is important for students to apply for a certificate before starting the coursework. *EDS Admission Requirements*: Applicants are required to have earned at least a baccalaureate degree and a master's degree from a regionally accredited US college or university or a degree from a non-US institution of higher education that is judged equivalent to a US baccalaureate degree and master's degree by the International Admissions office and have an undergraduate grade point average (GPA) of 3.50 (based on a 4-point scale) computed for all undergraduate credits from the applicant's most recent baccalaureate degree. Academic background must also be judged by the program coordinator as adequate for enrollment in graduate courses in education and educational technology. A prospective student may apply at any time and should follow the general graduate application procedure for degree-seeking students (see Graduate Admission Regulations). Admission to the program is based on official transcripts from all colleges attended; a letter of application including background in educational technology/education/training/instructional design or thorough explanation of change in fields, how the Ed.S. degree will ameliorate current knowledge and professional practice, and a specific project the applicant would consider doing as part of a culminating activity; a current resume or curriculum vitae; completion of the Program Development Form; and two letters of recommendation. *Ed.D. Admission Requirements*: Applicants are required to have earned at least a baccalaureate degree and a master's degree from a regionally accredited US college or university or a degree from a non-US institution of higher education that is judged equivalent to a US baccalaureate degree and master's degree by the International Admissions office and have an undergraduate grade point average (GPA) of 3.00 (based on a 4-point scale) computed for all undergraduate credits from the applicant's most recent baccalaureate degree and a graduate (GPA) of 3.50 (based on a 4-point scale) computed for all graduate credits. A prospective student may apply at any time and should follow the general graduate application procedure for degree-seeking students (see Graduate Admission Regulations). Admission to the program is based on official transcripts from all colleges attended; a letter of application that adheres to the guidelines linked from the Ed.D. Program Application page; a current resume or curriculum vitae; official Graduate Record Examinations (GRE) General Test scores (test must have been taken in the last 5 years); a writing sample; and three letters of recommendation.

Degree Requirements—*MET* https://www.boisestate.edu/education-edtech/met/#program-requirements. Program requirements: EDTECH 501 Introduction to Educational Technology 3. EDTECH 502 The Internet for Educators 3. EDTECH 503 Instructional Design 3. EDTECH 504 Theoretical Foundations of Educational Technology 3. EDTECH 505 Evaluation for Educational Technologists 3. Electives 15 Culminating Activity: EDTECH 592 Portfolio 3. Total 33 EDS https://www.boisestate.edu/education-edtech/eds-et/#program-requirements. Program requirements: course number and title credits core requirements: EDTECH 602 Emerging Trends in Educational Technology 3. EDTECH 604 Leadership in Educational Technology 3. EDTECH 650 Research in Educational Technology 3. EDTECH 651 Introduction to Statistics for Educational Technology 3. Cognate: Available cognates include technology integration, blended and online teaching and learning, educational games and simulations, e-learning design, and technology leadership. 9 Electives: 9 culminating activity: EDTECH 680 Education Specialist Final Project 3. Total 33 *Ed.D.* https://www.boisestate.edu/education-edtech/edd-et/#program-requirements. Program

Graduate Programs in Learning, Design, Technology, Information, or Libraries

requirements: course number and title credits core courses: EDTECH 601 Doctoral Studies Orientation 3. EDTECH 603 Global and Cultural Perspectives in Educational Technology 3. EDTECH 604 Leadership in Educational Technology 3. EDTECH 606 Research Writing 3. Research courses: EDTECH 650 Research in Educational Technology 3. EDTECH 651 Introduction to Statistics for Educational Technology 3. EDTECH 652 Quantitative Research Methods 3. EDTECH 653 Qualitative Research Methods 3. Research elective: A graduate-level research course applicable to education, educational technology, or a related field. Three cognate areas: A series of three graduate courses (from a relevant field) that are connected by a common thread or theme. Nine electives: Graduate courses in education, educational technology, or a related field; all courses are selected with student input and approved by the supervisory committee. Twelve innovation experience: EDTECH 640 Innovative Practices in Educational Technology 3. Doctoral seminar: EDTECH 698 Seminar in Educational Technology 4. Culminating examination: EDTECH 691 Doctoral Comprehensive Examination 1. Culminating activity: EDTECH 693 Dissertation 10. Total 66

Number of Full-Time Faculty—13; **Number of Other Faculty**—7

Name of Institution—Boise State University
Name of Department or Program—Organizational Performance and Workplace Learning
Program Website (URL)—https://www.boisestate.edu/opwl/
Name of Contact Person—Yonnie Chyung
Email Address of Contact Person—ychyung@boisestate.edu
Program Description—The online Master of Science (M.S.) degree in Organizational Performance and Workplace Learning (OPWL) is intended to prepare students for careers in the areas of instructional design, training and development, e-learning, workplace performance improvement, organizational development, program evaluation, and performance consulting.
Admission Requirements—Bachelor's degree, official transcripts, statement of purpose, completed application
Degree Requirements—https://www.boisestate.edu/opwl/programs-courses/ms--degree/. Core credits: OPWL 529 Needs Assessment 4. OPWL 530 Evaluation 4. OPWL 535 Principles of Adult Learning 4. OPWL 536 Foundations of Organizational Performance and Workplace Learning 4. OPWL 537 Instructional Design 4. OPWL 560 Workplace Performance Improvement 4. Total core credits 24. Thesis option: OPWL 531 Quantitative Research in Organizations 3. OPWL 597 Special Topics: Survey Design and Data Analysis, 1-credit. OPWL 597 Special Topics: Interviews|Focus Groups and Data Analysis, 1-credit. OPWL 597 Special Topics: Data Visualization, 1-credit 3. OPWL 593 Thesis (oral defense required) 6. Portfolio option: OPWL 531 Quantitative Research in Organizations OR OPWL 597 Special Topics: Survey Design and Data Analysis, 1-credit. OPWL 597 Special Topics: Interviews|Focus Groups and Data Analysis, 1-credit. OPWL 597 Special Topics: Data Visualization, 1-credit 3. Electives 8:

OPWL 592 Portfolio (oral defense required) 1. Total thesis or portfolio option credits 12. Total 36

Number of Full-Time Faculty—8; **Number of Other Faculty**—8

Name of Institution—The George Washington University

Name of Department or Program—Educational Technology Leadership

Program Website (URL)—https://gsehd.gwu.edu/programs/masters-educational-technology-leadership

Name of Contact Person—Natalie Milman

Email Address of Contact Person—nmilman@gwu.edu

Program Description—The Education Technology Programs concentrate on education, technology, and leadership. Core courses cover fundamental topics of instructional design and technology leadership, while electives span from needs assessment to computer interface design. The Master's degree in Educational Technology is founded on three beliefs: (1) that leadership skills and technological competence are fundamental to the appropriate and successful utilization of technologies in educational settings; (2) that access to the requisite knowledge should be universal, despite the barriers of distance, personal physical limitations, and lifestyle; and (3) that educational technologies focus on improving human performance and learning.

Admission Requirements—Application requirements: online application; resume; statement of purpose; two letters of recommendation; transcripts; application fee (this program does not require Graduate Record Exam (GRE) or Miller Analogies Test (MAT) results for admission).

Degree Requirements—GW's online Master's in Educational Technology Leadership is a 36-credit-hour master's degree: Curriculum (36 credit hours). Core courses (24 credit hours): EDUC 6114 Introduction to Quantitative Research (3 credits). EDUC 6368 Leadership and Education (3 credits). EDUC 6401 Foundations in Educational Technology (3 credits). EDUC 6402 Trends and Issues in Educational Technology (3 credits). EDUC 6403 Educational Hardware Systems (3 credits). EDUC 6404 Managing Computer Applications (3 credits). EDUC 6405 Developing Multimedia Materials (3 credits). EDUC 6406 Instructional Design (3 credits). Elective courses (12 credit hours)—Select four courses: EDUC 6371 Education Policy (3 credits). EDUC 6421 Critical Issues in Distance Education (3 credits). EDUC 6422 Instructional Needs Assessment and Analysis (3 credits). EDUC 6424 Learning Technologies and Organizations (3 credits). EDUC 6425 Developing Effective Training with Technology (3 credits). EDUC 6426 Computer Interface Design for Learning (3 credits). EDUC 6427 Advanced Instructional Design (3 credits). EDUC 6428 Developing Digital Professional Portfolios (3 credits)

Number of Full-Time Faculty—3; **Number of Other Faculty**—10–12

Name of Institution—Purdue University

Name of Department or Program—Curriculum and Instruction, Learning Design, and Technology

Program Website (URL)—https://www.education.purdue.edu/academics/graduate-students/degrees-and-programs/graduate-programs/learning-design-technology/
Name of Contact Person—Tim Newby
Email Address of Contact Person—Newby@purdue.edu
Program Description—The learning design and technology program prepares you to master current, proven learning methods and educational technologies through a rigorous curriculum taught by internationally recognized faculty members. Our program accepts students from all different educational and professional backgrounds who have an interest in the field of educational technology and learning design. Our mission is to prepare individuals at the master's and doctoral levels to serve as outstanding educators and leaders in the field who have expertise in the design and evaluation of learning experiences that effectively integrate pedagogy and technology; conduct programs of cutting-edge research and scholarship related to learning technologies and design both within our program and through collaborations with colleagues within the College of Education, across the university, and with entities outside the university; and engage with schools, business-industry, and nonprofit organizations to broaden our impact and understanding of learning, technology, and design issues.
Admission Requirements—Both M.S. and Ph.D. admission requirements can be found here—https://www.purdue.edu/gradschool/prospective/gradrequirements/westlafayette/edci.html?_ga=2.255442632.1537721476.1588933527-1340347304.1588100285.
Degree Requirements—*M.S. Degree*: https://www.education.purdue.edu/academics/graduate-students/degrees-and-programs/graduate-programs/learning--design-technology/learning-design-technology-masters-program/; *Ph.D. Degree*: https://www.education.purdue.edu/academics/graduate-students/degrees-and-programs/graduate-programs/learning-design-technology/learning-design-technology-doctoral-program/
Number of Full-Time Faculty—8; **Number of Other Faculty**—32

Name of Institution—Winthrop University
Name of Department or Program—Learning Design and Technology
Program Website (URL)—https://www.winthrop.edu/graduateschool/master-of--education-in-learning-design-and-technology.aspx
Name of Contact Person—Marshall G. Jones
Email Address of Contact Person—jonesmg@winthrop.edu
Program Description— https://www.winthrop.edu/graduateschool/master-of-education-in-learning-design-and-technology.aspx
Admission Requirements -.
Degree Requirements -.
Number of Full-Time Faculty -; Number of Other Faculty -.

Name of Institution—University of Houston
Name of Department or Program—Learning, Design, and Technology

Program Website (URL)—Master's: https://uh.edu/education/degree-programs/cuin-ldt-med/; Ph.D.: https://uh.edu/education/degree-programs/cuin-phd/

Name of Contact Person—Sara McNeil, Susie Gronseth

Email Address of Contact Person—Sara McNeil (smcneil@uh.edu); Susie Gronseth (slgronseth@uh.edu)

Program Description—*Master's*: The Master's program in Curriculum and Instruction—Learning, Design, and Technology systematically prepares education, healthcare, and business professionals to create, deliver, and analyze instruction and improve performance using effective technology tools. The program provides opportunities to learn new and innovative skills to integrate the latest technologies in teaching and learning. There is a strong connection between course activities and implementing and improving practices in an instructional setting. The Learning, Design, and Technology program consists of ten courses—two Curriculum and Instruction core courses and eight Learning, Design, and Technology specialization courses. *Ph.D.*: The Ph.D. in Curriculum and Instruction is a 66-h doctoral program focused on urban education with a specialization in Learning, Design, and Technology. The program prepares aspiring scholars and researchers to meet today's educational challenges in multicultural urban settings. The Houston metropolitan area, with 1.5 million K-12 students, is a laboratory of practice for our Ph.D. students from nearby and from around the world, as UH is recognized as one of only three national Tier 1 Hispanic-serving public research universities and is designated as an Asian-American serving institution. Graduates of the Ph.D. program in Curriculum and Instruction typically pursue careers as university faculty members, researchers in educational settings, curriculum design experts, content area and program evaluation directors, and advocates for policy improvements. Innovation, diversity, and excellence characterize this Ph.D. program—where our location in the most diverse region in the country allows for inquiry on critical real-world issues.

Admission Requirements—*Master's*: All graduate applicants (regardless of citizenship status) must demonstrate proficiency in English to obtain admission to the University. Admission requirements for the College of Education require a minimum cumulative grade point average (GPA) of 2.6 for undergraduate coursework or over the last 60 credit hours of coursework. The GRE requirement can be waived for applicants to the Master's in Curriculum and Instruction degree program who have an overall undergraduate grade point average of 3.00 or higher (on a 4-point scale), a master's degree, or a terminal degree from 14 specified fields. The College's admission committees evaluate all credentials submitted by applicants to determine a student's ability and potential to succeed in graduate study. In addition, the committee is interested in the applicant's potential to contribute to his/her program of study and the University community as a whole. Applicants should submit all official transcripts from both undergraduate and graduate work; three letters of recommendation from professionals attesting to the student's suitability for master's-level study with specific references to pertinent competencies, aptitudes, and experiences; a statement of professional intent/career objective; and a resume or curriculum vita. *Ph.D.*: All official tran-

Graduate Programs in Learning, Design, Technology, Information, or Libraries

scripts from both undergraduate and graduate work. A preferred minimum 3.0 GPA on a 4.0 scale in upper division undergraduate coursework and graduate coursework. Official GRE scores taken within the last 5 years. Three letters of recommendation from professionals attesting to the student's suitability for doctoral level study with specific references to pertinent competencies, aptitudes, and experiences. One-page (minimum) statement of professional intent/career objective. A complete curriculum vita.

Degree Requirements—*Master's*: Ten courses and a capstone project. There are four required courses—Professional Seminar 1: Introduction to Educational Research, Community Education, and Technology. Professional Seminar 2: Educational Leadership/Professionalism, Study of Practice, and Social Justice/Equity—Seminar in Instructional Technology—Instructional Design. The other six courses can be any LDT master's-level courses. The Capstone Project provides students with the opportunity to apply, integrate, and synthesize key concepts learned from courses in the program. This project demonstrates the depth and breadth of educational growth through the program and highlights the knowledge and skills gained, as well as development as a reflective practitioner. Students identify an authentic and challenging technology-related problem and then design, develop, implement, and evaluate a proposed solution to meet that need. *Ph.D.*: The Ph.D. in Curriculum and Instruction is a 66-h doctoral program that establishes a link between research and practice, providing opportunities to investigate curriculum, instruction, assessment, and social justice issues within an urban education context. Ph.D. students engage in rigorous research, quality teaching, and contextual service to enhance education, curriculum and instruction, and community connections. The program area, core, and research courses, in addition to the dissertation process and other experiential opportunities, prepare students for positions in Tier 1 universities or other related areas that expect continued examination of research and practice in urban environments. + Curriculum and Instruction Core (24 h)—Issues in Urban Education—Social Justice and Equity—Learning, Design, and Technology—Curriculum Theory—Curriculum and Instruction Seminar—Advanced Internship—The State of the Curriculum Field in Education—Instructional Strategies for Teaching Adults + Research (15 h)—Introduction to Educational Research—Introduction to Quantitative Educational Research—Introduction to Qualitative Educational Research—6 Additional Hours of Advanced Research Courses + LDT Specialization (21 h) + Dissertation (6 h).

Number of Full-Time Faculty—6; **Number of Other Faculty**—5

Name of Institution—University of Florida
Name of Department or Program—Educational Technology in School of Teaching and Learning
Program Website (URL)—https://education.ufl.edu/educational-technology/
Name of Contact Person—Kara Dawson
Email Address of Contact Person—dawson@coe.ufl.edu

Program Description—Faculty and students in the UF Ed Tech program collaborate with colleagues at UF and around the world to facilitate, study, and disseminate ways in which learning, design, and innovative technologies within physical, virtual, and blended learning environments empower educators and learners and impact society.

Admission Requirements—Admission requirements vary by program. Please see https://education.ufl.edu/educational-technology/admission-requirements/.

Degree Requirements—Degree requirements vary by program. Please see https://education.ufl.edu/educational-technology/programs/.

Number of Full-Time Faculty—9; **Number of Other Faculty**—The number of adjunct faculty hired varies by semester based on teaching needs but is typically between one and four per semester.

Name of Institution—University of North Carolina, Charlotte

Name of Department or Program—Learning, Design, and Technology

Program Website (URL)—https://edld.uncc.edu/programs/learning-design-and-technology-program-0

Name of Contact Person—Beth Oyarzun

Email Address of Contact Person—Beth.Oyarzun@uncc.edu

Program Description—At UNC Charlotte, our Learning, Design, and Technology (LDT) program master's degrees and graduate certificates are in three concentrations to align your scholastic pursuits with your personal and professional objectives. The school specialist concentration prepares graduates to become licensed leaders of technology facilitation in K-12 schools and school districts, by providing professional development for other faculty members and modeling technology integration in the classroom. The online learning and teaching concentration is designed for individuals interested in pursuing online teaching positions in higher education as well as K-12 environments, such as specializing in learning management, distance education, educational media, or coordination of instructional technologies. The training and development concentration is geared toward applications in the corporate sector as well as government, military, or even nonprofit roles in instructional design and development, analysis and evaluation, content development, and more.

Admission Requirements—The admission process is competitive and determined by the following application components: Applicants are required to have a minimum of a B.A. or B.S. Degree from an accredited college or university; official transcripts; GRE or MAT scores (students who have completed either the LDT Graduate Certificate or at least four courses within the LDT Graduate Certificate with a GPA of 3.5 or above do not have to submit GRE or MAT scores); three letters of recommendation from professionals who are able to judge the quality of the applicant as a future student in this program; and statement of purpose of no more than 750 words in 12-point font and double spaced, written definitively, coherently, and incorporating thoughtful expression in response to: What skills and knowledge do you hope to acquire and develop as a result of this program? Characterize what you would contribute to the collective learning experiences of

Graduate Programs in Learning, Design, Technology, Information, or Libraries

your fellow students. Additional items required for those using this program to satisfy the North Carolina Department of Public Instruction (NCDPI) Instructional Technology Specialists: Computers (10877). This requirement is only for those who wish to earn the 077 license. Those who wish to work in other instructional technology settings (higher education, corporate, military, government) do not have to fulfill this requirement. A valid appropriate North Carolina teaching license A or G level (or equivalent from another state): In the online admission application, there is a field in which to specify the type of teaching license. Rather than uploading a copy of the teaching license into the application system, scan the license and email a copy to the Program Director. A minimum of 2–3 years' teaching experience is required.

Degree Requirements—M.Ed. in Learning, Design, and Technology is a 33-credit-hour program. Courses are delivered 100% online. Select one of the following concentrations: School Specialist Concentration (18 credit hours): EIST 5100—Technology Integration in Education (3). EIST 6100—Foundations of Learning, Design, and Technology (3). EIST 6135—Learning Media, Resources, and Technology (3). EIST 6110—Instructional Design (3). EIST 6130—Instructional Multimedia Development (3). RSCH 6101—Research Methods (3). Training and Development Concentration (18 credit hours): EIST 6100—Foundations of Learning, Design, and Technology (3). EIST 6121— Advanced Instructional Design (3). EIST 6110—Instructional Design (3). EIST 6130—Instructional Multimedia Development (3). EIST 6170—Human Performance Technology (3). RSCH 6101—Research Methods (3). Online Learning and Teaching Concentration (18 credit hours): EIST 6100—Foundations of Learning, Design, and Technology (3). EIST 6101—Learning Principles in Learning, Design, and Technology (3). EIST 6110—Instructional Design (3). EIST 6130—Instructional Multimedia Development (3). EIST 6150—Design, Development, and Evaluation of Online Learning Systems (3). RSCH 6101— Research Methods (3). Elective courses (9 credit hours): Select three of the following: EIST 6000—Topics in Learning, Design, and Technology (1–6). EIST 6101—Learning Principles in Learning, Design, and Technology (3). EIST 6120—Current Trends in Learning, Design, and Technology (3). EIST 6121— Advanced Instructional Design (3). EIST 6135—Learning Media, Resources, and Technology (3). EIST 6140—Instructional Video Development (3). EIST 6150—Design, Development, and Evaluation of Online Learning Systems (3). EIST 6160—Designing Learning Systems with Simulation and Game Technology (3). RSCH 7196—Program Evaluation Methods (3). Internship and Capstone Project (6 credit hours): EIST 6491—Internship in Learning, Design, and Technology (3). EIST 6492—Capstone Project in Learning, Design, and Technology.

Number of Full-Time Faculty—3; **Number of Other Faculty**—5

Name of Institution—Florida Gulf Coast University
Name of Department or Program—Department of Leadership, Research, and Technology. M.A. in Curriculum and Instruction, Educational Technology

Program Website (URL)—https://www.fgcu.edu/coe/programs/graduatepro-grams/educational-technology-ma

Name of Contact Person—Michele Garabedian Stork

Email Address of Contact Person—mistork@fgcu.edu

Program Description—The M.A. in C and I, Educational Technology is a virtual program that provides advanced study in education and training and is designed to serve both K-12 and business and industry environments.

Admission Requirements—Admission into this program involves a holistic view of a potential candidate's overall scholarship. Please note that this program does not require GRE or MAT results for admission consideration. If, however, a candidate's GPA falls below the required 3.0 average during his/her last 60 h of undergraduate work, the college committee MAY ask for other substantiating evidence of scholarship including reporting of one's score on either of these examinations. Admission requirements: A 4-year undergraduate degree from a regionally accredited institution. A grade point average (GPA) of 3.0 or higher on a 4.0 scale for the last 60 semester hours attempted accruing to the undergraduate degree, or an in-person, phone, or virtual interview (i.e., Skype Adobe Connect). Submission of three favorable recommendations from working professionals in the field. Performance in courses taken postbaccalaureate will be taken into consideration for admission to the College of Education Graduate Programs.

Degree Requirements—*Required courses* (21 credits): EDF 6284 Instructional Design (3). EME 5053 Intro to Ed Tech (3). EME 6207 Web Design and Development (3). EME 6209 Still and Time-Based Media (3). EME 6408 Universal Design for Learning (3). EME 6465 Interactive Learning (3). EME 6646 Digital Narrative and Cognition (3). Capstone experience (6 credits): EME 6235 Professional Practicum and EME 6940 Professional Internship* OR EDF 6481 Foundations of Ed Research (3) and EDG 6363 Capstone Seminar (3)** *Restricted electives* (9 credits): See program advisor for prior approval of elective courses. The following courses are grouped by areas of interest for advising purposes. Learning technologies: EME 6405 Technology Integration (3). EME 6607 Instructional Program Analysis (3). EME 6936 Current Trends in Ed Tech (3). Educational media: EME 6609 Instructional Media Resources (3). EME 6705 Collection and Acquisition (3). EME 6716 Media Services and Programs (3). Instructional design: EME 6607 Instructional Program Analysis (3). EME 6617 Instructional Design-eLearning (3). EME 6675 Design for Informal Learning (3). eLearning: EME 6417 Teaching in a Virtual Setting (3). EME 6617 Instructional Design for eLearning (3). EME 6696 Media Ecology (3). Entrepreneurship: ENT 6248 Lead and Promote New Ventures (3). ENT 6628 Technology and New Launch (3). ENT 6441 New Venture Launch (3). *Total credits required: 36 hours.*

Number of Full-Time Faculty—3; **Number of Other Faculty**—1

Name of Institution—North Carolina State University

Name of Department or Program—Learning Design and Technology

Graduate Programs in Learning, Design, Technology, Information, or Libraries 179

Program Website (URL)—https://ced.ncsu.edu/graduate/programs/doctoral/learning-design-and-technology/
Name of Contact Person—Kevin Oliver
Email Address of Contact Person—kmoliver@ncsu.edu
Program Description—Our research is guided by cognitive, social, and/or cultural theories of learning and by the existing body of research informing how people learn in specific disciplines and professional settings. The field at large along with individual programs of research is influenced by educational technology and psychology, cognitive science, instructional design, communications/message design, graphic design, computer science, adult workforce training, human factors, and anthropology. Students will utilize quantitative, qualitative, or mixed methods, along with emerging methods applicable to the study of contemporary learning environments (e.g., design-based research, learning analytics). The goal of your research as a doctoral student is to generate theory and standards of disciplinary or professional practice that help to solve critical educational problems. Our coursework emphasizes learning theories and processes, digital-applied research methods, and technology cognate areas selected by the student for emphasis.
Admission Requirements—Two official* copies of all undergraduate and graduate transcripts, including any nondegree studies (NDS) at NC State—GRE scores from within the last 5 years—TOEFL or IELTS scores for international applicants whose first language is not English—Academic writing sample—Description of research interests—Three (3) letters of reference. Unofficial transcripts are accepted for application review purposes, but we require official ones before an admitted student can begin graduate studies.
Degree Requirements—*Master's*: 30 semester hours (M.Ed.), 36 semester hours (M.S.), thesis required for M.S. program. *Ph.D.*: 60 h. Up to 12 h of graduate-level transfer credits may be applied to any master's program if the transfer credits are from Instructional Technology courses similar to those in the program. Transfer credits not accepted for doctoral program—60 new hours required at NC State.
Number of Full-Time Faculty—4; **Number of Other Faculty**—10

Name of Institution—University of Memphis
Name of Department or Program—Instructional Design and Technology
Program Website (URL)—https://www.memphis.edu/idt/index.php
Name of Contact Person—Clif Mims
Email Address of Contact Person—clifmims@memphis.edu
Program Description—Instructional Design, Educational Technology, Technology Integration, Web 2.0 and Social Media, Web-Based Instruction, Computer-Based Instruction, Mobile Learning, K-12 NTeQ Model, Professional Development, Pedagogical Agents.
Twitter: https://twitter.com/#!/umidt. Facebook: http://www.facebook.com/idt-memphis. IDT Program News: http://idtmemphis.wordpress.com/. Our master's degree is 30 credit hours, and is completely online. The IDT Studio (http://idtstu-

dio.org), staffed and run by IDT faculty and students, serves as an R&D space for coursework and research involving technologies such as digital media, WBT/CBT, pedagogical agents, gaming, and simulation. The IDT program and IDT Studio are connected to the Center for Multimedia Arts in the FedEx Institute of Technology. The IDT Studio brings in outside contract work from corporate partners to provide real-world experience to students. The IDT program is an active partner in the Martin Institute for Teaching Excellence (http://martininstitute.org). We have also partnered with the Institute for Intelligent Systems and the Tutoring Research Group (www.autotutor.org) to work on intelligent agent development and research.

Admission Requirements—Minimum standards which identify a pool of master's--level applicants from which each department selects students to be admitted: an official transcript showing a bachelor's degree awarded by an accredited college or university with a minimum GPA of 2.0 on a 4.0 scale, competitive MAT or GRE scores, GRE writing test, two letters of recommendation, graduate school, and departmental application. Doctoral students must also be interviewed by at least two members of the program.

Degree Requirements—M.S.: 30 h total. Internship, master's project or thesis, 3.0 GPA. Ed.D.: 54 h total. 45 in major, 9 in research; residency project; comprehensive exams; dissertation

Number of Full-Time Faculty—6; **Number of Other Faculty**—8

Name of Institution—University of Texas Rio Grande Valley

Name of Department or Program—Master of Education in Educational Technology

Program Website (URL)—https://www.utrgv.edu/edtech/

Name of Contact Person—Joseph Rene Corbeil

Email Address of Contact Person—rene.corbeil@utrgv.edu

Program Description—The M.Ed. in Educational Technology is a 30-h, 100% online, accelerated program designed to prepare persons in K-12, higher education, corporate, and military settings to develop the skills and knowledge necessary for the classrooms and boardrooms of tomorrow. Through a real-world project-based curriculum graduates of this program will have a much better understanding of the uses of technology and how they can be applied in instructional/training settings. In addition to earning an M.Ed. in Educational Technology, students also have the opportunity to earn a graduate certificate in E-Learning or Technology Leadership, or both.

Admission Requirements—1. Bachelor's degree from a regionally accredited institution in the United States or a recognized international equivalent in a similar or related field. 2. Undergraduate GPA of at least 3.0. If the applicant does not meet minimum undergraduate GPA criterion, GRE general test with minimum scores of 150 verbal, 141 quantitative, and 4.0 analytical is required for conditional admission. GRE test scores are valid for 5 years. 3. Official transcripts from each institution attended (must be submitted directly to UTRGV). 4. Submission of a letter of intent. 5. Submission of a resume.

Graduate Programs in Learning, Design, Technology, Information, or Libraries   181

Degree Requirements—*Required courses* (21 h): EDFR 6300: Research Methods in Education. EDTC 6320: Instructional Technology. EDTC 6321: Instructional Design. EDTC 6323: Multimedia/Hypermedia. EDTC 6325: Educational Communications. EDTC 6332: Practicum in Educational Technology. EDFR 6302/EPSY 6304: Foundations of Learning, Cognition, and Human Development. *Electives* (9 h): Students may use the elective courses to earn a graduate certificate in E-Learning or Technology Leadership, or both. *Graduate E-Portfolio*: The Master's e-Portfolio represents the final assessment used in lieu of the comprehensive examination. The e-Portfolio reflects progress and growth over time. Each student will select, review, evaluate, and show works that reflect the achievement of the five professional standards addressed in the M.Ed. program.

Number of Full-Time Faculty—3; **Number of Other Faculty**—3

Name of Institution—National University

Name of Department or Program—Master of Science Educational and Instructional Technology

Program Website (URL)—https://www.nu.edu/ourprograms/schoolofeducation/

Name of Contact Person—E. George Beckwith

Email Address of Contact Person—gbeckwith@nu.edu

Program Description—The Master of Science in Educational and Instructional Technology is designed for students who want to participate in the paradigm changes that technology is precipitating in both education and training, as human learning moves from print and classroom-based instruction to digital media. The history and effectiveness of change processes and the role of technology in human learning are key components of the program. Graduates will be prepared to enter education careers such as K-12 technology coordination, site administration, home school and virtual school instruction, and online instruction in higher education. Graduates will be prepared for the rapidly growing employment opportunities available to people skilled in applying emerging information and telecommunication technologies to solving instructional problems. These graduates will be capable of applying their knowledge and skills to any situation in which digital technologies hold the potential for improving instruction especially business, industry, and governmental agencies. This program emphasizes practical applications by offering extensive technical training in a variety of software. The program culminates with a final technology project that applies the theory and practice of educational and instructional technology.

Admission Requirements—Qualifications: Applicants for admission to a graduate or postbaccalaureate program, other than the Doctor of Nursing Practice, must meet one of the following five requirements: (1) Hold a bachelor's degree or higher from a regionally accredited college or university with an overall grade point average of 2.5 or better, or a grade point average of 2.75 or higher within the last 90 quarter units. (2) Hold a bachelor's degree or higher from a regionally accredited college or university with an overall grade point average of 2.0–2.49 and a satisfactory score on one of the following tests: "Minimum score of 550 on the Graduate Management Admission Test (GMAT)," Minimum scores of 152 (verbal) and 147 (quantitative) on the Graduate Record Examination (GRE)," and "Minimum score of 408–413 on the Miller Analogies Test," an approved, standardized program-specific exam.

Degree Requirements—To obtain a Master of Science in Educational and Instructional Technology students must complete 45 quarter units of graduate work. Where appropriate, students can transfer a maximum of 4.5 quarter units of graduate work completed at another regionally accredited institution to meet stated requirements in the program if the units were not used toward a conferred degree. Students should refer to the section on graduate admission requirements for specific information regarding application and evaluation. Core requirements (10 courses; 45 quarter units): EDT 600A Technology Foundations. EDT 601 Instructional Design. Prerequisite: EDT 600A. EDT 605 Education Theory and Technology. EDT 607 Media Based Learning Objects. Prerequisite: EDT 600A, EDT 601. and EDT 605. EDT 609 Developing Online Courseware. Prerequisite: EDT 600A, EDT 601, EDT 605, and EDT 607. EDT 613 Simulations and Virtual Reality Recommended: prior completion of EDT 600A, EDT 601, EDT 605, EDT 607, and EDT 609. EDT 631 Media and Instruction. Prerequisite: EDT 600A. EDT 632 Technology and Leadership. Prerequisite: EDT 600A, EDT 601, EDT 605, EDT 607, EDT 609, EDT 631, and completion of all core requirements. EDT 693 Instructional Eval. and Devl. Prerequisite: EDT 600A, EDT 601, EDT 605, EDT 607, EDT 609, EDT 613, EDT 631, and EDT 632. EDT 695 Capstone Project. Prerequisite: EDT 693.

Number of Full-Time Faculty—4; **Number of Other Faculty**—8

Name of Institution—Baker University

Name of Department or Program—Master of Science in Instructional Design and Performance Technology; Doctor of Education in Instructional Design and Performance Technology

Program Website (URL)—https://www.bakeru.edu/school-of-education/ms-idpt/; https://www.bakeru.edu/school-of-education/idpt/

Name of Contact Person—Regena Aye

Email Address of Contact Person—raye@bakerU.edu

Program Description—*M.S. Degree*: The online M.S. in IDPT program prepares students to plan, develop, and manage instructional materials and their emerging technologies, particularly in the growing field of online learning and training. Based on competencies from the International Board of Standards for Training, Performance, and Instruction, Baker developed the curriculum with input from an advisory panel with a wide range of backgrounds, including company presidents and CEOs, instructional design professionals, performance improvement consultants, project managers, multimedia learning specialists, e-learning developers, software engineers, and scholars in the field. *Ed.D. Degree*: The online Ed.D. in IDPT program prepares professionals to use instructional design and performance technology, particularly in the growing field of online learning and training, to lead and direct the training and performance in a variety of workplaces. It is the only online doctoral program of its type in the region. Based on

Graduate Programs in Learning, Design, Technology, Information, or Libraries   183

competencies from the International Board of Standards for Training, Performance, and Instruction, Baker developed the curriculum with input from an advisory panel with a wide range of backgrounds, including company presidents and CEOs, instructional design professionals, performance improvement consultants, project managers, multimedia learning specialists, e-learning developers, software engineers, and scholars in the field.

Admission Requirements—*M.S. Degree*: Bachelor's degree from an accredited institution; 2.75 cumulative undergraduate GPA; completed application form; $20 application fee; official transcripts* from all undergraduate institutions attended; official transcript indicating a bachelor's degree** conferred from a regionally accredited institution of higher education with a minimum cumulative grade point average of 2.75; and minimum TOEFL scores for international students. *Ed.D. Degree*: Completed application and $50 application fee; completed master's degree from a regionally accredited institution, with a final GPA equal to or greater than 3.50 on a 4.00 scale; an official transcript indicating completion of a graduate degree from a regionally accredited institution; submission of the names of four references (with contact information) who will complete the recommendation survey; writing samples that demonstrate advanced writing skills; and a score on a university critical thinking instrument that demonstrates well-developed critical thinking and problem-solving skills.

Degree Requirements—*M.S. Degree*: Completion of the approved 36-credit-hour M.S. in IDPT curriculum; a minimum graduate grade point average of 3.0 with no more than one course completed with a grade of C (D and F grades are not acceptable); completion a master's project in IDPT; completion of all coursework within 6 years of the date of initial enrollment. *Ed.D. Degree*: Successfully complete the approved 59-plus-credit-hour Ed.D. curriculum. Maintain a minimum graduate grade point average of 3.50 with no grade below a B. Successfully complete both Field Experience I and II, as evidenced by artifacts and reflections provided in the electronic portfolio, scoring "proficient" or higher. Satisfactorily complete both Field Experience I and II and receive recommendations from the educational mentor and university supervisor on the evaluation form with mean scores equal to or greater than 8.2 on a 10.0 scale. Successfully complete and defend the program electronic portfolio scoring at the proficient level or above. Successfully complete and defend the dissertation.

Number of Full-Time Faculty—*M.S. Degree*: 2; *Ed.D. Degree*: 4; **Number of Other Faculty**—*M.S. Degree*: 8; *Ed.D. Degree*: 5

Name of Institution—Indiana University
Name of Department or Program—Instructional Systems Technology
Program Website (URL)—https://education.indiana.edu/programs/instructional--systems-technology.html
Name of Contact Person—Krista Glazewski
Email Address of Contact Person—glaze@indiana.edu
Program Description—We improve human learning and performance in diverse contexts. Take an active role in designing instructional materials and strategies

that improve the way people acquire, process, and share information. In this program, you will work with leading experts in the field to observe and analyze learning environments, evaluate the effectiveness of different strategies for learning, and research which technologies—analog, digital, and conceptual—can make those environments and strategies more powerful.

Admission Requirements—Vary depending on the program. Please visit the program website.

Degree Requirements—*Master's Degree* (online or residential): 36 credit hours plus successful completion of a portfolio; *Ed.D. Degree* (online): 60 credit hours above the master's degree plus successful performance on qualifying exam and completion and defense of dissertation; *Ph.D. Degree* (residential): 90 credit hours plus successful performance on qualifying exam (dossier based) and successful completion and defense of dissertation

Number of Full-Time Faculty—10; **Number of Other Faculty**—4

Name of Institution—The University of Tennessee, Knoxville

Name of Department or Program—Department: Educational Psychology and Counseling (EPC); Program: IT Online (M.S. in Education in Instructional Technology)

Program Website (URL)—https://epc.utk.edu/it-online/

Name of Contact Person—Director: Craig D. Howard (cdh@utk.edu); Christine Tidwell for inquiries (ktidwell@utk.edu)

Email Address of Contact Person—Christine Tidwell for inquiries: ktidwell@utk.edu

Program Description—Blended program. Fees and tuition are now the same for in- and out-of-state students. See our brochure: https://epc.utk.edu/wp-content/uploads/sites/32/2018/09/2019-IT-Online-Program-at-a-Glance_web.pdf.

Admission Requirements—GRE is not required. A completed bachelor's degree is.

Degree Requirements—36 credits and completion of a master's portfolio

Number of Full-Time Faculty—2 in 2019–2020. One more to be hired in 2021; **Number of Other Faculty**—4

Name of Institution—University of South Alabama

Name of Department or Program—Instructional Design and Development

Program Website (URL)—https://www.southalabama.edu/colleges/ceps/cins/iddmain.html

Name of Contact Person—James P. Van Haneghan

Email Address of Contact Person—jvanhane@southalabama.edu

Program Description—Ph.D. in Instructional Design and Development; Master of Science in Instructional Design and Development

Admission Requirements—*M.S. Degree*: bachelor's degree, application, GRE or Miller Analogies Test, two letters of recommendation, personal statement; *Ph.D. Degree*: bachelor's degree or higher, application, GRE or Miller Analogies Test, three letters of recommendation, personal statement

Degree Requirements—*M.S. Degree*: 33 h. Thirty hours of courses and a 3-h capstone internship, research and development project, or thesis. *Ph.D. Degree*:

Admission with bachelor's or master's outside of instructional design requires 18-h prerequisite core (6 courses) be taken before admission to doctoral study. Before advancing to doctoral study, students must pass an oral exam on these core courses. Students with an M.S. in Instructional Design or closely related field start directly with the main portion of the doctoral program described below. The doctoral program consists of 60 h: 24 h of instructional core courses (including an internship), 15 h of educational research and data analysis coursework, 12 h of supporting coursework, and a minimum of 9 dissertation hours. Comprehensive exams are offered on the educational research and instructional core. Students must completely defend a doctoral dissertation that contributes to the field.

Number of Full-Time Faculty—5; **Number of Other Faculty**—4

Name of Institution—University of New Mexico

Name of Department or Program—Program of Organization, Information, and Learning Sciences

Program Website (URL)—https://oils.unm.edu/

Name of Contact Person—Victor Law

Email Address of Contact Person—vlaw@unm.edu

Program Description—We offer three programs, a Bachelor or Science, a Master of Arts, and Ph.D., an Ed Specialist Program, and professional certificates. A brief description of the *Master of Arts*: The Organization, Information, and Learning Sciences (OILS) Program offers a Master of Arts (MA) degree that gives students an opportunity to combine aspects of adult learning, learning sciences, organizational learning and development, and instructional technology that includes multimedia design and distance learning, principles of knowledge management and data management, and design, development, and evaluation of training. We offer five concentrations in our M.A. program that include Organization Development and Human Resource Development, Instructional Design and Technology, eLearning, Adult Education and Professional Development, and Learning Officer. All of the concentrations can be completed 100% online, and hybrid options are also offered. A brief description of the *Ph.D. Program*: The Ph.D. in Organization, Information, and Learning Sciences is a research degree. It is designed to develop the candidate's competencies to design, conduct, and report original theoretical and applied research in learning sciences, eLearning, organizational learning and development, instructional technology, and human performance technology. The Program of Study and the Dissertation reflect an emphasis on theoretical concepts, inquiry skills, and original research. Our Ph.D. program only has the face-to-face option.

Admission Requirements—*Undergraduate*: 2.75 Cumulative GPA Meet with the OILS Undergraduate Advisor to discuss degree program and to work on a proposal for Technical Studies Submit letter of intent along with OILS application. Letter of intent should state your reasons for applying to the Program along with education and career goals. *Master*: A Bachelor's Degree from an accredited college or university. At least a 3.0 GPA in the last 60 hours of undergraduate work.

Required documentation (see below). Goals or objectives that can be reasonably achieved through a degree in this program. It is recommended that applicants should talk to one of the OILS faculty before the application deadline. *Ph.D.*: A master's degree from an accredited college or university with a 3.5 GPA. Positive recommendations. GRE or GMAT test required. Goals or objectives that can be reasonably achieved through a degree in this program.

Degree Requirements—*Undergraduate*: Students majoring in Instructional Technology and Training will complete a minimum of 121 credit hours as follows: 37 credit hours (minimum) of University Core Requirements with a grade of "C" or better 9 credit hours of Management/Communication Skills. 30 credit hours of Technical Course Work. 45 credit hours of OILS undergraduate courses. *Master*: Students who choose Plan III (coursework only) are required to complete 15 credit hours of core courses, which include adult learning, instructional design, culture and global e-learning, program evaluation, and capstone and 15 credit hours of coursework from one of the concentrations. *Doctoral*: An OILS Ph.D. candidate must complete an approved program of studies of no less than 60 graduate credit hours of coursework plus 18 credit hours of dissertation. All candidates complete the required core courses (18 credit hours), concentration courses (24 credit hours), and research courses (18 credit hours). Details of the coursework requirements are shown in the Program of Study: https://oils.unm.edu/current-students/phd-program-students/program-study.

Number of Full-Time Faculty—7; **Number of Other Faculty**—24. Currently, we have three faculty from Department of Computer Science, Honors College, and School of Medicine holding secondary appointments. Eight library faculty are teaching and advising in OILS. In addition, we have 13 active part-time faculty.

Name of Institution—Western Kentucky University

Name of Department or Program—Instructional Design Program, School of Teacher Education

Program Website (URL)—https://www.wku.edu/id/

Name of Contact Person—Xiaoxia Huang

Email Address of Contact Person—xiaoxia.huang@wku.edu

Program Description—The Instructional Design program at Western Kentucky University is a fully online program, including an online Master of Science in Instruction Design and an online Graduate Certificate in Instructional Design. It also offers an Undergraduate Certificate in Interactive Training Design. The program prepares students to be instructional designers and learning technologists at different levels and in various settings, such as K-12, higher-ed, business, government agencies, and healthcare.

Admission Requirements—Admission with a baccalaureate or master's degree requires the following: (a) Applicants who hold a bachelor's degree from a regionally accredited college or university may apply for admission with an overall undergraduate GPA of 2.75 or least a 2.75 GPA on their last 60 h of appropriate undergraduate credit for the degree. (b) Or completed master's degree from an accredited college or university with GPA of 3.0 or higher.

Degree Requirements—The M.S. program includes one 3-h research course, 15 h of required courses, and 12 h of advisor-approved electives from selected professional emphasis areas. The program requires a total of 30 h. The Graduate Certificate program requires a total of 12 h, including 6 h of required courses and 6 h of advisor-approved electives from selected professional emphasis areas.

Number of Full-Time Faculty—1; **Number of Other Faculty -.**

Name of Institution—The University of Tampa

Name of Department or Program—Master of Science in Instructional Design and Technology

Program Website (URL)—https://www.ut.edu/graduate-degrees/graduate--education-programs/ms-in-instructional-design-and-technology

Name of Contact Person—Enilda Romero-Hall

Email Address of Contact Person—eromerohall@ut.edu

Program Description—The M.S. in Instructional Design and Technology addresses a growing field in learning and human performance and provides a multidisciplinary area of study that draws students from many disciplines and backgrounds. Instructional designers understand and utilize technologies as both product (e.g., Web-based courses) and process (e.g., iterative and formative approaches to learner assessment). Given the diverse career tracks in instructional design, this program offers students the flexibility to customize their course of study based on individual goals and interests. Graduates of the program are well prepared to practice their unique, multidisciplinary profession in a variety of settings, including business, K-12 schools, higher education, government, and military, or to pursue doctoral studies. Courses in the M.S. in Instructional Design and Technology program are offered in hybrid format.

Admission Requirements—Applicants must have earned a 4-year degree from a regionally accredited institution. Applicants must have an overall GPA of 3.0 out of a possible 4.0 and a minimum of 3.0 in the last 60 credit hours of undergraduate study or have successfully completed a master's degree from a regionally accredited institution. NOTE: GPAs below 3.0 will be reviewed for conditional admittance. Test of English as a Foreign Language (TOEFL) for applicants whose primary language is not English. Must meet one of the minimum requirements listed below: A minimum of 550 on the paper-based exam. A minimum of 213 on the computer-based exam. A minimum of 80 on the Internet-based exam. The IELTS exam may be used instead of the TOEFL exam with a minimum score of 6.5.

Degree Requirements—M.S. curriculum core courses (24 credit hours): Introduction to Instructional Design (4). Theories of Learning and Cognition for Instruction (4). Inquiry and Measurement (4). Trends and Issues in Instructional Design and Technology (4). Introduction to Systematic Instructional Design (4). Seminar in Instructional Design (2). Advanced Seminar in Instructional Design (2). Field Internship in Instructional Design and Technology (0). Elective courses (choose 12 credit hours): Introduction to Distance Learning (4). Design of Online Collaborative Learning (4). Introduction to Instructional Games and Simulations

(4). Principles of Learner Motivation (4). Media for Instruction (4). Open Learning Environments in the Twenty-First Century (3). Development of Multimedia Instruction (4). Introduction to Program Evaluation (4). Management of Instructional Development (4). Management of Change (4). Performance Systems Analysis (4). Total credit hours: 36.

Number of Full-Time Faculty—3; **Number of Other Faculty**—2

Name of Institution—Virginia Tech

Name of Department or Program—Instructional Design and Technology

Program Website (URL)—https://liberalarts.vt.edu/departments-and-schools/school-of-education/academic-programs/instructional-design-and--technology.html

Name of Contact Person—Ken Potter

Email Address of Contact Person—kpotter@vt.edu

Program Description—M.A., Ed.S. Ed.D., and Ph.D. in Instructional Design and Technology. Graduates of our Master's and Educational Specialist programs find themselves applying their expertise in a variety of rewarding, professional venues, for example, as instructional designers, trainers, or performance consultants in industrial settings and as teachers or technology coordinators in pre-K-12. Graduates of our doctoral program typically assume exciting roles as faculty in higher education, advancing research in the field and preparing the next generation of instructional technologists for the profession. Areas of emphasis are instructional design, distance education, and multimedia development. Facilities include computer labs, extensive digital video and audio equipment, distance education classroom, and computer graphics production areas.

Admission Requirements—Ed.D. and Ph.D.: 3.3 GPA from Master's degree, GRE scores, writing sample, three letters of recommendation, transcripts. MA.: 3.0 GPA undergraduate

Degree Requirements—Ph.D.: 90 h above B.S., 2-year residency; 12-h research classes, 30-h dissertation; Ed.D.: 90 h above B.S., 1-year residency; 12-h research classes; MA.: 30 h above B.S.

Number of Full-Time Faculty—6; **Number of Other Faculty**—5

Name of Institution—George Mason University

Name of Department or Program—Masters of Science in Learning Design and Technology

Program Website (URL)—https://learntech.gmu.edu/learning-design-technology/

Name of Contact Person—Shahron Williams van Rooij

Email Address of Contact Person—swilliae@gmu.edu

Program Description—Students graduate from the online M.S. in Learning Design and Technology at George Mason University ready to design and implement learning experiences that help people improve their performance with new knowledge, skills, and abilities. The core curriculum includes not only the basic competencies set forth by the International Board of Standards for Training, Performance, and Instruction (IBSTPI), but also the advanced and managerial competencies that prepare students for more senior roles. Graduates are able to

Graduate Programs in Learning, Design, Technology, Information, or Libraries

step into new roles such as learning or instructional designer, e-learning developer, and UX designer with new abilities to analyze and evaluate learning technologies, programs, and trends; collaborate with business leaders and subject matter experts; design and implement new learning solutions; and manage projects through their entire life cycle.

Admission Requirements—In order to apply, applicants must have earned a US--equivalent bachelor's degree from an accredited university with a minimum GPA of 3.0 on a 4.0 scale. Application materials include transcripts, professional resume, 750-word essay or statement describing academic and career goals and past experiences related to the intended program as well as personal and professional aspirations, and two letters of recommendation from professional persons.

Degree Requirements—Program requirements for the online master's in learning design program at Mason include 30 credit hours, 23 of which are core courses and 7 of which are electives. Courses for Mason's online M.S. in Learning Design and Technology program are offered in a convenient, part-time asynchronous format. An optional Learning Technologies Certificate with a Concentration in E-Learning is also be built into the curriculum. Required courses: EDIT 705 Instructional Design. EDIT 704 Instructional Technology Foundations and Theories of Learning. EDIT 706 Business of Learning Design and Technology. EDIT 730 Advanced Instructional Design. EDIT 732 Analysis and Design of Technology-Based Learning Environments. EDIT 751 Overview of Learning Analytics and Big Data. EDIT 752 Design and Implementation of Technology--Based Learning Environments. EDIT 601 Instructional Design and Technology (IDT) Portfolio. EDIT 701 Advanced Instructional Design and Technology (IDT) Portfolio. Elective options: EDIT 526 Web Accessibility and Design. EDIT 530 Scripting and Programming. EDIT 571 Visual Design and Applications. EDIT 573 Project Management. EDIT 574 Social Media and Digital Collaboration Applications. EDIT 575 E-Learning Design Applications. EDIT 576 Mobile Learning Applications. EDIT 611 Innovations in e-Learning. EDIT 710 Online Teaching Essentials. EDIT 772 Virtual Worlds, Augmented Reality, and Gaming Applications.

Number of Full-Time Faculty—4; **Number of Other Faculty**—6

Name of Institution—East Carolina University
Name of Department or Program—Instructional Technology
Program Website (URL)—https://education.ecu.edu/msite/instructional-technology/
Name of Contact Person—Patricia Slagter Van Tryon
Email Address of Contact Person—slagtervantryonp@ecu.edu
Program Description—Degrees offered 100% online within the Instructional Technology program at East Carolina University include the Master of Arts in Education in Instructional Technology (with recommendation for North Carolina license 077: Instructional Technology Specialist); Master of Science in Instructional Technology; as well as certificates in Computer-Based Instruction;

Digital Learning for Education Leaders; Distance Learning and Administration; and Special Endorsement in Computer Education.

Admission Requirements—Admission requirements include a completed application to the Graduate School, official transcripts for all postsecondary institutions attended, a statement of purpose, and three letters of recommendation from someone aware of your potential as a graduate student. Applicants must have an overall undergraduate GPA of 2.7 on a 4.0 scale (from an accredited college/ university).

Degree Requirements—The M.S. in Instructional Technology and M.A.Ed. in Instructional Technology each requires 36 student hours of successfully completed coursework. The graduate certificates in Computer-Based Instruction; Digital Learning for Education Leaders; Distance Learning and Administration; and Special Endorsement in Computer Education each requires 18 student hours of successfully completed coursework.

Number of Full-Time Faculty—8; **Number of Other Faculty**—4

Name of Institution—Piedmont College

Name of Department or Program—School of Education

Program Website (URL)—https://www.piedmont.edu/academics/education--master-arts/instructional-technology%2D%2Dma; https://www.piedmont.edu/eds-instructional-technology

Name of Contact Person—Randy Hollandsworth

Email Address of Contact Person—rhollandsworth@piedmont.edu

Program Description—The School of Education offers two master's degree programs in the area of Instructional Technology: one with an emphasis on instructional design and development in nonschool settings, and the other for individuals wishing to use their expertise in an educational setting. Piedmont College also offers two education specialist degrees … one for initial certification and the other for advanced certification. Both programs are designed to prepare and support professional educators to attain distinguished levels of both theory and practice and to become contributing members in the professional discourse of improving schooling in roles such as Technology Leader, Instructional Technology Coordinator, or Director of Instructional Technology.

Admission Requirements—The admission process begins with our Graduate Admissions Department; see info at https://www.piedmont.edu/apply.

Degree Requirements—Master of Arts (MA) degree in Instructional Technology—Instructional Design and Development (36 credits): Individuals who hold a bachelor's degree in any field and who desire to learn the fundamentals and skills of instructional design and human resource development for noneducational settings. No state P-12 certifications are associated with this degree; graduates seek professional roles in government, higher education, and corporate organizations as trainers, designers, online learning managers, and eLearning developers. Master of Arts (MA) degree in Instructional Technology—Initial Certification (42 credits): Certified educators who have two or more years' teaching experience and who seek initial certification in Instructional Technology. Candidates who successfully complete the program and who take and pass the Georgia Assessments for the Certification of Educators (GACE) assessments in Instructional Technology will be recommended for an initial Level 5 Service (S) certificate in Instructional Technology. Education Specialist (Ed.S.) degree in Instructional Technology—Initial Certification (33 credits): Certified educators who hold a master's degree or higher in a field of certification other than Instructional Technology and who seek initial certification and an advanced degree in Instructional Technology. Candidates who successfully complete the program and who take and pass the Georgia Assessments for the Certification of Educators (GACE) assessments in Instructional Technology will be recommended for an initial Level 6 Service (S) certificate in Instructional Technology. Education Specialist (Ed.S.) degree in Instructional Technology—Advanced Certification (30 credits): Certified educators who are currently certified in Instructional Technology and who wish to upgrade their skills and their certification. Candidates who complete the program can apply in their school districts and/or to the Georgia Professional Standards Commission (GaPSC) for a certificate/pay upgrade. All certifications will be upgraded to Level 6.

Number of Full-Time Faculty—1; **Number of Other Faculty**—3

Name of Institution—University of Minnesota

Name of Department or Program—Learning Technologies Program in the Department of Curriculum and Instruction

Program Website (URL)—https://www.cehd.umn.edu/ci/academics/LearningTechnologies/

Name of Contact Person—Bodong Chen

Email Address of Contact Person—chenbd@umn.edu

Program Description—The Learning Technologies Program at the University of Minnesota offers unique opportunities for educators and technology professionals to advance the field of educational technology. We offer Ph.D., M.A., M.Ed., professional certificate, and undergraduate minor programs. Students can earn degrees that help them successfully incorporate technology into the classroom, create a distance learning program, foster online learning, and develop digital literacy. Students benefit from a rich, broad-based curriculum and faculty members with both research-based and practical expertise.

Admission Requirements—Vary depending on program. Please visit the program website.

Degree Requirements—Vary depending on program. Please visit the program website.

Number of Full-Time Faculty—2 tenured faculty, 3 full-time lecturers; **Number of Other Faculty -.**

Name of Institution—Brigham Young University

Name of Department or Program—Instructional Psychology and Technology (IP&T)

Program Website (URL)—https://education.byu.edu/ipt

Name of Contact Person—Stephen C. Yanchar

Email Address of Contact Person—stephen_yanchar@byu.edu

Program Description—Instructional Psychology and Technology deals with identifying and implementing improvements in instruction and understanding the principles that influence these improvements. IP&T applies these principles to solve instructional problems, which occur in educational settings, including public schools and universities, government, church, military, business, and industry. The program requires students to attain skills in the following areas: Research Instructional Design and Development Evaluation and Measurement. Students participate in department seminars, interact with other students in group projects and informal study, collaborate with faculty, and participate in a wide variety of internship experiences. All majors are accepted.

Admission Requirements—Master's program application requirements: To apply to the master's program, you will need the following: letter of intent, three letters of recommendation from those who can affirm your ability to succeed in the academic rigor of a graduate program, transcripts, and GRE scores or evidence of experience in the field. Ph.D. program application requirements: To apply to the Ph.D. program, you will need the following: letter of intent, three letters of recommendation from those who can affirm your ability to succeed in the academic rigor of a graduate program, transcripts, and GRE scores. Once you are ready to apply, you can complete the application at https://gradstudies.byu.edu/.

Degree Requirements—36–39 credits, 18 credits of core courses, 8 credits of specialized courses, 3 credits of internship, 1 credit of seminar. Internship: To meet this requirement students may register for 1–3 credit hours of IP&T 599R during any semester or term. Thesis/project work: Master's students must complete a total of 6 h of master's project or thesis credit in order to graduate. These credits may be taken over a period of one or two semesters, as the student prepares the prospectus, conducts the project, and writes the report. Oral exam: The final oral examination should be scheduled with the Department Secretary. An oral exam may take from 1 to 4 h, but typically lasts about 2 h.

Number of Full-Time Faculty—10; **Number of Other Faculty**—3

Name of Institution—University of Wyoming

Name of Department or Program—Learning, Design, and Technology

Program Website (URL)—https://www.uwyo.edu/clad/instech/

Name of Contact Person—Mia Williams

Email Address of Contact Person—mwill114@uwyo.edu

Program Description—Our program emphasizes instructional design, distance delivery, rural environments, and learning in a variety of settings. Graduates from our degree program secure employment in PK-12 classrooms; school media and technology centers, and school district administrative offices; public, corporate, and government centers and training agencies; college and university faculty and administrative positions; design and development labs; product support teams; and consulting firms. Our mission is to assist professionals in effectively developing, implementing, and evaluating systems, tools, strategies, and environments that enhance learning.

Admission Requirements—For Master's Degree Domestic Students: GPA: 3.0 GRE: no requirement. Rolling admission: international students: TOEFL: 550 min written or 80 min online, OR IELTS: 6.5 min overall score. GRE: no requirement. Rolling admission

Degree Requirements—The University of Wyoming Learning, Design, and Technology master's degree program is 33 credit hours, including a capstone course and e-portfolio.

Number of Full-Time Faculty—2; **Number of Other Faculty**—8

Name of Institution—The University of the West Indies Open Campus
Name of Department or Program—MSc Instructional Design and Technology
Program Website (URL)—https://open.uwi.edu/programmes/msc-instructional-design-and-technology
Name of Contact Person—https://open.uwi.edu/programmes/msc-instructional-design-and-technology
Email Address of Contact Person -.
Program Description—https://open.uwi.edu/programmes/msc-instructional-design-and-technology
Admission Requirements -.
Degree Requirements -.
Number of Full-Time Faculty -; Number of Other Faculty -.

Name of Institution—University of Georgia
Name of Department or Program—Career and Information Studies
Program Website (URL)—https://coe.uga.edu/academics/concentrations/learning-design-and-technology
Name of Contact Person—Theodore J. Kopcha
Email Address of Contact Person—tjkopcha@uga.edu
Program Description—Our programs develop informed leaders through teaching, research, and service in learning, design, and technology.
Admission Requirements—Purpose statement, three letters of reference, GREs (a waiver can be requested), CV, or resume
Degree Requirements—33 credit hours with a course in applied instructional design and technology
Number of Full-Time Faculty—7; **Number of Other Faculty**—2

Name of Institution—Mississippi State University
Name of Department or Program—Instructional Systems and Workforce Development
Program Website (URL)—http://www.iswd.msstate.edu/
Name of Contact Person—Trey Martindale
Email Address of Contact Person—treymartindale@gmail.com
Program Description -.
Admission Requirements—https://www.iswd.msstate.edu/graduate/phd/admissions Departmental graduate admission requirements, general requirements, and prerequisites for admission into the graduate program include all the general

requirements of the graduate school. In addition, scores from all sections of the GRE must be submitted. GRE may be waived if you have a 3.5 GPA or higher. International students must obtain a minimum TOEFL score of 550 PBT (213 CBT or 79 iBT) or a minimum IELTS score of 6.5; components of the admission packet; Ph.D. program application to the graduate degree program; GRE scores (waived if the student has a 3.50 or higher); three letters of recommendation (preferably from faculty and administrators who can comment about your scholarly ability); and statement of purpose (a minimum of one page, single spaced): In the statement, please make sure to address the following: describe the purpose of applying for the Ph.D. degree in this program area, identify your research interest, and discuss your career goals. Applicants with a graduate GPA of 3.50 or higher on previous graduate work from an accredited institution may qualify for a waiver of the GRE/GMAT requirement. Official transcripts from all colleges and universities attended. A copy of professional resume. Ph.D. applicants who pass the initial screening will be contacted for an online interview.

Degree Requirements—https://www.iswd.msstate.edu/graduate/phd; https://www.iswd.msstate.edu/graduate/msit

Number of Full-Time Faculty—9; **Number of Other Faculty**—5

Name of Institution—Athabasca University

Name of Department or Program—Centre for Distance Education

Program Website (URL)—cde.athabascau.ca

Name of Contact Person—Mohamed Ally

Email Address of Contact Person—mohameda@athabascau.ca

Program Description—Doctor of Education in Distance Education, Master of Distance Education, Graduate Diploma in Distance Education Technology, Graduate Diploma in Instructional Design, Graduate Certificate in Instructional Design

Admission Requirements—Doctorate of Education in Distance Education Admission requirements for the doctoral program includes both academic and experiential elements. * Completion of a master's degree, preferably with a thesis or research project, in a relevant field or area of study (e.g., education or distance education, psychology or educational psychology, instructional technology, adult education, curriculum and instruction, and the like) from a recognized university, normally with a GPA of at least 3.7 or 85% (Graduate Grading Policy). * Significant experience in open or distance learning, which demonstrates that the student is capable of study at a distance, and of completing high-quality original research with distance supervision only. Master of Distance Education Applicants to the MDE program must hold a baccalaureate degree from a recognized postsecondary education institution. If the potential applicant does not have a degree but believes that his/her education and experience are equivalent to an undergraduate degree, then it is the responsibility of the applicant to put forward this position in writing as part of the application process. Graduate Diploma in Distance Education Technology: Applicants to the GDDET program must hold a baccalaureate degree from a recognized postsecondary education institution. If the potential applicant does not have a degree but believes that his/her education and experience are equivalent to an undergraduate degree, then it is the responsibility of the applicant to put forward this position in writing as part of the application process. Graduate Diploma in Instructional Design: Applicants to the GDID program must hold a baccalaureate degree from a recognized postsecondary education institution. If the potential applicant does not have a degree but believes that his/her education and experience are equivalent to an undergraduate degree, then it is the responsibility of the applicant to put forward this position in writing as part of the application process. Graduate Certificate in Instructional Design: Applicants to the GCID program must hold a baccalaureate degree from a recognized postsecondary education institution. If the potential applicant does not have a degree but believes that his/her education and experience are equivalent to an undergraduate degree, then it is the responsibility of the applicant to put forward this position in writing as part of the application process.

Degree Requirements—*Doctor of Education in Distance Education*: The Doctor of Education in Distance Education program will address the needs of a wide range of practitioners, scholars, and researchers who operate in the distance education arena. The doctorate will provide critical direction as distance education evolves and expands. The primary goal of the doctoral program is to provide students with a complete and rigorous preparation to assume senior responsibilities for planning, teaching, directing, designing, implementing, evaluating, researching, and managing distance education programs. *Master of Distance Education*: Athabasca University's Master of Distance Education (MDE) program is designed to provide a common base of skills, knowledge, and values regarding distance education and training, independent of any special area of interest. *Graduate Diploma in Distance Education*: Athabasca University's Graduate Diploma in Distance Education Technology: GDDET is a focused, 18-credit (six courses) program designed to provide a solid grounding in the current principles and practices of technology use in distance education and training. The program structure and course content emphasize the concepts and skills required of practitioners who are employed as instructors, teachers, trainers, decision makers, planners, managers, and administrators in distance education or "virtual" programs. The emphasis of the GDDET is on the user of technology for the preparation, delivery, and management of instruction. *Graduate Diploma in Instructional Design*: The Graduate Diploma in Instructional Design is an 18-credit program comprised of six courses. For those who wish to pursue instructional design as a profession, this Diploma program provides more depth and breadth than the certificate. *Graduate Certificate in Instructional Design*: The Graduate Certificate in Instructional Design is a 9-credit program, comprised of three courses. For those wanting to enhance their instructional design expertise, the Certificate program is an expedient way to obtain the appropriate skills and knowledge.

Number of Full-Time Faculty—11; **Number of Other Faculty**—15

Name of Institution—University of Calgary

Name of Department or Program—Office of Graduate Programs, Faculty of Education

Program Website (URL)—http://ucalgary.ca/gpe/

Name of Contact Person—Michele Jacobsen

Email Address of Contact Person—dmjacobs@ucalgary.ca

Program Description—In a knowledge-based economy, the Ph.D., Ed.D., M.A., and M.Ed. programs in the educational technology specialization in Educational Research at the University of Calgary have proven valuable to public and private sector researchers, postsecondary faculty, school teachers and school leaders, military/industrial trainers, health educators, instructional designers, managers, and leaders. A spectrum of entrepreneurs and educational experts have successfully completed our graduate programs in educational technology and are using their research, knowledge, and competencies in schools, higher education, and a range of corporate and private workplaces today. Our graduates have careers as practitioners and scholars in the top government, industry, K-12, and higher education institutions as professors, education and training leaders, teachers, and instructors—worldwide. Your academic and professional career growth is possible through our innovative, student-centered programs and supervision processes in this growing, vibrant area. Degree programs can be completed on campus, in blended formats, or completely online.

The Educational Technology Specialization is interdisciplinary and is addressed to at least two audience: (a) postsecondary teachers and leaders, and school leaders and classroom teachers who are interested in the study and practice of educational technology to facilitate learning or who are interested in technology leadership positions or who are interested in academic careers in higher education, and (b) those who are interested in instructional design and development in settings both within and outside elementary/secondary/tertiary schools, e.g., instructional developers and faculty developers in colleges, institutes of technology and universities, military/industrial trainers, health educators, and private training consultants. Graduate students in the educational technology specialization have the opportunity to investigate a broad spectrum of knowledge building, participatory cultures, instructional design, and development theories and practices as they apply to current and emergent technologies and to explore new directions in instructional design and development and evaluation as they emerge in the literature and in practice.

Admission Requirements—The Master of Education (MEd) is a course-based professional degree. The M.Ed. program is available in online formats. Admission requirements normally include a completed 4-year bachelor's degree and a 3.0 GPA. The Master of Arts (MA) is a thesis-based degree with a residency requirement that is intended to prepare students for further research. Admission requirements normally include a completed 4-year bachelor's degree and a 3.3 GPA. The Doctor of Education (Ed.D.) is a thesis-based degree intended to prepare scholars of the profession for careers in leadership and teaching. The Ed.D. program is available in the online format. Admission requirements normally include a completed master's degree and a 3.5 GPA. The Doctor of Philosophy (Ph.D.) is

Graduate Programs in Learning, Design, Technology, Information, or Libraries

a thesis-based degree with a residency requirement intended to prepare scholars of the discipline for careers in research and teaching. The Ph.D. program is available for full-time, on-campus engagement in apprenticeship. Admission requirements normally include a completed master's thesis and a 3.5 GPA.

Degree Requirements—Program requirements for the Master of Education (M. Ed.) program are completion of a minimum of 6 full-course equivalents (12 half-courses). In Educational Technology, Master of Education Students complete 7 half-courses in the specialization of educational technology and 5 half-courses in educational research methodology and action research. The Master of Education cohort-based degree consists of a total of 36 credits (12 half-courses). Graduate students are required to complete their courses in a prescribed sequence. Students are expected to complete all program requirements within 2 years. Program requirements for the Master of Arts (MA) thesis program include (a) one full-course equivalent (two half-courses) in research methods; (b) a minimum of one full-course equivalent (two half-courses) in the student's area of specialization; (c) additional graduate courses or seminars determined by the supervisor in consultation with the student; and (d) a master's thesis and an oral examination on the thesis. The Education Doctorate (EDD) in Educational Technology is a 3-year cohort-based program consisting of a) coursework, b) candidacy examination, and c) dissertation. Year 1 is designed primarily to develop students' competencies as "critical consumers of educational research" and skills to conduct practitioner inquiry. As outlined within the program to which the student has applied, first-year students must complete (a) two half-courses in research: EDER 701.06, and either EDER 701.07 or EDER 701.08, (b) two half-courses in the student's specialization area. Year 2 is designed to engage students in an in-depth analysis of an identified problem of practice through diverse academic disciplines (e.g., leadership, adult learning). Specialization coursework exposes students to context-specific best practices and cutting-edge research and emphasizes the application of theory and research to practice within collaborators of practice. As outlined within the program to which the student has applied, students must complete (a) two half-courses in the student's specialization area, (b) two specialization collaborators of practice half-courses, and (c) comprehensive candidacy examination. Year 3 is designed to support students in synthesizing their Year 2 inquiry projects into a dissertation. Students work collaboratively with faculty and practitioners from their field to complete a dissertation that addresses a contemporary issue in education. As outlined within the program to which the student has applied, students must complete (a) Dissertation Seminar I, (b) Dissertation Seminar II, (c) Doctoral Dissertation Program. Requirements for the on-campus Doctor of Philosophy (Ph.D.) program include (a) three 600-or 700-level half-courses in research methods; (b) in addition, Ph.D. students in the Educational Technology specialization are required to complete EDER 771 and two half-courses at the 700 level in technology; (c) candidacy examination; and (d) dissertation.

Number of Full-Time Faculty—8; **Number of Other Faculty**—72

Name of Institution—University of British Columbia
Name of Department or Program—Master of Educational Technology Degree Program
Program Website (URL)—http://met.ubc.ca
Name of Contact Person—David Roy
Email Address of Contact Person—info@met.ubc.ca
Program Description—This innovative online program provides an excellent environment in which to learn the techniques of instructional design including the development and management of programs for international and intercultural populations. Attracting students from more than 30 countries, the program provides a unique opportunity to learn and collaborate with professionals and colleagues from around the world. The MET curriculum is designed for K-12 teachers, college and university faculty, course designers, and adult and industry educators.
MET fully online graduate degree. MET Graduate Certificate in Technology-Based Distributed Learning. MET Graduate Certificate in Technology-Based Learning for Schools
Admission Requirements—Please see website.
Degree Requirements—Master's Program: 10 courses. Graduate Certificates: 5 courses
Number of Full-Time Faculty—9; **Number of Other Faculty**—8

Name of Institution—University of New Brunswick

Name of Department or Program—Faculty of Education
Program Website (URL)—http://www.unbf.ca/education/
Name of Contact Person—Ellen Rose
Email Address of Contact Person—erose@unb.ca
Program Description—Courses are offered in instructional design theories and processes, cultural studies in instructional design, instructional design processes, needs assessment, designing constructivist learning environments, instructional message design, and instructional design for online learning. In addition, students are allowed to take other courses in the Faculty of Education or other applicable areas.
Students can choose the course, project, or thesis stream. UNB's M.Ed. in Instructional Design is very flexible, allowing students to customize their own learning experiences in order to meet their particular learning outcomes. While this is not an online program, several of the Instructional Design courses, and many other relevant courses in the Faculty of Education, are available online.
Admission Requirements—Applicants must have an undergraduate degree in education or a relevant field, a grade point average of at least 3.0 (B, or its equivalent), and at least 1 year of teaching or related professional experience. Applicants whose first language is not English must submit evidence of their proficiency in the use of English language. The minimum proficiency levels accepted by the Faculty of Education are scores of 650 on the TOEFL (280 computer based) and 5.5 on the TWE.

Graduate Programs in Learning, Design, Technology, Information, or Libraries 199

Degree Requirements—Course route: 10 3-credit-hour courses. Project route: 8 3-credit-hour courses and one project/report. Thesis route: 5 3-credit-hour courses and one thesis. Required courses: ED 6221 Instructional Design Theories and ED 6902 Introduction to Research in Education.

Number of Full-Time Faculty—1; **Number of Other Faculty**—2

Name of Institution—University of Saskatchewan
Name of Department or Program—Educational Technology and Design
Program Website (URL)—http://www.edct.ca
Name of Contact Person—richard.schwier@usask.ca
Email Address of Contact Person—Richard A. Schwier
Program Description—We offer a general educational technology degree, but with a particular emphasis on instructional design in all coursework.

Almost all of our courses are delivered in flexible formats. Courses can be taken completely online or blended with classroom experiences. A few courses are only offered face to face, but an entire program can be taken online. Many of our courses emphasize authentic learning options, where students work on projects with clients.

Admission Requirements—A professional bachelor's degree or the equivalent of a 4-year Bachelor of Arts. Normally, we require a minimum of 1 year of practical experience in education or a related field. An average of 70% in your most recent 60 credit units of university coursework.

Degree Requirements—M.Ed. (course-based) students need to complete 30 credit units of graduate-level coursework for the degree. M.Ed. (project) students require 24 credit units of graduate-level coursework and the project seminar (ETAD 992.6) supervised by a faculty member in the program. M.Ed. (thesis) students need to complete 21 units of graduate-level coursework and a thesis supervised by a faculty member in the program and a committee.

Number of Full-Time Faculty—4; **Number of Other Faculty**—2

Name of Institution—The University of Hong Kong
Name of Department or Program—Faculty of Education
Program Website (URL)—http://web.edu.hku.hk/programme/mite/
Name of Contact Person—Mark King
Email Address of Contact Person—mite@cite.hku.hk
Program Description—The Master of Science in Information Technology in Education [MSc(ITE)] program offers the following three specialist strands: e--leadership, e-learning, and learning technology design.

The program aims to provide an investigation into Web 2.0, mobile learning, and other emerging learning and teaching technology applications, an opportunity to apply technology in learning and teaching, an opportunity to work in technology--rich learning environment, an exploration of the cultural, administrative, theoretical, and practical implications of technology in education, an introduction to research in technology for education, and an opportunity for those wishing to develop leadership capabilities in the use of technology in education.

Admission Requirements—Applicants should normally hold a recognized bachelor's degree or qualifications of equivalent standard. Applicants may be required to sit for a qualifying examination.

Degree Requirements—To complete the following modules in 1-year full-time study or no more than 4 years of part-time studies: 3 core modules—2 modules from a specialist strand plus either of the following: one independent project and two elective modules, or one dissertation.

Number of Full-Time Faculty—20; **Number of Other Faculty**—90

Name of Institution—Université de Poitiers
Name of Department or Program—Ingénierie des médias pour léducation
Program Website (URL)—http://ll.univ-poitiers.fr/dime/
Name of Contact Person—Jean-François CERISIER
Email Address of Contact Person—cerisier@univ-poitiers.fr
Program Description—EUROMIME: European Master in Media Engineering for Education (Erasmus Mundus master) EUROMIME is a European Master in Media Engineering for Education. It trains project managers in the field of design, development, and implementation of educational and training programs resorting to computer-mediated environments. It also trains researchers specializing the study of the use of these technologies. The master, which gives the right to continuing to doctoral studies, prepares students to work in various settings such as business firms, government agencies, as well as universities. Many of the graduate students work in public or private settings involved in projects related to distance education. MIME: national Master in Media Engineering for Education.

The EUROMIME consortium is composed of seven universities, three in south-west Europe (Université de Poitiers—France; Universidad Nacional de Educación a Distancia, Madrid—España; Universidade Técnica de Lisboa—Portugal) and four in Latin America (Universidad de Los Lagos, Osorno—Chile; Pontificia Universidad Católica del Perú—Lima; Universidade de Brasilia—Brazil; Universidad Nacional Autónoma de México—Mexico). More information: http://www.euromime.org/en/home.

Admission Requirements—Application and interview
Degree Requirements—Bachelor's degree
Number of Full-Time Faculty—25; **Number of Other Faculty**—25

Name of Institution—Ewha Womans University

Name of Department or Program—Educational Technology Department
Program Website (URL)—https://cms.ewha.ac.kr/user/indexMain.action?siteId=et
Name of Contact Person—Myunghee Kang
Email Address of Contact Person—et2670@hanmail.net
Program Description—Theory and Practice of Instructional Technology e-Leaning Design and Development, Quality Assurance HRD/HPT Program development

Undergraduate Master's Program, Ph.D. Program, Special Master's Program for In-- Service Teachers

Admission Requirements—Portfolio Interview English Competency

Degree Requirements—24 credit hours of coursework for Master's 60 credit hours of coursework for Ph.D. and Qualifying Exam Dissertation

Number of Full-Time Faculty—8; **Number of Other Faculty**—2

Name of Institution—Andong National University

Name of Department or Program—Department of Educational Technology, College of Education

Program Website (URL)—http://edutech.andong.ac.kr/~try/2009-10/main1.html

Name of Contact Person—Yong-Chil Yang

Email Address of Contact Person—ycyang@andong.ac.kr

Program Description—Instruction Systems Design and e-HRD major for Master's Degree Educational Technology major for Ph.D.

- Only Department supported by the Ministry of Education in Korea * B.A., M.A. and Ph.D. programs are offered * Established in 1996 * Inexpensive tuition and living expenses * Small class size

Admission Requirements—Fluent commanding English or Korean language

Degree Requirements—B.A. degree for Master M.A. degree in Education for Ph.D.

Number of Full-Time Faculty—5; **Number of Other Faculty**—9

Name of Institution—Universiti Sains Malaysia

Name of Department or Program—Centre for Instructional Technology and Multimedia

Program Website (URL)—http://www.ptpm.usm.my

Name of Contact Person—Wan Mohd. Fauzy Wan Ismail

Email Address of Contact Person—Fauzy@usm.my

Program Description—Instructional Design Web/Internet Instruction and Learning Educational Training/Resource Management Instructional Training Technology/ Evaluation Instructional System Development Design and Development of Multimedia/Video/Training Materials Instructional and Training Technology Constructivism in Instructional Technology E-Learning Systems, Learning Management Systems

Master's in Instructional Technology—entering its third academic year 2004–2005— full-time—1–2 years, part-time—2–4 years. Teaching programs—Postgraduate programs and research consultancy—services on the application of educational/ instructional design technology in teaching and learning Training and Diffusion, Continuing Education in support of Lifelong Learning Academic Support Services—services to support research, teaching, and learning activities and centers within the university

Admission Requirements—Bachelor's and Master's degree from accredited institution or relevant work experience

Degree Requirements—Part-time, full-time

Number of Full-Time Faculty -; **Number of Other Faculty** -.

Name of Institution—Taganrog State Pedagogical Institute
Name of Department or Program—Media Education (Social Pedagogic Faculty)
Program Website (URL)—http://www.tgpi.ru
Name of Contact Person—Alexander Fedorov
Email Address of Contact Person—tgpi@mail.ru
Program Description—Media Education, Media Literacy, Media Competence
Admission Requirements—Various per year, please see http://www.tgpi.ru
Degree Requirements—admission after high school
Number of Full-Time Faculty—10; **Number of Other Faculty**—20

Name of Institution—Keimyung University
Name of Department or Program—Department of Education
Program Website (URL)—https://newcms.kmu.ac.kr/pedagogy/index.do
Name of Contact Person—Wooyong Eom
Email Address of Contact Person—weom@kmu.ac.kr
Program Description -
Admission Requirements -
Degree Requirements -
Number of Full-Time Faculty—9; **Number of Other Faculty**—0

Name of Institution—University of Balearic Islands
Name of Department or Program—Sciences of Education
Program Website (URL)—http://www.uib.es
Name of Contact Person—Jesus Salinas
Email Address of Contact Person—jesus.salinas@uib.es
Program Description—Doctorado Interuniversitario de Tecnología Educativa [Interuniversity Doctorate of Educational Technology. University of Sevilla, University of Murcia, University of Balearic Islands and Rovira i Virgili Universitity—Master en Tecnología Educativa. E-learning y gestión del conocimiento [Master in Educational Technology. E-learning and knowlegde management] . University of Balearic Islands and Universitat Rovira i Virgili—Especialista Universitario en Tecnología Educativa. Diseño y elaboración de medios didácticos multimedia [Specialist in Educational Technology. Design and development of didactic multimedia environments]. "Curso de Dirección y gestión pedagógica de entornos virtuales" [course of direction and pedagogical management of virtual environments]. University of Balearic Islands, Rovira I Virgili University, University of Sevilla, University Central of Venezuela, University of Panamá, Higher Institute Polytechnic Jose Antonio Echevarria.
Admission Requirements -
Degree Requirements -
Number of Full-Time Faculty—6; **Number of Other Faculty**—9

Name of Institution—University of Geneva
Name of Department or Program—TECFA—Master of Science in Learning and Teaching Technologies

Program Website (URL)—http://tecfa.unige.ch

Name of Contact Person—Daniel Peraya

Email Address of Contact Person—Daniel.Peraya@unige.ch

Program Description—Basics in information and communication technologies. Design of computer-supported learning technology. Mediated communication and e-learning. User-centered design and ergonomics. Research methods in educational technologies. Blended education (face-to-face sessions alternately with tutored distance periods). 120 ECTS, 2-year program. Learning approach: mostly project based, with authentic project design and collaborative work. French language

http://edutechwiki.unige.ch/en/Main_Page

Admission Requirements—Applicants should qualify to be admitted in master program at the University of Geneva. For more information, see http://tecfaetu. unige.ch/maltt/staf.php3?id_article=27

Degree Requirements—Bachelor's degree. Training or experience in training, education, or psychology

Number of Full-Time Faculty—4; **Number of Other Faculty**—1

Name of Institution—Università della Svizzera italiana

Name of Department or Program—New Media in Education Laboratory and Red-Ink Doctoral School

Program Website (URL)—www.newmine.org

Name of Contact Person—Lorenzo Cantoni, Luca Botturi

Email Address of Contact Person—luca.botturi@lu.unisi.ch

Program Description—Red-ink is a doctoral school whose name stands for "Rethinking Education in the Knowledge Society." It strives to understand the complex issues related to the introduction, management, and impact of educational technologies and eLearning in the perspective of the new context of the knowledge society. To this purpose, RED-INK federates three Swiss universities in order to establish an outstanding multidisciplinary research team at national level, with expected international visibility and impact. The RED-INK doctoral school is funded by the pro*doc program of the Swiss National Research Fund, started in 2008, and will award its first doctoral degrees in 2010.

Admission Requirements—Completed master's degree in educational technology or related field

Degree Requirements -

Number of Full-Time Faculty—3; **Number of Other Faculty**—0

Name of Institution—Utrecht University

Name of Department or Program—Educational Sciences

Program Website (URL)—http://www.uu.nl/NL/Informatie/master/edsci/Pages/study.aspx

Name of Contact Person—Mieke Brekelmans

Email Address of Contact Person—m.brekelmans@uu.nl

Program Description—The 2-year (120 EC) program concentrates on the theory, use, and effects of innovative teaching and learning arrangements aimed at meaningful, enjoyable learning through the application of different theories, paradigms, and media. Research projects use both experimental design-based and longitudinal approaches and combine qualitative and quantitative analyses of interaction processes and learning products in different teaching and/or learning environments.

The program combines high-level coursework with hands-on research skill and competence development. Students take courses on various theories of learning, instruction, and teaching, and are trained in advanced research techniques and statistical methods to study the design and effectiveness of innovative teaching and learning arrangements. Research seminars help students develop their academic skills. Participation in a senior faculty members research project introduces each student to "hands-on" research. Throughout the program, various electronic learning environments are used to support students in their collaborative study assignments, and to allow them to experiment with these innovative learning and instruction tools. The program offers a systematic theoretical and empirical analysis of educational phenomena and problems. It emphasizes three goals: helping students develop (1) a strong foundation in research and in theories of learning, instruction, and teaching; (2) competence in conducting high-quality educational research; and (3) capacities and skills to apply basic knowledge and specific research methods from various domains to the study of learning in interaction in education. The program concludes with writing a master's thesis in the form of a draft research article for international publication.

Admission Requirements—Applicants should hold a B.A. or B.Sc. in one of the relevant social or behavioral sciences (such as education, psychology, cognitive science, informatics, artificial intelligence) or in a domain relevant to teaching in schools (e.g., math, science, linguistics, history). It is required of applicants to have successfully completed several undergraduate courses on statistics in order to have a basic knowledge of multivariate analysis at the beginning of their first semester. There is a summer school for students who do not meet this requirement. Students meeting the above criteria who have a GPA of at least 2.85 (Dutch equivalent: 7.0) are encouraged to apply for admission. Students will be selected on the basis of their Grade Point Average (GPA) and an essay on their motivation and their recommendations; in some cases, an intake interview will also be conducted. All courses are taught in English; therefore all students are required to provide proof of their English language proficiency. Examples of accepted minimum English language test scores: TOEFL paper: 580. TOEFL computer: 237. TOEFL Internet: 93.

Degree Requirements—Completion of all courses and thesis

Number of Full-Time Faculty—12; **Number of Other Faculty**—7

Name of Institution—Middle East Technical University

Name of Department or Program—Computer Education and Instructional Technology

Program Website (URL)—http://www.ceit.metu.edu.tr

Name of Contact Person—M. Yasar Ozden

Email Address of Contact Person—myozden@metu.edu.tr
Program Description—Computer education, instructional technology
Admission Requirements -
Degree Requirements -
Number of Full-Time Faculty—20; **Number of Other Faculty**—40

Name of Institution—Hacettepe University
Name of Department or Program—Computer Education and Instructional Technology
Program Website (URL)—http://www.ebit.hacettepe.edu.tr/
Name of Contact Person—Arif Altun
Email Address of Contact Person—altunar@hacettepe.edu.tr
Program Description—The CEIT department has been established in 1998. Innovations and improvements in technology have changed so many things in people's life. There have been huge improvements in terms of diffusion of information. Computers continue to make an ever-increasing impact on all aspects of education from primary school to university and in the growing areas of open and distance learning. In addition, the knowledge and skills related to computers have become essential for everybody in the information age. However, at all levels in society there is a huge need for qualified personnel equipped with the skills that help them to be successful in their personal and professional life. The department aims to train students (prospective teachers) who would teach computer courses in K-12 institutions. It also provides individuals with professional skills in the development, organization, and application of resources for the solution of instructional problems within schools.
The department has M.S. and Ph.D. programs. The research areas are learning objects and ontologies, diffusion of innovation, computerized testing, e-learning environments, design, development, and assessment.
Admission Requirements—B.S. in education or computer-related fields
Degree Requirements—B.S.
Number of Full-Time Faculty—10; **Number of Other Faculty**—12

Name of Institution—Anadolu University
Name of Department or Program—Computer Education and Instructional Technology
Program Website (URL)—http://www.anadolu.edu.tr/akademik/fak_egt/bilgveo-grttekegt/eindex.htm
Name of Contact Person—H. Ferhan Odabasi
Email Address of Contact Person—fodabasi@anadolu.edu.tr
Program Description—The basic aim of the department is to equip students, with up-to-date knowledge about computer and other information technologies, required for K-12 computer teachers. Graduated students of the department can be employed in public or private schools of the Ministry of National Education, as teachers, instructional technologists, or academicians in the universities. The department offers bachelor's, master's, and doctorate programs. Both department staff and students collaborate with international schools in terms of teach-

ing and research through exchange programs. Some of the themes, having been studied by academic staff of the department, are computer-assisted instruction, computer-assisted language instruction, educational technology, computer use in education and school systems, effects of technology on individuals, computer anxiety, industrial design, using Internet in education, instructional design, instructional software design, statistics, professional development, ICT action competence, technology integration into education, technology integration into special education, safe Internet use, cyberbullying and digital storytelling, and mobile learning.

Computer Education and Instructional Technologies Department has two computer labs. Technical properties of the computers in both of the labs are up to date. In addition, students can use the main library which is around 100 m to department building. Students may reach many books and journals about computers and instructional technologies and have access to various databases and electronic journals. There is a nonsmoking cafeteria for students in the faculty building where they can find snacks, sandwiches, and hot and cold drinks. There is also a small room for the smokers. There is a main student cafeteria for students on the campus. There are also fast-food restaurants on the campus.

Admission Requirements—High School Diploma plus required scores from the Student Selection Examination administered by Student Selection and Placement Centre and successful completion of qualification examinations. For foreign students, High School Diploma plus required scores from the Foreign Student Examination and successful completion of qualification examinations. Associate Degree plus placement by Student Selection and Placement Centre according to the score obtained in the Student Selection Examination and the student's preferences. In addition, may apply to master's or doctorate programs in any field or proficiency in fine arts programs. May apply to bachelor's degree completion programs in related fields of study in Distance Education System.

Degree Requirements—For bachelor's degree, students are selected by Student Selection and Placement Center according to the student scores in the Student Selection Exam. About 50 students are admitted to the department each year. The duration of the program is 4 years. Students must pass all courses and obtain a minimum Grade Point Average (GPA) of 2.00 before they can graduate. The official language of instruction is Turkish. Students who want to learn English can attend a 1-year English preparatory school before taking the department courses. The students are required to take courses and prepare and defend a thesis based on their research. It takes approximately 2 years to complete the master's degree. The doctorate degree requires coursework and research. The students will conduct original research, prepare a dissertation, and then make an oral defense of their completed research. Students require about 4 years beyond the master's degree to complete a doctorate program.

Number of Full-Time Faculty—12; **Number of Other Faculty**—9

Name of Institution—University of Manchester

Name of Department or Program—M.A.: Digital Technologies, Communication, and Education
Program Website (URL)—http://www.MAdigitaltechnologies.com
Name of Contact Person—Andrew Whitworth
Email Address of Contact Person—andrew.whitworth@manchester.ac.uk
Program Description—Educators from any sector are catered for by the program: that is, primary, secondary (K-12), tertiary/higher education, adult education, corporate training, home educators, private tutors, and so on.
The goals of this program are to promote the use of digital technologies, broadcast media, and/or interpersonal, group, or organizational communications techniques to enhance practice and the professional and academic development of educators in technology-rich environments. There is, therefore, a particular focus on professional development techniques, enquiry-based and problem-based learning, and transformations of practice as well as work with practical EMT techniques (such as Web design, Flash, and video production). Students will study the history of educational media and technology, and its impact on the organization and management of education as well as on pedagogy. The course is available to study in both face-to-face and distance modes.
Admission Requirements—A first degree to at least a 2:2 (UK degree classification) or equivalent. IELTS score of at least 6.5 and preferably 7.0, or 600 in TOEFL. Teaching experience is desirable, though not mandatory.
Degree Requirements -
Number of Full-Time Faculty—2; **Number of Other Faculty**—3

Name of Institution—The Ohio State University
Name of Department or Program—Cultural Foundations, Technology, and Qualitative Inquiry
Program Website (URL)—http://ehe.osu.edu/epl/academics/cftqi/technology.cfm
Name of Contact Person—Rick Voithofer
Email Address of Contact Person—voithofer.2@osu.edu
Program Description—The Technology area in CFTQI offers both M.A. and Ph.D. degrees. This interdisciplinary educational technology program focuses on intersections of learning, technology, and culture in formal and informal education and in society at large. Some of the settings addressed in the program include K-12 environments, distance education, e-learning, online education, higher education, urban education, private and nonprofit organizations, museums, and community-based organizations and programs. Students in the program are exposed to a variety of technologies and media including educational multimedia, computer-based instruction, pod/video casts, blogs and wikis, educational games, Web-based instruction, video, and electronic portfolios. Recent areas of focus studied by faculty and students include educational technology, digital divides, and diverse populations; implications of Web 2.0 technologies for education and globalization; online educational research; education policy and technology; visual culture and visual media multiliteracies, learning, and technology; games and simulations technology; virtuality; and student identities. Students in

this area integrate theoretical and practical studies of technologies and media through pedagogical, social, cultural, economic, historical, and political inquiry and critique, in addition to the production of educational media and cultural artifacts.

http://www.facebook.com/pages/Ohio-State-University-Educational-Technology-Program/138548946182406

Admission Requirements—Please see http://ehe.osu.edu/epl/academics/cftqi/downloads/cftqi-checklist.pdf

Degree Requirements—Please see http://ehe.osu.edu/epl/academics/cftqi/degree-req.cfm

Number of Full-Time Faculty—3; **Number of Other Faculty**—2

Name of Institution—Widener University
Name of Department or Program—Instructional Technology
Program Website (URL)—http://www.educator.widener.edu
Name of Contact Person—Kathleen A. Bowes
Email Address of Contact Person—kabowes@Widener.Edu
Program Description—Instructional Technology, Educational Leadership
Wideners Instructional Technology program has three branches: (1) Master's of Education in Instructional Technology, (2) Instructional Technology Specialist Certification (PA nonteaching certificate), and (3) Doctor of School Administration with an Instructional Technology Tract. Most courses are hybrids.
Admission Requirements—3.0 undergraduate, MAT's three letters of recommendation, writing sample
Degree Requirements—undergraduate degree
Number of Full-Time Faculty—1; **Number of Other Faculty**—4

Name of Institution—University of Alabama
Name of Department or Program—School of Library and Information Studies
Program Website (URL)—http://www.slis.ua.edu
Name of Contact Person—Joan Atkinson, Director; Gordy Coleman, Coordinator of School Media Program
Email Address of Contact Person—vwright@bamaed.ua.edu
Program Description—M.L.I.S. degrees in a varied program including school, public, academic, and special libraries. Ph.D. in the larger College of Communication and Information Sciences; flexibility in creating individual programs of study. Also a Master of Fine Arts Program in Book Arts (including history of the book)
M.L.I.S. is one of 56 accredited programs in the United States and Canada.
Admission Requirements—M.L.I.S.: 3.0 GPA; 50 MAT or 1000 GRE and an acceptable score on analytical writing. Doctoral: 3.0 GPA; 60 MAT or 1200 GRE and an acceptable score on analytical writing
Degree Requirements—Master's: 36 semester hours. Doctoral: 48–60 semester hours plus 24-h dissertation research
Number of Full-Time Faculty—; **Number of Other Faculty** -

Name of Institution—University of Central Arkansas
Name of Department or Program—Leadership Studies
Program Website (URL)—http://www.coe.uca.edu/
Name of Contact Person—Stephanie Huffman
Email Address of Contact Person—steph@uca.edu
Program Description—M.S. in Library Media and Information Technologies is School Library Media program.
Admission Requirements—Transcripts, GRE scores, and a copy of the candidates teaching certificate
Degree Requirements—36 semester hours, practicum (for School Library Media), and a professional portfolio
Number of Full-Time Faculty—4; **Number of Other Faculty**—2

Name of Institution—California State University at East Bay
Name of Department or Program—Educational Technology Leadership
Program Website (URL)—http://edtech.csueastbay.edu
Name of Contact Person—Bijan Gillani
Email Address of Contact Person—bijan.gillani@csueastbay.edu
Program Description—Advances in the field of technology and the explosive growth of the Internet in recent years have revolutionized the way instruction is delivered to students. In parallel with these technological advances, the field of Learning Sciences has made phenomenal contributions to how people learn. For the most part, the advances in these two fields (technology and learning sciences) have gone their separate ways. A synergy of these two fields would enable educators and instructional designers to design and develop more effective educational materials to be transmitted over the Internet. To provide a solution for this synergy we the Institute of Learning Sciences and Technology focuses on providing a systematic and more intelligent approach to the design of e-learning environments by applying the research findings in the field of Learning Sciences to the design and development of technological environments.
How do people learn? What are learning theories? What are the instructional principles that we can derive from learning theories? How can we apply these instructional principles to the design of meaningful learning with existing and emerging technology? How do we make these principles accessible to faculty who wish to use technology more effectively? How do we develop pedagogically sound learning environments that prepare students to pursue meaningful lifework that has local and global contribution?
Admission Requirements—A completed University Graduate Application (online only). Two official copies of each transcript (mail to the enrollment office). Statement of residency (mail to the department). A department application form (mail to the department). Two letters of recommendations (mail to the department), GPA 3.0
Degree Requirements—(1) Completion of required 24 units of core courses. (2) Completion of 16 units of elective courses. (3) Completion of master's degree project or thesis project. (4) Completion of graduate checklist (online and forms)

Number of Full-Time Faculty—3; **Number of Other Faculty**—3

Name of Institution—California State University-San Bernardino
Name of Department or Program—Department of Science, Mathematics, and Technology Education
Program Website (URL)—http://www.csusb.edu/coe/programs/inst_tech/index.htm
Name of Contact Person—Amy Leh
Email Address of Contact Person—aleh@csusb.edu
Program Description—Technology integration, online instruction, instructional design, STEM education
Preparing educators in K-12, corporate, and higher education
Admission Requirements—Bachelor's degree, 3.0 GPA, completion of university writing requirement
Degree Requirements—48 units including a master's project (33 units completed in residence); 3.0 GPA; grades of "C" or better in all courses
Number of Full-Time Faculty—4; **Number of Other Faculty**—2

Name of Institution—San Diego State University
Name of Department or Program—Educational Technology
Program Website (URL)—http://edtec.sdsu.edu/
Name of Contact Person—Marcie Bober
Email Address of Contact Person—bober@mail.sdsu.edu
Program Description—Certificate in Instructional Technology. Advanced Certificate in Distance Learning, and Software Design. Master's degree in Education with an emphasis on Educational Technology. Doctorate in Education with an emphasis on Educational Technology (a joint program with the University of San Diego).
Focuses on design of intervention to improve human performance via strategies that combine theory and practice in relevant, real-world experiences. Offers both campus and online programs.
Admission Requirements—Please refer to SDSU Graduate bulletin at http://libweb.sdsu.edu/bulletin/. Requirements include a minimum score of 950 on the GRE (verbal + quantitative), and 4.5 on the analytical. See our website at http://edtec.sdsu.edu for more information.
Degree Requirements—36 semester hours for the master's (including 6 prerequisite hours). 15 to 18 semester hours for the certificates
Number of Full-Time Faculty -; **Number of Other Faculty** -

Name of Institution—San Jose State University
Name of Department or Program—Instructional Technology
Program Website (URL)—http://sweeneyhall.sjsu.edu/depts/it
Name of Contact Person—Robertta Barba
Email Address of Contact Person—rbarba@email.sjsu.edu
Program Description—Master's degree in education with an emphasis on Instructional Technology

Admission Requirements—Baccalaureate degree from approved university, appropriate work experience, minimum GPA of 2.5, and minimum score of 550 on TOEFL (Test of English as a Foreign Language). 36 semester hours (which includes 6 prerequisite hours)

Degree Requirements—30 units of approved graduate studies

Number of Full-Time Faculty -; **Number of Other Faculty** -

Name of Institution—University of Southern California, Rossier School of Education

Name of Department or Program—Educational Psychology and Instructional Technology

Program Website (URL)—http://www.usc.edu/dept/education/academic/masters/index.htm

Name of Contact Person—For Admissions Info (soeinfo@usc.edu), for general program info (rsoemast@usc.edu), for specific program info (rueda@usc.edu)

Email Address of Contact Person—rsoemast@usc.edu

Program Description—The Educational Psychology/Instructional Technology program focuses on learning and motivation, emphasizing the study of new information and performance technologies used to improve instruction among diverse student populations. To understand human learning, educational psychologists' study areas include motivation; developmental and individual differences; social, cultural, and group processes; instructional technology; and evaluation of instruction. Students will be prepared to apply a wide range of computer and telecommunications technologies in achieving educational goals within school, community, corporate, and public settings.

Distinctive Features—Focus on learning and motivation with a strong emphasis on technology and a major concern with urban education settings. Major objective is to learn how to diagnose and solve learning and motivation problems, especially those characteristic of urban learning settings. Faculty are well known in the field and are active researchers. Special emphasis upon instructional design, human performance at work, systems analysis, and computer-based training.

Admission Requirements—Bachelor's degree, 1000 GRE

Degree Requirements—Program of study: 28 units, 7 core courses, and 2 elective courses. Core courses: EDPT 576 Technology in Contemporary Education and Training. EDPT 550 Statistical Inference. EDPT 502 Learning and Individual Differences. EDPT 510 Human Learning. EDPT 540 Introduction to Educational Measurement and Evaluation. EDPT 571 Instructional Design. CTSE 593A and B Master's Seminar. Electives (two classes): EDPT 511 Human Motivation in Education. EDPT 520 Human Lifespan Development. EDPT 570 Language and Cultural Diversity in Learning. CTSE 573 Management of Instructional Resources. EDPA 671 The Computer and Data Processing Education

Number of Full-Time Faculty -; **Number of Other Faculty** -

Name of Institution—Azusa Pacific University

Name of Department or Program—EDUCABS—Advanced Studies

Program Website (URL)—http://www.apu.edu

Name of Contact Person—Kathleen Bacer

Email Address of Contact Person—kbacer@apu.edu

Program Description—Educational technology, online learning, infusing technology in teaching/learning environments, digital learning for the twenty-first-century learner.

100% Online Master of Arts in Educational Technology program designed for the K-12 educator

Admission Requirements—Undergraduate degree from accredited institution with at least 12 units in education, 3.0 GPA

Degree Requirements—36-unit program

Number of Full-Time Faculty—2; **Number of Other Faculty**—8

Name of Institution—San Francisco State University

Name of Department or Program—College of Education, Department of Instructional Technology

Program Website (URL)—www.itec.sfsu.edu

Name of Contact Person—Kim Foreman

Email Address of Contact Person—kforeman@sfsu.edu

Program Description—Master's degree with emphasis on Instructional Multimedia Design, Training and Designing Development, and Instructional Computing. The school also offers an 18-unit Graduate Certificate in Training Systems Development, which can be incorporated into the master's degree. This program emphasizes the instructional systems approach to train teachers, trainers, and e-learning professionals by providing practical design experience in the field. Most of our courses are delivered both face to face and online.

Admission Requirements—Bachelor's degree, appropriate work experience, 2.5 GPA, purpose statement, two letters of recommendation, interview with the department chair

Degree Requirements—30 semester hours, field study project, or thesis. Three to nine units of prerequisites, assessed at entrance to the program

Number of Full-Time Faculty—3; **Number of Other Faculty**—9

Name of Institution—University of Colorado Denver

Name of Department or Program—School of Education and Human Development

Program Website (URL)—http://www.ucdenver.edu/academics/colleges/SchoolOfEducation/Academics/MASTERS/ILT/Pages/eLearning.aspx

Name of Contact Person—Brent Wilson

Email Address of Contact Person—brent.wilson@cudenver.edu

Program Description—M.A. in Information and Learning Technologies (ILT)—includes options for eLearning, K-12 Teaching, Instructional Design/Adult Learning, and School Librarianship. Graduate certificates are available in eLearning Design and Implementation (15 graduate credits), and Digital Storytelling (9 graduate credits). The Ed.D. in Educational Equity is available with concentration in adult education and professional learning, where students can focus on learning technologies. A Ph.D. program option is also available for those choosing careers in higher education and research. The ILT program

Graduate Programs in Learning, Design, Technology, Information, or Libraries   213

focuses on design and use of digital learning resources and social support for online learning. Master's students prepare a professional portfolio, published online, that showcases their skills and accomplishments. The doctoral program is cross-disciplinary, drawing on expertise in technology, adult learning, professional development, social justice, systemic change, research methods, reflective practice, and cultural studies.

Admission Requirements—M.A. and Ph.D.: satisfactory GPA, GRE, writing sample, letters of recommendation, transcripts. See website for more detail.

Degree Requirements—M.A.: 30 semester hours including 27 h of core coursework; professional portfolio; field experience. Ed.D.: 50 semester hours of coursework and labs, plus 20 dissertation hours; dissertation

Number of Full-Time Faculty—3; **Number of Other Faculty**—8

Name of Institution—Fairfield University
Name of Department or Program—Educational Technology
Program Website (URL)—http://www.fairfield.edu
Name of Contact Person—Dr. Elizabeth Langran, Director, Educational Technology Program; Dr. Gayle Bogel, Assistant Professor of Educational Technology
Email Address of Contact Person—graded@mail.fairfield.edu
Program Description—M.A. in Educational Technology; certification (initial and cross-endorsement) in School Library Media. Emphasis on theory, practice, and new instructional developments in computers in education, multimedia, school/media, and applied technology in education
Admission Requirements—See http://fairfield.edu/gseap/gseap_policies.html.
Degree Requirements—33 credits. Additional coursework for certification
Number of Full-Time Faculty—2; **Number of Other Faculty**—5

Name of Institution—University of Connecticut
Name of Department or Program—Educational Psychology
Program Website (URL)—http://www.epsy.uconn.edu/
Name of Contact Person—Michael Young
Email Address of Contact Person—myoung@UConn.edu
Program Description—M.A. in Educational Technology (portfolio or thesis options), 1-year partially online master's (summer, fall, spring, summer), 6th-year certificate in Educational Technology, and Ph.D. in Learning Technology
M.A. can be on campus or two summers (on campus) and fall-spring (online) that can be completed in a year. The Ph.D. emphasis on Learning Technology is a unique program at UConn. It strongly emphasizes cognitive science and how technology can be used to enhance the way people think and learn. The Program seeks to provide students with knowledge of theory and applications regarding the use of advanced technology to enhance learning and thinking. Campus facilities include $2 billion twenty-first-century UConn enhancement to campus infrastructure, including a new wing to the Neag School of Education. Faculty research interests include interactive video for anchored instruction and situated learning, telecommunications for cognitive apprenticeship, technology-mediated

interactivity for learning by design activities, and, in cooperation with the National Research Center for Gifted and Talented, research on the use of technology to enhance cooperative learning and the development of gifted performance in all students.

Admission Requirements—Admission to the graduate school at UConn, GRE scores (or other evidence of success at the graduate level). Previous experience in a related area of technology, education, or experience in education or training

Degree Requirements—Completion of plan of study coursework, comprehensive exam (portfolio based on multiple requirements), and completion of an approved dissertation

Number of Full-Time Faculty -; **Number of Other Faculty** -

Name of Institution—Florida Institute of Technology

Name of Department or Program—Science and Mathematics Education Department

Program Website (URL)—http://www.fit.edu/catalog/sci-lib/comp-edu.html#master-info

Name of Contact Person—David Cook

Email Address of Contact Person—dcook@fit.edu

Program Description—Master's degree in Computer Education. Ph.D. degree in Science Education with options for research and major technical area concentrations in Computer Science, Computer Education, and Instructional Technology. Flexible program depending on student experience

Admission Requirements—Master's: 3.0 GPA for regular admission. Ph.D.: Master's degree and 3.2 GPA

Degree Requirements—Master's: 33 semester hours (15 in computer and/or technology education, 9 in education, 9 electives); practicum; no thesis or internship required or 30 semester hours. For thesis option: Ph.D.: 42 semester hours (includes dissertation and research; also requires 21 graduate hours in computer science/computer information systems, 6 of which may be applicable to the required 42 h)

Number of Full-Time Faculty—2; **Number of Other Faculty**—4

Name of Institution—Barry University

Name of Department or Program—Department of Educational Computing and Technology, School of Education

Program Website (URL)—http://www.barry.edu/ed/programs/masters/ect/default.htm

Name of Contact Person—Donna Lenaghan

Email Address of Contact Person—dlenaghan@bu4090.barry.edu

Program Description—M.S. and Ed.S. in Educational Technology Applications and Ph.D. degree in Educational Technology Leadership. These programs and courses prepare educators to integrate computer/technologies in their disciplines and/or train individuals to use computers/technologies. The focus is on improving the teaching and learning process thought integration of technologies into curricula and learning activities.

Graduate Programs in Learning, Design, Technology, Information, or Libraries 215

Admission Requirements—GRE scores, letters of recommendation, GPA, interview, achievements

Degree Requirements—M.S. or Ed. S.: 36 semester credit hours. Ph.D.: 54 credits beyond the master's including dissertation credits

Number of Full-Time Faculty -; **Number of Other Faculty** -

Name of Institution—Florida State University

Name of Department or Program—Educational Psychology and Learning Systems

Program Website (URL)—http://insys.fsu.edu

Name of Contact Person—Mary Kate McKee, Program Coordinator

Email Address of Contact Person—mmckee@oddl.fsu.edu

Program Description—M.S. and Ph.D. in Instructional Systems with specializations for persons planning to work in academia, business, industry, government, or military, both in the United States and in international settings. Core courses include systems and materials development, performance improvement, online learning, development of multimedia, project management, psychological foundations, current trends in instructional design, and research and statistics. Internships are recommended. Strong alumni network. M.S. courses available both on campus and online.

Admission Requirements—M.S.: 3.0 GPA in last 2 years of undergraduate program, 1000 GRE (verbal plus quantitative), 550 TOEFL (for international applicants). Ph.D.: 1100 GRE (V + Q), 3.5 GPA in last 2 years; international students, 550 TOEFL

Degree Requirements—M.S.: 36 semester hours, 2–4-h internship, comprehensive exam preparation of professional portfolio

Number of Full-Time Faculty—4; **Number of Other Faculty**—4

Name of Institution—University of Central Florida

Name of Department or Program—College of Education—ERTL

Program Website (URL)—http://www.education.ucf.edu/insttech/

Name of Contact Person—Dr. Atsusi Hirumi, Dr. Glenda Gunter

Email Address of Contact Person—atsusi.hirumi@ucf.edu

Program Description—Graduate certificates in (a) Instructional Design of Simulations, (b) Educational Technology, and (c) e-Learning Professional Development. M.A. in Instructional Design and Technology with professional tracks in Instructional Systems, Educational Technology and e-Learning, Ph.D. in Education with Instructional Design and Technology track. Ed.D. in Education with Instructional Design and Technology concentration. There are approximately 120 students in M.A. program, 5 in Ed.D. and 30 in Ph.D. programs.

All programs rely heavily on understanding of fundamental competencies as reflected by NCATE, ASTD, AECT, AASL, and ISTE. There is an emphasis on the practical application of theory through intensive hands-on experiences. Orlando and the surrounding area are home to a plethora of high-tech companies, military training and simulation organizations, and tourist attractions. UCF, established in 1963, now has in excess of 36,000 students, representing more than 90 countries. It has been ranked as one of the leading "most-wired" universities in North America.

Admission Requirements—GRE score of 1000 for consideration for doctoral program. No GRE required for M.A. or graduate certificate programs. GPA of 3.0 or greater in last 60 h of undergraduate degree for M.A. program; TOEFL of 550 (270 computer-based version) if English is not the first language; three letters of recommendation; resume; statement of goals; residency statement; and health record. Financial statement if coming from overseas

Degree Requirements—M.A. in Instructional Technology/Instructional Systems, 39 semester hours; M.A. in Instructional Technology/Educational Technology, 39 semester hours; M.A. in Instructional Technology/eLearning, 39 semester hours. Practicum required in all three programs; thesis, research project, or substitute additional coursework. Ph.D. and Ed.D. require between 58 and 69 h beyond the master's for completion.

Number of Full-Time Faculty—3; **Number of Other Faculty**—5

Name of Institution—University of South Florida

Name of Department or Program—Instructional Technology Program, Secondary Education Department, College of Education

Program Website (URL)—http://www.coedu.usf.edu/it

Name of Contact Person—Dr. William Kealy, Graduate Certificates; Dr. Frank Breit, Master's program; Dr. Ann Barron, Education Specialist program; Dr. James White, Doctoral program

Email Address of Contact Person—IT@coedu.usf.edu

Program Description—Graduate Certificates in Web Design, Instructional Design, Multimedia Design, School Networks, and Distance Education; M.Ed., Ed.S., and Ph.D. in Curriculum and Instruction with emphasis on Instructional Technology. Many students gain practical experience in the Florida Center for Instructional Technology (FCIT), which provides services to the Department of Education and other grants and contracts; the Virtual Instructional Team for the Advancement of Learning (VITAL), which provides USF faculty with course development services; and Educational Outreach. The College of Education is one of the largest in the United States in terms of enrollment and facilities. As of Fall 1997, a new, technically state-of-the-art building was put into service. The University of South Florida has been classified by the Carnegie Foundation as a Doctoral/Research University-Extensive.

Admission Requirements—See http://www.coedu.usf.edu/it

Degree Requirements—See http://www.coedu.usf.edu/it

Number of Full-Time Faculty -; **Number of Other Faculty** -

Name of Institution—Georgia State University

Name of Department or Program—Middle-Secondary Education and Instructional Technology

Program Website (URL)—http://edtech.gsu.edu

Name of Contact Person—Stephen W. Harmon

Email Address of Contact Person—swharmon@gsu.edu

Program Description—M.S. and Ph.D. in Instructional Design and Technology. Endorsement in Online Teaching and Learning. Focus on research and practical application of instructional technology in educational and corporate settings. Online M.S. in Instructional Design and Technology available

Admission Requirements—M.S.: Bachelor's degree, 2.5 undergraduate GPA, 800 GRE, 550 TOEFL. Ph.D.: Master's degree, 3.30 graduate GPA, 500 verbal plus 500 quantitative GRE, or 500 analytical GRE.

Degree Requirements—M.S.: 36 sem. hours, internship, portfolio, comprehensive examination. Ph.D.: 66 sem. hours, internship, comprehensive examination, dissertation

Number of Full-Time Faculty—5; **Number of Other Faculty**—2

Name of Institution—Valdosta State University
Name of Department or Program—Curriculum, Leadership, and Technology
Program Website (URL)—http://www.valdosta.edu/coe/clt/
Name of Contact Person—Ellen Wiley
Email Address of Contact Person—ewiley@valdosta.edu
Program Description—M.Ed. in Instructional Technology with two tracks: Library/Media or Technology Applications; Online Ed.S. in Instructional Technology with two tracks: Library/Media or Technology Applications; Ed.D. in Curriculum and Instruction

The program has a strong emphasis on systematic design and technology in M.Ed., Ed.S., and Ed.D. Strong emphasis on change leadership, reflective practice, applied research in Ed.S. and Ed.D.

Admission Requirements—M.Ed.: 2.5 GPA, 800 GRE. Ed.S.: Master's degree, 3 years of experience, 3.0 GPA, 850 GRE, MAT 390, and less than 5 years old. Ed.D.: Master's degree, 3 years of experience, 3.50 GPA, 1000 GRE

Degree Requirements—M.Ed.: 33 semester hours. Ed.S.: 27 semester hours. Ed.D.: 54 semester hours

Number of Full-Time Faculty—12; **Number of Other Faculty**—4

Name of Institution—University of Hawaii-Manoa
Name of Department or Program—Department of Educational Technology
Program Website (URL)—http://etec.hawaii.edu
Name of Contact Person—Catherine P. Fulford
Email Address of Contact Person—edtech-dept@hawaii.edu
Program Description—M.Ed. in Educational Technology. This nationally accredited program prepares students to create resources for teaching and learning through diverse media as well as integrate technology into educational environments. Educational Technology (ETEC) provides theoretical knowledge and scientific principles that can be applied to problems that arise in a social context; prepares individuals to devise effective messages, teams, materials, devices, techniques, and settings; and involves the study of theory and practice of design, development, utilization, management, and evaluation of processes and resources for learning. Practitioners in educational technology, whether they are teachers, trainers, developers, administrators, or support personnel, seek innovative and

effective ways of organizing the teaching and learning process through the best possible application of technological developments. The program places emphasis on applications of technology in educational settings rather than simple technical skills. Individuals from diverse backgrounds can immediately apply what they learn to their particular context. Upon graduation, these new professionals will have a clearer vision of how they can prepare learners for the future. ETEC graduates are found in many learning environments including K-12 and higher education, government, business, industry, and health occupations.

Admission Requirements—A baccalaureate degree from an accredited institution in any field of study is acceptable to the Department, provided that the students' undergraduate scholastic record is acceptable to the Graduate Division. A "B" average (i.e., 3.0 on a 4-point scale) in the last 60 semester hours of the undergraduate program is required for regular admission. Students from foreign countries must submit the results of the Test of English as a Foreign Language (TOEFL). The minimum score is 600, representing approximately the 77th percentile rank. Students must submit an "Intent to Apply for Admission Form," a "Graduate Program Supplemental Information Form," and a "Statement of Objectives Form." These are available on the ETEC website. Three letters of recommendation, to be submitted with the application for admission, should evaluate the applicant's potential in the field of educational technology, not only his/her academic abilities to do graduate work. All applicants should submit a resume, and additional materials, documentation, or samples of work relevant to the evaluation and selection process.

Degree Requirements—The ETEC M.Ed. program requires a minimum of 36 semester credit hours, with 7 required and 5 elective ETEC courses. All required and most elective courses are 3 credits each. Full-time students usually complete their coursework in two academic years. Students attending part-time may take three or more years to finish program requirements. Of the seven required courses, four comprise the core of the Educational Technology program. Students are required to complete the core courses in sequence during the first year. The program is designed as a cohort system in which students admitted at the same time take initial courses together to build a sense of support and professional community. In the final year of the program the students will complete an electronic portfolio and final master's project.

Number of Full-Time Faculty—7; **Number of Other Faculty**—7

Name of Institution—University of Northern Iowa

Name of Department or Program—Instructional Technology Program

Program Website (URL)—http://www.uni.edu/itech

Name of Contact Person—Leigh E. Zeitz

Email Address of Contact Person—leigh.zeitz@uni.edu

Program Description—M.A. in Curriculum and Instruction: Instructional Technology. The Instructional Technology Master's is designed to prepare educators for a variety of professional positions in K-12 and adult learning/corporate educational settings. This is a hands-on program that requires students to apply the theoretical foundations presented in the courses. The UNI Instructional Technology Master's program is available both online and on campus. A 2-year cohort is initiated during the summer in even-numbered years. The program's practical perspective prepares professionals for fulfilling technology leadership roles. On a PK-12 level, these roles include technology coordinators, master teachers, special education media specialists, and county educational specialists. On an adult and corporate level, the roles include instructors at vocational-technical schools, community colleges, and universities. They can work as trainers in the corporate world as well as higher education. Many of our graduates have also become successful instructional designers throughout the country. The master's degree is aligned with the AECT/ECIT standards and is focused on addressing specific career choices.

Admission Requirements—Bachelor's degree, 3.0 undergraduate GPA, 500 TOEFL Licensure as a teacher is not required for admission to the master's program. The bachelor's degree may be in any field.

Degree Requirements—35 semester credits. Research paper (literature review, project report, journal article, or research report on original research) is required. A thesis option is available. An online digital portfolio will be created by each student to share and reflect upon the student's learning experiences in the program.

Number of Full-Time Faculty—2; **Number of Other Faculty**—3

Name of Institution—Governors State University
Name of Department or Program—College of Arts and Sciences
Program Website (URL)—http://www.govst.edu/hpt
Name of Contact Person—Mary Lanigan
Email Address of Contact Person—mlanigan@govst.edu
Program Description—M.A. in Communication and Training with HP&T major— Program concentrates on building instructional design skills. Most classes are delivered in a hybrid format of online and face to face. Some classes are almost all online.

Instructional Design overview: front-end analysis including both needs and task; design and delivery using various platforms; evaluation skills and how to predict behavior transfer; various technologies; consulting; project management; systems thinking; principles of message design; and more

Admission Requirements—Undergraduate degree in any field; 2.75 GPA and a statement of purpose

Degree Requirements—36 credit hours. All in instructional and performance technology; internship or advanced field project required. Metropolitan Chicago area based

Number of Full-Time Faculty—1; **Number of Other Faculty**—3

Name of Institution—Southern Illinois University at Carbondale
Name of Department or Program—Department of Curriculum and Instruction
Program Website (URL)—http://idt.siu.edu/
Name of Contact Person—Sharon Shrock

Email Address of Contact Person—sashrock@siu.edu

Program Description—M.S.Ed. in Curriculum and Instruction (with specializations in Instructional Design and Instructional Technology); Ph.D. in Education (with concentration in Instructional Technology). All specializations are oriented to multiple education settings. The ID program emphasizes nonschool (primarily corporate) learning environments, human performance technology, and criterion-referenced performance assessment. The IT program covers many essential skills and tools leading to the production of e-learning and performance assessment using digital games and other virtual learning environments.

Admission Requirements—M.S.: Bachelor's degree, 2.7 undergraduate GPA, transcripts. Ph.D.: Master's degree, 3.25 GPA, GRE scores, three letters of recommendation, transcripts, writing sample

International students without a degree from a US institution must submit TOEFL score.

Degree Requirements—M.S.: 32 credit hours with thesis; 36 credit hours without thesis. Ph.D.: 40 credit hours beyond the master's degree in courses, 24 credit hours for the dissertation

Number of Full-Time Faculty—3; **Number of Other Faculty**—1

Name of Institution—University of Illinois at Urbana-Champaign

Name of Department or Program—Curriculum, Technology, and Education Reform (CTER) Program, Department of Educational Psychology

Program Website (URL)—http://cter.ed.uiuc.edu

Name of Contact Person—Doe-Hyung Kim

Email Address of Contact Person—cter-info-L@listserv.illinois.edu

Program Description—Ed.M. in Educational Psychology with emphasis on Curriculum, Technology, and Education Reform. This Master of Education program is geared toward teachers and trainers interested in learning more about the integration of computer-based technology in the classroom. This online set of project-based courses offers an opportunity to earn a coherent, high-quality master's degree online, with most interactions through personal computers and Internet connections at home or workplace.

Admission Requirements—Application to the Graduate College, three letters of recommendation, personal statement. For more information go to http://cterport.ed.uiuc.edu/admissions_folder/application_procedures_html.

Degree Requirements—Eight courses (5 requirements + 3 electives) required for Ed.M.

Number of Full-Time Faculty—4; **Number of Other Faculty**—2

Name of Institution—Northern Illinois University

Name of Department or Program—Educational Technology, Research, and Assessment

Program Website (URL)—http://www.cedu.niu.edu/etra

Name of Contact Person—Jeffrey B. Hecht

Email Address of Contact Person—edtech@niu.edu

Program Description—M.S.Ed. in Instructional Technology with concentrations in Instructional Design, Distance Education, Educational Computing, and Media Administration; Ed.D. in Instructional Technology, emphasizing instructional design and development, computer education, media administration, and preparation for careers in business, industry, and higher education. In addition, Illinois state certification in school library media is offered in conjunction with either degree or alone. Program is highly individualized. All facilities were remodeled and modernized in 2002–2003 featuring five smart classrooms and over 110 students use desktop and laptop computers. Specialized equipment for digital audio and video editing, website and CD creation, and presentations. All students are encouraged to create portfolios highlighting personal accomplishments and works (required at master's). Master's program started in 1968, and doctorate in 1970.

Admission Requirements—M.S.Ed.: 2.75 undergraduate GPA, GRE verbal and quantitative scores, two references. Ed.D.: 3.25 M.S. GPA, writing sample, three references, interview

Degree Requirements—M.S.Ed.: 39 h, including 30 in instructional technology; portfolio. Ed.D.: 63 h beyond master's, including 15 h for dissertation

Number of Full-Time Faculty -; **Number of Other Faculty** -

Name of Institution—Southern Illinois University Edwardsville
Name of Department or Program—Instructional Technology Program
Program Website (URL)—http://www.siue.edu/education/edld/it/index.shtml
Name of Contact Person—Melissa Thomeczek
Email Address of Contact Person—mthomec@siue.edu
Program Description—The Educational Technologies option enables teachers and other school personnel to learn how to plan, implement, and evaluate technology--based instruction and learning activities in p-12 settings. Students pursuing this option will become knowledgeable users of technology as well as designers of curriculum and instruction that effectively utilize and integrate technology to improve student learning. Students interested in leadership roles in educational technology, such as those wishing to become technology coordinators in schools or school districts, can work toward meeting the standards for the Illinois State Board of Education's (ISBE) Technology Specialist endorsement through this program. The Library Information Specialist option enables teachers and other school personnel to learn how to plan, implement, and evaluate library information-based activities in P-12 settings. Students pursuing this option will become knowledgeable users of library information as well as designers of curriculum and instruction that effectively utilize and integrate library information to improve student learning. Students interested in Library Information Specialist endorsement can work toward meeting the standards for the Illinois State Board of Education's Library Information Specialist endorsement through this program. The Instructional Design and Performance Improvement option focuses on skills necessary for careers in the areas of instructional technology, performance technology, instructional design, training, and performance consulting.

Emphasis is placed on systematic instructional design and on the use of various media and technologies for learning and instruction. Students in this option may also focus on the design and development of online learning and other performance improvement strategies. The Interactive Multimedia Technologies option is appropriate for people wishing to pursue the design and development of various interactive multimedia and Web-based learning experiences. This option prepares students for careers with publishing and production companies, consulting firms, and other businesses that produce engaging multimedia applications for learning and other opportunities. Coursework focuses on theories and methods for designing compelling user experiences, developing skills with tools for Web and other delivery media, and project management strategies. Several unique features of the program provide students with opportunities for important practical experiences that complement coursework. Juried presentations provide students with an opportunity to share their work with a jury of professors and peers and defend their work in light of their own goals and the content of their degree program. Design studios provide students with opportunities to work on real-world projects for a variety of real clients in order to develop skills in collaboration, design, development tools and techniques, and project management.

Admission Requirements—The requirements for admission are a bachelor's degree and a GPA of 3.0 or above during their last 2 years of undergraduate work.

Degree Requirements—36 semester hours; thesis or final project options

Number of Full-Time Faculty—4; **Number of Other Faculty**—1

Name of Institution—Indiana State University

Name of Department or Program—Department of Curriculum, Instruction, and Media Technology

Program Website (URL) -

Name of Contact Person—James E. Thompson

Email Address of Contact Person—espowers@isugw.indstate.edu

Program Description—Master's degree in Instructional Technology with education focus or with noneducation focus; Specialist Degree program in Instructional Technology; Ph.D. in Curriculum, Instruction with specialization in Media Technology

Admission Requirements -

Degree Requirements—Master's: 32 semester hours, including 18 in media; thesis optional; Ed.S.: 60 semester hours beyond bachelor's degree; Ph.D.: approximately 100 h beyond bachelor's degree

Number of Full-Time Faculty -; **Number of Other Faculty** -

Name of Institution—Clarke College

Name of Department or Program—Graduate Studies

Program Website (URL)—http://www.clarke.edu

Name of Contact Person—Margaret Lynn Lester

Email Address of Contact Person—llester@clarke.edu

Program Description—M.A.E. (two tracks: Instructional Leadership and Literacy)

The Instructional Leadership track of this program offers hybrid courses in educational technology. Courses are offered through WEB-ST and face to face. Outcomes are aligned with the National Educational Technology Standards for Educators.

Admission Requirements—Completed graduate application, official transcripts, photocopy of all teaching certificates and licenses, 2.75 GPA (4-point scale), two letters of reference, interview, statement of goals, and $25 application fee (minimum TOEFL score of 550 if English is not the first language)

Degree Requirements—9 h in Research Core; 9 h in Instructional Core; and 18 h in Instructional Leadership Track

Number of Full-Time Faculty -; **Number of Other Faculty** -

Name of Institution—Iowa State University
Name of Department or Program—College of Education
Program Website (URL)—http://www.educ.iastate.edu/
Name of Contact Person—Niki Davis
Email Address of Contact Person—pkendall@iastate.edu
Program Description—M.Ed., M.S., and Ph.D. in Curriculum and Instructional Technology. Features: Prepares candidates as practitioners and researchers in the field of curriculum and instructional technology. All areas of specialization emphasize appropriate and effective applications of technology in teacher education. M.Ed. program also offered at a distance (online and face-to-face learning experiences).

Practicum experiences related to professional objectives, supervised study, and research projects tied to long-term studies within the program, development, and implementation of new techniques, teaching strategies, and operational procedures in instructional resource centers and computer labs, program emphasis on technologies for teachers.

Admission Requirements—Admission requirements: M.Ed. and M.S.: Bachelor's degree, top half of undergraduate class, official transcripts, three letters, autobiography. Ph.D.: top half of undergraduate class, official transcripts, three letters, autobiography, GRE scores, scholarly writing sample

Degree Requirements—Degree requirements: M.Ed.: 32 credit hours (7 research, 12 foundations, 13 applications and leadership in instructional technology); and action research project. M.S.: 36 credit hours (16 research, 12 foundations, 8 applications and leadership in instructional technology) and thesis. Ph.D.: 78 credit hours (minimum of 12 research, minimum of 15 foundations, additional core credits in conceptual, technical, and advanced specialization areas, minimum of 12 dissertation); portfolio; and dissertation

Number of Full-Time Faculty -; **Number of Other Faculty** -

Name of Institution—Emporia State University
Name of Department or Program—School of Library and Information Management
Program Website (URL)—http://slim.emporia.edu
Name of Contact Person—Daniel Roland

Email Address of Contact Person—idt@emporia.edu

Program Description—Master's of Library Science (ALA-accredited program); Master's in Legal Information Management—in partnership with the University of Kansas School of Law—50 semester hours or 15-h certificate. School Library Certification program, which includes 27 h of the M.L.S. program; Ph.D. in Library and Information Management. B.S. in Information Resource Studies Information Management Certificate—18 h of MLS curriculum Library Services Certificates—6 separate 12-h programs of undergraduate work available for credit or noncredit. Areas include Information Sources and Services; Collection Management; Technology; Administration; Youth Services; and Generalist. The Master of Library Science program is also delivered to satellite campus sites in Denver, Salt Lake City, Portland, and Oregon. New programs tend to start every 3 years in each location. New programs include Denver—Summer 2004, Portland—Spring 2005, and Salt Lake City—Fall 2005.

Admission Requirements—Undergrad GPA of 3.0 or better for master's degrees, 3.5 or better for PhD. GRE score of 1000 points combined in verbal and analytical sections for master's degrees, 1100 for PhD. GRE can be waived for students already holding a graduate degree in which they earned a 3.75 GPA or better. Admission interview.

Degree Requirements—M.L.S.: 42 semester hours. Ph.D.: total of 55–59 semester hours beyond the masters

Number of Full-Time Faculty -; **Number of Other Faculty** -

Name of Institution—Kansas State University

Name of Department or Program—Curriculum and Instruction

Program Website (URL)—http://coe.ksu.edu/ecdol

Name of Contact Person—Rosemary Talab

Email Address of Contact Person—talab@ksu.edu

Program Description—The Educational Computing, Design, and Online Learning Program has these specializations: I. M.S. in Curriculum and Instruction with specialties in (1) Educational Computing, Design, and Online Learning (online option) and (2) Digital Teaching and Learning (online). II. Ph.D. in Curriculum and Instruction with specialty in Educational Computing, Design, and Online Learning (online). III. KSU Graduate School Certificate in Digital Teaching and Learning Master's program started in 1982; doctoral in 1987; and certificate in 1999. All coursework for the Certificate, M.A., and Ph.D. can be taken online. ECDOL is an online program that focuses on research, theory, practice, ethics, and design of learning environments, with an emphasis on emerging technologies. Coursework includes instructional design, virtual learning environments, game-based learning, design and evaluation of online courses, etc. Classes are offered regularly on a rotating basis. A cohort group is begun each fall for the Professional Seminar 1 and 2 academic year via videoconferencing, in which major areas of the field (change and ID models, distance education and online learning, etc.) are explored, as well as various delivery methods and technologies. E-portfolios are required at the certificate and master's degree levels. The

Ph.D. program allows the student to tailor the classes to individual needs. At the certificate and master's degree levels the DTL program offers classroom teachers leadership opportunities as technology facilitators and lead teachers, with course-work available in integrating emerging technologies into instruction to improve student achievement through a blend of practical technology skills with research and theory. The master's degree-level ECDOL program is offered to those who have B.A.s in other fields who wish to pursue a specialty in instructional design or prepare for the Ph.D. in ECDOL or who wish to design instructional environments in online and virtual learning environments. The KSU Graduate School Certificate in Digital Teaching and Learning is a 15-h completely online program for the classroom teacher with uniform exit outcomes and an e-portfolio requirement. The emphasis is on the application of technological and pedagogical theory, knowledge, and practical application skills that can be directly translated into the classroom. The ECDOL program, as a whole, is on Twitter (#Proseminar1) and on Facebook (KSUECDOL) http://www.facebook.com/group.php?gid=113228718719613, though the group is private.

Admission Requirements—M.S. in ECDOL: B average in undergraduate work, midrange scores on TOEFL. M.S./Certificate in DTL: B average in undergraduate work and teaching experience. Ph.D.: B average in undergraduate and graduate work, GRE, three letters of recommendation, experience, or basic courses in educational computing.

Degree Requirements—Certificate is 15 h and requires an e-portfolio and technology project DTL is a 15-h KSU Graduate School Certificate program; e-portfolio and project are required. M.S.: 31 semester hours (minimum of 15 in specialty); thesis, internship, or practicum are not required, but all three are possible; e-portfolio and project are required. The Ph.D. degree is 36–42 h, with 30 h of research, for a total of 60 h, minimum. Certificate: 15-h M.S. 31-h Ph.D.: 60 semester hours are required, and 30 h is taken from the student's master's program. There is a minimum of 21 h in Educational Computing, Design, and Online Learning or related area approved by committee and 30 h for dissertation research.

Number of Full-Time Faculty—1; **Number of Other Faculty**—5

Name of Institution—University of Louisville
Name of Department or Program—Workforce and Human Resource Education Program
Program Website (URL)—http://louisville.edu/education/departments/elfh/whre
Name of Contact Person—Rod Githens
Email Address of Contact Person—rod.githens@louisville.edu
Program Description—B.S. in Workforce Leadership (specialization in Training and Development) (100% online or face to face); M.S. in Human Resource Education (100% online or face to face); M.Ed. in Instructional Technology (please note: this program is offered for educators in P-12 settings through the Department of Teaching and Learning); Ph.D. in Educational Leadership and Organizational Development (specialization in Human Resource Development)

Our program is Relevant, Rigorous, and Research based: Relevant: The program has a strong emphasis on hands-on, applied projects that provide direct application to the field. Our instructors have practitioner experience in the field and many currently work in HR-related positions in Louisville and around the country. Rigorous: Expect to work hard and complete challenging assignments. Our goal is to help you develop the skills to think unconventionally about conventional problems. Research based: The program is designed around research-based competencies from the American Society for Training and Development, International Society for Performance Improvement, and the Society for Human Resource Management. Faculty members have strong theoretical and conceptual backgrounds that guide both their teaching and their practical approach to the field.

Admission Requirements—Master's degree: 3.0 GPA, 800 GRE, two letters of recommendation, goal statement, resume. Ph.D.: 3.5 GPA, 1000 GRE, letters of recommendation, goal statement, resume

Degree Requirements—See program websites: B.S. in Workforce Leadership: http://louisville.edu/education/degrees/files/bs-wl-tdc-curriculum.pdf. M.S. in Human Resource Education: http://louisville.edu/education/degrees/ms-hre.html. M.Ed. in Instructional Technology: http://louisville.edu/education/degrees/med-it.html. Ph.D. in Educational Leadership and Organization Development (HRD Specialty): http://louisville.edu/education/degrees/files/phd-elod-hr.pdf

Number of Full-Time Faculty—11; **Number of Other Faculty**—14

Name of Institution—Louisiana State University
Name of Department or Program—School of Library and Information Science
Program Website (URL)—http://slis.lsu.edu
Name of Contact Person—Beth Paskoff
Email Address of Contact Person—bpaskoff@lsu.edu
Program Description—Archives, academic libraries, information technology, medical libraries, public libraries, special libraries, youth services, Louisiana School Library Certification. Dual degrees are available in Systems Science and in History.
Distance education courses are available at seven locations in Louisiana.
Admission Requirements—Bachelor's degree, prefer 3.00 GPA GRE scores: prefer 500+ on verbal
Degree Requirements—M.L.I.S.: 40 h, comprehensive exam, completion of degree program in 5 years
Number of Full-Time Faculty—11; **Number of Other Faculty** -

Name of Institution—Boston University
Name of Department or Program—School of Education
Program Website (URL)—http://www.bu.edu/sed; http://www.bu.edu/emt
Name of Contact Person—David B. Whittier
Email Address of Contact Person—whittier@bu.edu
Program Description—Ed.M., CAGS (Certificate of Advanced Graduate Study) in Educational Media and Technology; Ed.D. in Curriculum and Teaching,

Specializing in Educational Media and Technology; preparation for Massachusetts public school License as Instructional Technology Specialist

The Master's Program prepares graduates for professional careers as educators, instructional designers, developers of educational materials, and managers of the human and technology-based resources necessary to support education and training with technology. Graduates are employed in PK-12 schools, higher education, industry, medicine, public health, government, publishing, and a range of services such as finance and insurance. Students come to the program from many different backgrounds and with a wide range of professional goals. The doctoral program sets the study of Educational Media and Technology within the context of education and educational research in general, and curriculum and teaching in particular. In addition to advanced work in the field of Educational Media and Technology, students examine and conduct research and study the history of educational thought and practice. Graduates make careers in education as professors and researchers, technology directors and managers, and developers of technology-based materials and systems. Graduates who work in both educational and noneducational organizations are often responsible for managing the human and technological resources required to create learning experiences that include the development and delivery of technology-based resources and distance education.

Admission Requirements—All degree programs require either the GRE or the MAT test score completed within the past 5 years and recommendations. Specific programs also include Ed.M.: undergraduate degree and GPA. For CAGS, in addition to above, an earned Ed.M. is required. For Ed.D. three letters of recommendation, test scores, transcripts, earned master's degree, and two writing samples (a statement of goals and qualifications and an analytical essay) are required.

Degree Requirements—Ed.M.: 36 credit hours (including 26 h from required core curriculum, 10 from electives). CAGs: 32 credits beyond Ed.M., one of which must be a curriculum and teaching course and a comprehensive exam. Ed.D.: 60 credit hours of courses selected from Educational Media and Technology, curriculum and teaching, and educational thought and practice with comprehensive exams; coursework and apprenticeship in research; dissertation

Number of Full-Time Faculty—1; **Number of Other Faculty**—10

Name of Institution—Fitchburg State University

Name of Department or Program—Division of Graduate and Continuing Education

Program Website (URL)—www.fitchburgstate.edu

Name of Contact Person—Randy Howe

Email Address of Contact Person—rhowe@fitchburgstate.edu

Program Description—M.Ed. in Educational Leadership and Management with specialization in Technology Leadership. Collaborating with professionals working in the field both for organizations and as independent producers, Fitchburg offers a unique M.Ed. program. The objectives are to develop in candidates the knowledge and skills for the effective implementation of technology within business, industry, government, not-for-profit agencies, health services, and education.

Admission Requirements—MAT or GRE scores, official transcript(s) of a baccalaureate degree, two or more years of experience in communications or media or education, three letters of recommendation

Degree Requirements—39 semester credit hours

Number of Full-Time Faculty—5; **Number of Other Faculty**—7

Name of Institution—Lesley University

Name of Department or Program—Technology in Education

Program Website (URL)—http://www.lesley.edu/soe/111tech.html

Name of Contact Person—George Blakeslee

Email Address of Contact Person—gblakesl@lesley.edu

Program Description—M.Ed. in Technology in Education; CAGS/Ed.S. in Technology in Education; Ph.D. in Educational Studies with specialization in Technology in Education.

M.Ed. program is offered off-campus at 70+ sites in 21 states; contact 617-349-8311 for information. The degree is also offered completely online. Contact Maureen Yoder, myoder@lesley.edu, or (617)348-8421 for information. Or check our website: URL above.

Admission Requirements—Completed bachelor's teaching certificate.

Degree Requirements—M.Ed.: 33 semester hours in technology, integrative final project in lieu of thesis, no internship or practicum. CAGS: 36 semester hours. Ph.D. requirements available on request

Number of Full-Time Faculty -; **Number of Other Faculty** -

Name of Institution—Harvard University

Name of Department or Program—Graduate School of Education

Program Website (URL)—http://www.gse.harvard.edu/tie

Name of Contact Person—Joseph Blatt, Director, Technology, Innovation, and Education Program; Irene Pak, Program Coordinator, Technology, Innovation, and Education Program

Email Address of Contact Person—pakir@gse.harvard.edu

Program Description—The Technology, Innovation, and Education Program (TIE) at Harvard prepares students to contribute to the thoughtful design, implementation, and assessment of educational media and technology initiatives. Graduates of the program fill leadership positions in a wide range of fields, including design and production, policy development and analysis, technology integration and administration, research, and evaluation, and teaching with new technologies. Some distinctive features of studying educational technology in TIE include the following: * Focus on learning and teaching: Our approach puts learning and teaching at the center, with technology as the means, not the mission. Our courses examine cutting-edge technologies that bridge distance and time, the research behind them, and the design that goes into them—but we always center on the cognitive, affective, and social dimensions of learning, not

Graduate Programs in Learning, Design, Technology, Information, or Libraries

on hardware or fashion. * A world-class faculty: Our faculty combines internationally recognized researchers with leading professionals in design and evaluation. We are all committed teachers and learners, dedicated to supporting you as a student and helping you craft a course of study that meets your goals. * A curriculum that builds leaders: Our curriculum bridges three broad strands of design, implementation, and research. Design courses apply learning principles to creating software, networks, digital video and television, handheld applications, and multiuser virtual environments. Implementation courses focus on using new technologies to bring about transformative changes in educational practice. Courses on research emphasize formulating evaluation designs that are both rigorous and practical. To deepen connections between theory and practice, TIE students often undertake an internship in one of the many research projects, educational technology firms, or media production organizations in the Boston area. * A diverse community of learners: Our community includes students of all ages, from all parts of the globe, with varied professional backgrounds and experience in technology. The upshot is that students have endless opportunities to learn from one another, exchanging insights about the potential role for learning technologies in different settings and cultures. More information about the program, our faculty, and the student experience is available on our website, http://www.gse.harvard.edu/tie.

Courses in design, technology policy and leadership, research, and evaluation, leading to the Ed.M. degree in Technology, Innovation, and Education. The program offers access to other courses throughout Harvard University, and at MIT, as well as many internship opportunities in the Greater Boston media and technology community.

Admission Requirements—GRE scores, 600 TOEFL, academic transcripts, three letters of recommendation, and a statement of purpose. Students interested in further information about the TIE Program should visit our website, http://www.gse.harvard.edu/tie, which includes a link to the Harvard Graduate School of Education online application.

Degree Requirements—32 semester credits

Number of Full-Time Faculty—5; **Number of Other Faculty**—6

Name of Institution—McDaniel College (formerly Western Maryland College)

Name of Department or Program—Graduate and Professional Studies

Program Website (URL)—http://www.mcdaniel.edu

Name of Contact Person—Ramona N. Kerby

Email Address of Contact Person—rkerby@mcdaniel.edu

Program Description—M.S. in Education with an emphasis on school librarianship

Admission Requirements—3.0 Undergraduate GPA, 3 reference checklist forms from principal and other school personnel, acceptable application essay, acceptable praxis test scores

Degree Requirements—37 credit hours, including professional digital portfolio.

Number of Full-Time Faculty—1; **Number of Other Faculty**—5

Name of Institution—Towson University
Name of Department or Program—College of Education
Program Website (URL)—http://grad.towson.edu/program/master/istc-ms/
Name of Contact Person—Jeffrey M. Kenton
Email Address of Contact Person—jkenton@towson.edu
Program Description—M.S. degrees in Instructional Development, and Educational Technology (Contact Liyan Song: lsong@towson.edu); M.S. degree in School Library Media (Contact, David Robinson: derobins@towson.edu); Ed.D. degree in Instructional Technology (Contact, William Sadera, bsadera@towson.edu) (http://grad.towson.edu/program/doctoral/istc-edd/)
Excellent labs. Strong practical hands-on classes. Focus of M.S. program: Students produce useful multimedia projects for use in their teaching and training. Many group activities within courses. School library media degree confers with Maryland State Department of Education certification as a Pre-K-12 Library Media Specialist. Innovative Ed.D. program with online hybrid courses and strong mix of theory and practical discussions.
Admission Requirements—Bachelor's degree from accredited institution with 3.0 GPA (conditional admission granted for many applicants with a GPA over 2.75). Doctoral requirements are listed: http://grad.towson.edu/program/doctoral/istc--edd/ar-istc-edd.asp.
Degree Requirements—M.S. degree is 36 graduate semester hours without thesis. Ed.D. is 63 h beyond the M.S. degree.
Number of Full-Time Faculty—17; **Number of Other Faculty**—5

Name of Institution—Eastern Michigan University
Name of Department or Program—Teacher Education
Program Website (URL)—http://www.emich.edu
Name of Contact Person—Nancy L. Copeland
Email Address of Contact Person—ncopeland@emich.edu
Program Description—M.A. and Graduate Certificate in Educational Media and Technology. The mission of this program is to prepare professionals who are capable of facilitating student learning in a variety of settings. The program is designed to provide students with both the knowledge base and the application skills that are required to use technology effectively in education. Focusing on the design, development, utilization, management, and evaluation of instructional systems moves us toward achieving this mission. Students who complete the educational technology concentration will be able to (a) provide a rationale for using technology in the educational process; (b) identify contributions of major leaders in the field of educational media technology and instructional theory, and the impact that each leader has had on the field; (c) assess current trends in the area of educational media technology and relate the trends to past events and future implications; (d) integrate technology into instructional programs; (e) teach the operation and various uses of educational technology in instruction; (f) act as consultants/facilitators in educational media technology; (g) design and develop instructional products to meet specified needs; and (h) evaluate the

Graduate Programs in Learning, Design, Technology, Information, or Libraries

231

effectiveness of instructional materials and systems. Courses in our 30-credit-hour Educational Media and Technology (EDMT) program include technology and reflective teacher, technology and student-centered learning, technology-- enhanced learning environments, issues and emerging technologies, instructional design, development of online materials, psychology of the adult learner, principles of classroom learning, curriculum foundations, research seminar, and seminar in educational technology. Since Spring 2003, all of the EDMT courses have been taught online. The program can be completed online. Students who do not want to receive a master's degree can apply for admission to our 20-credit-hour Educational Media and Technology certificate. The EDMT courses for the certificate are also offered online.

Admission Requirements—Individuals seeking admission to this program must (1) comply with the Graduate School admission requirements; (2) score 550 or better on the TOEFL and 5 or better on TWE, if a non-native speaker of English; (3) have a 2.75 undergraduate grade point average, or a 3.30 grade point average in 12 h or more of work in a master's program; (4) solicit two letters of reference; and (5) submit a statement of professional goals.

Degree Requirements—In order to graduate, each student is expected to (1) complete all work on an approved program of study (30 semester hours); (2) maintain a "B" (3.0 GPA) average or better on coursework taken within the program; (3) get a recommendation from the faculty adviser; (4) fill out an application for graduation and obtain the adviser's recommendation; (5) meet all other requirements for a master's degree adopted by the Graduate School of Eastern Michigan University; and (6) complete a culminating experience (research, instructional development, or evaluation project) as determined by the student and faculty adviser.

Number of Full-Time Faculty—5; **Number of Other Faculty** -

Name of Institution—Michigan State University
Name of Department or Program—College of Education
Program Website (URL)—http://edutech.msu.edu
Name of Contact Person—Leigh Wolf
Email Address of Contact Person—edutech@msu.edu
Program Description—M.A. in Educational Technology with Learning, Design, and Technology specialization. Extensive opportunities to work with faculty in designing online courses and online learning environments
Admission Requirements—Please visit http://edutech.msu.edu/apply_masters.html.
Degree Requirements—30 semester hours, Web-based portfolio
Number of Full-Time Faculty—6; **Number of Other Faculty**—6

Name of Institution—Wayne State University
Name of Department or Program—Instructional Technology
Program Website (URL)—http://coe.wayne.edu/aos/it/
Name of Contact Person—Timothy W. Spannaus
Email Address of Contact Person—tspannaus@wayne.edu

Program Description—M.Ed. degrees in Instructional Design, Performance Improvement and Training, K-12 Technology Integration, and Interactive Technologies. Ed.D. and Ph.D. programs to prepare individuals for leadership in academic, business, industry, health care, and K-12 school setting as professor, researcher, instructional design, and development specialists; media or learning resources managers or consultants; specialists in instructional video; and Web-based instruction and multimedia specialists. The school also offers a 6-year specialist degree program in Instructional Technology. The IT program offers certificates in Online Learning, Educational Technology, and University Teaching. Guided experiences in instructional design and development activities in business and industry are available. Specific classes use a variety of technologies, including blogs, wikis, Twitter, Facebook, Google docs, and many others. M.Ed. programs are available face to face and online.

Admission Requirements—Ph.D.: Master's degree, 3.5 GPA, GRE, strong academic recommendations, interview

Degree Requirements—Ph.D. 113 cr. hours, including IT core and electives, research courses, graduate seminars, 30 cr. dissertation. M.Ed.: 36 semester hours, including required project; internship recommended

Number of Full-Time Faculty—6; **Number of Other Faculty**—10

Name of Institution—Northwest Missouri State University

Name of Department or Program—Department of Computer Science/ Information Systems

Program Website (URL)—http://www.nwmissouri.edu/csis

Name of Contact Person—Nancy Zeliff

Email Address of Contact Person—nzeliff@nwmissouri.edu

Program Description—M.S.Ed. in Instructional Technology. Certificate Program in Instructional Technology. These degrees are designed for industry trainers and computer educators at the elementary, middle school, high school, and junior college level.

Admission Requirements—3.0 undergraduate GPA, 700 GRE (V + Q)

Degree Requirements—32 semester hours of graduate courses in computer science, education, and instructional technology courses. Fifteen hours of computer education and instructional technology courses for the certificate

Number of Full-Time Faculty—5; **Number of Other Faculty**—7

Name of Institution—St. Cloud State University

Name of Department or Program—College of Education

Program Website (URL)—http://www.stcloudstate.edu/cim

Name of Contact Person—Merton E. Thompson

Email Address of Contact Person—cim@stcloudstate.edu

Program Description—Undergraduate major and minor in Information Media. Undergraduate certificate in Instructional Technology. Master's degrees in Information Technologies, Educational Media, and Instructional Design and Training. Graduate certificates in Instructional Technology, Design for E--

Graduate Programs in Learning, Design, Technology, Information, or Libraries

learning, and School Library Media. Most courses are available online as well as face to face.

Admission Requirements—Acceptance to Graduate School, written and oral preliminary examination

Degree Requirements—Master's: 42 semester credits with thesis; 39 semester credits with starred paper or portfolio; 200-h practicum is required for library media licensure. Coursework for licensure may be applied to Educational Media Master's program.

Number of Full-Time Faculty—5; **Number of Other Faculty**—21

Name of Institution—University of Missouri-Columbia

Name of Department or Program—School of Information Science and Learning Technologies

Program Website (URL)—http://sislt.missouri.edu

Name of Contact Person—Julie Caplow

Email Address of Contact Person—caplowj@missouri.edu

Program Description—The Educational Technology program takes a theory-based approach to designing, developing, implementing, and researching computer-mediated environments to support human activity. We seek individuals who are committed to lifelong learning and who aspire to use advanced technology to improve human learning and performance. Graduates of the program will find opportunities to use their knowledge and competencies as classroom teachers, media specialists, district technology specialists and coordinators, designers and developers of technology-based learning and information systems, training specialists for businesses, medical settings, and public institutions, as well as other creative positions. The curriculum at the master's and specialist levels has two focus areas: Technology in Schools and Learning Systems Design and Development, with coursework tailored to each focus area. For information regarding our Ph.D., see http://education.missouri.edu/SISLT/PhD/index.php.
Both focus areas are available online via the Internet or on the MU campus. The Technology in Schools focus area is based on the ISTE competencies and culminates in an online portfolio based on these competencies. Several courses are augmented by technical resources developed at MU, including a technology integration knowledge repository and online collaboration tools. The Learning Systems Design and Development focus area links to business, military, and government contexts. This focus area offers a challenging balance of design and development coursework, in addition to coursework dealing with needs assessment and evaluation. For information regarding our Ph.D., see http://sislt.missouri.edu/phd.

Admission Requirements—Master's: Bachelor's degree, GRE (V > 500; A > 500; W > 3.5). Ed.S.: Master's degree, GRE (V > 500; A > 500; W > 3.5). Ph.D.: 3.5 graduate GPA, GRE (V > 500; A > 500; W > 3.5). See website for details.

Degree Requirements—Master's and Ed.S.: Minimum of 30 graduate credit hours required for the degree; 15 h of upper division coursework. Maximum of 6 h of transfer credit. Ph.D.

Number of Full-Time Faculty—10; **Number of Other Faculty**—8

Name of Institution—The University of Southern Mississippi
Name of Department or Program—Instructional Technology and Design
Program Website (URL)—http://dragon.ep.usm.edu/~it
Name of Contact Person—Taralynn Hartsell
Email Address of Contact Person—Taralynn.Hartsell@usm.edu
Program Description—The Department of Technology Education at the University of Southern Mississippi has two graduate programs relating to Instructional Technology and Design. The Master's of Science in Instructional Technology is a 33–36-h program, and the Ph.D. of Instructional Technology and Design is a 60–75-h program. The Master's of Science concentrates more on the technology application and integration aspect that helps students learn both hands-on application of technology and theoretical and historical aspects related to the field of study. A majority of the coursework in the program can be completed online (about 70%), and the remaining coursework is hybrid or blended in nature (about 60% online and 40% traditional). The Ph.D. program is a new advanced study program for those wishing to pursue their education in the application of technology and design, research, and leadership (began in Fall 2009). The Ph.D. program also has two emphasis areas that meet students' needs: instructional technology or instructional design. A majority of the coursework in the program can be completed online (between 60 and 80% depending upon emphasis area selected), and the remaining coursework is hybrid or blended in form (about 60% online and 40% traditional).
Admission Requirements—Please review the IT website for more information on the application procedures for each program: http://dragon.ep.usm.edu/~it. The GRE is mandatory for graduate programs.
Degree Requirements—Please review the IT website for more information on degree requirements for each program: http://dragon.ep.usm.edu/~it.
Number of Full-Time Faculty—4; **Number of Other Faculty**—2

Name of Institution—University of Montana
Name of Department or Program—School of Education
Program Website (URL)—http://www.umt.edu
Name of Contact Person—Sally Brewer
Email Address of Contact Person—sally.brewer@mso.umt.edu
Program Description—M.Ed. and specialist degrees; K-12 School Library Media specialization with Library Media endorsement. Not represented in the rest of this is that we also have a Master's in Curricular Studies with an option in Instructional Design for Technology. Dr. Martin Horejsi is the coordinator of this program. His phone is 406.243.5785. His email is martin.horejsi@umontana. edu. This program is 37 credits and can be taken totally online. There are three full-time faculty members in this program. Combined online program with the University of Montana-Western in Dillon, MT. 25 credits.
Admission Requirements—(Both degrees) GRE, letters of recommendation, 2.75 GPA

Graduate Programs in Learning, Design, Technology, Information, or Libraries

Degree Requirements—M.Ed.: 37 semester credit hours (18 overlap with library media endorsement). Specialist: 28 semester hours (18 overlap)
Number of Full-Time Faculty—3; **Number of Other Faculty**—1

Name of Institution—University of North Carolina
Name of Department or Program—School of Information and Library Science
Program Website (URL)—http://www.ils.unc.edu/
Name of Contact Person—Sandra Hughes-Hassell
Email Address of Contact Person—smhughes@email.unc.edu
Program Description—Master of Science Degree in Library Science (M.S.L.S.) with specialization in school library media. Post-Master's certification program
Rigorous academic program plus field experience requirement; excellent placement record
Admission Requirements—Competitive admission based on all three GRE components (quantitative, qualitative, analytical), undergraduate GPA (plus graduate work if any), letters of recommendation, and student statement of career interest and school choice
Degree Requirements—48 semester hours, field experience, comprehensive exam, master's paper
Number of Full-Time Faculty—31; **Number of Other Faculty**—1

Name of Institution—University of Nebraska at Kearney
Name of Department or Program—Teacher Education
Program Website (URL)—http://www.unk.edu/academics/ecampus. aspx?id=6217
Name of Contact Person—Scott Fredrickson
Email Address of Contact Person—fredricksons@unk.edu
Program Description—M.S.Ed. in Instructional Technology, M.S.Ed. in Library Media
Two main emphasis areas—Instructional Technology and School Library Media. The Instructional Technology track has an Information Technology endorsement module, and the School Library track has a module to obtain a School Library endorsement. To obtain either endorsement requires a current teaching certificate; however the degree itself does not.
Admission Requirements—Graduate Record Examination or completion of an electronic portfolio meeting department requirements, acceptance into graduate school, and approval of Instructional Technology Committee
Degree Requirements—36 credit hours, 18 of which are required and 18 are elective (30 h is required for either endorsement with 6 h of electives), and a capstone Instructional Technology project
Number of Full-Time Faculty—5; **Number of Other Faculty**—24

Name of Institution—University of Nebraska-Omaha
Name of Department or Program—College of Education Department of Teacher Education
Program Website (URL)—http://www.unomaha.edu/libraryed/

Name of Contact Person—Rebecca J. Pasco

Email Address of Contact Person—rpasco@unomaha.edu

Program Description—Undergraduate Library Science Program (public, academic, and special libraries), School Library Endorsement (undergraduate and graduate), M.S. in Secondary Education with School Library concentration, M.S. in Elementary Education with School Library concentration, M.S. in Reading with School Library concentration, Master's in Library Science Program (cooperative program with the University of Missouri).

Web-assisted format (combination of online and on-campus) for both undergraduate and graduate programs. School Library programs nationally recognized by American Association of School Librarians (AASL): Public, Academic, and Special Libraries programs and Cooperative UNO/University of Missouri MLS program that is ALA accredited

Admission Requirements—As per the University of Nebraska at Omaha undergraduate and graduate admission requirements

Degree Requirements—School Library Endorsement (undergraduate and graduate)—30-h M.S. in Secondary and Elementary Education with School Library endorsement—36-h M.S. in Reading with School Library endorsement—36-h Master's in Library Science Program (cooperative program with the University of Missouri at Columbia)—42 h

Number of Full-Time Faculty—2; **Number of Other Faculty**—10

Name of Institution—Rutgers, the State University of New Jersey

Name of Department or Program—School of Communication and Information

Program Website (URL)—http://www.comminfo.rutgers.edu/

Name of Contact Person—Dr. Kay Cassell, Director, Master of Library and Information Science, Department of Library and Information Studies, School of Communication, Information and Library Studies. Dr. Michael Lesk, Chair

Email Address of Contact Person—kcassell@rutgers.edu

Program Description—The Master of Library and Information Science (M.L.I.S.) program provides professional education for a wide variety of service and management careers in libraries, information agencies, information industry, and business, industry, government, research, and similar environments where information is a vital resource. Specializations include school library media; services for children and youth; digital libraries; information retrieval/information systems; and knowledge management (http://comminfo.rutgers.edu/master-of--library-and-information-science/curriculum-overview.html).

The M.L.I.S. program, available both on campus and online, is organized around six themes in the field of library and information science: human-information interaction; information access; information and society; information systems; management; and organization of information. Six lead courses, one in each area, form the foundation of the curriculum and offer general knowledge of the major principles and issues of the field. Two or more central courses in each theme offer basic understanding and competencies in important components of the field. Specialization courses in each theme allow students to develop expertise in preparation for specific career objectives. The specialization in School Librarianship is certified with the NJ Department of Education. All students in the New Brunswick M.L.I.S. program work with an adviser to plan a course of study appropriate for their interests and career objectives.

Admission Requirements—A bachelor's degree or its equivalent from a recognized institution of higher education with a B average or better; GRE scores; personal statement which presents a view of the library and information science profession and applicants' aspirations and goals in the library and information science professions; three letters of recommendation which focus on the applicant's academic capacity to undertake a rigorous program of graduate study

Degree Requirements—A minimum of 36 credits, or 12 courses, is required to earn the M.L.I.S. degree. All students are required to enroll in two noncredit classes, 501—Introduction to Library and Information Professions in their first semester and 502—Colloquium in a later semester. There are no language requirements for the M.L.I.S. degree, and there is no thesis or comprehensive examination.

Number of Full-Time Faculty—22; **Number of Other Faculty**—15

Name of Institution—Appalachian State University
Name of Department or Program—Department of Curriculum and Instruction
Program Website (URL)—http://edtech.ced.appstate.edu
Name of Contact Person—Robert Muffoletto
Email Address of Contact Person—muffoletto@appstate.edu; riedlre@appstate.edu
Program Description—M.A. in Educational Media and Technology with three areas of concentration: Computers, Media Literacy, and Media Production. A plan of study in the Internet distance teaching is offered online. Two certificate programs: (1) Distance Learning—internet delivered—(2) Media Literacy. Business, university, community college, and public-school partnership offers unusual opportunities for learning. The programs are focused on developing learning environments over instructional environments.
Admission Requirements—Undergraduate degree
Degree Requirements—36 graduate semester hours. We also have certificates in (1) Distance Learning and (2) Media Literacy.
Number of Full-Time Faculty -; **Number of Other Faculty** -

Name of Institution—Buffalo State College
Name of Department or Program—Computer Information Systems Department
Program Website (URL)—http://www.buffalostate.edu/cis/x471.xml
Name of Contact Person—Stephen E. Gareau
Email Address of Contact Person—gareause@buffalostate.edu
Program Description—M.S. in Education in Educational Technology. This program is designed for K-12 and higher education educators, as well as trainers from business and industry, who wish to develop and expand their knowledge and skills in the development and application of various educational technolo-

gies. A wide range of media and tools are covered in the program, including text, graphics, audio, video, animation, models, simulations, games, and Web tools.

Admission Requirements—Bachelor's degree from accredited institution, undergraduate 3.0 GPA, three letters of recommendation, one letter from applicant

Degree Requirements—36 semester hours. See http://www.buffalostate.edu/cis/x471.xml for full details.

Number of Full-Time Faculty—3; **Number of Other Faculty**—2

Name of Institution—Fordham University

Name of Department or Program—M.A. Program in Public Communications in the Department of Communication and Media Studies

Program Website (URL)—http://www.fordham.edu

Name of Contact Person—Fred Wertz, Department Chair, Tom McCourt, Director of Graduate Studies

Email Address of Contact Person—andersen@fordham.edu

Program Description—The M.A. in Public Communications has three concentrations: (1) Media Analysis and Criticism; (2) Industries, Publics, and Policy; and (3) Screen Arts and Culture.

Extensive Internship program: full-time students can complete program in 12 months, but many students take 18 months to complete the program.

Admission Requirements—3.0 undergraduate GPA. Fellowship applicants must take the GREs.

Degree Requirements—10 courses, (30) credits, and either a media project or a research paper or an M.A. Thesis to complete the degree

Number of Full-Time Faculty—12; **Number of Other Faculty**—4

Name of Institution—Ithaca College

Name of Department or Program—School of Communications

Program Website (URL)—http://www.ithaca.edu/gps/gradprograms/comm/

Name of Contact Person—Howard K. Kalman, Chair, Graduate Program in Communications; Roy H. Park, School of Communications

Email Address of Contact Person—hkalman@ithaca.edu

Program Description—M.S. in Communications. Students in this program find employment in such areas as instructional design/training, Web development, corporate/community/public relations and marketing, and employee communication. The program can be tailored to individual career goals. Program is interdisciplinary, incorporating organizational communication, instructional design, management, and technology.

Admission Requirements—3.0 GPA, recommendations, statement of purpose, resume, application forms and transcripts, TOEFL 550 (or 213 computer scored; 80 on the iBT version) where applicable

Degree Requirements—36 semester hours including capstone seminar

Number of Full-Time Faculty—6; **Number of Other Faculty** -

Name of Institution—State University College of Arts and Science at Potsdam

Name of Department or Program—Organizational Leadership and Technology

Graduate Programs in Learning, Design, Technology, Information, or Libraries 239

Program Website (URL)—http://www.potsdam.edu/olt
Name of Contact Person—Anthony Betrus
Email Address of Contact Person—betrusak@potsdam.edu
Program Description—M.S. in Education in Instructional Technology with concentrations in Educational Technology Specialist, K-12 Track Educational Technology Specialist, Non-K-12 Track Organizational Performance, Leadership, and Technology. Live instruction. Evening 12-week courses. Group Work Internships
Admission Requirements—(1) Submission of an official transcript of an earned baccalaureate degree from an accredited institution. (2) A minimum GPA of 2.75 (4.0 scale) in the most recent 60 credit hours of coursework. (3) Submission of the Application for Graduate Study (w/$50 nonrefundable fee). (4). For students seeking the Educational Technology Specialist Certification, a valid NYS Teaching Certificate is required.
Degree Requirements—36 semester hours, including internship or practicum; culminating project required
Number of Full-Time Faculty—3; **Number of Other Faculty**—3

Name of Institution—Wright State University
Name of Department or Program—College of Education and Human Services, Department of Educational Leadership
Program Website (URL)—http://www.cehs.wright.edu/academic/educational_leadership/lib-media/index.php
Name of Contact Person—Susan Berg
Email Address of Contact Person—susan.berg@wright.edu
Program Description—M.Ed. or M.A. in Computer/Technology or Library Media. Ohio licensure available in multiage library media (ages 3–21). Computer/technology endorsement. Above licensure only available on a graduate basis. Multiage library media licensure available in two tracks: initial (no previous teaching license) and advanced (with current teaching license in another field). The computer/technology endorsement must be added to a current teaching license.
Admission Requirements—Completed application with nonrefundable application fee, Bachelor's degree from accredited institution, official transcripts, 2.7 overall GPA for regular status (conditional acceptance possible), statement of purpose, satisfactory scores on MAT or GRE
Degree Requirements—M.Ed. requires a comprehensive portfolio; M.A. requires a 6-h thesis
Number of Full-Time Faculty—3; **Number of Other Faculty**—5

Name of Institution—Ohio University
Name of Department or Program—Instructional Technology
Program Website (URL)—http://www.cehs.ohio.edu/academics/es/it/index.htm
Name of Contact Person—David Richard Moore
Email Address of Contact Person—moored3@ohio.edu

Program Description—M.Ed. in Computer Education and Technology. Ph.D. in Curriculum and Instruction with a specialization in Instructional Technology also available; call for details (740-593-4561) or visit the website http://www. ohio.edu/education/dept/es/it/index.cfm. Master's program is a blended online delivery.

Admission Requirements—Bachelor's degree, 3.0 undergraduate GPA, 35 MAT, 500 GRE (verbal), 500 GRE (quantitative), 550 TOEFL, three letters of recommendation, paper describing future goals and career expectations from completing a degree in our program

Degree Requirements—Master's—36 semester credits, electronic portfolio, or optional thesis worth 2–10 credits or alternative seminar research paper. Students may earn two graduate degrees simultaneously in education and in any other field. Ph.D.—66 h with 15 h being dissertation work

Number of Full-Time Faculty—4; **Number of Other Faculty** -

Name of Institution—University of Cincinnati

Name of Department or Program—College of Education

Program Website (URL)—http://www.uc.edu/

Name of Contact Person—Richard Kretschmer

Email Address of Contact Person—richard.kretschmer@uc.edu

Program Description—M.Ed. or Ed.D. in Curriculum and Instruction with an emphasis on Instructional Design and Technology; Educational Technology degree programs for current professional, technical, critical, and personal knowledge

Admission Requirements—Bachelor's degree from accredited institution, 2.8 undergraduate GPA; GRE 1500 or better

Degree Requirements—54 qtr. hours, written exam, thesis, or research project (12–15-credit-hour college core; 12–15 C&I; 18–27-credit-hour specialization; 3–6-credit-hour thesis or project)

Number of Full-Time Faculty -; **Number of Other Faculty** -

Name of Institution—The University of Oklahoma

Name of Department or Program—Instructional Psychology and Technology, Department of Educational Psychology

Program Website (URL)—http://education.ou.edu/ipt/

Name of Contact Person—H. Michael Crowson

Email Address of Contact Person—mcrowson@ou.edu

Program Description—Master's degree with emphases on Instructional Design and Technology (includes tracks: Instructional Design; and Interactive Learning Technologies), and Instructional Psychology and Technology (includes tracks: Instructional Psychology and Technology; Teaching and Assessment; Teaching and Learning; and Integrating Technology in Teaching). Doctoral degree in Instructional Psychology and Technology. Strong interweaving of principles of instructional psychology with instructional design and development. Application

Graduate Programs in Learning, Design, Technology, Information, or Libraries 241

of IP&T in K-12, vocational education, higher education, business and industry, and governmental agencies

Admission Requirements—Master's: acceptance by IPT program and graduate college based on minimum 3.00 GPA for last 60 h of undergraduate work or last 12 h of graduate work; written statement that indicates goals and interests compatible with program goals. Doctoral: minimum 3.25 GPA, GRE scores, written statement that indicates goals and interests compatible with program goals, writing sample, and letters of recommendation

Degree Requirements—Master's: 36-h coursework with 3.0 GPA; successful completion of thesis or comprehensive exam. Doctorate: see program description from institution or http://education.ou.edu/ipt/

Number of Full-Time Faculty—11; **Number of Other Faculty** -

Name of Institution—Bloomsburg University

Name of Department or Program—Instructional Technology and Institute for Interactive Technologies

Program Website (URL)—http://iit.bloomu.edu

Name of Contact Person—Timothy L. Phillips

Email Address of Contact Person—tphillip@bloomu.edu

Program Description—M.S. in Instructional Technology—Corporate Concentration M.S. in Instructional Technology—Instructional Technology Specialist Concentration (education M.S. Instructional Technology—Instructional Game and Interactive Environments Concentration (currently under development) eLearning Developer Certificate.

M.S. in Instructional Technology with emphasis on preparing for careers as Instructional Technologist in corporate, government, healthcare, higher education, and K-12 educational settings. The program is highly applied and provides opportunities for students to work on real-world projects as part of their coursework. Our program offers a corporate concentration and an Instructional Technology Specialist Concentration for educators. The program offers a complete master's degree online as well as on campus. Graduate assistantships are available for full-time students. The program is closely associated with the nationally known Institute for Interactive Technologies.

Admission Requirements—Bachelor's degree

Degree Requirements—33 semester credits (27 credits + 6 credit thesis, or 30 credits + 3 credit internship)

Number of Full-Time Faculty—4; **Number of Other Faculty**—3

Name of Institution—Drexel University

Name of Department or Program—The iSchool at Drexel, College of Information Science and Technology

Program Website (URL)—http://www.ischool.drexel.edu

Name of Contact Person—David E. Fenske

Email Address of Contact Person—info@ischool.drexel.edu

Program Description—The ALA-accredited Master of Science (MS) in Library and Information Science curriculum prepares professionals for information--

providing organizations. In April 2009, the M.S. was ranked 9th among library science programs in the nation, according to U.S. News & World Report's "America's Best Graduate Schools." The M.S. degree qualifies students for a wide variety of positions, including school library media specialist. Students may formally declare a concentration in School Library Media, Youth Services, Competitive Intelligence and Knowledge Management, Digital Libraries, or Information and Library Services. The School Library Media concentration is for students who wish to work in K-12 school library programs in both public and private schools. Designed to prepare graduates to be eligible for certification as school librarians by the Pennsylvania Department of Education (PDE), the program meets the requirements of the State of Pennsylvania and provides a strong basis for seeking certification in other states as well. Three course sequences are available within the concentration: one for students who have no prior teaching certification from PDE; one for students who have prior teaching certification from PDE and who wish to add school librarian certification to their credentials; and one for students with ALA-accredited master's degrees who wish to seek school librarian certification from PDE. In addition to the concentrations outlined above, students may choose to specialize in Healthcare Informatics or Archival Management. In keeping with the flexibility and personal planning emphasis of the College's M.S., students may also select a "no concentration" option. The College also offers a Master of Science in Information Systems (MSIS), a Master of Science in Software Engineering (MSSE), and a Ph.D. There is an Advanced Certificate in Information Studies and Technology which is a nondegree program providing specialized training beyond the master's degree, and an online Certificate in Healthcare Informatics providing knowledge and skills in the application of information technology (IT) in the provision of health care. The M.S. degree (as well as the MSIS and MSSE) is offered on campus and online. Students may take the degree completely on campus, completely online, or as a mixture of the two. Currently, all courses in the School Library Media Concentration except the Field Study (INFO 891) are offered online. INFO 891 must be completed in approved sites and is augmented with an online seminar.

Admission Requirements—Admission requirements for the master's program: Official Graduate Record Exam (GRE) scores (may be waived with a 3.2 GPA CUM or in the last half (credits) of a completed undergraduate or graduate degree; department decision). For a full list of admission requirements, visit the website at www.ischool.drexel.edu.

Degree Requirements—15 courses. Additional coursework is required for those seeking teaching certification in Pennsylvania.

Number of Full-Time Faculty—38; **Number of Other Faculty**—73

Name of Institution—Lehigh University
Name of Department or Program—Teaching, Learning, and Technology
Program Website (URL)—http://www.lehigh.edu/education/tlt/
Name of Contact Person—MJ Bishop

Email Address of Contact Person—TLTProgram@Lehigh.edu

Program Description—M.S. in Instructional Technology: Emphasizes design, development, implementation, integration, and evaluation of technology for teaching and learning. The degree is well suited to both designers (producers) and implementers (consumers) of instructional technologies. Graduate certificate in Technology Use in the Schools: This 12-credit grad certificate focuses on integrating technology into daily practice in the schools. Ph.D. in Teaching and Learning, concentration in Instructional Design and Technology: Emphasizes cognitive processes and their implications for the design, development, and evaluation of technology-based teaching and learning products in a variety of settings. High level of integration with teacher education and certification, leading to a practical and quickly applicable program of study. Our Integrated Professional Development School approach offers further opportunities to get into the schools and work on solving meaningful teaching and learning problems, not just "tech support." Both masters and doctoral students collaborate with faculty on projects and studies (including national presentation and publication).

Admission Requirements—M.S. (competitive): 3.0 undergraduate GPA or 3.0 graduate GPA, GREs recommended, transcripts, at least two letters of recommendation, statement of personal and professional goals, application fee. Application deadlines: July 15 for fall admission, December 1 for spring admission, April 30 for summer admission. Ph.D. (highly competitive): 3.5 graduate GPA, GREs required. Copy of two extended pieces of writing (or publications); statement of future professional goals; statement of why Lehigh is the best place to meet those goals; identification of which presentations, publications, or research by Lehigh faculty attracted applicants to Lehigh. Application deadline: February 1 (admission only once per year from competitive pool)

Degree Requirements—M.S.: 30 credits; thesis option. Ph.D.: 48 credits past master's (including dissertation). Qualifying exam (written and oral) + general examination research project (publication quality) + dissertation

Number of Full-Time Faculty—5; **Number of Other Faculty**—1

Name of Institution—The University of Rhode Island

Name of Department or Program—Graduate School of Library and Information Studies

Program Website (URL)—http://www.uri.edu/artsci/lsc

Name of Contact Person—E. Gale Eaton

Email Address of Contact Person—geaton@mail.uri.edu

Program Description—M.L.I.S. degree with specialties in School Library Media Services, Information Literacy Instruction, Youth Services Librarianship, Public Librarianship, Academic Librarianship, and Special Library Services. Fifteen-credit Post-Baccalaureate Certificate in Information Literacy Instruction

Admission Requirements—Undergraduate GPA of 3.0, score in 50th percentile or higher on SAT or MAT, statement of purpose, current resume, letters of reference

Degree Requirements—42 semester-credit program offered in Rhode Island and regionally in Worcester, MA, and Durham, NH

Number of Full-Time Faculty—7; **Number of Other Faculty**—36

Name of Institution—University of South Carolina Aiken and University of South Carolina Columbia

Name of Department or Program—Aiken: School of Education; Columbia: Department of Educational Psychology

Program Website (URL)—http://edtech.usca.edu

Name of Contact Person—Thomas Smyth

Email Address of Contact Person—smyth@usca.edu

Program Description—Master of Education in Educational Technology (A Joint Program of the University of South Carolina Aiken and Columbia)

The Master's Degree in Educational Technology is designed to provide advanced professional studies in graduate-level coursework to develop capabilities essential to the effective design, evaluation, and delivery of technology-based instruction and training (e.g., software development, multimedia development, assistive technology modifications, Web-based development, and distance learning). The program is intended (1) to prepare educators to assume leadership roles in the integration of educational technology into the school curriculum and (2) to provide graduate-level instructional opportunities for several populations (e.g., classroom teachers, corporate trainers, educational software developers) that need to acquire both technological competencies and understanding of sound instructional design principles and techniques. The program is offered entirely online as high-quality, interactive, Web-based courses. There are occasional synchronous online meetings, but the vast majority of the program is asynchronous. Candidates present a program portfolio for review by the faculty at the end of the program.

Admission Requirements—Application to the Educational Technology Program can be made after completion of at least the bachelor's degree from a college or university accredited by a regional accrediting agency. The standard for admission will be based on a total profile for the applicant. The successful applicant should have an undergraduate grade point average of at least 3.0, a score of 45 on the Miller Analogies Test, or scores of 450 on both the verbal and quantitative portions of the Graduate Record Exam, a well-written letter of intent that matches the objectives of the program and includes a description of previous technology experience, and positive letters of recommendation from individuals who know the professional characteristics of the applicant. Any exceptions for students failing to meet these standards shall be referred to the Admissions Committee for review and final decision.

Degree Requirements—36 semester hours, including instructional theory, computer design, and integrated media

Number of Full-Time Faculty—3; **Number of Other Faculty**—3

Name of Institution—Dakota State University

Name of Department or Program—Educational Technology

Program Website (URL)—http://www.dsu.edu/mset/index.aspx

Name of Contact Person—Mark Hawkes

Email Address of Contact Person—mark.hawkes@dsu.edu

Program Description—The MSET program offers two specializations: Distance Education and Technology Systems. These specializations are indicated on the official transcript. Students who wish to choose one of these specializations or the technology endorsement must take designated electives as follows: Distance Education: CET 747 Web and ITV Based Applications of Dist Ed (3 credit hours). CET 749 Policy and Management of Distance Education (3 credit hours). CET 769 Adult Learning for Distance Education (3 credit hours). Technology systems: CET 747 Web and ITV Based Applications of Dist Ed (3 credit hours). CET 750 Multimedia II (2 credit hours). CET 753 Network Management in Educational Institutions (3 credit hours). CET 758 Advanced Instructional Programming (2 credit hours). K-12 Educational Technology Endorsement: Individuals who hold or are eligible for teaching certification may earn the K-12 Educational Technology Endorsement by completing specified courses within the MSET program.

The Master of Science in Educational Technology (MSET) is an instructional technology program designed to meet the rapidly increasing demand for educators who are trained to integrate computer technologies into the curriculum and instruction. As computers and technology have become a significant part of the teaching and learning process, addressing the information needs of teachers has become the key to integrating technology into the classroom and increasing student learning. The primary emphasis of the master's program is to prepare educators who can create learning environments that integrate computing technology into the teaching and learning process. The MSET degree is an advanced degree designed to equip educators to be leaders in educational technology, current in teaching and learning processes and practices, current in research technologies and designs, knowledgeable of technologies and programming skills, and knowledgeable of current, technology-based educational tools and products. Specifically, by the end of the program MSET students will understand the capabilities of the computer and its impact upon education. They will be proficient in the use and application of computer software and will be able to demonstrate proficiency in using computers and related technologies to improve their own and their students' learning needs. The program integrates a highly technological environment with a project-based curriculum. Its focus is supported by an institutionally systemic belief that there is a substantial role for technology in teaching and learning in all educational environments.

Admission Requirements—Baccalaureate degree from an institution of higher education with full regional accreditation for that degree. Satisfactory scores on the GRE. The test must have been taken within the last 5 years. The GRE test can be waived if one of the following conditions is met: A cumulative grade point average of 3.25 or higher on a 4.0 scale for a baccalaureate degree from a regionally accredited college or university in the United States. Official admission into and demonstrated success in a regionally accredited graduate program in the United States. Demonstrated success is defined as grades of A or B in at least 12 h of graduate work. OR Graduation from a regionally accredited college/

university in the United States at least 15 years ago or more. Other factors (such as student maturity, references, or special expertise) may also be used to determine admission to the program. Also see program-specific admission requirements for additional requirements. Demonstrated basic knowledge of computers and their applications for educational purposes: Basic knowledge can be demonstrated in one of the following ways: technology endorsement from an accredited university, or in-service position as full- or part-time technology coordinator in a public school. A personal statement of technological competency: The statement should not exceed two pages and should be accompanied by supporting documentation or electronic references, e.g., URL.

Degree Requirements—The program requires a total of 36 credits beyond the baccalaureate degree. All students must take the following: 25 h of required courses. Eleven hours of electives. It is possible to specialize in either Distance Education or Technology Systems by selecting the designated electives for that specialization. You can also get a K-12 Educational Technology Endorsement. It is also possible to select the thesis option from among the electives. MSET courses are offered using a variety of distance delivery methods. Currently, one required course and one elective course have a limited-length hands-on campus requirement. These courses are offered in summer and the residency requirement is limited to 1 week per course. Alternatives may be available for the distance student.

Number of Full-Time Faculty—3; **Number of Other Faculty**—5

Name of Institution—Texas A&M University

Name of Department or Program—Educational Technology Program, Department of Educational Psychology

Program Website (URL)—http://educ.coe.tamu.edu/~edtc

Name of Contact Person—Ronald D. Zellner for program information/Carol Wagner for admission materials

Email Address of Contact Person—zellner@tamu.edu

Program Description—M.Ed. in Educational Technology; EDCI Ph.D. program with specializations in Educational Technology and in Distance Education; Ph.D. in Educational Psychology Foundations: Learning and Technology. The purpose of the Educational Technology Program is to prepare educators with the competencies required to improve the quality and effectiveness of instructional programs at all levels. A major emphasis is placed on multimedia instructional material development and techniques for effective distance education and communication. Teacher preparation with a focus on field-based instruction and school-to-university collaboration is also a major component. The program goal is to prepare graduates with a wide range of skills to work as professionals and leaders in a variety of settings, including education, business, industry, and the military. Program facilities include laboratories for teaching, resource development, and production. Computer, video, and multimedia development are supported in a number of facilities. The college and university also maintain facilities for distance education material development and fully equipped classrooms for

Graduate Programs in Learning, Design, Technology, Information, or Libraries 247

course delivery to nearby collaborative school districts and sites throughout the state.

Admission Requirements—M.Ed.: Bachelor's degree (range of scores, no specific cutoffs), 400 GRE Verbal, 550 (213 computer version) TOEFL; Ph.D.: 3.0 GPA, 450 GRE Verbal. Composite score from GRE verbal and quantitative and GPA, letters of recommendation, general background, and student goal statement

Degree Requirements—M.Ed.: 39 semester credits, oral exam; Ph.D.: coursework varies with student goals—degree is a Ph.D. in Educational Psychology Foundations with specialization in educational technology

Number of Full-Time Faculty—3; **Number of Other Faculty** -

Name of Institution—East Tennessee State University

Name of Department or Program—College of Education, Department of Curriculum and Instruction

Program Website (URL)—http://www.etsu.edu/coe/cuai/emet-ma.asp

Name of Contact Person—Harold Lee Daniels

Email Address of Contact Person—danielsh@etsu.edu

Program Description—(1)—M.Ed. in School Library Media. (2)—M.Ed. in Educational Technology. (3)—School Library Media Specialist add-on certification for those with current teaching license and a master's degree. (4)—M.Ed. in Classroom Technology for those with teaching license

Two (MAC & PC) dedicated computer labs (45+ computers). Online and evening course offerings for part-time, commuter, and employed students. Student pricing/campus licensing on popular software (MS, Adobe, Macromedia, etc.). Off-site cohort programs for classroom teachers. Extensive software library (900 + titles) with review/checkout privileges

Admission Requirements—Bachelor's degree from accredited institution with undergraduate GPA of 3.0 or higher, transcripts, personal application essay, interview, and in some cases GRE

Degree Requirements—36 semester hours, including 12 h in common core of instructional technology and media, 18 professional content hours, and 5-credit-hour practicum (200 field experience hours)

Number of Full-Time Faculty—4; **Number of Other Faculty**—4

Name of Institution—Texas Tech University

Name of Department or Program—Instructional Technology

Program Website (URL)—http://edit.educ.ttu.edu

Name of Contact Person—Steven Crooks

Email Address of Contact Person—Steven.Crooks@ttu.edu

Program Description—M.Ed. in Instructional Technology; completely online M. Ed. in Instructional Technology; Ed.D. in Instructional Technology. Program is NCATE accredited and follows ISTE and AECT guidelines

Admission Requirements—Holistic evaluation based on GRE scores (doctorate only), GPA, student goals, and writing samples

Degree Requirements—M.Ed.: 39 h (21-h instructional technology core, 12-h instructional technology electives, 6-h education foundations and research).

Ed.D.: 93 h (60 h in educational technology, 21 h in education or resource area, 12 h in dissertation)

Number of Full-Time Faculty—4; **Number of Other Faculty**—2

Name of Institution—University of North Texas

Name of Department or Program—Technology and Cognition (College of Education)

Program Website (URL)—http://www.cecs.unt.edu

Name of Contact Person—Dr. Mark Mortensen and Mrs. Donna Walton, Computer Education and Cognitive Systems; Dr. Jon Young, Chair, Department of Technology and Cognition

Email Address of Contact Person—iyoung@unt.edu

Program Description—M.S. in Computer Education and Cognitive Systems—two emphasis areas: Instructional Systems Technology and Teaching and Learning with Technology. Ph.D. in Educational Computing. See www.cecs.unt.edu. Unique applications of theory through research and practice in curriculum integration of technology, digital media production, and Web development. See www.cecs.unt.edu.

Admission Requirements—Toulouse Graduate School Requirements, 18 h in education, acceptable GRE: 405 V and 489 A, three analytical writing for M.S. degree. Increased requirements for Ph.D. program

Degree Requirements—36 semester hours (12-h core, 12-h program course requirement based on M.S. track, 12-h electives). See www.cecs.unt.edu.

Number of Full-Time Faculty -; **Number of Other Faculty** -

Name of Institution—Utah State University

Name of Department or Program—Department of Instructional Technology and Learning Sciences, Emma Eccles Jones College of Education and Human Services

Program Website (URL)—http://itls.usu.edu

Name of Contact Person—Mimi Recker

Email Address of Contact Person—mimi.recker@usu.edu

Program Description—M.S. and M.Ed. with concentrations in the areas of Instructional Technology, Learning Sciences, Multimedia, Educational Technology, and Information Technology/School Library Media Administration. Ph.D. in Instructional Technology and Learning Sciences is offered for individuals seeking to become professionally involved in instructional/learning sciences research and development in higher education, corporate education, public schools, community colleges, and government. M.Ed. programs in Instructional Technology/School Library Media Administration and Educational Technology are also available completely online. The doctoral program is built on a strong master's and specialist program in Instructional Technology. All doctoral students complete a core with the remainder of the course selection individualized, based upon career goals.

Admission Requirements—M.S. and Ed.S.: 3.0 GPA, a verbal and quantitative score at the 40th percentile on the GRE or 43 MAT, three written recommendations. Ph.D.: relevant master's degree, 3.0 GPA, verbal and quantitative score at the 40th percentile on the GRE, three written recommendations, essay on research interests

Degree Requirements—M.S.: 39 sem. hours; thesis or project option. Ed.S.: 30 sem. hours if M.S. is in the field, 40 h if not. Ph.D.: 60 total hours, dissertation, 3 sem. residency, and comprehensive examination

Number of Full-Time Faculty—10; **Number of Other Faculty**—1

Name of Institution—University of Virginia

Name of Department or Program—Instructional Science and Technology Program, Department of Curriculum and Instruction, Curry School of Education

Program Website (URL)—curry.edschool.virginia.edu/it.

Name of Contact Person—Karen Dwier

Email Address of Contact Person—kdg9g@virginia.edu

Program Description—In the University of Virginia's Curry School of Education's Ph.D. program, Instructional Science and Technology (IT) is not just a program; it is a key theme in the identity of the entire school and is influential across the university. Twenty faculty members from across the Curry School and University come together to focus on IT, and students have rich learning opportunities across a range of focal areas:

Instructional Design and Interactive Development

Web 2.0 Convergence, Educational Multimedia

Technology Leadership, Technology, and Teaching

Science, Technology, Engineering, and Mathematics (STEM) Education

Consumer Health Education, Gender, and Technology

Games/Play/Flow, Museums, and Education

M.Ed., Ed.S., Ed.D., and Ph.D. degrees are offered.

The IT program is situated in a major research university with linkages to multiple disciplines. Faculty in the program hold leadership positions with the Center for Advanced Study of Teaching and Learning (CASTL) and the Center for Technology and Teacher Education, among others. Our students work closely with faculty in a collegial environment on both time-tested and leading-edge practices. You will find yourself working with the most talented students from virtually every discipline and background, learning team leadership skills, and forming lifelong friendships. The University of Virginia is one of the top-ranked public universities in the nation, and the Curry School is nationally recognized for its leadership and innovation, particularly in IT. We are the recipient of the American Association of Colleges for Teacher Education (AACTE) Innovative Use of Technology Award for modeling innovative use of technology for others in the profession as well as a recipient of the first International Society for Technology in Education (ISTE) Distinguished Achievement Award for integration of technology into teacher education, among other awards and recognition.

Faculty and students are active in national organizations such as the Association for Educational Communications and Technology (AECT), Society for Information Technology and Teacher Education (SITE), and the American Educational

Research Association (AERA). Graduates in IT from the Curry School are creating positive change through positions in research and development and instructional innovation around the world. We invite you to discover, create, and change with us.

Admission Requirements—Admission to any graduate program requires undergraduate degree from accredited institution in any field, undergraduate GPA 3.0, and TOEFL (if applicable): 600 paper based, 250 computer based

For admission to the Master of Education (M.Ed.), Educational Specialist (Ed.S.), and Doctor of Education (Ed.D.) degrees, minimum 1000 GRE (V + Q)

For admission to the Doctor of Philosophy (Ph.D.) program, minimum GRE 1100 (V + Q). Ph.D. admissions are highly competitive and fully funded, to provide mentored, 4-year program based on research, development, and scholarship.

Degree Requirements—M.Ed.: 36 semester hours. Ed.S.: 60 semester hours beyond undergraduate degree

Ed.D.: 72 semester hours including 48 h of coursework, 12 h of internship experience, and a 12-h capstone project

Ph.D.: 76 semester hours of coursework and research internship, plus 24 h of dissertation research. All graduate degrees require a comprehensive examination. The Ph.D. also requires completion of a preliminary examination and a juried pre-dissertation presentation or publication.

Number of Full-Time Faculty—4; **Number of Other Faculty**—16

Name of Institution—University of Washington

Name of Department or Program—College of Education

Program Website (URL)—http://www.educ.washington.edu/COE/c-and-i/c_and_i_med_ed_tech.htm

Name of Contact Person—William Winn

Email Address of Contact Person—billwinn@u.washington.edu

Program Description—M.Ed., Ed.D., and Ph.D. for individuals in business, industry, higher education, public schools, and organizations concerned with education or communication (broadly defined). Emphasis on design of materials and programs to encourage learning and development in school and nonschool settings; research and related activity in such areas as interactive instruction, Web-based learning, virtual environments, use of video as a tool for design and development. Close collaboration with program in cognitive studies.

Admission Requirements—M.Ed.: goal statement (2–3 papers), writing sample, 1000 GRE (verbal plus quantitative), undergraduate GPA indicating potential to successfully accomplish graduate work. Doctoral: GRE scores, letters of reference, transcripts, personal statement, master's degree or equivalent in field appropriate to the specialization with 3.5 GPA, 2 years of successful professional experience and/or experience related to program goals desirable

Degree Requirements—M.Ed.: 45 qtr. hours (including 24 in technology); thesis or project recommended, exam optional. Ed.D.: see http://www.educ.washington.edu/COEWebSite/programs/ci/EdD.html; Ph.D.: http://www.educ.washington.edu/COEWebSite/students/prospective/phdDescrip.html

Graduate Programs in Learning, Design, Technology, Information, or Libraries 251

Number of Full-Time Faculty -; **Number of Other Faculty** -

Name of Institution—University of Alaska Southeast
Name of Department or Program—Educational Technology Program
Program Website (URL)—http://uas.alaska.edu/education/experienced
Name of Contact Person—Marsha Gladhart
Email Address of Contact Person—marsha.gladhart@uas.alaska.edu
Program Description—Educational Technology

- Distance program * Standards-based learning * Integration of the most current technologies * Collaboration with other teachers * Instructors with K-12 teaching experience * Focus on improving student learning * Use of technology as a tool to assist learning

Admission Requirements—# A completed graduate application and $60 processing fee. # Official academic transcript indicating baccalaureate degree and a GPA of 3.0. # Two general recommendations written by former or current professors, employers, or supervisors who are familiar with your work and performance. Each recommendation must be submitted using the Letter of Recommendation for Graduate Programs form. # A recommendation documenting your ability to meet the educational technology standards required for entry to the program. This recommendation should be completed by an administrator, supervisor, or technology leader. # Statement of professional objectives. # A copy of a current teaching or administrative certificate
Degree Requirements—Official academic transcript indicating baccalaureate degree and a GPA of 3.0
Number of Full-Time Faculty—2; **Number of Other Faculty**—5

Name of Institution—University of Arkansas
Name of Department or Program—Educational Technology
Program Website (URL)—http://etec.uark.edu
Name of Contact Person—Cheryl Murphy
Email Address of Contact Person—cmurphy@uark.edu
Program Description—The program prepares students for a variety of work environments by offering core courses that are applicable to a multitude of professional venues. The program also allows for specific emphasis area studies via open-ended assignments and course electives that include courses particularly relevant to higher education, business/industry, or K-12 environments. The primary focus of the program is on the processes involved in instructional design, training and development, media production, and utilization of instructional technologies. Because technology is continually changing, the program emphasizes acquisition of a process over the learning of specific technologies. Although skills necessary in making Educational Technology products are taught, technology changes rapidly; therefore, a primary emphasis on making technological products would lead to the acquisition of skills that are quickly outdated. However, learning the principles and mental tools critical to producing successful training and education will endure long after "new" technologies have become

obsolete. That is why the University of Arkansas ETEC program focuses on the processes as opposed to specific technologies.

The Educational Technology Program is a 33-h non-thesis online master's program that prepares students for professional positions as educational technologists of education, business, government, and health professions. Because the program is offered online, there are no on-campus requirements for the completion of this degree.

Admission Requirements—The Educational Technology online master's program admits students in the fall, spring, and summer. Applications and all accompanying documents must be submitted within 3 months of the desired starting semester to ensure adequate processing time. To qualify for admission applicants must have an earned bachelor's degree and an undergraduate GPA of 3.0 within the last 60 h of coursework. Specific application materials can be found at http://etec.uark.edu/1069.htm. Applicants for the M.Ed. degree must have met all requirements of graduate school admission, completed a bachelor's degree, and earned a 3.0 GPA in all undergraduate coursework or obtained an acceptable score on the Graduate Record Examinations or Miller Analogies Test. A graduate school application, ETEC Program Application, writing sample, autobiographical sketch, and letters of recommendation are required for admission consideration.

Degree Requirements—Beginning fall 2012, in addition to general admission requirements students must complete a minimum of 34 h to include 22 semester hours of educational technology core courses; nine semester hours of educational technology electives; and three semester hours of research. Additionally, a Culminating Student Portfolio must be successfully completed during the last semester of coursework. There are no on-campus requirements for the completion of this degree, although approved courses that meet the research requirements may be taken on campus if desired.

Number of Full-Time Faculty—2; **Number of Other Faculty**—3

Name of Institution—University of Arkansas at Little Rock
Name of Department or Program—Learning Systems Technology
Program Website (URL)—http://ualr.edu/med/LSTE/
Name of Contact Person—Elizabeth Vaughn-Neely
Email Address of Contact Person—eivaughn@ualr.edu
Program Description—The Learning Systems Technology master's degree prepares you for the design, production, and application of these new methods, including creating and designing the following learning products: * documents and electronic displays * interactive tutorials for Web-based delivery * instructional blogs * useful Web pages * complete instructional packages using digital images and film clips * courses using a variety of online course management systems * learning resource centers. This program is offered entirely online.
Admission Requirements—Admission to the LSTE master's program requires the following: * a baccalaureate degree from a regionally accredited institution with substantially the same undergraduate programs as the University of Arkansas at

Little Rock with an overall GPA of 3.0 or 3.25 for the last 60 h. * A 3.0 GPA on the last 60 h (including postbaccalaureate hours or a 2.7 GPA on all undergraduate hours taken for the baccalaureate degree). * Successful application to the UALR graduate school. * Academic evaluation by the LSTE program coordinator. After you have completed your online application to the graduate school, your folder with all of your transcripts will be sent to the program coordinator for evaluation. The program coordinator will then send you a letter with your status in the process. Once you get your letter of acceptance you will be able to start the program in any semester: fall, spring, or summer. If you have any questions, please contact the program coordinator.

Degree Requirements—The 36 graduate credit hours include * 9 Educational Foundations hours * 18 Learning Technologies hours * up to 3 elective courses (Foundations, English writing, Learning Technologies, or other content area approved by the adviser). No more than 6 h earned within the last 3 years of transfer credit will be accepted in the program.

Number of Full-Time Faculty—1; **Number of Other Faculty**—5

Name of Institution—California State Polytechnic University
Name of Department or Program—Educational Multimedia Design
Program Website (URL)—www.csupomona.edu/emm
Name of Contact Person—Shahnaz Lotfipour
Email Address of Contact Person—slotfipour@csupomona.edu
Program Description—Design and production of e-learning materials and educational multimedia software (including audio, video, animation, Web programming (three levels), graphics, etc.) for educational and corporate training environments using the sound instructional principles and strategies. Hands-on training, project-based, combination of online and hybrid courses, internship possibilities in educational and corporate settings
Admission Requirements—Undergraduate GPA of 3.0, three strong letters of recommendations for this program, and satisfying graduate writing test (GWT) within the first couple of quarters
Degree Requirements—B.A. or B.S. in any area
Number of Full-Time Faculty—3; **Number of Other Faculty**—5

Name of Institution—California State University Monterey Bay (CSUMB)
Name of Department or Program—Master of Science in Instructional Science and Technology (IST)
Program Website (URL)—http://itcd.csumb.edu/mist
Name of Contact Person—Bude Su
Email Address of Contact Person—mist@csumb.edu
Program Description—Interdisciplinary collaboration that integrates learning science and information technology is the hallmark of the IST graduate program and a CSUMB core value. Recognizing that the use of technology is critical to the design, development, and delivery of instruction in the twenty-first century, IST integrates modern learning technology and pedagogy to create educational experiences adequate for the contemporary world. This technology infusion

models best practices to learners. Rather than setting aside one course that deals solely with ethics and social responsibility, our curriculum integrates ethical reflection and practice throughout the program. All required courses incorporate the basic concepts and concerns of ethics into their design, development, and delivery. Multiculturalism and globalism are infused into the IST curriculum, including discussion of diversity in the conduct of instructional design and diversity in the understanding of ethics. Applied learning is critical to the IST program, and we use an integrated pedagogy that builds on each semester's outcome. Please see the program curriculum outline in the Degree Requirements section, and visit our website for more details at http://www.csumb.edu/mist/.

Admission Requirements—(1) Complete and submit an application form at CSUMENTOR.edu and $55.00 application fee payable to CSUMB. (A) Select fall 2012 as the application term. B. Select M.S. in Instructional Science and Technology program to continue. (2) Submit all required supporting documents. All supporting documents should be submitted to School of Information Technology and Communication Design Attention: MIST Program, Building 18, Room 150,100 Campus Center Seaside, CA 93955 A. Submit two official copies of each of the following: (1) Transcripts of all college coursework taken * Have two official transcripts from all colleges and universities you have attended mailed directly to the MIST Program at the address listed above. (We recommend that you request that an additional copy be mailed directly to you at home and that you leave that envelope unopened until you have confirmation that we have received our copies.) * A GPA of 3.0 is expected for the most recent 60 units of college-level work attempted. GPA between 2.5 and 3.0 may be considered with substantial alternative demonstration of the ability to succeed in the program. (2) Test scores (TOEFL, GRE, etc.) (if applicable) * We recommend that you take the GRE test to improve your competitive standing, but it is not required. CSUMB's school code for ETS is 1945. * For those students required to demonstrate English proficiency: the IST program requires a TOEFL score of 575 for admission. Selected applicants with TOEFL scores between 525 and 574 and applicants demonstrating English proficiency with test scores other than TOEFL must pass a writing workshop offered by ITCD before the first day of classes as a condition of admission. Applicants with TOEFL scores below 525 will not be considered. * CSUMB minimum requirements for English proficiency for applicants with degrees from foreign universities are listed on the Admissions and Recruitment website at http://ar.csumb.edu/site/x5362.xml#requirements. (3) Foreign Credential Evaluation (if applicable) * All transcripts from schools outside the United States must be sent, at the applicant's expense, to a foreign credential evaluation service. A detailed "course-by-course" report is required for all programs. Three credential evaluation services accepted by CSU Monterey Bay are (1) World Education Services, WES, http://www.wes.org/; (2) American Association of Collegiate Registrars and Admissions Offices, AACRAO, http://www.aacrao.org/credential/; and (3) International Education Research Foundation, IERF, http://www.ierf.org/. * CSUMB minimum requirements for foreign credential evaluation for applicants with degrees from foreign universities are listed on the Admissions and Recruitment website at http://ar.csumb.edu/site/x5362.xml#requirements. (B) Submit an original "Statement of Purpose" (one copy is sufficient). * Include a 1000–2000-word statement of purpose (statement of educational and professional goals) that demonstrates your writing ability. (C) Submit two or three letters of reference (one copy of each is sufficient). * Include two or three letters of recommendation from individuals familiar with your professional and academic work. For more detailed information, please visit our website at http://www.csumb.edu/mist.

Degree Requirements—The Master of Science in Instructional Science and Technology degree requires 24 semester hours of core courses, 4 semester hours of an elective, and 4 semester hours for the culminating capstone experience or thesis [learn more at CSUMB.EDU/capstone]. As the title signifies, the core courses are a cluster of instructional design, instructional systems, and best educational practices that represent the core of the collaborative program. By guiding you toward the Learning Outcomes (LOs) listed below, these courses provide you with the skills necessary to become an effective instructional designer and e-learning developer in today's high-tech, global marketplace. Given the complexities that emanate from strong and growing global forces and conflicting values, we discuss international and ethical issues in all courses. The IST program consists of four terms that must be taken sequentially covering the following courses and outcomes. IST 522: Instructional Design, IST 524: Instructional Technology, LO 1 Instructional Technology, and LO 2 Instructional Design Students are introduced to the field and profession of Instructional Science and Technology. Topics include but are not limited to history, current issues, future trends, and an overview of how the components of the field fit together. Students investigate and apply instructional design models to carry out small-scale projects and generate a detailed instructional design document. Students are encouraged to incorporate projects from their current employment into the class assignments. Term II courses: IST 520: Learning Theories. IST 526: Interactive Multimedia Instruction. LO 3 Learning Theories. LO 4 Interactive Multimedia. Students learn to evaluate and select appropriate learning theories and instructional principles and apply them for the design and implementation of instruction and training. Students construct a functioning learning module using interactive multimedia software, information technology, and media. Term III courses: IST 622: Assessment and Evaluation. IST 626: Advanced Instructional Design. LO 2 Instructional Design. LO 5 Assessment and Evaluation. Students work on authentic instructional design projects individually or in small groups. Students engage in a real-world design experience that deals with and balance numerous additional variables, including project management, effective communication with clients, time management, application of professional knowledge and skills, and producing of professional level products. Students are introduced to the theoretical framework of assessment as it applies to learner performance, effectiveness of curriculum design, and effectiveness of instructional delivery. Students develop techniques for judging the performance of instructional delivery and conduct appropriate usability, reliability, and efficiency tests of instructional and learning management systems. Term IV courses: IST 699: Graduate Capstone Minimum of four elective upper division or graduate-level credits, approved by program coordinator and faculty adviser, related to the field of instructional science and technology. LO 6 Breadth of Knowledge. LO 7 Instructional Science and Technology Capstone Project or Thesis. Students complete a capstone project or thesis that connects with their careers as the culminating experience. Examples include a field study, a client-driven project, or applied research.

Number of Full-Time Faculty—8; **Number of Other Faculty**—12

Name of Institution—California State University, East Bay

Name of Department or Program—Online Teaching and Learning

Program Website (URL)—http://www.ce.csueastbay.edu/degree/education/index. shtml?intid=fhome_otlm

Name of Contact Person—Nan Chico

Email Address of Contact Person—nan.chico@csueastbay.edu

Program Description—A professional development degree for experienced K-12, college/university faculty, and corporate or nonprofit trainers at institutions creating new, or building on old, online course and program degrees, workshops, and trainings. A major focus is learning how to design courses around accessibility issues.

Courses are in blackboard; students are given a blackboard shell of their own to design or may choose among other course management systems. We focus on best practices in online teaching and learning, using a CMS and varieties of other social media. Not cohort based, admission is quarterly; maximum 2 courses per quarter; may skip 1–2 consecutive quarters.

Admission Requirements—B.A. or B.S. degree from a regionally accredited US institution, in any major; GPA 3.0 in last 60 semester units or last 90 quarter units. Selection is also based on mandatory Letter of Intent.

Degree Requirements—Four 5-week courses taken over two quarters (which earn the Certificate in Online Teaching and Learning); two 10-week electives, four 10-week required courses, the last of which is a capstone project. Each course earns 4.5 quarter units; all required courses must earn a "B" or better; overall GPA must be 3.0 or better. Total of 10 courses, 45 units.

Number of Full-Time Faculty -; **Number of Other Faculty**—9

Name of Institution—California State University, Fresno

Name of Department or Program—M.A. in Education and Certificate of Advanced Study in Educational Technology

Program Website (URL)—http://www.csufresno.edu/kremen/ci/graduate/ma--education.html

Name of Contact Person—Roy M. Bohlin

Email Address of Contact Person—royb@csufresno.edu

Program Description -

Admission Requirements -

Degree Requirements—Bachelor's degree

Number of Full-Time Faculty—6; **Number of Other Faculty**—4

Name of Institution—Metropolitan State College of Denver
Name of Department or Program—Department of Special Education, Early
 Childhood Education, Reading, and Educational Technology
Program Website (URL)—http://www.mscd.edu/~ted
Name of Contact Person—Miri Chung
Email Address of Contact Person—mchung3@mscd.edu
Program Description -
Admission Requirements -
Degree Requirements -
Number of Full-Time Faculty—2; **Number of Other Faculty**—1

Name of Institution—Regis University
Name of Department or Program—School of Education and Counseling
Program Website (URL)—www.regis.edu
Name of Contact Person—Carole Hruskocy
Email Address of Contact Person—chruskoc@regis.edu
Program Description—Instructional Technology Curriculum, Instruction, and
 Assessment Professional Leadership Adult Learning, Training, and Development
 Self-Designed Reading Space Studies. The majority of our programs are offered
 in the online format.
Admission Requirements—Essay Letters of Recommendation Minimum
 GPA of 2.75
Degree Requirements -
Number of Full-Time Faculty—15; **Number of Other Faculty** -

Name of Institution—University of Bridgeport
Name of Department or Program—Instructional Technology
Program Website (URL)—http://www.bridgeport.edu/imsit
Name of Contact Person—Jerald D. Cole
Email Address of Contact Person—jcole@bridgeport.edu
Program Description—Master's and Professional Diploma (6th Year) Instructional
 Technology Tracks: (1) teacher, (2) trainer, (3) developer, (4) technology educa-
 tion, (5) technology leadership
Open-Source Curriculum and Software Model. (2) Cross Platform Mobil Tablet
 Computing Initiative. (3) Social Constructionist Pedagogy. (4) Hybrid and online
 courses. (5) Cohort based. (6) Tuition-free internships for teacher track
Admission Requirements—Online application, essay on experience and objec-
 tives for study, two letters of reference, praxis 1 for teacher track, TOEFL for
 non-native English speakers, transcripts, phone interview
Degree Requirements—4 core courses, 2 distribution requirements, 1 research, 1
 practicum, 4 electives
Number of Full-Time Faculty—14; **Number of Other Faculty**—21

Name of Institution—Ball State University
Name of Department or Program—Master of Arts in Curriculum and Educational
 Technology

Program Website (URL)—http://www.bsu.edu/edstudies/edtech/
Name of Contact Person—Jon M. Clausen
Email Address of Contact Person—jmclaus@bsu.edu
Program Description—Specialization tracks in curriculum or educational technology

The Master of Arts in Curriculum and Educational Technology is a 30-h program designed for educators seeking to integrate technology into K-12 curriculum and other instructional contexts where teaching and learning occur. Graduates are prepared to become leaders within their instructional contexts by coursework and experiences that focus on the development of a conceptual framework in which technology is an embedded aspect of the teaching and learning process. The program prepares graduates to utilize technology to meet learning needs of students and to critically examine technology's ever-changing presence within schools and society.

Admission Requirements—Prospective students should apply to the graduate college and provide official transcripts from all universities/colleges attended. A student seeking admittance for a master's degree must meet the following minimum criteria: hold an earned bachelor's degree from a college or university that is accredited by its regional accrediting association and have one of the following: an undergraduate cumulative GPA of at least 2.75 on a scale of 4.0 or a cumulative GPA of at least 3.0 on a 4.0 scale in the latter half of the baccalaureate. Additional information regarding application and admission to the graduate college can be found at the following website: http://www.bsu.edu/gradschool.

Degree Requirements—Successful completion of 30 graduate hours
Number of Full-Time Faculty—8; **Number of Other Faculty**—4

Name of Institution—Purdue University, Calumet
Name of Department or Program—Instructional Technology
Program Website (URL)—http://www.purduecal.edu/education/grad/it.html
Name of Contact Person—Janet Buckenmeyer
Email Address of Contact Person—buckenme@purduecal.edu
Program Description—Instructional Technology and Instructional Design

The Instructional Technology program at Purdue University, Calumet, is a practitioner-based program. Students entering the program may be teachers but do not need a teaching license to enroll. The program does not lead to PK-12 licensure.

Admission Requirements—3.0 GPA; three letters of recommendation; essay; two official copies of all transcripts
Degree Requirements -
Number of Full-Time Faculty—3; **Number of Other Faculty**—1

Name of Institution—Emporia State University
Name of Department or Program—Instructional Design and Technology
Program Website (URL)—http://idt.emporia.edu
Name of Contact Person—Marcus D. Childress
Email Address of Contact Person—mchildre@emporia.edu

Program Description—Distance learning, online learning, corporate education, P-12 technology integration

All program courses are offered online. The online Master of Science in Instructional Design and Technology program prepares individuals for leadership in the systematic design, development, implementation, evaluation, and management of technology-rich learning in a variety of settings. Individuals obtaining the IDT degree serve as instructional designers/trainers in business, industry, health professions, and the military and are charged with training, development, and e-learning programs within their organizations. Other graduates hold leadership positions in P-12 and postsecondary institutions. In addition to positions in the workplace, graduates regularly choose to pursue their Ph.D. degrees in IDT at top-ranked universities. IDT faculty members hold leadership positions on the Association for Educational Communications and Technology (AECT) board of directors, executive committee, and research and theory division. Forms and application materials are available at the website http://idt.emporia.edu. Other social media contacts: Ning—http://idtesu.ning.com/. Twitter—http://twitter.com/idtesu. Blogspot—http://idtesu.blogspot.com/. YouTube—http://www.youtube.com/idtesu.

Admission Requirements—Graduate application, official transcripts, GPA of 2.75 or more based on a 4-point scale in the last 60 semester hours of undergraduate study, resume, two current recommendations, writing competency. The program admits on a rolling basis. The departmental admission committee reviews and decides on applications as they are received, until there are no remaining openings.

Degree Requirements—36 credit hours: 21 cr. core, 6 cr. research, 9 cr. electives
Number of Full-Time Faculty—6; **Number of Other Faculty**—4

Name of Institution—Pittsburg State University
Name of Department or Program—Master's Degree in Educational Technology
Program Website (URL)—http://www.pittstate.edu
Name of Contact Person—Sue Stidham
Email Address of Contact Person—jstidham@pittstate.edu
Program Description—Library Media licensure
Admission Requirements -
Degree Requirements -
Number of Full-Time Faculty—3; **Number of Other Faculty** -

Name of Institution—Morehead State University
Name of Department or Program—Educational Technology Program
Program Website (URL)—www.moreheadstate.edu/education
Name of Contact Person—Christopher T. Miller
Email Address of Contact Person—c.miller@morehead-st.edu
Program Description—Master of Arts in Education degree focuses on technology integration, multimedia, distance education, educational games, and instructional design. Educational Leadership Doctor of Education in Educational Technology Leadership is a practitioner-based doctoral degree program focused

260   K. H. Chien et al.

on the development of leaders in the field of educational technology. Master's program is fully online. Ed.D. program is fully online but requires a 1-week face-to-face seminar course each year.

Admission Requirements—Admission requirements for master's degree: * Standard or provisional teaching certification, a statement of eligibility for teaching, or letter describing your role as educational support. Those students who fit the criteria of educational support will be able to obtain the master's degree, but it cannot be used for initial teacher certification. * A GRE minimum combined score of 750 (verbal and quantitative) and 2.5 on the analytic writing portion or a minimum 31 raw score (381–386 scaled score) on the Miller Analogies Test. * For students who have not met testing requirements for admission into the program, but who have successfully completed 12 h of coursework required for the program with a 3.5 or above GPA, the department chair may waive the testing requirement. * The testing requirement is waived for students who have already completed a master's degree. * A minimum of 2.75 undergraduate GPA. * Demonstrated competency of computer fluency (i.e., undergraduate or graduate computer competency course or computer competency assessment). Ed.D. admission requirements: * GRE, Miller Analogies Test (MAT), or GMAT scores including GRE writing score or on-demand writing sample. * Official transcripts of all undergraduate and graduate coursework. * Documentation of a master's degree from an institution accredited by a nationally recognized accreditation body. * Resume or vita documenting years of related professional/leadership or educational technology, instructional design, and training experience. * Letter of introduction/interest stating professional goals, leadership style, and educational philosophy. * Recommendation forms: at least three professional references from persons in a position to evaluate the applicant's potential for success in a doctoral program. At least one to be completed by immediate or up-line supervisor or (for Ed. Tech track) professional familiarity with candidates' use of technology, instructional design, and training. Other recommendation forms to be completed by professional colleagues or university faculty who are familiar with the applicant. * Documentation of previous statistical methodology, research-related coursework or evidence of use, and application of data-informed decision-making to determine possible need for statistical methodology coursework. * International students and ESL students must meet university minimum TOEFL score or its equivalent. * No more than 24 h of previously completed postgraduate work from MSU may be counted in the Ed.D. program.

Degree Requirements—Master's program degree requirements. * Satisfy general degree requirements. * Must submit a professional portfolio demonstrating work completed within the program during the final semester of graduate work. * Must apply for graduation in the Graduate Office, 701 Ginger Hall, in the beginning of the term that completion is anticipated. * Maintain a 3.0 GPA in all courses taken after completing the bachelor's degree. *Must be unconditionally admitted. Ed.D. degree requirements: * Satisfy all degree requirements. * The student must successfully complete and defend a qualifying examination to enroll in Ed.D. 899 capstone courses and continue within the doctoral program.

Graduate Programs in Learning, Design, Technology, Information, or Libraries 261

* Students are required to successfully complete and defend a doctoral capstone. * Students must apply for graduation with the Graduate Office at the beginning of the semester in which they intend to complete. * Maintain a cumulative 3.0 GPA in all courses taken. Must be unconditionally admitted. If a student is not unconditionally admitted after completing 12 graduate hours, he/she will not be permitted to register for additional credit hours. * Students are encouraged to complete the program within the cohort time limit. The maximum allowed time for completion is 10 years. * A total of 18 h will be permitted to be transferred from other universities.

Number of Full-Time Faculty—2; **Number of Other Faculty**—2

Name of Institution—University of Massachusetts, Amherst

Name of Department or Program—Learning, Media, and Technology Master's Program/Math Science and Learning Technology Doctoral Program

Program Website (URL)—http://www.umass.edu/education/academics/tecs/ed_tech.shtml

Name of Contact Person—Florence R. Sullivan

Email Address of Contact Person—fsullivan@educ.umass.edu

Program Description—The Master of Education concentration in Learning, Media, and Technology prepares students to understand, critique, and improve technology- and media-based learning and teaching. The program is structured such that students construct solid knowledge of theories of learning and instruction, as well as theories of the design and use of educational technologies and media. Just as importantly, we offer a number of courses and research experiences through which students develop facility with applied aspects of technology--centered educational practices (e.g., authoring software systems, utilizing tools such as Director and Flash). By encountering multiple opportunities for the analysis, design, and testing of educational technology/media, students develop a principled approach to technology- and media-based instruction and learning. The Math, Science, and Learning Technology doctoral program prepares graduate students to improve the learning and instruction of Science, Technology, Engineering, and Mathematics (STEM) disciplines. To achieve that goal, we are deeply committed to research and scholarship, using both basic and applied research. We put a premium on developing principled approaches to affect educational practice and pursuing rigorous theory building about educational phenomena. We apply such knowledge in developing state-of-the-art instructional designs. These efforts grow from an understanding of educational practice and close work with practitioners in both formal and informal learning settings. Importantly we recognized that certain social groups have been historically marginalized from STEM disciplines, education, and work. We seek to understand the processes and structures contributing to the systematic exclusion of these groups and to actively contribute to correcting such inequities. Our work draws from a variety of disciplines including cognitive science, sociology, anthropology, learning sciences, psychology, and computer science.

In the master's program, we consider media and technology both as tools in learning and teaching specific disciplines (e.g., mathematics and science) and as objects of study in and of themselves. With regard to the former, and in line with the affiliated faculty's expertise, students explore the educational uses of a variety of technological forms (e.g., robotics systems for learning engineering, physics, programming, and arts) and computer-based environments (e.g., software systems for learning scientific image processing). As for the latter, students actively engage in designing and using various learning technologies and media, including Web-based environments, computer-mediated communications systems, computer-based virtual worlds, and new media for new literacies. The features of the doctoral program of study are: * provide an interconnected locus of intellectual activity for graduate students and faculty; * increase equity (in gender, ethnicity, and opportunities) in recruitment, admission, and retention of students and faculty and pursue issues of equity in science education; * teach relevant courses, seminars, and independent studies in mathematics and science education; * conduct pertinent research studies in mathematics and science learning, teaching, curriculum development, and assessment; * build a base of scholarship, disseminate new knowledge, and apply it actively in education; * provide apprenticeship opportunities for graduate students; * understand and support effective practice in mathematics and science education; * coordinate outreach efforts with K-12 schools and related projects; * collaborate with faculty in the department, school, and university as well as in the wider profession throughout the Commonwealth of Massachusetts, nationally, and internationally.

Admission Requirements—For the master's program—GPA of 2.75 or higher, TESOL test score of 80 points or higher, excellent letters of recommendation, clear statement of purpose. For the doctoral program—earned master's degree in math, natural sciences, learning technology, or education; GPA of 2.75 or higher; TESOL test score of 80 points or higher; excellent letters of recommendation; clear statement of purpose

Degree Requirements—Master's degree—33 credit hours and thesis. Doctoral degree—36 credit hours beyond the master's degree, 18 dissertation credit hours, successful completion of comprehensive exams, successful completion of doctoral dissertation

Number of Full-Time Faculty—8; **Number of Other Faculty**—2

Name of Institution—Oakland University
Name of Department or Program—Master of Training and Development Program
Program Website (URL)—www2.oakland.edu/sehs/hrd/
Name of Contact Person—Chaunda L. Scott
Email Address of Contact Person—ouhrdmtd@gmail.com
Program Description—The Master of Training and Development Program at Oakland University provides a unique blend of knowledge and skills in all aspects of training and development. Students can choose between two areas of emphasis: * Instructional Design and Technology * Organizational Development and Leadership.

Graduate Programs in Learning, Design, Technology, Information, or Libraries 263

The Master of Training and Development Program develops practitioners with the knowledge and skills required to enhance individual performance. Graduates of the program will be able to lead interventions associated with diagnosing performance problems and opportunities. Graduates will also be able to design and implement individual and organizational solutions and evaluate results. All courses are taught by outstanding faculty who have diverse backgrounds and experience in business and academia. The Master of Training and Development Program completed in two- and one-half years. Graduates of the program will be qualified to work as human resource development professionals. Including directors of training centers, organizational development consultants, instructional designers, and performance technologists.

Admission Requirements—Official transcripts for undergraduate and graduate coursework showing a bachelor's degree from a regionally accredited institution and a cumulative GPA of 3.0 or higher. A formal statement, between 100 and 1500 words, highlighting work and life experience—preferably 1 year or longer that have led to the desire to pursue the Master of Training and Development Degree. Three letters of recommendations to attest to the quality and scope of the applicant's academic and professional ability and an interview will be required.

Degree Requirements—The completion of 36 approved credits with an overall GPA of 3.0 or better and a grade of 2.8 or above in each additional course. The completion of five core courses is also required: HRD 530 Instructional Design, HRD 506 Theoretical Foundations of Training and Development, HRD 507 Needs Assessment, HRD 605 Program Evaluation, and HRD 611 Program Administration.

Number of Full-Time Faculty—4; **Number of Other Faculty**—2

Name of Institution—University of Michigan
Name of Department or Program—Department of Educational Studies
Program Website (URL)—http://www.soe.umich.edu/learningtechnologies/
Name of Contact Person—Barry J. Fishman
Email Address of Contact Person—fishman@umich.edu
Program Description—Ph.D. in Learning Technologies, M.A. in Educational Studies with a focus on Digital Media and Education

The Learning Technologies Program at the University of Michigan integrates the study of technology with a focus on a substantive content area. A unique aspect of the program is that your learning and research will engage you in real-world educational contexts. You will find that understanding issues related to a specific content area provides an essential context for meaningful research in learning. Your understanding of technology, school contexts, and a content area will place you among the leaders who design and conduct research on advanced technological systems that change education and schooling. The doctoral specialization in Learning Technologies must be taken in conjunction with a substantive concentration designed in consultation with your advisor. Current active concentrations include Science, Literacy, Culture and Gender, Teacher Education, Design and Human-Computer Interaction, Policy, and Social Studies. Other areas are possible. The Master's Degree in Educational Studies with a focus on Digital Media and Education at the University of Michigan prepares professionals for leadership roles in the design, development, implementation, and research of powerful technologies to enhance learning. Our approach to design links current knowledge and research about how people learn with technological tools that enable new means of organizing and evaluating learning environments. Course and project work reflect the latest knowledge and practice in learning, teaching, and technology. Core courses prepare students to use current understandings about learning theory, design principles, research methodologies, and evaluation strategies in educational settings ranging from classrooms to Web-based and distributed learning environments. Faculty work with students to shape programs that meet individual interests. Practical experience is offered through internships with area institutions.

Admission Requirements—GRE, B.A. for M.A., or Ph.D.; TOEFL (minimum score of 84) for students from countries where English is not the primary language

Degree Requirements—M.A.: 30 h beyond B.A., Ph.D.: 60 h beyond B.A. or 30 h beyond master's plus research paper/qualifying examination, and dissertation

Number of Full-Time Faculty—3; **Number of Other Faculty**—5

Name of Institution—Bemidji State University
Name of Department or Program—Professional Education
Program Website (URL)—http://www.bemidjistate.edu
Name of Contact Person—Shari Olson
Email Address of Contact Person—solson@bemidjistate.edu
Program Description -
Admission Requirements -
Degree Requirements -
Number of Full-Time Faculty—; **Number of Other Faculty** -

Name of Institution—University of Missouri, Columbia
Name of Department or Program—School of Information Science and Learning Technologies
Program Website (URL)—www.coe.missouri.edu/~sislt
Name of Contact Person—John Wedman
Email Address of Contact Person—sislt@missouri.edu
Program Description—The Educational Technology emphasis area prepares educators and technologists for excellence and leadership in the design, development, and implementation of technology in education, training, and performance support. The program offers three focus areas: Technology in Schools, Networked Learning Systems, and Training Design and Development. Each focus area has its own set of competencies, coursework, and processes.

All three focus areas are available online via the Internet or on the MU campus. The Technology in Schools focus area is based on the ISTE competencies and culminates in an online portfolio based on these competencies. Several courses are augmented by technical resources developed at MU, including a technology

Graduate Programs in Learning, Design, Technology, Information, or Libraries 265

integration knowledge repository and online collaboration tools. The Networked Learning Systems focus area offers a truly challenging and innovative set of technical learning experiences. Students have opportunities to work on large--scale software development projects, acquiring valuable experience and broadening their skill set. The Digital Media ZONE supports anytime/anywhere technical skill development. The Training and Development focus area links to business, military, and government contexts. The curriculum is offered by faculty with extensive experience in these contexts and is grounded in the problems and processes of today's workplace. Ed.S. and Ph.D. programs are also available.

Admission Requirements—Bachelor's degree with 3.0 in last 60 credit hours of coursework. GRE (V > 500; A > 500; W > 3.5), TOEFL of 540 (207 computer--based test) (if native language is not English), letters of reference

Degree Requirements—Master's: 30–34 credit hours; 15 h at 400 level. Specific course requirements vary by focus area.

Number of Full-Time Faculty -; **Number of Other Faculty** -

Name of Institution—University of Missouri, Kansas City
Name of Department or Program—Curriculum and Instructional Leadership
Program Website (URL)—http://r.web.umkc.edu/russelldl/
Name of Contact Person—Donna Russell
Email Address of Contact Person—russelldl@umkc.edu
Program Description—3D Virtual Learning Environments
Admission Requirements -
Degree Requirements -
Number of Full-Time Faculty—30; **Number of Other Faculty**—15

Name of Institution—University of North Carolina, Wilmington
Name of Department or Program—Master of Science in Instructional Technology, Department of Instructional Technology, Foundations and Secondary Education
Program Website (URL)—http://www.uncw.edu/ed/mit
Name of Contact Person—Mahnaz Moallem
Email Address of Contact Person—moallemm@uncw.edu
Program Description—The Master of Science degree in Instructional Technology (MIT) program provides advanced professional training for teachers and school technology coordinators; business and industry personnel such as executives, trainers, and human resource development employees; persons in the healthcare field; and community college instructors. The program focuses on the theory and practice of design and development, utilization, management, and evaluation of processes and resources for learning. It emphasizes product development and utilization of advanced technology and provides applied training in the total design, development, implementation, and evaluation of educational and training programs.

As an exciting and innovative program, MIT provides students the opportunity to gain skills and knowledge from educational and applied psychology, instructional systems design, computer science, systems theory, and communication theory, allowing for considerable flexibility to tailor individual needs across other academic disciplines. Students from diverse fields can plan programs which are consistent with their long-range academic and professional goals. MIT courses are offered both on campus and online, allowing professionals to earn their degrees and/or certificates by taking MIT on-campus courses, or MIT online courses, or a combination of both types. In addition, the MIT program is directed toward preparing students to function in a variety of roles to be performed in a broad range of settings, including business and industry, human services, health institutions, higher education, government, military, and public and private K-12 education.

Admission Requirements—Students desiring admission into the graduate program in instructional technology must present the following: a bachelor's degree from an accredited college or university or its equivalent from a foreign institution of higher education based on a 4-year program; a strong academic record (an average GPA of 3.0 or better is expected) in the basic courses required in the area of the proposed graduate study academic potential as indicated by satisfactory performance on standardized test scores (e.g., Miller Analogies Test or Graduate Record Examination); the MAT or GRE must have been taken within the last 5 years; three recommendations from individuals who are in a position to evaluate the student's professional competence as well as potential for graduate study; a statement of career goals and degree objectives; a letter describing educational and professional experiences, their reasons for pursuing graduate study, and the contributions that the student hopes to make after completing the degree; and North Carolina essential and advanced technology competencies. Individuals who fall below a specified criterion may be admitted if other factors indicate potential for success. Individuals with identified deficiencies may be accepted provisionally with specified plans and goals for the remediation of those deficiencies. Such remediation may include a requirement of additional hours beyond those normally required for the degree.

Degree Requirements—Applicants should submit the following to the UNCW Graduate School: Official graduate application (use the following link https:// app.applyyourself.com/?id=uncw-grad to apply electronically). Official transcripts of all college work (undergraduate and graduate). The transcripts should be mailed directly to UNCW Graduate School. Official scores on the Miller Analogies Test (MAT) or Graduate Record Examination (GRE). Scores more than 5 years old will not be accepted. The UNCW institution code for the MAT and GRE is 5907. Three recommendations from individuals in professionally relevant fields, addressing the applicant's demonstrated academic skills and/or potential for successful graduate study. Evidence of a bachelor's degree at the time of entrance. International students: TOEFL score of 550 or higher or IELTS (International English Language Testing System) score of 217 or better (computerized test), 550 or better (paper test), or a minimum score of 79 on the Internet-based test (TOEFL iBT) or IELTS minimum score of 6.5 or 7.0 to be eligible for a teaching assistantship. Letter of application and a statement of professional goals describing applicant's educational and professional experiences, reasons

Graduate Programs in Learning, Design, Technology, Information, or Libraries 267

for pursuing a master's degree in instructional technology, and contributions that the applicant hopes to make after degree completion.

Number of Full-Time Faculty—5; **Number of Other Faculty**—6

Name of Institution—University of North Dakota
Name of Department or Program—Instructional Design and Technology
Program Website (URL)—idt.und.edu
Name of Contact Person—Richard Van Eck
Email Address of Contact Person—richard.vaneck@und.edu
Program Description—Serious Games, Game-Based Learning, K-12 Technology Integration, Human Performance Technology, eLearning Problem-Based Learning

Online Hybrid with synchronous and asynchronous learning. Master's and certificates fully available at a distance Three graduate certificates (K-12 Technology Integration; Corporate Training and Performance; eLearning) M.S. and M.Ed. Ph.D. Interdisciplinary studies. Research opportunities: Northern Plains Center for Behavioral Research Odegard School of Aerospace Sciences (Aviation and Radar simulators; Unmanned Aerial Systems Training).

Admission Requirements—See idt.und.edu
Degree Requirements—See idt.und.edu
Number of Full-Time Faculty—3; **Number of Other Faculty**—1

Name of Institution—Valley City State University
Name of Department or Program—School of Education and Graduate Studies
Program Website (URL)—www.vcsu.edu/graduate
Name of Contact Person—Terry Corwin
Email Address of Contact Person—terry.corwin@vcsu.edu
Program Description—The Master of Education program has four concentrations that focus on technology and the learner: Teaching and Technology concentration, Technology Education concentration, Library and Information Technologies concentration, and Teaching English Language Learners concentration.

This is a completely online program which focuses on how technology can be used in a school setting to enhance student learning.

Admission Requirements—(1) Baccalaureate degree with a 3.0 undergraduate GPA or a test is required. (2) Three letters of recommendation. (3) Written goals statement. (4) Resume. (5) $35 fee for application

Degree Requirements—Completion of 32–37 credits depending on concentration. Action Research report. Final portfolio demonstrating program core values

Number of Full-Time Faculty—12; **Number of Other Faculty**—5

Name of Institution—New York Institute of Technology
Name of Department or Program—Department of Instructional Technology and Educational Leadership
Program Website (URL)—http://www.nyit.edu/education
Name of Contact Person—Sarah McPherson
Email Address of Contact Person—smcphers@nyit.edu

Program Description—M.S. in Instructional Technology for Educators for Educational Technology Specialist Certification, and for Professional Trainers; Certificates in Computers in Education, Teaching Twenty-First Century Skills, Science Technology Engineering Mathematics (STEM); Advanced Certificate: Virtual Education; Advanced Diploma Educational Leadership and Technology for School Building and Advanced Certificate for District Leader; M.S. in Childhood Education.

Courses offered in Long Island, New York City, and upstate New York in partnership with NYS Teacher Centers, School Districts, and related to special grant funding graduate courses. Program is offered 100% online statewide, nationally, and internationally. Technology integration in content areas for K-12 teachers; Leadership and Technology for school building and district administrators; Professional Trainer for corporate training, government, and nonprofit agencies. All courses are hands-on instruction in technology labs; online courses; hybrid courses; evening, weekend, and summer courses.

Admission Requirements—Bachelor's degree from accredited college with 3.0 cumulative average; Advanced Diploma and Advanced Certificate require master's for admission.

Degree Requirements—36 credits with 3.0 GPA for Master of Science, 18 credits with 3.0 GPA for Certificates; Advanced Diploma 33 credits and Advanced Certificate, 15 credits

Number of Full-Time Faculty—6; **Number of Other Faculty**—50

Name of Institution—Richard Stockton College of New Jersey

Name of Department or Program—Master of Arts in Instructional Technology (MAIT)

Program Website (URL)—http://intraweb.stockton.edu/eyos/page.cfm?siteID=73&pageID=47

Name of Contact Person—Jung Lee

Email Address of Contact Person—leej@stockton.edu

Program Description—The Master of Arts in Instructional Technology offered by the Richard Stockton College of New Jersey is designed to bring the best instructional technologies into both public and corporate curricula. With a strong theoretical foundation, the degree enables graduates to use technology as a tool to enhance learning and training.

The program serves (1) students who seek or will continue employment in the P-12 schools; (2) students who wish to pursue coordinator or supervisor positions in P-12 schools and districts; and (3) students seeking or holding careers in business, industry, or nonprofit organizations.

Admission Requirements—Minimum 3.0 GPA, relevant experience, reference letters and GRE General Exam scores or MAT (Miller Analogies Test scores).

Degree Requirements—11 graduate courses (33 credits) including capstone project course

Number of Full-Time Faculty—3; **Number of Other Faculty**—5

Name of Institution—Seton Hall University

Graduate Programs in Learning, Design, Technology, Information, or Libraries 269

Name of Department or Program—College of Education and Human Services
Program Website (URL)—http://www.shu.edu/academics/education/ma--instructional-design/index.cfm
Name of Contact Person—Rosemary W. Skeele
Email Address of Contact Person—edstudies@shu.edu
Program Description—The Instructional Design program assists teachers to improve their professional performance as educators and instructional and curriculum designers, and to assume instructional leadership roles in their place of employment. Students are accepted from many instructional environments, including K-12, college, and adult education. The program emphasizes a theoretical base for instructional design and exposure to a broad array of the most current instructional methods, strategies, technologies, and materials. Seton Hall University is a recognized leader in the use of a variety of modern techniques and computer-based technologies for teaching and learning.
The Instructional Design Program is nationally recognized by the Association for Educational Communications and Technology. The program is structured to meet the specific goals of each student and provide them with an opportunity to acquire content knowledge and skills that are state of the art, enabling them to expand their personal competence and to achieve higher levels of professional excellence. The program is unique in that it allows students, under the guidance of faculty mentors, to design a master's program that satisfies their interests and career objectives.
Admission Requirements—Official undergraduate and graduate transcripts from each accredited college or university attended; two letters of reference from professional and/or academic contacts attesting to your academic abilities and personal qualifications; a two-page, double-spaced, typed statement of goals; current professional vitae/resume; Miller Analogies Test (MAT) or Graduate Record Examination (GRE) scores, within the past 5 years (note: candidates who already possess an advanced degree do not need to submit entrance exam scores); a $50 nonrefundable fee.
Degree Requirements—The Instructional Design Program is a 36-credit program that yields a Master of Arts degree. Students are engaged in concentration courses, electives, as well as a capstone course that must be taken during their final semester. Throughout the program, students gain knowledge and experiences in the foundations of education, professional education, and technology studies, which enhance the professional preparation of teachers and trainers.
Number of Full-Time Faculty -; **Number of Other Faculty** -

Name of Institution—Montclair State University
Name of Department or Program—Department of Curriculum and Teaching
Program Website (URL)—http://cehs.montclair.edu
Name of Contact Person—Vanessa Domine
Email Address of Contact Person—dominev@mail.montclair.edu
Program Description—MSU offers (1) an M.Ed. degree program in Educational Technology (EDTC); (2) a post-bac certification program for Associate School

Library Media Specialists (ALMS); and (3) an advanced certification program for School Library Media Specialists (SLMS).

All three programs draw from the same pool of educational technology courses and can be completed together in a carefully assembled program of approximately 46 graduate credits. Three areas comprise coursework: philosophical foundations, pedagogical design and integration, and practical design and application. In the M.Ed. program, students can choose to emphasize in one of the three areas: (A) administration, policy, and leadership; (B) organizational planning and development; and (C) curriculum and technology integration.

Admission Requirements—Students can apply in person or online to the Graduate School (http://www.montclair.edu/graduate). The M.Ed. program requires submission of GRE scores, letters of recommendation, and a project sample. The ALMS program requires a bachelor's degree and standard NJ teaching license. The SLMS program requires a master's degree, a standard NJ teaching license, and at least 1 year of successful teaching as an associate school library media specialist.

Degree Requirements—The M.Ed. program requires 33 credits of coursework and field experience. The ALMS program requires 18–21 credits of coursework and field experience. The SLMS program requires 36 credits of coursework and field experience.

Number of Full-Time Faculty -; **Number of Other Faculty** -

Name of Institution—New York University

Name of Department or Program—Educational Communication and Technology Program (Ph.D.) and Digital Media Design for Learning Program (M.A., Adv. Cert.), Steinhardt School of Culture, Education, and Human Development

Program Website (URL)—http://steinhardt.nyu.edu/alt/ect

Name of Contact Person—Christopher Hoadley (Program Director); Jan Plass (Doctoral Program Coordinator)

Email Address of Contact Person—ectdmdl@nyu.edu

Program Description—M.A., Advanced Certificate, in Digital Media Design for Learning, and Ph.D. in Educational Communication and Technology: for the preparation of individuals as educational media designers, developers, media producers, and/or researchers in education, business and industry, health and medicine, community services, government, museums, and other cultural institutions, and to teach or become involved in the administration of educational communications and educational technology or learning sciences programs in higher education, including instructional television, multimedia, Web 2.0, serious games, and simulations. The program also offers a post-M.A. 30-point Certificate of Advanced Study in Education.

Features—Emphasizes theoretical foundations, especially a cognitive science and learning sciences perspective of learning and instruction, and their implications for designing media-based learning environments and materials. All efforts focus on video, multimedia, instructional television, Web-based technology and simulations and games, participation in special research and production projects, and

Graduate Programs in Learning, Design, Technology, Information, or Libraries   271

field internships. Uses an apprenticeship model to provide doctoral students and advanced M.A. students with research opportunities in collaboration with faculty.

Admission Requirements—M.A.: Bachelor's degree or international equivalent required. Typically, 3.0 undergraduate GPA, statement of purpose (no GRE required). Ph.D.: Master's degree or international equivalent required. 3.0 GPA, 1100 GRE, responses to essay questions, interview related to academic or professional preparation and career goals. (TOEFL required for international students.)

Degree Requirements—M.A.: 36 semester credit hours including specialization, elective courses, thesis, English essay examination. Ph.D.: 57 semester credit hours beyond M.A., including specialization, foundations, research, content seminar, and elective coursework; candidacy papers; dissertation; English essay examination. Full-time or part-time study available; no online option available

Number of Full-Time Faculty—4; **Number of Other Faculty**—4

Name of Institution—Syracuse University

Name of Department or Program—Instructional Design, Development, and Evaluation Program, School of Education

Program Website (URL)—http://idde.syr.edu

Name of Contact Person—Nick Smith

Email Address of Contact Person—nlsmith@syr.edu

Program Description—Certificates in Educational Technology and Adult Lifelong Learning, M.S., M.S. in Instructional Technology, C.A.S., and Ph.D. degree programs in Instructional Design, Educational Evaluation, Human Issues in Instructional Development, Technology Integration, and Educational Research and Theory (learning theory, application of theory, and educational media research). Graduates are prepared to serve as curriculum developers, instructional designers, program and project evaluators, researchers, resource center administrators, technology coordinators, educational technology specialist, distance learning design and delivery specialists, trainers and training managers, and higher education faculty.

The courses and programs are typically project centered. Collaborative project experience, fieldwork, and internships are emphasized throughout. There are special-issue seminars, as well as student- and faculty-initiated mini-courses, seminars and guest lecturers, faculty-student formulation of department policies, and multiple international perspectives. International collaborations are an ongoing feature of the program. The graduate student population is highly diverse.

Admission Requirements—Certificates and M.S.: undergraduate transcripts, recommendations, personal statement, and interview recommended; TOEFL for international applicants; GRE recommended. Certificate of Advanced Study: Relevant master's degree from accredited institution or equivalent, GRE scores, recommendations, personal statement, TOEFL for international applicants; interview recommended. Doctoral: Relevant master's degree from accredited institution or equivalent, GRE scores, recommendations, personal statement, TOEFL for international applicants; interview strongly encouraged

Degree Requirements—Certificates: 15 and 24 semester hours. M.S.: 36 semester hours, portfolio required. M.S. in Instructional Technology: 37 semester hours, practicum, and portfolio required. C.A.S.: 60 semester hours, exam, and project required. Ph.D.: 90 semester hours, research apprenticeship, portfolio, qualifying exams, and dissertation required
Number of Full-Time Faculty—4; **Number of Other Faculty**—6

Name of Institution—East Stroudsburg University
Name of Department or Program—Instructional Technology, Media Communication and Technology Department
Program Website (URL)—www.esu.edu/gradmcom
Name of Contact Person—Beth Rajan Sockman
Email Address of Contact Person—bsockman@po-box.esu.edu
Program Description—The graduate programs are designed to develop the technology literacy of educators and prepare specialists to work in K-12 schools, school districts, or instructional technology personnel in education, business, or industry. Students can obtain a Master's of Education degree in Instructional Technology and/or a Pennsylvania Instructional Technologist Specialist Certificate. Students interested in PK-12 education may choose to concentrate in Technology Integration.
The program provides students with an opportunity to take courses from ESU University. Students who successfully complete the program become proficient in using technology in teaching. Students can choose courses that explore that following areas: * Desktop publishing * Interactive Web design (including Web 2.0 applications) * Graphics * Video * New and emerging technologies * Instructional design * Learning theories * Research in instructional technology.
Admission Requirements—For M.Ed. degree: * Two letters of recommendation * Portfolio or interview (interview is granted after the application is received) * For full admission a minimum overall undergraduate 2.5 QPA * Rolling deadline for certification: * Contact the graduate coordinator for additional admission information to comply with Pennsylvania Department of Education requirements * Minimum overall undergraduate QPA 3.0 (Pennsylvania Act 354) * If not 3.0 QPA, then completion of nine credits of Media Communication and Technology Department courses with prior written approval of department faculty adviser * Two letters of recommendation * Rolling deadline
Degree Requirements—Total = 33 credits # Take courses and learn—Take 30 credits of courses for the master's and learn based on your needs. You will learn to use and implement technologies outside average person's experience. # Create, Submit, and Present your Portfolio—This is the time to display your learning in a professional manner. In the portfolio you articulate your goals and may identify learning goals for your internship. Click here for the Portfolio Guidelines. # Complete an Internship—You complete a 90-h internship that extends your knowledge base—3 credits. # Complete Portfolio and Graduate
Number of Full-Time Faculty—7; **Number of Other Faculty**—3

Name of Institution—Penn State Great Valley School of Graduate Professional Studies

Name of Department or Program—Education Division/Instructional Systems Program

Program Website (URL)—http://www.sgps.psu.edu

Name of Contact Person—Doris Lee

Email Address of Contact Person—ydl1@psu.edu

Program Description—Instructional Systems/Designs

Admission Requirements—On-line application, MAT/GRE scores, two letters of recommendations

Degree Requirements—36 credits

Number of Full-Time Faculty—10; **Number of Other Faculty**—15

Name of Institution—Temple University

Name of Department or Program—Department of Psychological Studies in Education

Program Website (URL)—http://www.temple.edu/education/

Name of Contact Person—Susan Miller

Email Address of Contact Person—susan.miller@temple.edu

Program Description—Instructional and Learning Technology (ILT) is a new master's program within the Educational Psychology Program in the Department of Psychological Studies in Education. As such, ILT is designed to address conceptual as well as technical issues in using technology for teaching and learning. Program areas include (a) instructional theory and design issues, (b) application of technology, and (c) management issues.

Instructional theory and design topics include psychology of the learner, cognitive processes, instructional theories, human development, and individual differences as well as psychological and educational characteristics of technology resources, and identification of strengths and weaknesses of instructional technology resources. The application of technology area focuses on clarification of instructional objectives, identification of resources to facilitate learning, operation and application of current and emergent technologies, facility using graphic design, multimedia, video, distributed learning resources, WWW, and print publishing. Management and consultation are structured around defining instructional needs; monitoring progress; evaluating outcomes; designing technology delivery systems; preparing policy statements, budgets, and facility design criteria; managing skill assessment and training; understanding legal and ethical issues; and managing and maintaining facilities.

Admission Requirements—Bachelor's degree from an accredited institution, GRE (MAT) scores, three letters of recommendation, transcripts from each institution of higher learning attended (undergraduate and graduate), goal statement

Degree Requirements—Coursework (33 h: 5 core courses, 3 technology electives, 3 cognate area courses). Practicum in students' area of interest. Comprehensive Exam Portfolio of Certification Competencies (for students interested in PA Department of Ed Certification as Instructional Technology Specialist)

274 K. H. Chien et al.

Number of Full-Time Faculty -; **Number of Other Faculty** -

Name of Institution—Texas A&M University, Commerce
Name of Department or Program—Department of Educational Leadership
Program Website (URL)—http://www.tamu-commerce.edu/
Name of Contact Person—Sue Espinoza
Email Address of Contact Person—Sue_Espinoza@tamu-commerce.edu
Program Description—M.S. or M.Ed. degrees in Educational Technology--
Leadership and in Educational Technology-Library Science Certification pro-
grams—School Librarian and Technology Applications, both approved by the
Texas State Board for Educator Certification.
Programs may be completed totally online, although some courses may also be
offered in Web-enhanced formats, and one or more electives may be offered only
face to face.
Admission Requirements—Apply to the Graduate School at Texas A&M
University.
Commerce: For school library certification, must also apply to the professional cer-
tification program.
Degree Requirements—36 h for each master's degree; each program contains core
courses, and specialization area courses are selected in consultation with advisor,
who is assigned when each student is admitted to the program.
Number of Full-Time Faculty—3; **Number of Other Faculty**—6

Name of Institution—University of Texas at Brownsville
Name of Department or Program—Educational Technology
Program Website (URL)—http://edtech.utb.edu
Name of Contact Person—J. Rene Corbeil
Email Address of Contact Person—Rene.Corbeil@UTB.edu
Program Description—E-Learning Instructional Design Web-Based Instruction
Multimedia Design
The Online M.Ed. in Educational Technology is a 36-h program designed to prepare
persons in K-12, higher education, corporate, and military settings to develop the
skills and knowledge necessary for the classrooms of tomorrow. Graduates of
this program will have a much better understanding of the uses of technology and
how they can be applied in instructional/training settings. The program focuses
on the theory, research, and applications related to the field of educational technology and is intended to help individuals—use instructional technology (computers, telecommunications, and related technologies) as resources for the
delivery of instruction—serve as facilitators or directors of instructional technology in educational settings and/or be developers of instructional programs and
materials for new technologies—design instructional materials in a variety of
media. In addition to earning an M.Ed. in Educational Technology, students
working in K-12 environments also have the opportunity to complete the Master
Technology Teacher (MTT) Program and test for the MTT Certificate. The program is provided through the four MTT elective courses offered as an option in

the degree program. An E-Learning Certificate is also available for individuals working in higher education or at e-learning industries.

Admission Requirements—Proof of a baccalaureate degree from a 4-year institution which has regional accreditation. GPA of 2.5 or higher (3.0 GPA for "unconditional" admission; between 2.5 and 2.9 for "conditional" admission). Application essay/statement of goals. Please provide a carefully considered statement of (1) your academic and professional objectives and (2) explain how graduate study will help you to attain your goals. Note: The GRE is no longer required.

Degree Requirements—The M.Ed. in Educational Technology consists of 24 h from core courses plus 12 h of electives for a total of 36 h. Students can select the 12 h of electives based upon their professional needs and academic interests (e.g., Master Technology Teacher—MTT Certificate, e-Learning Certificate, or 12 h in a specific content area such as reading, mathematics, science) with adviser approval. Core courses: (24 h) EDTC 6320—Educational Technology. EDTC 6321—Instructional Design. EDTC 6323—Multimedia/Hypermedia. EDTC 6325—Educational Communications. EDTC 6329—Selected Topics in Educational Technology. EDTC 6332—Practicum in Educational Technology. EDCI 6300—Foundations of Research in Education. EDCI 6304—Learning and Cognition. Electives: (12 h) EDCI 6301—Instructional Technology in Teaching. EDCI 6336—Problems in Education: International Technology Issues. EDTC 6340—Applications of Advanced Technologies in the Pk-12 Classroom. EDTC 6341—Student-Centered Learning Using Technology. EDTC 6342—Technology Leadership. EDTC 6343—Master Teacher of Technology Practicum*. EDTC 6351—Web-Based Multimedia in Instruction. EDTC 6358—Theory and Practice of e-Learning.

Number of Full-Time Faculty—4; **Number of Other Faculty**—2

Name of Institution—Old Dominion University
Name of Department or Program—Instructional Design and Technology
Program Website (URL)—http://education.odu.edu/eci/idt/
Name of Contact Person—Gary R. Morrison
Email Address of Contact Person—gmorriso@odu.edu
Program Description—Our faculty engages students in a rigorous course of study tailored to meet individual educational and career interests. Research opportunities and coursework ensure that all students receive a solid foundation in Instructional Design Theory, Human Performance Technology, Gaming and Simulation, Distance Education Evaluation, and Assessment Trends and Issues in Instructional Technology Quantitative and Qualitative Research.

All of our courses are offered via distance using a hybrid format. Classroom instruction uses a virtual classroom that allows all students to participate in a face-to--face classroom. A reduced tuition rate is available for students living outside of Virginia who are accepted into the program.

Admission Requirements—M.S. degree: GRE scores or MAT scores; transcripts for undergraduate and graduate courses Ph.D.: GRE scores, transcripts for undergraduate and graduate courses, letters of recommendation, and an essay describing professional goals

Degree Requirements—M.S. program is 30–36-h Ph.D. program is a post-master's degree consisting of 60 h.

Number of Full-Time Faculty—4; **Number of Other Faculty** -

Name of Institution—Concordia University, Wisconsin

Name of Department or Program—Educational Technology

Program Website (URL)—http://www.cuw.edu/go/edtech

Name of Contact Person—Bernard Bull

Email Address of Contact Person—bernard.bull@cuw.edu

Program Description—Digital culture, designing digital-age learning experiences, and social/spiritual/ethical implications of technology. Courses are available via e-learning or face to face. Some cohorts are also offered at off-campus sites in Wisconsin and beyond. In addition, we run occasional thematic cohorts where a group of students work through the program together over an 18–24-month period, all agreeing to focus their thesis or culminating project upon the cohort theme (e.g., new literacies, bridging the digital divide, global education, discipleship in the digital age).

Admission Requirements—To be considered for admission, a student must have a bachelor's degree from an accredited college or university and have a minimum GPA of 3.00 in the undergraduate program.

Degree Requirements—Required courses: EDT 970—Integrating Technology in the Classroom (3). EDT 889—Applying Technology in the Content Areas (3). EDT 908—Critical Issues in Educational Technology (3). EDT 892—Instructional Design (3). EDT 893—Theories of Learning and Design (3). EDT 815—Research in Educational Technology (3). EDT 927, 928, 929—Portfolio I, II, and III (0). EDT 895—Capstone Project (3). OR EDT 890—Thesis Completion Seminar (3). Electives: EDT 805—Online Teaching and Learning (3). EDT 814—Educational Ministry in the Digital World (3). EDT 894—Digital Literacy (3). EDT 907—Multimedia for the Classroom (3). EDT 939—School Leadership in Technology (3). EDT 940—Networking, Support, and Delivery Systems for Schools (3). EDT 957—Building Online Learning Communities (Web 2.0/Learning 2.0) (3). EDT 971—Grants and Funding for Educational Technology Initiatives (3). EDT 804—Strategies for Teaching and Learning with Interactive Whiteboards (1). Other electives as approved by the program director.

Number of Full-Time Faculty—3; **Number of Other Faculty**—6

Name of Institution—University of Wisconsin-Madison

Name of Department or Program—Curriculum and Instruction, School of Education

Program Website (URL)—http://www.education.wisc.edu/ci/

Name of Contact Person—Kurt D. Squire

Email Address of Contact Person—kdsquire@wisc.edu

Program Description—M.S. and Ph.D. degree programs to prepare Educational Technology faculty and professionals. Ongoing research includes studying the impact of contemporary gaming practices on learning, schooling, and society; understanding ways in which online play spaces align (or fail to align) with practices valued outside the game (i.e., informal scientific reasoning, collaborative problem-solving, and media literacy); interrogating the implementation of technology-rich innovations in local and international schools as well as the role of culture in the design of instruction; and using photography as a research method in education.

Educational technology courses are processed through social, cultural, historical, and design-based frames of reference. Current curriculum emphasizes new media theories, critical cultural and visual culture theories, and constructivist theories of instructional design and development. Many courses are offered in the evening.

Admission Requirements—Master's and Ph.D.: previous experience in Instructional Technology preferred, previous teaching experience, 3.0 GPA on last 60 undergraduate credits, acceptable scores on GRE, 3.0 GPA on all graduate work

Degree Requirements—M.S.: 24 credits plus thesis and exam (an additional 12 credits of Educational Foundations if no previous educational background); Ph.D.: 1 year of residency beyond the bachelor's; major, minor, and research requirements; preliminary exam; dissertation; and oral exam

Number of Full-Time Faculty—4; **Number of Other Faculty** -

Part V
Mediagraphy

Introduction

Sheng-Shiang Tseng

1 Contents

This resource lists journals and other resources of interest to practitioners, researchers, students, and others concerned with educational technology and educational media. The primary goal of this section is to list current publications in the field. The majority of materials cited here were published in 2016 or mid-2019. Media-related journals include those listed in past issues of EMTY, as well as new entries in the field. This chapter is not intended to serve as a specific resource location tool, although it may be used for that purpose in the absence of database access. Rather, readers are encouraged to peruse the categories of interest in this chapter to gain an idea of recent developments within the field. For archival purposes, this chapter serves as a snapshot of the field of instructional technology publications. Readers must bear in mind that technological developments occur well in advance of publication and should take that fact into consideration when judging the timeliness of resources listed in this chapter.

2 Selection

Items were selected for the mediagraphy in several ways. The EBSCO Host Databases were used to locate most of the journal citations. Others were taken from the journal listings of large publishing companies. Items were chosen for this list when they met one or more of the following criteria: reputable publisher, broad

---

S.-S. Tseng (✉)
Graduate Institute of Curriculum and Instruction, Tamkang University, New Taipei City, Taiwan

© The Author(s), under exclusive license to Springer Nature Switzerland AG 2021
R. M. Branch et al. (eds.), *Educational Media and Technology Yearbook*,
Educational Media and Technology Yearbook 43,
https://doi.org/10.1007/978-3-030-71774-2_13

circulation, coverage by indexing services, peer review, and coverage of a gap in the literature. The author chose items on subjects that seem to reflect the instructional technology field as it is today. Because of the increasing tendency for media producers to package their products in more than one format and for single titles to contain mixed media, titles are no longer separated by media type. The author makes no claims as to the comprehensiveness of this list. It is, instead, intended to be representative.

3 Obtaining Resources

Media-related periodicals: The author has attempted to provide various ways to obtain the resources listed in this mediagraphy, including telephone and fax numbers, web and postal addresses, as well as email contacts. Prices are also included for student (stud), individual (indiv), K-12 educator (k12), and institutional (inst) subscriptions. The information presented reflects the most current information available at the time of publication.

ERIC Documents: As of December 31, 2003, ERIC was no longer funded. However, ERIC documents can still be read and copied from their microfiche form at any library holding an ERIC microfiche collection. The identification number beginning with ED (for example, ED 332677) locates the document in the collection. Document delivery services and copies of most ERIC documents can also continue to be available from the ERIC Document Reproduction Service. Prices charged depend on the format chosen (microfiche or paper copy), length of the document, and method of shipping. Online orders, fax orders, and expedited delivery are available.

To find the closest library with an ERIC microfiche collection, contact ACCESS ERIC, 1600 Research Blvd, Rockville, MD 20850–3172, USA; (800) LET-ERIC (538–3742); email: acceric@inet.ed.gov.

To order ERIC documents, contact:

ERIC Document Reproduction Services (EDRS)
7420 Fullerton Rd., Suite 110, Springfield, VA 22153–2852, USA
(800) 433-ERIC (433–3742); (703) 440–1400
Fax: (703) 440–1408
Email: service@edrs.com

Journal articles: Photocopies of journal articles can be obtained in one of the following ways: (1) from a library subscribing to the title, (2) through interlibrary loan, (3) through the purchase of a back issue from the journal publisher, or (4) from an article reprint service such as ProQuest Microfilm.

ProQuest Microfilm, 789 E. Eisenhower Parkway, PO Box 1346
Ann Arbor, MI 48106–1346, USA
(734) 761–4700
Fax: (734) 997–4222

Introduction

Email: sandra.piver@proquest.com

Journal articles can also be obtained through the Institute for Scientific Information (ISI).

ISI Document Solution
PO Box 7649
Philadelphia, PA 19104–3389, USA
(800) 336–4474, option 5
Fax: (215) 222–0840 or (215) 386–4343
Email: ids@isinet.com

4 Arrangement

Mediagraphy entries are classified according to major subject emphasis under the following headings:

- Artificial Intelligence, Robotics, and Electronic Performance Support Systems
- Computer-Assisted Instruction
- Distance Education
- Educational Research
- Educational Technology
- Information Science and Technology
- Instructional Design and Development
- Learning Sciences
- Libraries and Media Centers
- Media Technologies
- Professional Development
- Simulation, Gaming, and Virtual Reality
- Special Education and Disabilities
- Telecommunications and Networking

Mediagraphy

Sheng-Shiang Tseng

1 Artificial Intelligence, Robotics, and Electronic Performance Support Systems

Artificial Intelligence Review. Springer Science+Business Media, PO Box 2485, Secaucus, NJ 07096-2485. http://www.springer.com/journal/10462, tel: 800-777-4643, fax: 201-348-4505, service-ny@springer.com [8/year; $99 indiv (online)] Publishes reports and evaluations, as well as commentary on issues and development in artificial intelligence foundations and current research.

AI Magazine. Association for the Advancement of Artificial Intelligence, 2275 East Bayshore Road, Suite 160, Palo Alto, California 94303. http://www.aaai.org/Magazine, tel: 650-328-3123, fax: 650-321-4457, info08@aaai.org [4/year; $75 stud (print), $145 indiv (print), $285 inst (print), $290 inst (online)] Proclaimed "journal of record for the AI community," this magazine provides full-length articles on new research and literature, but is written to allow access to those reading outside their area of expertise.

International Journal of Human-Computer Interaction. Taylor & Francis Group, Customer Services Department, 325 Chestnut St, Suite 800, Philadelphia, PA 19106. http://www.tandfonline.com/hihc, tel: 800-354-1420, fax: 215-625-2940, subscriptions@tandf.co.uk [12/year; $292 indiv (print), $306 indiv (print + online), $2305 inst (online), $2634 inst (print + online)] Addresses the cognitive, creative, social, health, and ergonomic aspects of interactive computing.

International Journal of Robotics Research. Sage Publications, 2455 Teller Rd., Thousand Oaks, CA 91320. http://ijr.sagepub.com, tel: 805-499-9774, journals@sagepub.com [14/year; $250 indiv (print), $2558 inst (online), $2785 inst

S.-S. Tseng (✉)
Graduate Institute of Curriculum and Instruction, Tamkang University, New Taipei City, Taiwan

© The Author(s), under exclusive license to Springer Nature Switzerland AG 2021
R. M. Branch et al. (eds.), *Educational Media and Technology Yearbook*,
Educational Media and Technology Yearbook 43,
https://doi.org/10.1007/978-3-030-71774-2_14

(print), $2842 inst (print + online)] Interdisciplinary approach to the study of robotics for researchers, scientists, and students. The first scholarly publication on robotics research.

Journal of Intelligent and Robotic Systems. Springer Science+Business Media, PO Box 2485, Secaucus, NJ 07096-2485. http://www.springer.com/journal/10846, tel: 800-777-4643, fax: 201-348-4505, service-ny@springer.com [16/year; $199 indiv (/online)] Main objective is to provide a forum for the fruitful interaction of ideas and techniques that combine systems and control science with artificial intelligence and other related computer science concepts. It bridges the gap between theory and practice.

Journal of Interactive Learning Research. Association for the Advancement of Computing in Education, PO Box 1545, Chesapeake, VA 23327-1545. http://www.aace.org/pubs/jilr, tel: 757-366-5606, fax: 703-997-8760, info@editlib.org [4/year; $125 indiv, $215 inst] Publishes articles on how intelligent computer technologies can be used in education to enhance learning and teaching. Reports on research and developments, integration, and applications of artificial intelligence in education.

Knowledge-Based Systems. Elsevier, Inc., Journals Customer Service, 3251 Riverport Lane, Maryland Heights, MO 63043. http://www.elsevier.com/locate/knosys, tel: 877-839-7126, fax: 314-447-8077, journalcustomerservice-usa@elsevier.com [12/year; $247 indiv, $2189 inst (print)] Interdisciplinary application-oriented journal on fifth-generation computing, expert systems, and knowledge-based methods in system design.

Minds and Machines. Springer Science+Business Media, PO Box 2485, Secaucus, NJ 07096-2485. http://www.springer.com/journal/11023, tel: 800-777-4643, fax: 201-348-4505, service-ny@springer.com [4/year; $99 indiv] Discusses issues concerning machines and mentality, artificial intelligence, epistemology, simulation, and modeling.

2 Computer-Assisted Instruction

AACE Journal. Association for the Advancement of Computing in Education, PO Box 1545, Chesapeake, VA 23327-1545. http://www.aace.org/pubs/jilr, tel: 757-366-5606, fax: 703-997-8760, info@editlib.org [4/year; $125 indiv, $215 inst] Publishes articles dealing with issues in instructional technology.

CALICO Journal. Computer-Assisted Language Instruction Consortium, 214 Centennial Hall, Texas State University, San Marcos, TX 78666. http://calico.org, tel: 512-245-1417, fax: 512-245-9089, info@calico.org [3/year; $20 stud, $65 indiv, $50 k12, $105 inst] Provides information on the applications of technology in teaching and learning languages.

Children's Technology Review. Active Learning Associates, 120 Main St, Flemington, NJ 08822. http://childrenstech.com, tel: 800-993-9499, fax: 908-284-0405, lisa@childrenstech.com [12/year; $60 indiv (online)] Provides reviews and other information about software to help parents and educators more effectively use computers with children.

Computers and Composition. Elsevier, Inc., Journals Customer Service, 3251 Riverport Lane, Maryland Heights, MO 63043. http://www.elsevier.com/locate/ compcom, tel: 877-839-7126, fax: 314-447-8077, journalcustomerservice-usa@ elsevier.com [4/year; $98 indiv, $669 inst] International journal for teachers of writing that focuses on the use of computers in writing instruction and related research.

Computers & Education. Elsevier, Inc., Journals Customer Service, 3251 Riverport Lane, Maryland Heights, MO 63043. http://www.elsevier.com/locate/ compedu, tel: 877-839-7126, fax: 314-447-8077, journalcustomerservice-usa@ elsevier.com [12/year; $476 indiv, $3354 inst] Presents technical papers covering a broad range of subjects for users of analog, digital, and hybrid computers in all aspects of higher education.

Computer Assisted Language Learning. Taylor & Francis Group, Customer Services Department, 325 Chestnut St, Suite 800, Philadelphia, PA 19106. http:// www.tandfonline.com/ncal, tel: 800-354-1420, fax: 215-625-2940, subscriptions@tandf.co.uk [6/year; $307 indiv (print), $944 inst (online), $1078 inst (print + online)] An intercontinental and interdisciplinary journal which leads the field in its dedication to all matters associated with the use of computers in language learning (L1 and L2), teaching, and testing.

Computers in Human Behavior. Elsevier, Inc., Journals Customer Service, 3251 Riverport Lane, Maryland Heights, MO 63043. http://www.elsevier.com/locate/ comphumbeh, tel: 877-839-7126, fax: 314-447-8077, journalcustomerservice-usa@elsevier.com [12/year; $377 indiv, $2704 inst] Scholarly journal dedicated to examining the use of computers from a psychological perspective.

Computers in the Schools. Taylor & Francis Group, Customer Service Department, 325 Chestnut Street, Suite 800, Philadelphia, PA 19106. http://www.tandf.co.uk/ journals/titles/07380569, tel: 800-354-1420, fax: 215-625-2940, subscriptions@ tandf.co.uk [4/year; $163 indiv (online), $879 inst (online), $186 indiv (print + online), $1005 inst (print + online)] Features articles that combine theory and practical applications of small computers in schools for educators and school administrators.

Center for Digital Education. e.Republic, Inc., 100 Blue Ravine Rd., Folsom, CA 95630. http://www.centerdigitaled.com/, tel: 800-940-6039 ext 1319, fax: 916-932-1470, subscriptions@erepublic.com [4/year; free] Explores the revolution of technology in education.

Dr. Dobb's Journal. United Business Media LLC, Customer Service, PO Box 1093, Skokie, IL 60076. http://www.ddj.com, tel: 888-664-3332, fax: 847-763-9606, drdobbsjournal@halldata.com [12/year; free to qualified applicants] Articles on the latest in operating systems, programming languages, algorithms, hardware design and architecture, data structures, and telecommunications; in-Departmenth hardware and software reviews.

Instructor. Scholastic Inc., PO Box 420235, Palm Coast, FL 32142-0235. http:// www.scholastic.com/teachers/instructor, tel: 866-436-2455, fax: 215-625-2940, instructor@emailcustomerservice.com [6/year; $8)] Features articles on applications and advances of technology in education for K-12 and college educators and administrators.

Interactive Learning Environments. Taylor & Francis Group, Customer Services Department, 325 Chestnut St, Suite 800, Philadelphia, PA 19106. http://www.tandf.co.uk/journals/titles/10494820, tel: 800-354-1420, fax: 215-625-2940, subscriptions@tandf.co.uk [6/year; $420 indiv (print), $1212 inst (online), $1386 inst (print + online)] Explores the implications of the Internet and multimedia presentation software in education and training environments that support collaboration among groups of learners or co-workers.

Journal of Computer Assisted Learning. John Wiley & Sons, Inc., Journal Customer Services, 350 Main St, Malden, MA 02148. http://onlinelibrary.wiley.com/journal/10.1111/(ISSN)1365-2729, tel: 800-835-6770, fax: 781-388-8232, cs-agency@wiley.com [6/year; $269 indiv (print + online), $1866 inst (print/online), $2240 inst (print + online)] Articles and research on the use of computer-assisted learning.

Journal of Educational Computing Research. Baywood Publishing Co., Inc., 26 Austin Ave, PO Box 337, Amityville, NY 11701-0337. http://journals.sagepub.com/home/jec, tel: 800-638-7819, fax: 631-691-1770, info@baywood.com [8/year; $307 indiv (online), $843 indiv (print), $774 inst (online), $860 inst (print + online)] Presents original research papers, critical analyses, reports on research in progress, design and development studies, article reviews, and grant award listings.

Journal of Educational Multimedia and Hypermedia. Association for the Advancement of Computing in Education, PO Box 1545, Chesapeake, VA 23327-1545. http://www.aace.org/pubs/jemh, tel: 757-366-5606, fax: 703-997-8760, info@editlib.org [4/year; $175 indiv, $215 inst] A multidisciplinary information source presenting research about and applications for multimedia and hypermedia tools.

Journal of Research on Technology in Education. International Society for Technology in Education, 180 West 8th Ave., Suite 300, Eugene, OR 97401-2916. http://www.iste.org/jrte, tel: 800-336-5191, fax: 541-434-8948, iste@iste.org [4/year; $109 indiv (member price)] Contains articles reporting on the latest research findings related to classroom and administrative uses of technology, including system and project evaluations.

Language Resources and Evaluation. Springer Science+Business Media, PO Box 2485, Secaucus, NJ 07096-2485. http://www.springer.com/journal/10579, tel: 800-777-4643, fax: 201-348-4505, service-ny@springer.com [4/year; $99 indiv] Contains papers on computer-aided studies, applications, automation, and computer-assisted instruction.

MacWorld. Mac Publishing, Macworld Subscription Services, PO Box 37781, Boone, IA 50037. http://www.macworld.com, tel: 800-288-6848, fax: 515-432-6994, subhelp@macworld.com [12/year; $19.97] Describes hardware, software, tutorials, and applications for users of the Macintosh microcomputer.

System. Elsevier, Inc., Journals Customer Service, 3251 Riverport Lane, Maryland Heights, MO 63043. http://www.journals.elsevier.com/system, tel: 877-839-7126, fax: 314-447-8077, journalcustomerservice-usa@elsevier.com [8/year; $167 indiv, $1134 inst] International journal covering educational technology and applied linguistics with a focus on foreign language teaching and learning.

Social Science Computer Review. Sage Publications, 2455 Teller Rd., Thousand Oaks, CA 91320. http://ssc.sagepub.com, tel: 800-818-7243, fax: 800-583-2665, journals@sagepub.com [4/year; $150 indiv (print), $972 inst (online), $1058 inst (print), $1080 inst (online + online)] Interdisciplinary peer-reviewed scholarly publication covering social science research and instructional applications in computing and telecommunications; also covers societal impacts of information technology.

Wireless Networks. Springer Science+Business Media, PO Box 2485, Secaucus, NJ 07096-2485. http://www.springer.com/journal/11276, tel: 800-777-4643, fax: 201-348-4505, service-ny@springer.com [8/year; $99 indiv] Devoted to the technological innovations that result from the mobility allowed by wireless technology.

3 Distance Education

American Journal of Distance Education. Taylor & Francis Group, Customer Services Department, 325 Chestnut St, Suite 800, Philadelphia, PA 19106. http://www.tandf.co.uk/journals/titles/08923647, tel: 800-354-1420, fax: 215-625-2940, subscriptions@tandf.co.uk [4/year; $109 indiv (print + online), $383 inst (online), $438 inst (print + online)] Created to disseminate information and act as a forum for criticism and debate about research on and practice of systems, management, and administration of distance education.

Journal of E-learning & Distance Education. Canadian Network for Innovation in Education, BCIT Learning & Teaching Centre, British Columbia Institute of Technology, 3700 Willingdon Ave, Burnaby, BC, V5G 3H2, Canada. http://www.jofde.ca, tel: 604-454-2280, fax: 604-431-7267, journalofde@gmail.com [at least 2/year; free] Aims to promote and encourage scholarly work of empirical and theoretical nature relating to distance education in Canada and throughout the world.

Journal of Library & Information Services in Distance Learning. Taylor & Francis Group, Customer Service Department, 325 Chestnut Street, Suite 800, Philadelphia, PA 19106. http://www.tandf.co.uk/journals/titles/1533290X, tel: 800-354-1420, fax: 215-625-2940, subscriptions@tandf.co.uk [4/year; $97 indiv (online), $110 indiv (print + online), $248 inst (online), $284 inst (print + online)] Contains peer-reviewed articles, essays, narratives, current events, and letters from distance learning and information science experts.

Journal of Research on Technology in Education. International Society for Technology in Education, 180 West 8th Ave., Suite 300, Eugene, OR 97401-2916.

http://www.iste.org/jrte, tel: 800-336-5191, fax: 541-434-8948, iste@iste.org [4/year; $109, member] Contains articles reporting on the latest research findings related to classroom and administrative uses of technology, including system and project evaluations.

Open Learning. Taylor & Francis Group, Customer Services Department, 325 Chestnut St, Suite 800, Philadelphia, PA 19106. http://www.tandf.co.uk/journals/titles/02680513, tel: 800-354-1420, fax: 215-625-2940, subscriptions@tandf.co.uk [3/year; $152 indiv (print), $433 inst (online), $495 inst (print + online)] Academic, scholarly publication on aspects of open and distance learning anywhere in the world. Includes issues for debate and research notes.

4 Educational Research

American Educational Research Journal. Sage Publications, 2455 Teller Rd., Thousand Oaks, CA 91320. http://aer.sagepub.com, tel: 800-818-7243, fax: 800-583-2665, journals@sagepub.com [6/year; $79 indiv (print + online), $985 inst (online), $1072 inst (print), $1094 inst (print + online)] Reports original research, both empirical and theoretical, and brief synopses of research.

Asia-Pacific Education Researcher. Springer Science+Business Media, PO Box 2485, Secaucus, NJ 07096-2485. http://www.springer.com/journal/40299, tel: 800-777-4643, fax: 201-348-4505, service-ny@springer.com [4/year; $99 indiv] Reports on the successful educational systems in the Asia-Pacific Region and on the national educational systems that are underrepresented.

Educational Research. Taylor & Francis Group, Customer Services Department, 325 Chestnut St, Suite 800, Philadelphia, PA 19106. http://www.tandf.co.uk/journals/titles/00131881, tel: 800-354-1420, fax: 215-625-2940, subscriptions@tandf.co.uk [4/year; $255 indiv, $679 inst (online), $776 inst (print + online)] Reports on current educational research, evaluation, and applications.

Educational Researcher. Sage Publications, 2455 Teller Rd., Thousand Oaks, CA 91320. http://edr.sagepub.com, tel: 800-818-7243, fax: 800-583-2665, journals@sagepub.com [9/year; $68 indiv (print + online), $526 inst (online), $572 inst (print), $584 inst (print + online)] Contains news and features of general significance in educational research.

Innovations in Education and Teaching International. Taylor & Francis Group, Customer Services Department, 325 Chestnut St, Suite 800, Philadelphia, PA 19106. http://www.tandfonline.com/riie, tel: 800-354-1420, fax: 215-625-2940, subscriptions@tandf.co.uk [6/year; $252 indiv, $828 inst (online), $947 inst (print + online)] Essential reading for all practitioners and decision makers who want to stay in good practice in higher education through staff and educational development and subject-related practices.

Journal of Interactive Learning Research. Association for the Advancement of Computing in Education, PO Box 1545, Chesapeake, VA 23327-1545. http://www.aace.org/pubs/jilr, tel: 757-366-5606, fax: 703-997-8760, info@editlib.org

[4/year; $175 indiv, $215 inst] Publishes articles on how intelligent computer technologies can be used in education to enhance learning and teaching. Reports on research and developments, integration, and applications of artificial intelligence in education.

Research in Science & Technological Education. Taylor & Francis Group, Customer Services Department, 325 Chestnut St, Suite 800, Philadelphia, PA 19106. http://www.tandf.co.uk/journals/titles/02635143, tel: 800-354-1420, fax: 215-625-2940, subscriptions@tandf.co.uk [3/year; $578 indiv, $2639 inst (online), $3016 inst (print + online)] Publication of original research in the science and technological fields. Includes articles on psychological, sociological, economic, and organizational aspects of technological education.

5 Educational Technology

Appropriate Technology. Research Information Ltd., Grenville Court, Britwell Rd., Burnham, Bucks SL1 8DF, United Kingdom. http://www.researchinformation.co.uk/apte.php, tel: +44 (0) 1628 600499, fax: +44 (0) 1628 600488, info@researchinformation.co.uk [4/year; $104 indiv, $332 inst] Articles on less technologically advanced, but more environmentally sustainable solutions to problems in developing countries.

British Journal of Educational Technology. John Wiley & Sons, Inc., Journal Customer Services, 350 Main St, Malden, MA 02148. http://onlinelibrary.wiley.com/journal/10.1111/(ISSN)1467-8535, tel: 800-835-6770, fax: 781-388-8232, cs-agency@wiley.com [6/year; $250 indiv (print + online), $1774 inst (print/online), $2129 inst (print + online)] Published by the National Council for Educational Technology, this journal includes articles on education and training, especially theory, applications, and development of educational technology and communications.

Canadian Journal of Learning and Technology. Canadian Network for Innovation in Education (CNIE), 260 Dalhousie St., Suite 204, Ottawa, ON, K1N 7E4, Canada. http://www.cjlt.ca, tel: 613-241-0018, fax: 613-241-0019, cjlt@ucalgary.ca [3/year; free] Concerned with all aspects of educational systems and technology.

Educational Technology. Educational Technology Publications, Inc., 700 Palisade Ave, Englewood Cliffs, NJ 07632-0564. http://www.bookstoread.com/etp, tel: 800-952-2665, fax: 201-871-4009, edtecpubs@aol.com [6/year; $259] Covers telecommunications, computer-aided instruction, information retrieval, educational television, and electronic media in the classroom.

Educational Technology Research & Development. Springer Science+Business Media, PO Box 2485, Secaucus, NJ 07096-2485. http://www.springer.com/journal/11423, tel: 800-777-4643, fax: 201-348-4505, service-ny@springer.com [6/year; $99 indiv] Focuses on research, instructional development, and applied theory in the field of educational technology.

International Journal of Technology and Design Education. Springer Science+Business Media, PO Box 2485, Secaucus, NJ 07096-2485. http://www.springer.com/journal/10798, tel: 800-777-4643, fax: 201-348-4505, service-ny@springer.com [4/year; $99 indiv] Publishes research reports and scholarly writing about aspects of technology and design education.

Journal of Computing in Higher Education. Springer Science+Business Media, PO Box 2485, Secaucus, NJ 07096-2485. http://www.springer.com/journal/12528, tel: 800-777-4643, fax: 201-348-4505, service-ny@springer.com [3/year; $99 indiv] Publishes scholarly essays, case studies, and research that discuss instructional technologies.

Journal of Educational Technology Systems. Baywood Publishing Co., Inc., 26 Austin Ave, Box 337, Amityville, NY 11701-0337. http://journals.sagepub.com/home/ets, tel: 800-638-7819, fax: 631-691-1770, info@baywood.com [4/year; $147 indiv (print + online), $527 inst (online), $574 inst (online), $586 inst (print + online)] Deals with systems in which technology and education interface; designed to inform educators who are interested in making optimum use of technology.

Journal of Interactive Media in Education. Open University, Knowledge Media Institute, Milton Keynes MK7 6AA, United Kingdom. http://www-jime.open.ac.uk, tel: +44 (0) 1908 653800, fax: +44 (0) 1908 653169, jime@open.ac.uk [irregular; free] A multidisciplinary forum for debate and idea sharing concerning the practical aspects of interactive media and instructional technology.

Journal of Science Education and Technology. Springer Science+Business Media, PO Box 2485, Secaucus, NJ 07096-2485. http://www.springer.com/journal/10956, tel: 800-777-4643, fax: 201-348-4505, service-ny@springer.com [6/year; $99 indiv] Publishes studies aimed at improving science education at all levels in the USA.

Science Communication. Sage Publications, 2455 Teller Rd., Thousand Oaks, CA 91320. http://scx.sagepub.com, tel: 800-818-7243, fax: 800-583-2665, journals@sagepub.com [8/year; $194 indiv (print), $1202 inst (online), $1308 inst (print), $1335 inst (print + online)] An international, interdisciplinary journal examining the nature of expertise and the translation of knowledge into practice and policy.

Social Science Computer Review. Sage Publications, 2455 Teller Rd., Thousand Oaks, CA 91320. http://ssc.sagepub.com, tel: 800-818-7243, fax: 800-583-2665, journals@sagepub.com [4/year; $150 indiv (print), $972 inst (online), $1058 inst (print), $1080 inst (print + online)] Interdisciplinary peer-reviewed scholarly publication covering social science research and instructional applications in computing and telecommunications; also covers societal impacts of information technology.

TechTrends. Springer Science+Business Media, PO Box 2485, Secaucus, NJ 07096-2485. http://www.springer.com/journal/11528, tel: 800-777-4643, fax: 201-348-4505, service-ny@springer.com [6/year; $99, indiv] Targeted at leaders in education and training; features authoritative, practical articles about technology and its integration into the learning environment.

Mediagraphy 293

T.H.E. Journal. PO Box 2166, Skokie, IL 60076. http://www.thejournal.com, tel: 866-293-3194, fax: 847-763-9564, thejournal@1105service.com [9/year; free] For educators of all levels; focuses on a specific topic for each issue, as well as technological innovations as they apply to education.

6 Information Science and Technology

Canadian Journal of Information and Library Science. University of Toronto Press, Journals Division, 5201 Dufferin St, Toronto, ON, M3H 5T8, Canada. http://www.utpjournals.com/cjils, tel: 416-667-7777, fax: 800-221-9985, journals@utpress.utoronto.ca [4/year; $93 indiv] Published by the Canadian Association for Information Science to contribute to the advancement of library and information science in Canada.

E-Content. Information Today, Inc., 143 Old Marlton Pike, Medford, NJ 08055-8750. http://www.econtentmag.com, tel: 800-300-9868, fax: 609-654-4309, custserv@infotoday.com [10/year; $119, free to qualified applicants] Features articles on topics of interest to online database users; includes database search aids.

Information Processing & Management. Elsevier, Inc., Journals Customer Service, 3251 Riverport Lane, Maryland Heights, MO 63043. http://www.elsevier.com/locate/infoproman, tel: 877-839-7126, fax: 314-447-8077, journalcustomerservice-usa@elsevier.com [6/year; $337 indiv, $2992 inst (print)] International journal covering data processing, database building, and retrieval.

Information Services & Use. IOS Press, Nieuwe Hemweg 6B, 1013 BG Amsterdam, The Netherlands. http://www.iospress.nl/journal/information-services-use/, tel: +31 20 688 3 [4/year; $590 indiv] An international journal for those in the information management field. Includes online and off-line systems, library automation, micrographics, videotex, and telecommunications.

The Information Society. Taylor & Francis Group, Customer Services Department, 325 Chestnut St, Suite 800, Philadelphia, PA 19106. http://www.tandf.co.uk/journals/titles/01972243, tel: 800-354-1420, fax: 215-625-2940, subscriptions@tandf.co.uk [5/year; $242 indiv, $588 inst (online), $672 inst (print + online)] Provides a forum for discussion of the world of information, including transborder data flow, regulatory issues, and impact of the information industry.

Information Technology and Libraries. American Library Association, Subscriptions, 50 E Huron St, Chicago, IL 60611-2795. http://www.ala.org/lita/ital, tel: 800-545-2433, fax: 312-944-2641, subscription@ala.org [4/year; free] Articles on library automation, communication technology, cable systems, computerized information processing, and video technologies.

Information Today. Information Today, Inc., 143 Old Marlton Pike, Medford, NJ 08055-8750. http://www.infotoday.com/it, tel: 609-654-6266, fax: 609-654-4309, custserv@infotoday.com [10/year; $99.95] Newspaper for users and producers of electronic information services. Includes articles and news about the industry, calendar of events, and product information.

Internet Reference Service Quarterly. Taylor & Francis Group, Customer Services Department, 325 Chestnut St, Suite 800, Philadelphia, PA 19106. http://www.tandf.co.uk/journals/WIRS, tel: 800-354-1420, fax: 215-625-2940, subscriptions@tandf.co.uk [4/year; $112 indiv (online), $128 indiv (print + online), $273 inst (online), $312 inst (print + online)] Discusses multidisciplinary aspects of incorporating the Internet as a tool for reference service.

Journal of Access Services. Taylor & Francis Group, Customer Services Department, 325 Chestnut St, Suite 800, Philadelphia, PA 19106. http://www.tandf.co.uk/journals/WJAS, tel: 800-354-1420, fax: 215-625-2940, subscriptions@tandf.co.uk [4/year; $103 indiv (online), $118 indiv (print + online), $273 inst (online), $312 inst (print + online)] Explores topics and issues surrounding the organization, administration, and development of information technology on access services and resources.

Journal of the Association for Information Science and Technology. John Wiley & Sons, Inc., Journal Customer Services, 350 Main St, Malden, MA 02148. http://onlinelibrary.wiley.com/journal/10.1002/(ISSN)1532-2890,   tel: 800-835-6770, fax: 781-388-8232, cs-agency@wiley.com [12/year; $3186 inst (print/online), $3824 inst (print + online)] Provides an overall forum for new research in information transfer and communication processes, with particular attention paid to the context of recorded knowledge.

Journal of Database Management. IGI Global, 701 E Chocolate Ave, Suite 200, Hershey, PA 17033-1240. http://www.igi-global.com/journal/journal-database-management-jdm/1072, tel: 866-342-6657, fax: 717-533-8661, cust@igi-global.com [4/year; $260 indiv (print/online), $310 indiv (print + online), $730 inst (print/online), $880 inst (print + online)] Provides state-of-the-art research to those who design, develop, and administer DBMS-based information systems.

Journal of Documentation. Emerald Group Publishing Inc., Brickyard Office Park, 84 Sherman Street, Cambridge, MA 02140. http://www.emeraldinsight.com/loi/jd, tel: 617-945-9130, fax: 617-945-9136, america@emeraldinsight.com [6/year; inst prices vary] Focuses on theories, concepts, models, frameworks, and philosophies in information sciences.

Journal of Interlibrary Loan, Document Delivery & Electronic Reserve. Taylor & Francis Group, Customer Services Department, 325 Chestnut St, Suite 800, Philadelphia, PA 19106. http://www.tandf.co.uk/journals/titles/1072303X, tel: 800-354-1420, fax: 215-625-2940, subscriptions@tandf.co.uk [5/year; $138 indiv (online), $158 indiv (print + online), $516 inst (online), $589 inst (print + online)] A forum for ideas on the basic theoretical and practical problems regarding all aspects of library resource sharing faced by planners, practitioners, and users of network services.

Journal of Library Metadata. Taylor & Francis Group, Customer Services Department, 325 Chestnut St, Suite 800, Philadelphia, PA 19106. http://www.tandf.co.uk/journals/titles/19386389, tel: 800-354-1420, fax: 215-625-2940, subscriptions@tandf.co.uk [4/year; $109 indiv (online), $125 indiv (print +

online), \$326 inst (online), \$372 inst (print + online)] A forum for the latest research, innovations, news, and expert views about all aspects of metadata applications and information retrieval in libraries.

7 Instructional Design and Development

Human-Computer Interaction. Taylor & Francis Group, Customer Services Department, 325 Chestnut St, Suite 800, Philadelphia, PA 19106. http://www.tandf.co.uk/journals/titles/07370024, tel: 800-354-1420, fax: 215-625-2940, subscriptions@tandf.co.uk [4/year; \$122 indiv, \$1011 inst (online), \$1156 inst (online + print)] A journal of theoretical, empirical, and methodological issues of user science and of system design.

Instructional Science. Springer Science+Business Media, PO Box 2485, Secaucus, NJ 07096-2485. http://www.springer.com/journal/11251, tel: 800-777-4643, fax: 201-348-4505, service-ny@springer.com [6/year; \$99 indiv] Promotes a deeper understanding of the nature, theory, and practice of the instructional process and the learning resulting from this process.

International Journal of Human-Computer Interaction. Taylor & Francis Group, Customer Services Department, 325 Chestnut St, Suite 800, Philadelphia, PA 19106. http://www.tandf.co.uk/journals/titles/10447318, tel: 800-354-1420, fax: 215-625-2940, subscriptions@tandf.co.uk [12/year; \$292 indiv (print), \$306 indiv (print + online), \$2305 inst (online), \$2634 inst (print + online)] Addresses the cognitive, social, health, and ergonomic aspects of work with computers. It also emphasizes both the human and computer science aspects of the effective design and use of computer interactive systems.

Journal of Educational Technology Systems. Baywood Publishing Co., Inc., 26 Austin Ave, PO Box 337, Amityville, NY 11701-0337. https://us.sagepub.com/en-us/nam/journal-of-educational-technology-systems/journal202400, tel: 800-638-7819, fax: 631-691-1770, info@baywood.com [4/year; \$147 individ (print + online), \$527 inst (online), \$574 inst (print), \$586 inst (print + online)] Deals with systems in which technology and education interface; designed to inform educators who are interested in making optimum use of technology.

Journal of Technical Writing and Communication. Baywood Publishing Co., Inc., 26 Austin Ave, PO Box 337, Amityville, NY 11701-0337. https://us.sagepub.com/en-us/nam/journal-of-technical-writing-and-communication/journal202406, tel: 800-638-7819, fax: 631-691-1770, info@baywood.com [4/year; \$147 indiv (online), \$527 inst (online), \$574 inst (print), \$586 inst (print + online)] Essays on oral and written communication, for purposes ranging from pure research to needs of business and industry.

Journal of Visual Literacy. International Visual Literacy Association, Dr. David R. Moore, IVLA Executive Treasurer, Ohio University, 250 McCracken Hall, Athens, OH 45701. http://www.tandfonline.com/loi/rjvl20, tel: 740-597-1322, jvleditor@ohio.edu [2/year; \$234 indiv (online), \$268 inst (print + online)]

Explores empirical, theoretical, practical, and applied aspects of visual literacy and communication.

Performance Improvement. John Wiley & Sons, Inc., Journal Customer Services, 350 Main St, Malden, MA 02148. http://onlinelibrary.wiley.com/journal/10.100 2/(ISSN)1930-8272, tel: 800-835-6770, fax: 781-388-8232, cs-agency@wiley.com [10/year; $98 indiv (print), $109 indiv (print + online), $510 inst (print/online), $612 inst (print + online)] Promotes performance science and technology. Contains articles, research, and case studies relating to improving human performance.

Performance Improvement Quarterly. John Wiley & Sons, Inc., Journal Customer Services, 350 Main St, Malden, MA 02148. http://www3.interscience.wiley.com/journal/117865970/home, tel: 800-835-6770, fax: 781-388-8232, cs-agency@wiley.com [4/year; 67 indiv (print), $289 inst (print/online), $347 inst (print + online)] Presents the cutting edge in research and theory in performance technology.

Training. Lakewood Media Group, PO Box 247, Excelsior, MN 55331. http://www.trainingmag.com, tel: 877-865-9361, fax: 847-291-4816, ntrn@omeda.com [6/year; $79, free to qualified applicants] Covers all aspects of training, management, and organizational development, motivation, and performance improvement.

8   Learning Sciences

International Journal of Computer-Supported Collaborative Learning. Springer Science+Business Media, PO Box 2485, Secaucus, NJ 07096-2485. http://www.springer.com/journal/11412, tel: 800-777-4643, fax: 201-348-4505, service-ny@springer.com [4/year; $99 indiv] Promotes a deeper understanding of the nature, theory, and practice of the uses of computer-supported collaborative learning.

Journal of the Learning Sciences. Taylor & Francis Group, Customer Services Department, 325 Chestnut St, Suite 800, Philadelphia, PA 19106. http://www.tandf.co.uk/journals/titles/10508406, tel: 800-354-1420, fax: 215-625-2940, subscriptions@tandf.co.uk [4/year; $103 indiv (print + online), $948 inst (online), $1084 inst (print + online)] Provides a forum for the discussion of research on education and learning, with emphasis on the idea of changing one's understanding of learning and the practice of education.

International Journal of Science Education. Taylor & Francis Group, Customer Services Department, 325 Chestnut St, Suite 800, Philadelphia, PA 19106. http://www.tandfonline.com/tsed, tel: 800-354-1420, fax: 215-625-2940 subscriptions@tandf.co.uk [18/year; $1484 indiv (print), $4381 inst (online), $5006 (print + online)] Special emphasis is placed on applicable research relevant to educational practice, guided by educational realities in systems, schools, colleges, and universities.

Mediagraphy

9 Libraries and Media Centers

Collection Building. Emerald Group Publishing Inc., Brickyard Office Park, 84 Sherman Street, Cambridge, MA 02140. http://www.emeraldinsight.com/loi/cb, tel: 617-945-9130, fax: 617-945-9136, america@emeraldinsight.com [4/year; inst prices vary] Provides well-researched and authoritative information on collection maintenance and development for librarians in all sectors.

Computers in Libraries. Information Today, Inc., 143 Old Marlton Pike, Medford, NJ 08055-8750. http://www.infotoday.com/cilmag/default.shtml, tel: 609-654-6266, fax: 609-654-4309, custserv@infotoday.com [10/year; $104] Covers practical applications of microcomputers to library situations and recent news items.

The Electronic Library. Emerald Group Publishing Inc., Brickyard Office Park, 84 Sherman Street, Cambridge, MA 02140. http://www.emeraldgrouppublishing.com/el.htm, tel: 617-945-9130, fax: 617-945-9136, america@emeraldinsight.com [6/year; inst prices vary] International journal for minicomputer, microcomputer, and software applications in libraries; independently assesses current and forthcoming information technologies.

Government Information Quarterly. Elsevier, Inc., Journals Customer Service, 3251 Riverport Lane, Maryland Heights, MO 63043. http://www.elsevier.com/locate/govinf, tel: 877-839-7126, fax: 314-447-8077, journalcustomerservice-usa@elsevier.com [4/year; $226 indiv, $1029 inst (print)] International journal of resources, services, policies, and practices.

Information Outlook. Special Libraries Association, Information Outlook Subscriptions, 1700 Eighteenth Street, NW, Washington, DC 20009-2514. http://www.sla.org/access-membership/io, tel: 703-647-4900, fax: 1-202-234-2442, magazine@sla.org [12/year; $240 member] Discusses administration, organization, and operations. Includes reports on research, technology, and professional standards.

The Journal of Academic Librarianship. Elsevier, Inc., Journals Customer Service, 3251 Riverport Lane, Maryland Heights, MO 63043. http://www.elsevier.com/locate/jacalib, tel: 877-839-7126, fax: 314-447-8077, journalcustomerservice-usa@elsevier.com [6/year; $177 indiv (print), $591 inst (print)] Results of significant research, issues, and problems facing academic libraries, book reviews, and innovations in academic libraries.

Journal of Librarianship and Information Science. Sage Publications, 2455 Teller Rd., Thousand Oaks, CA 91320. http://lis.sagepub.com, tel: 800-818-7243, fax: 800-583-2665, journals@sagepub.com [4/year; $126 indiv (print), $905 inst (online), $986 inst (print), $1006 inst (print + online)] Deals with all aspects of library and information work in the United Kingdom and reviews literature from international sources.

Journal of Library Administration. Taylor & Francis Group, Customer Services Department, 325 Chestnut St, Suite 800, Philadelphia, PA 19106. http://www.tandf.co.uk/journals/titles/01930826, tel: 800-354-1420, fax: 215-625-2940, subscriptions@tandf.co.uk [8/year; $273 (online), $312 indiv (print + online), $1016 inst (online), $1161 inst (print + online)] Provides information on all aspects of effective library management, with emphasis on practical applications.

Library & Information Science Research. Elsevier, Inc., Journals Customer Service, 3251 Riverport Lane, Maryland Heights, MO 63043. http://www.elsevier.com/locate/lisres, tel: 877-839-7126, fax: 314-447-8077, journalcustomerservice-usa@elsevier.com [4/year; $188 indiv (print), $779 inst (print)] Research articles, dissertation reviews, and book reviews on issues concerning information resource management.

Library Hi Tech. Emerald Group Publishing Inc., Brickyard Office Park, 84 Sherman Street, Cambridge, MA 02140. http://www.emeraldinsight.com/loi/lht, tel: 617-945-9130, fax: 617-945-9136, america@emeraldinsight.com [4/year; inst prices vary] Concentrates on reporting on the selection, installation, maintenance, and integration of systems and hardware.

Library Hi Tech News. Emerald Group Publishing Inc., Brickyard Office Park, 84 Sherman Street, Cambridge, MA 02140. http://www.emeraldinsight.com/loi/lhtn, tel: 617-945-9130, fax: 617-945-9136, america@emeraldinsight.com [10/year; inst prices vary] Supplements Library Hi Tech and updates many of the issues addressed in-Departmenth in the journal; keeps the reader fully informed of the latest developments in library automation, new products, network news, new software and hardware, and people in technology.

Library Journal. Media Source, Inc., 160 Varick Street, 11th Floor, New York, NY 10013. http://www.libraryjournal.com, tel: 800-588-1030, fax: 712-733-8019, LJLcustserv@cds-global.com [20/year; $102 indiv] A professional periodical for librarians, with current issues and news, professional reading, a lengthy book review section, and classified advertisements.

The Library Quarterly: Information, Community, Policy. University of Chicago Press, Journals Division, PO Box 37005, Chicago, IL 60637. http://www.journals.uchicago.edu/LQ, tel: 877-705-1878, fax: 877-705-1879, subscriptions@press.uchicago.edu [$27 students (online), $48 indiv (print), $49 indiv (online), $54 indiv (print + online), $253 inst (print), $403 inst (online), $685 inst (print + online)] Scholarly articles of interest to librarians.

Library Resources & Technical Services. American Library Association, Subscriptions, 50 E Huron St, Chicago, IL 60611-2795. http://www.ala.org/ala/mgrps/divs/alcts/resources/lrts/index.cfm, tel: 800-545-2433, fax: 312-944-2641, subscription@ala.org [4/year; inst prices vary] Scholarly papers on bibliographic access and control, preservation, conservation, and reproduction of library materials.

Library Trends. Johns Hopkins University Press, PO Box 19966, Baltimore, MD 21211-0966. http://www.press.jhu.edu/journals/library_trends, tel: 800-548-1784, fax: 410-516-3866, jrnlcirc@press.jhu.edu [4/year; $80 indiv (print), $85 indiv (online), $175 inst (print)] Each issue is concerned with one aspect of library and information science, analyzing current thought and practice and examining ideas that hold the greatest potential for the field.

Public Libraries. American Library Association, Subscriptions, 50 E Huron St, Chicago, IL 60611-2795. http://www.ala.org/pla/publications/publiclibraries, tel: 800-545-2433, fax: 312-944-2641, subscription@ala.org [6/year; $65 indiv] News and articles of interest to public librarians.

Public Library Quarterly. Taylor & Francis Group, Customer Services Department, 325 Chestnut St, Suite 800, Philadelphia, PA 19106. http://www.tandf.co.uk/journals/WPLQ, tel: 800-354-1420, fax: 215-625-2940, subscriptions@tandf.co.uk [4/year; $152 indiv (online), $174 indiv (print + online), $468 inst (online), $536 inst (print + online)] Addresses the major administrative challenges and opportunities that are faced by the nation's public libraries.

Reference and User Services Quarterly. American Library Association, Subscriptions, 50 E Huron St, Chicago, IL 60611-2795. https://journals.ala.org/index.php/rusq, tel: 800-545-2433, fax: 312-944-2641, subscription@ala.org [4/year; inst prices vary] Disseminates information of interest to reference librarians, bibliographers, adult service librarians, those in collection development and selection, and others interested in public services.

The Reference Librarian. Taylor & Francis Group, Customer Services Department, 325 Chestnut St, Suite 800, Philadelphia, PA 19106. http://www.tandf.co.uk/journals/wref, tel: 800-354-1420, fax: 215-625-2940, subscriptions@tandf.co.uk [4/year; $328 indiv (online), $375 indiv (print + online), $1325 inst (online), $1514 inst (print + online)] Each issue focuses on a topic of current concern, interest, or practical value to reference librarians.

Reference Services Review. Emerald Group Publishing Inc., Brickyard Office Park, 84 Sherman Street, Cambridge, MA 02140. http://www.emeraldinsight.com/loi/rsr, tel: 617-945-9130, fax: 617-945-9136, america@emeraldinsight.com [4/year; inst prices vary] Dedicated to the enrichment of reference knowledge and the advancement of reference services. It prepares its readers to understand and embrace current and emerging technologies affecting reference functions and information needs of library users.

School Library Journal. Media Source, Inc., 160 Varick Street, 11th Floor, New York, NY 10013. http://www.slj.com, tel: 800-595-1066, fax: 712-733-8019, sljcustserv@cds-global.com [12/year; $89 indiv] For school and youth service librarians. Reviews about 4000 children's books and 1000 educational media titles annually.

School Library Monthly. Libraries Unlimited, Inc., PO Box 291846, Kettering OH 45429. http://www.schoollibrarymedia.com, tel: 800-771-5579, fax: 937-890-0221, schoollibrarymonthly@sfsdayton.com [12/year; $89 indiv] A vehicle for distributing ideas for teaching library media skills and for the development and implementation of library media skill programs.

School Library Research. American Library Association and American Association of School Librarians, Subscriptions, 50 E Huron St, Chicago, IL 60611-2795. http://www.ala.org/aasl/slr, tel: 800-545-2433, fax: 312-944-2641, subscription@ala.org [annual compilation; free online] For library media specialists, district supervisors, and others concerned with the selection and purchase of print and nonprint media and with the development of programs and services for preschool through high school libraries.

Teacher Librarian. The Scarecrow Press, Inc., 4501 Forbes Blvd, Suite 200, Lanham, MD 20706. http://www.teacherlibrarian.com, tel: 800-462-6420, fax: 800-338-4550, admin@teacherlibrarian.com [5/year; $62 indiv] "The journal for school library professionals"; previously known as Emergency Librarian. Articles, review columns, and critical analyses of management and programming issues.

10 Media Technologies

Broadcasting & Cable. NewBay Media, LLC., 28 E. 28th St, 12th Floor, New York, NY 10016. http://www.broadcastingcable.com, tel: 800-554-5729, fax: 712-733-8019, bcbcustserv@cdsfulfillment.com [47/year; $169 indiv] All-inclusive newsweekly for radio, television, cable, and allied business.

Educational Media International. Taylor & Francis Group, Customer Services Department, 325 Chestnut St, Suite 800, Philadelphia, PA 19106. http://www.tandf.co.uk/journals/titles/09523987, tel: 800-354-1420, fax: 215-625-2940, subscriptions@tandf.co.uk [4/year; $188 indiv (print), $667 inst (online), $762 inst (print + online)] The official journal of the International Council for Educational Media.

Historical Journal of Film, Radio and Television. Taylor & Francis Group, Customer Services Department, 325 Chestnut St, Suite 800, Philadelphia, PA 19106. http://www.tandf.co.uk/journals/titles/01439685, tel: 800-354-1420, fax: 215-625-2940, subscriptions@tandf.co.uk [4/year; $564 indiv (print), $1489 inst (online), $1703 inst (print + online)] Articles by international experts in the field, news and notices, and book reviews concerning the impact of mass communications on political and social history of the twentieth century.

Journal of Educational Multimedia and Hypermedia. Association for the Advancement of Computing in Education, PO Box 1545, Chesapeake, VA 23327-1545. http://www.aace.org/pubs/jemh, tel: 757-366-5606, fax: 703-997-8760, info@editlib.org [4/year; 4/year; $175 indiv, $215 inst] A multidisciplinary information source presenting research about and applications for multimedia and hypermedia tools.

Journal of Popular Film and Television. Taylor & Francis Group, Customer Service Department, 325 Chestnut Street, Suite 800, Philadelphia, PA 19106. http://www.tandf.co.uk/journals/titles/01956051, tel: 800-354-1420, fax: 215-625-2940, subscriptions@tandf.co.uk [4/year; $84 indiv (print + online), $224 inst (online), $255 (print + online)] Articles on film and television, book reviews, and theory. Dedicated to popular film and television in the broadest sense. Concentrates on commercial cinema and television, film and television theory or criticism, filmographies, and bibliographies. Edited at the College of

Arts and Sciences of Northern Michigan University and the Department of Popular Culture, Bowling Green State University.

Learning, Media & Technology. Taylor & Francis Group, Customer Services Department, 325 Chestnut St, Suite 800, Philadelphia, PA 19106. http://www. tandf.co.uk/journals/titles/17439884, tel: 800-354-1420, fax: 215-625-2940, subscriptions@tandf.co.uk [4/year; $673 indiv (print), $2265 inst (online), $2589 inst (print + online)] This journal of the Educational Television Association serves as an international forum for discussions and reports on developments in the field of television and related media in teaching, learning, and training.

Media & Methods. American Society of Educators, 1429 Walnut St, Philadelphia, PA 19102. http://www.media-methods.com, tel: 215-563-6005, fax: 215-587-9706, info@media-methods.com [5/year; $35 indiv] The only magazine published for the elementary school library media and technology specialist. A forum for K-12 educators who use technology as an educational resource, this journal includes information on what works and what does not, new product reviews, tips and pointers, and emerging technologies.

Multichannel News. NewBay Media, LLC., 28 E. 28th St. 12th Floor, New York, NY 10016. http://www.multichannel.com, tel: 888-343-5563, fax: 712-733-8019, mulcustserv@cdsfulfillment.com [47/year; $249 indiv] A newsmagazine for the cable television industry. Covers programming, marketing, advertising, business, and other topics.

MultiMedia & Internet@Schools. Information Today, Inc., 143 Old Marlton Pike, Medford, NJ 08055-8750. http://www.mmischools.com, tel: 609-654-6266, fax: 609-654-4309, custserv@infotoday.com [5/year; $50 indiv] Reviews and evaluates hardware and software. Presents information pertaining to basic troubleshooting skills.

Multimedia Systems. Springer Science+Business Media, PO Box 2485, Secaucus, NJ 07096-2485. http://www.springer.com/journal/00530, tel: 800-777-4643, fax: 201-348-4505, service-ny@springer.com [6/year; $99 indiv] Publishes original research articles and serves as a forum for stimulating and disseminating innovative research ideas, emerging technologies, state-of-the-art methods, and tools in all aspects of multimedia computing, communication, storage, and applications among researchers, engineers, and practitioners.

Telematics and Informatics. Elsevier, Inc., Journals Customer Service, 3251 Riverport Lane, Maryland Heights, MO 63043. http://www.elsevier.com/locate/tele, tel: 877-839-7126, fax: 314-447-8077, journalcustomerservice-usa@elsevier.com [4/year; $165 indiv (print), $1899 inst (print)] Publishes research and review articles in applied telecommunications and information sciences in business, industry, government, and educational establishments. Focuses on important current technologies, including microelectronics, computer graphics, speech synthesis and voice recognition, database management, data encryption, satellite television, artificial intelligence, and ongoing computer revolution.

11 Professional Development

Journal of Digital Learning in Teacher Education. International Society for Technology in Education, Special Interest Group for Teacher Educators, 180 West 8th Ave., Suite 300, Eugene, OR 97401. http://www.iste.org/jdlte, tel: 800-336-5191, fax: 541-302-3778, iste@iste.org [4/year; $89 member] Contains refereed articles on preservice and in-service training, research in computer education and certification issues, and reviews of training materials and texts.

Journal of Technology and Teacher Education. Association for the Advancement of Computing in Education, PO Box 1545, Chesapeake, VA 23327-1545. http://www.aace.org/pubs/jtate/, tel: 757-366-5606, fax: 703-997-8760, info@editlib.org [4/year; $125 indiv, $215 inst] Serves as an international forum to report research and applications of technology in preservice, in-service, and graduate teacher education.

12 Simulation, Gaming, and Virtual Reality

Simulation & Gaming. Sage Publications, 2455 Teller Rd., Thousand Oaks, CA 91320. http://sag.sagepub.com, tel: 800-818-7243, fax: 800-583-2665, journals@sagepub.com [6/year; $171 indiv (online), $1393 inst (online), $1532 inst (print + online)] An international journal of theory, design, and research focusing on issues in simulation, gaming, modeling, role-playing, and experiential learning.

13 Special Education and Disabilities

Journal of Special Education Technology. Technology and Media Division, JSET, PO Box 3853, Reston, VA 20195. http://www.tamcec.org/jset, tel: 703-709-0136, fax: 405-325-7661, info@exinn.net [4/year; $93 indiv (online), $101 indiv (print), $103 (print + online), $261 inst (online), $284 inst (print), $290 inst (print + online)] Provides information, research, and reports of innovative practices regarding the application of educational technology toward the education of exceptional children.

Mediagraphy

14 Telecommunications and Networking

Canadian Journal of Learning and Technology. Canadian Network for Innovation in Education (CNIE), 260 Dalhousie St., Suite 204, Ottawa, ON, K1N 7E4, Canada. http://www.cjlt.ca, tel: 613-241-0018, fax: 613-241-0019, cjlt@ucalgary.ca [3/year; free] Concerned with all aspects of educational systems and technology.

Computer Communications. Elsevier, Inc., Journals Customer Service, 3251 Riverport Lane, Maryland Heights, MO 63043. http://www.elsevier.com/locate/comcom, tel: 877-839-7126, fax: 314-447-8077, journalcustomerservice-usa@elsevier.com [24/year; $3331 inst (online/print)] Focuses on networking and distributed computing techniques, communications hardware and software, and standardization.

EDUCAUSE Review. EDUCAUSE, 4772 Walnut St, Suite 206, Boulder, CO 80301-2536. http://er.educause.edu/, tel: 303-449-4430, fax: 303-440-0461, ersubs@educause.edu [6/year; free online] Features articles on current issues and applications of computing and communications technology in higher education. Reports on EDUCAUSE consortium activities.

International Journal on E-Learning. Association for the Advancement of Computing in Education, PO Box 1545, Chesapeake, VA 23327-1545. http://www.aace.org/pubs/ijel, tel: 757-366-5606, fax: 703-997-8760, info@editlib.org [4/year; $175 indiv, $215 inst] Reports on current theory, research, development, and practice of telecommunications in education at all levels.

The Internet and Higher Education. Elsevier, Inc., Journals Customer Service, 3251 Riverport Lane, Maryland Heights, MO 63043. http://www.elsevier.com/locate/iheduc, tel: 877-839-7126, fax: 314-447-8077, journalcustomerservice-usa@elsevier.com [4/year; $103 indiv (print), $706 inst (print)] Designed to reach faculty, staff, and administrators responsible for enhancing instructional practices and productivity via the use of information technology and the Internet in their institutions.

Internet Reference Services Quarterly. Taylor & Francis Group, Customer Services Department, 325 Chestnut St, Suite 800, Philadelphia, PA 19106. http://www.tandf.co.uk/journals/titles/10875301, tel: 800-354-1420, fax: 215-625-2940, subscriptions@tandf.co.uk [4/year; $112 indiv (online), $128 indiv (print + online), $273 inst (online), $312 inst (print + online)] Describes innovative information practice, technologies, and practice. For librarians of all kinds.

Internet Research. Emerald Group Publishing Inc., Brickyard Office Park, 84 Sherman Street, Cambridge, MA 02140. http://www.emeraldinsight.com/loi/intr, tel: 617-945-9130, fax: 617-945-9136, america@emeraldinsight.com [5/year; inst prices vary] A cross-disciplinary journal presenting research findings related to electronic networks, analyses of policy issues related to networking, and descriptions of current and potential applications of electronic networking for communication, computation, and provision of information services.

Online Searcher. Information Today, Inc., 143 Old Marlton Pike, Medford, NJ 08055-8750. http://www.infotoday.com/online, tel: 609-654-6266, fax: 609-654-4309, custserv@infotoday.com [6/year; $139 indiv] For online information system users. Articles cover a variety of online applications for general and business use.

Index

A

Active learning classrooms (ACLs), 7
Adaptech Research Network, 77–79
Admission requirements, 151
AECT Legends & Legacies Project, 69
AECT's HistoryMakers Project, 69
Agency for Instructional Technology (AIT), 79
Aiken: School of Education; Columbia: Department of Educational Psychology, 244
American Association of Colleges for Teacher Education (AACTE), 80
American Association of Community Colleges (AACC), 80, 81
American Association of School Librarians (AASL), 81
American Educational Research Association (AERA), 82
American Educational Research Journal, 290
American Foundation for the Blind (AFB), 83
American Journal of Distance Education, 289
American Library Association (ALA), 83, 84
American Society for Training & Development (ASTD), 84, 85
Anadolu University, 205
Andong National University, 201
Appalachian State University, 237
Appropriate Technology, 291
Arizona State University, 155
Artificial intelligence (AI), 5, 285
Artificial intelligence, robotics, and electronic performance support systems, 283

Asia-Pacific Education Researcher, 290
Associate School Library Media Specialists (ALMS), 269–270
Association for Childhood Education International (ACEI), 85, 86
Association for Computers and the Humanities (ACH), 86
Association for Continuing Higher Education (ACHE), 86, 87
Association for Educational Communications and Technology (AECT), 17, 63–66, 87, 88, 160
Association for Experiential Education (AEE), 88, 89
Association for Library and Information Science Education (ALISE), 89
Association for Library Collections & Technical Services (ALCTS), 89, 90
Association for Library Service to Children (ALSC), 90, 91
Association for Talent Development (ATD), 3–5
Association of American Publishers (AAP), 91, 92
Association of College and Research Libraries (ACRL), 92, 93
Association of Specialized and Cooperative Library Agencies (ASCLA), 93, 94
Athabasca University, 194
Augmented reality (AR), 7
Authentic learning experiences, 25
Azusa Pacific University, 211

B

Babson Survey Research Group, 3
Baker University, 182
Ball State University, 257
Barry University, 214
Bemidji State University, 264
Blended learning designs, 8
Bloomsburg University, 241
Boise State University, 168, 171
Boston University, 226
Bricolage-form applications, 14
Brigham Young University, 191
British Journal of Educational Technology, 43, 291
Broadcasting & Cable, 300
Buffalo State College, 237

C

California State Polytechnic University, 253
California State University, 256
California State University Monterey Bay (CSUMB), 253
California State University-San Bernardino, 210
Canadian Journal of Information and Library Science, 293
Canadian Journal of Learning and Technology, 291, 303
Canadian Library Association/Association canadienne des bibliothèques (CLA/ACB), 94, 95
Canadian Museums Association/Association des musées canadiens (CMA/AMC), 95
Career and Information Studies, 193
Center for Advanced Study of Teaching and Learning (CASTL), 249
Center for Digital Education, 287
Centre for Distance Education, 194, 195
Centre for Educational Technology (CET), 96
Centre for Instructional Technology and Multimedia, 201
Certificate in Instructional Technology, 210
Cherokee language, 68
Children's Technology Review, 286
Chromebooks, 10
Clarke College, 222
Close Up Foundation (CUF), 96, 97
Coax television-based classrooms, 14
Collection Building, 297
College of Arts and Sciences, 219
College of Education, 215, 223, 230–232, 240, 250

College of Education and Human Services, 269
College of Education and Human Services, Department of Educational Leadership, 239
College of Education Department of Teacher Education, 235
College of Education, Department of Instructional Technology, 212
College of Information Science and Technology, 241
Communication technology, 59
Communications and technology, 68
Competencies, 17–19, 22, 24
Computer AND, 44
Computer-assisted instruction, 283, 286–289
Computer Assisted Language Instruction Consortium (CALICO), 97
Computer Assisted Language Learning, 287
Computer communications, 303
Computer Education and Instructional Technology, 204–206
Computer Information Systems Department, 237
Computers & Education, 287
Computers and Composition, 287
Computers and Education, 54
Computers in Human Behavior, 287
Computers in Libraries, 297
Concordia University, 161, 276
Consortium of College and University Media Centers (CCUMC), 97, 98
Corporate training and development
  instructional content, 5
  instructional delivery methods, 5
  instructional designers' professional prospects, 6
  learning expenditures, 4, 5
Council for Exceptional Children (CEC), 98, 99
Counseling and tutoring sessions, 14
Cultural Foundations, Technology, and Qualitative Inquiry (CFTQI), 207
Currency and accuracy, 151
Curriculum and Instruction, 224
Curriculum and Instructional Leadership, 265
Curriculum and Instruction, Learning Design, and Technology, 172, 173
Curriculum and Instruction, Learning Technologies, 159
Curriculum and Instruction, School of Education, 276
Curriculum development, 96, 136
Curriculum, Leadership, and Technology, 217

Index

Curriculum, Technology, and Education Reform (CTER) Program, 220
Curry School of Education, 249

D

Dakota State University, 244
Data analysis, 45
Data retrieval, 45
Degree requirements, 151
Department of Communication and Media Studies, 238
Department of Computer Science/Information Systems, 232
Department of Curriculum and Instruction, 219, 237, 247, 249
Department of Curriculum and Teaching, 269
Department of Curriculum, Instruction, and Media Technology, 222
Department of Education, 202
Department of Educational Computing and Technology, School of Education, 214
Department of Educational Leadership, 274
Department of Educational Psychology, 240
Department of Educational Studies, 263
Department of Educational Technology, 201, 217
Department of Instructional Design and Technology (IDT), 165, 166
Department of Instructional Technology and Educational Leadership, 267
Department of Instructional Technology and Learning Sciences, 248
Department of Instructional Technology, Foundations and Secondary Education, 265
Department of Leadership, Research, and Technology, 177
Department of Library Science and Technology, 157
Department of Psychological Studies in Education, 273
Department of Science, Mathematics, and Technology Education, 210
Department of Special Education, Early Childhood Education, Reading, and Educational Technology, 257
Design and technology, 75
Design thinking, 22
Digital Learning Collaborative, 8
Digital Media Design for Learning Program (M.A., Adv. Cert.), 270
Distance AND, 44

Distance education, 68, 69, 283, 289, 290
Division of Graduate and Continuing Education, 227
Doctor of Education in Distance Education program, 195
Doctor of Education in *Educational Technology*, 169
Doctor of Education in Instructional Design and Performance Technology, 182, 183
Doctorate in Instructional Systems Design and Technology, 158
Doctorate of Education in Distance Education Admission, 194
Domestic programs, 44
Drexel University, 241

E

East Carolina University, 189
Eastern Michigan University, 230
East Stroudsburg University, 272
East Tennessee State University, 247
East-West Center, 99, 101
EBSCO Host Databases, 281
E-Content, 293
Ed.S. in Instructional Technology, Media, and Design, 167, 168
EDUCABS, 211
Education Development Center (EDC), 101
Education Division/Instructional Systems Program, 273
Education Doctorate (EDD) in Educational Technology, 197
Education Northwest, 101, 102
Education Specialist (Ed.S.) degree in Instructional Technology, 191
Education Specialist (Ed.S.) in Educational Technology, 168
Education Specialist in Educational Technology program, 169
Education Technology Programs, 172
Education Week, 3, 8
Educational Communication and Technology Program (Ph.D.), 270
Educational Communications (EC), 102
Educational Computing, Design, and Online Learning Program, 224
Educational environments. Educational Technology (ETEC), 217
Educational media, 59
Educational Media and Technology Yearbook, 59
Educational Media International, 300

Educational Multimedia Design, 253
Educational Psychology, 213
Educational Psychology and Counseling (EPC), 184
Educational Psychology and Instructional Technology program, 211
Educational Psychology and Learning Systems, 215
Educational research, 283, 290, 291
Educational Sciences, 203
Educational technology, 161, 168, 169, 210, 213, 244, 251, 274, 276, 283, 291, 292
Educational Technology and Design, 199
Educational Technology and Society, 54
Educational Technology Department, 200
Educational Technology in School of Teaching and Learning, 175, 176
Educational Technology Leadership, 172, 209
Educational Technology Media Yearbook, 43, 45
Educational Technology program, 164, 165, 233, 251, 259
Educational Technology Program, Department of Educational Psychology, 246
Educational technology publications, 48
Educational Technology Research & Development, 291
Educational Technology Specialization, 196
Educational Technology Use in Schools Report, 9
Educational Technology, Research, and Assessment, 220
EDUCAUSE Center for Analysis and Research (ECAR) study, 6, 7
EDUCAUSE Review, 303
Edvantia, 103
Emporia State University, 223, 258
EMTY, 281
ENC Learning Inc, 103, 104
ERIC Document Reproduction Service, 282
ERIC documents, 282
ETEC M.Ed. program, 218
European Master in Media Engineering for Education (Erasmus Mundus master), 200
Ewha Womans University, 200

F

Face-to-face education, 13, 15
Faculty of Education, 196, 198–200
Fairfield University, 213
Film Arts Foundation, 104

First Lego League Robotics, 33
FIRST Robotics, 33
Fischler College of Education and School of Criminal Justice, 157
Fitchburg State University, 227
Florida Center for Instructional Technology (FCIT), 216
Florida Gulf Coast University, 177
Florida Institute of Technology, 214
Florida State University, 215
Fordham University, 238
Full-time, part-time, and adjunct faculty, 151

G

Gaming, 283
Gartner Incorporated, 3
Gartner Trend Insight Report, 5
General Instructional Design and Technology Emphasis, 154
George Lucas Educational Foundation (GLEF), 145, 146
George Mason University, 188
Georgia Assessments for the Certification of Educators (GACE) assessments, 191
Georgia Professional Standards Commission (GaPSC), 191
Georgia Southern University, 166
Georgia State University, 216
Google Scholar, 44
Government Information Quarterly, 297
Governors State University, 219
Graduate and Professional Studies, 229
Graduate Certificate in Instructional Design, 186, 194, 195
Graduate Diploma in Distance Education Technology (GDDET), 194, 195
Graduate Diploma in Instructional Design, 194, 195
Graduate Diploma in Instructional Technology, 161
Graduate Management Admission Test (GMAT), 181
Graduate Program Supplemental Information Form, 218
Graduate Record Exam (GRE), 172, 182
Graduate School of Education, 228
Graduate School of Library and Information Studies, 243
Graduate Studies, 222
Grand Valley State University, 158
Great Plains National ITV Library, 104, 105

Index

H

Hacettepe University, 205
Harvard University, 228
Health Sciences Communications Association (HeSCA), 105
Higher education
  faculty use of technology for instruction, 7
  students use of technology for learning, 8
  teaching and learning online, 8
  technology on campus, classrooms, and online, 6, 7
High-quality educational services, 98
Historical Journal of Film, Radio and Television, 300
Human-computer, 285, 295
Human learning, 156, 181, 211, 233

I

IDT program, 68
Illinois State Board of Education's (ISBE) Technology Specialist, 221
Indiana State University, 222
Indiana University, 183
Information Outlook, 297
Information Processing & Management, 293
Information science and technology, 283, 293, 294
Information Services & Use, 293
Information Today, 293
Ingénierie des médias pour léducation, 200
Innovations in Education and Teaching International, 290
Inside Higher Ed and Gallup, 3
Institute for Scientific Information (ISI), 283
Institute for the Future (IFTF), 105, 106
Instructional and Learning Technology (ILT), 273
Instructional Coordinators and Training and Development Specialists, 6
Instructional design
  authentic practice, 25
  competencies, 17, 18
  definition, 17
  design thinking, 22
  frequency of course offerings programs, 20–21
  ID models, 18
  performance improvement, 23, 24
  problem-solving process, 21
  project management models, 24
  recommendations for future research, 21
  reflective practice, 24

user experience design, 22, 23
Instructional design and development, 184, 283, 295, 296
Instructional Design and Technology (IDT), 153, 154, 179, 180, 188, 258, 267, 275
Instructional Design program, 186, 269
Instructional Design, Development, and Evaluation Program, 271
Instructional Leadership track, 223
Instructional Psychology and Technology (IP&T), 191, 240
Instructional Science, 295
Instructional Science and Technology Program, 249
Instructional Systems and Workforce Development, 193
Instructional Systems Technology, 183
Instructional technology
  corporate training and development
    instructional content, 5
    instructional delivery methods, 5
    instructional designers' professional prospects, 6
    learning expenditures, 4
  higher education
    faculty use of technology for instruction, 7
    students use of technology for learning, 8
    teaching and learning online, 8
    technology on campus, classrooms, and online, 6
  K-12 Education, 8–10
  overall developments, 4
Instructional Technology, 166, 189, 190, 208, 210, 231, 239, 247, 257, 258
Instructional Technology and Design, 234
Instructional Technology and Distance Education, 157
Instructional Technology and Institute for Interactive Technologies, 241
Instructional Technology Council (ITC), 106, 107
Instructional Technology Program, 216, 218, 221
Instructional Technology, Media Communication and Technology Department, 272
Intent to Apply for Admission Form, 218
Interactive Learning Environments, 288
International Academic Forum (IAFOR) conferences, 69

310　Index

International Association for Language
　　Learning Technology (IALLT),
　　107, 108
International Association of School
　　Librarianship (IASL), 108, 109
International Board of Standards for Training,
　　Performance and Instruction
　　(IBSTPI), 17, 188
International Center of Photography
　　(ICP), 109
International Council for Educational Media
　　(ICEM), 109–111
International Development, 69
International Journal of Computer-Supported
　　Collaborative Learning, 296
International Journal of Human-Computer
　　Interaction, 285, 295
International Journal of Robotics
　　Research, 285
International Journal of Science
　　Education, 296
International Journal of Technology and
　　Design Education, 292
International Journal on E-Learning, 303
International Recording Media Association
　　(IRMA), 111
International Society for Performance
　　Improvement (ISPI), 112
International Society for Technology in
　　Education (ISTE), 160, 249
International Standard Serial Number
　　(ISSN), 45
International Visual Literacy Association
　　(IVLA), 113
Internet and higher education, 303
Internet of Things (IoT), 5
Internet Reference Service Quarterly, 294, 303
Internet Research, 303
Iowa State University, 223
iSchool at Drexel, 241
IT jobs, 69
Ithaca College, 238

J

Journal articles, 282, 283
Journal inclusion criteria, 44
Journal of Access Services, 294
Journal of Computer Assisted Learning, 288
Journal of Computing in Higher
　　Education, 292
Journal of Database Management, 294
Journal of Digital Learning in Teacher
　　Education, 302

Journal of Documentation, 294
Journal of Educational Computing
　　Research, 288
Journal of Educational Multimedia and
　　Hypermedia, 288, 300
Journal of Educational Technology Systems,
　　292, 295
Journal of E-learning & Distance
　　Education, 289
Journal of Intelligent and Robotic
　　Systems, 286
Journal of Interactive Learning Research,
　　286, 290
Journal of Interactive Media in Education, 292
Journal of Interlibrary Loan, Document
　　Delivery & Electronic Reserve, 294
Journal of Librarianship and Information
　　Science, 297
Journal of Library & Information Services in
　　Distance Learning, 289
Journal of Library Administration, 297
Journal of Library Metadata, 294
Journal of Popular Film and Television, 300
Journal of Research on Technology in
　　Education, 288, 289
Journal of Science Education and
　　Technology, 292
Journal of Special Education Technology, 302
Journal of Technical Writing and
　　Communication, 295
Journal of Technology and Teacher
　　Education, 302
Journal of the Association for Information
　　Science and Technology, 294
Journal of the Learning Sciences, 296
Journal of Visual Literacy, 295

K

K-12 education, 14
　　technology availability and use in
　　　classrooms, 9, 10
　　trends to watch, 10
Keeping Pace with Digital Learning Report, 9
Keimyung University, 202
Kent State University, 164
Knowledge Alliance, 113, 114
Knowledge-Based Systems, 286

L

Language preservation, 68
Language Resources and Evaluation, 288
Leadership Studies, 209

Index

Learning Design and Technologies, 155, 156, 173, 178
Learning management system (LMS), 7
Learning Point Associates, 114, 115
Learning sciences, 283, 296
Learning Systems Technology, 252
Learning technologies (LT), 75, 85, 96, 107, 136, 159
Learning Technologies Program in the Department of Curriculum and Instruction, 191
Learning, Design, and Technology (LDT), 156, 157, 173–177, 192, 193
Learning, Media & Technology, 301
Learning, Media, and Technology Master's Program, 261
Lehigh University, 242
Lesley University, 228
Libraries and media Centers, 283, 297–300
Library & Information Science Research, 298
Library Administration and Management Association (LAMA), 115, 116
Library and Information Technology Association (LITA), 115
Library Hi Tech, 298
Library Journal, 298
Library Resources & Technical Services, 298
Library Trends, 298
Lister Hill National Center for Biomedical Communications (LHNCBC), 116, 117
Literacy and Technology/Educational Technology, 158
Live web chat, 14
Louisiana State University, 226

M

M.A. and Graduate Certificate in Educational Media and Technology, 230
M.A. in Communication and Training with HP&T major, 219
M.A. in Curriculum and Instruction, 218
M.A. in Curriculum and Instruction, Educational Technology, 177
M.A. in Education and Certificate of Advanced Study in Educational Technology, 256
M.A. in Educational Media and Technology, 237
M.A. in Educational Technology, 162
M.A. in Technology, Innovation, and Pedagogy, 155

M.A. Program in Public Communications, 238
M.A. Digital Technologies, Communication, and Education, 207
M.Ed. degree program in Educational Technology (EDTC), 269
M.Ed. in Computer Education and Technology, 240
M.Ed. in Educational Technology, 160, 180, 217, 246
M.Ed. in Instructional Technology, 225
M.Ed. in Instructional Technology, Media, and Design, 167
M.Ed. or Ed.D. in Curriculum and Instruction, 240
M.Ed. or M.A. in Computer/Technology or Library Media, 239
M.Ed. program, 156, 157, 164–168, 177, 179–181, 191, 196–199, 216–218, 223, 227, 228, 232, 235, 239, 240, 247–250, 267, 270, 272, 274
M.Ed. program in learning design and technologies, 156
M.S. degrees in Instructional Development and Educational Technology, 230
M.S. in Communications, 238
M.S. in Computer Education and Cognitive Systems, 248
M.S. in Education in Educational Technology, 237
M.S. in Education in Instructional Technology, 239
M.S. in Education in Instructional Technology (IT Online), 184
M.S. in Elementary Education with School Library concentration, 236
M.S. in Human Resource Education, 225
M.S. in Instructional Technology, 241
M.S. in Reading with School Library concentration, 236
M.S. in Secondary Education with School Library concentration, 236
MacWorld, 288
Management systems, 14
Management training, 68
Master of Arts (MA) degree in Instructional Technology, 190
Master of Arts in Curriculum and Educational Technology, 257
Master of Arts in Educational Technology, 161
Master of Arts in Instructional Technology (MAIT), 268
Master of Distance Education (MDE) program, 195

Master of Education in Educational
Technology, 160, 180
Master of Education in Instructional Systems
Design and Technology, 157, 158
Master of Educational Technology, 168
Master of Educational Technology Degree
Program, 198, 199
Master of Library and Information Science
(M.L.I.S.), 208, 226, 236, 237, 243
Master of Science (MS) in Library and
Information Science
curriculum, 241
Master of Science Degree in Library Science
(M.S.L.S.), 235
Master of Science Educational and
Instructional Technology, 181, 182
Master of Science in Educational Technology
(MSET) program, 245
Master of Science in Information Systems
(MSIS), 242
Master of Science in Instructional Design and
Performance Technology, 182, 183
Master of Science in Instructional Design and
Technology, 187
Master of Science in Instructional Science and
Technology, 253, 255
Master of Science in Instructional
Technology, 265
Master of Science in Learning and Teaching
Technologies, 202
Master of Science in Software Engineering
(MSSE), 242
Master of Training and Development
Program, 262
Master Technology Teacher (MTT)
Program, 274
Master's Degree in Educational Technology,
244, 259
Master's degree in Instructional
Technology, 222
Master's in Legal Information
Management, 224
Master's in Library Science Program, 236
Master's of Library Science, 224
Master's of Science in Instructional
Technology, 234
Master's program in Curriculum and
Instruction—Learning, Design, and
Technology, 174
Masters of Science in Learning Design and
Technology, 188
Math Science and Learning Technology
Doctoral Program, 261

McDaniel College, 229
Media & Methods, 301
Media AND, 44
Media Communications Association-
International (MCA-I), 117, 118
Media Education (Social Pedagogic
Faculty), 202
Media technologies, 281, 283, 300, 301
Mediagraphy, 281–283
Media-related journals, 281
Media-related organizations, 75
Media-related periodicals, 282
Medical Library Association (MLA), 118
MET admission requirements, 169
Metropolitan State College of Denver, 257
Michigan State University, 231
Mid-continent Research for Education and
Learning (McREL), 119
Middle East Technical University, 204
Middle-Secondary Education and Instructional
Technology, 216
Miller Analogies Test (MAT), 172, 244
Minds and Machines, 286
Minorities in Media (MIM), 119, 120
Mississippi State University, 193
Modularized and disaggregated degrees, 7
Montclair State University, 269
Morehead State University, 259
MSc Instructional Design and Technology, 193
Multichannel News, 301
MultiMedia & Internet@Schools, 301
Multimedia Systems, 301

N
NASA Jet Propulsion Lab, 69
National Aeronautics and Space
Administration (NASA), 120, 121
National Alliance for Media Arts and Culture
(NAMAC), 121
National Association for Visually Handicapped
(NAVH), 121, 122
National Association of Media and
Technology Centers (NAMTC),
122, 123
National Commission on Libraries and
Information Science (NCLIS), 123
National Communication Association (NCA),
123, 124
National Council for Accreditation of Teacher
Education (NCATE) standards, 17
National Council of Teachers of English
(NCTE), 124, 125

Index 313

National EBS Association (NEBSA), 125
National Education Policy Center, 8
National Endowment for the Humanities (NEH), 126
National Federation of Community Broadcasters (NFCB), 126, 127
National Film Board of Canada (NFBC), 127
National Freedom of Information Coalition (NFOIC), 127, 128
National Gallery of Art (NGA), 128
National PTA, 128, 129
National Public Broadcasting Archives (NPBA), 129
National Science Foundation grant, 69
National Telemedia Council (NTC), 130
National University, 181
Native American Public Telecommunications (NAPT), 130, 131
Natural Science Collections (NSC) Alliance, 131, 132
Networking, 303–304
New England School Library Association (NESLA), 132
New Media in Education Laboratory and Red-Ink Doctoral School, 203
New York Festivals (NYF), 132, 133
New York Institute of Technology, 267
New York University, 270
North Carolina Department of Public Instruction (NCDPI) Instructional Technology Specialists, 177
North Carolina State University, 178
Northern Illinois University, 220
Northwest College and University Council for the Management of Educational Technology (NW/MET), 133
Northwest Missouri State University, 232
Nova Southeastern University, 157

O
Oakland University, 262
Office of Graduate Programs, 196
Ohio State University, 207
Ohio University, 239
Old Dominion University, 275
Online Computer Library Center (OCLC), 134
Online Searcher, 304
Online Teaching and Learning, 256
Online tutoring sessions, 14–16
Ontario Film Association (OLA), 134, 135
Open Learning, 290
Organization, Information, and Learning Sciences (OILS) Program, 185

Organizational Leadership and Technology, 238
Organizational Performance and Workplace Learning (OPWL), 171
Overall developments, 4

P
Pacific Film Archive (PFA), 135
Pacific Resources for Education and Learning (PREL), 135–138
Penn State Great Valley School of Graduate Professional Studies, 273
Pennsylvania State University, 156
Performance Improvement Quarterly, 296
Ph.D. in Educational Leadership and Organizational Development, 225
Photography and film, 68
Piedmont College, 190
Pittsburg State University, 259
Positive attitude, 67
Professional development, 157, 176, 206, 207, 213, 256, 283, 302
Professional instructional design education programs, 21
Program description, 151
Program of Organization, Information, and Learning Sciences, 185
Program representatives, 151
Programmed Teaching Research and Development Center, 64
Programmed Tutoring projects, 64
Project management models, 24
ProQuest Microfilm, 282
Public Library Quarterly, 299
Purdue University, 172, 258
Python script, 45

R
RED-INK doctoral school, 203
Reference and User Services Association (RUSA), 138
Reference and User Services Quarterly, 299
Reference Services Review, 299
Reflective practice, 24
Regis University, 257
Remote tutoring sessions, 15
Research and communications, 68
Research and Development Division, 70
Research and outreach programs, 70
Research and pedagogy, 69
Research and psychology, 64
Research for Better Schools (RBS), 138, 139

Rethinking Education in the Knowledge Society (RED-INK), 203
Richard Stockton College of New Jersey, 268
Robotics education
    danger zone, 34
    development, 34
    eight robotic lessons for 5th grade, 34
    Honduras
        pre- and posttest overall scores, 38, 39
        reflection, 40
        STEM, 38
    Tanzania
        qualitative study, 40
        students and teachers, 41
    United States
        data collection and analysis, 36, 37
        five sites, 35
        mathematical curriculum, 35, 36
        reflection, 37
Robotics research, 286

S
Saba Meeting, 14
Sam Houston State University, 157
San Diego State University, 210
San Francisco State University, 212
San Jose State University, 210
School Library Journal, 299
School Library Media Specialists (SLMS), 270
School Library Monthly, 299
School Library Research, 299
School of Communication and Information, 236
School of Communications, 238
School of Education, 190, 226, 234
School of Education and Counseling, 257
School of Education and Graduate Studies, 267
School of Education and Human Development, 212
School of Information and Library Science, 235
School of Information Science and Learning Technologies, 233, 264
School of Library and Information Management, 223
School of Library and Information Science, 226
School of Library and Information Studies, 208
School of Teacher Education, 186
Science and Mathematics Education Department, 214
Science Communication, 292
Science, technology, engineering, and math (STEM), 38, 40, 41, 261
Sciences of Education, 202
Scopus scholarship database, 43
SERVE Center, 139, 140
Seton Hall University, 268
Significant skills, 68
Simulation, 283
Simulation & Gaming, 302
Simulation, gaming, and virtual reality, 302
Skills in instructional technology, 157
Skype, 14
Social Science Computer Review, 289, 292
Society for Photographic Education (SPE), 140, 141
Society of Cable Telecommunications Engineers (SCTE), 141, 142
Society of Photo Technologists (SPT), 142
Sociology, 64
Southern Illinois University at Carbondale, 219
Southern Illinois University Edwardsville, 221
Southwest Educational Development Laboratory (SEDL), 142, 143
Speak Up Survey, 9
Special education and disabilities, 283, 302
Special Libraries Association (SLA), 143, 144
St. Cloud State University, 232
Staff development and research, 96
State of the Industry Report survey, 4, 5
State of the States Report, 9
State University College of Arts and Science at Potsdam, 238
State University of New Jersey, 236
Statement of Objectives Form, 218
Steinhardt School of Culture, Education, and Human Development, 270
Student-centered programs, 196
Student council (StuCo) meetings, 14
Student group meetings, 14
Student Selection Examination, 206
Study groups, 14
Synchronous distance education
    face-to-face education, 13
    live web chat, 14
    remote tutoring sessions, 15
    student group meetings, 14
    video meetings, 14
    webinars, 15
Syracuse University, 271

Index

T

Taganrog State Pedagogical Institute, 202
Teacher Education, 230, 235
Teacher Librarian, 300
Teachers and Writers Collaborative (T&W), 144, 145
Teaching assignments, 64
Teaching, Learning, and Technology, 242
Team projects, 14
Technology AND, 44
Technology and Cognition (College of Education), 248
Technology in Education, 228
Technology, Innovation, and Education Program (TIE), 228
Technology, Innovation, and Pedagogy, 155
TechTrends, 292
Telecommunication, 287, 289, 291–293, 301, 303–304
Telecommunications and networking, 283, 303
Telematics and Informatics, 301
Temple University, 273
Texas A&M University, 246, 274
Texas Tech University, 247
TOEFL admission score, 154
Towson University, 230
Training, 296
2020 scholarship rankings
    countries producing most scholarship, 51
    data analysis, 45
    data retrieval, 45
    database selection, 44
    frequent author keywords in articles, 54–55
    journal inclusion criteria, 44
    top-cited articles, 52–53
    universities producing most scholarship, 51, 52
    US authors publications
        medal count score, 45, 46
        top global authors, 47
        top most cited global authors, 45, 49, 50

U

Undergraduate Library Science Program, 236
Undergraduate major and minor in Information Media, 232
UNI Instructional Technology Master's program, 219
United States Office of Occupational Statistics and Employment Projections, 6
Università della Svizzera italiana, 203
Université de Poitiers, 200

Universiti Sains Malaysia, 201
University Continuing Education Association (UCEA), 147
University of Alabama, 208
University of Alaska Southeast, 251
University of Arkansas, 251
University of Arkansas at Little Rock, 252
University of Balearic Islands, 202
University of Bridgeport, 257
University of British Columbia, 198
University of Calgary, 195, 196
University of Central Arkansas, 209
University of Central Florida, 215
University of Cincinnati, 240
University of Colorado Denver, 212
University of Connecticut, 213
University of Delaware, 160
University of Florida, 175
University of Geneva, 202
University of Georgia, 193
University of Hawaii-Manoa, 217
University of Hong Kong, 199
University of Houston, 173
University of Illinois at Urbana-Champaign, 220
University of Louisville, 225
University of Manchester, 206
University of Massachusetts, 261
University of Memphis, 179
University of Michigan, 263
University of Minnesota, 191
University of Missouri, 264, 265
University of Missouri-Columbia, 233
University of Montana, 234
University of Nebraska at Kearney, 235
University of Nebraska-Omaha, 235
University of New Brunswick, 198
University of New Mexico, 185
University of North Carolina, 176, 235, 265
University of North Dakota, 267
University of North Texas, 248
University of Northern Colorado, 155
University of Northern Iowa, 218
University of Oklahoma, 240
University of Rhode Island, 243
University of Saskatchewan, 199
University of South Alabama, 184
University of South Carolina Aiken, 244
University of South Carolina Columbia, 244
University of South Florida, 216
University of Southern California, 211
University of Southern Mississippi, 234
University of Tampa, 187
University of Texas at Brownsville, 274

Index

University of Texas Rio Grande Valley, 180
University of the West Indies Open
  Campus, 193
University of Toledo, 166
University of Virginia, 249
University of Washington, 250
University of West Florida, 165
University of West Georgia, 167
University of Wisconsin-Madison, 276
University of Wyoming, 192
Utah State University, 248
Utrecht University, 203

V

Valdosta State University, 217
Valley City State University, 267
Videodiscs, 68
Virginia Tech, 188
Virtual Instructional Team for the
  Advancement of Learning
  (VITAL), 216

Virtual reality (VR), 7, 283

W

Wayne State University, 231
Webinars, 15
Western Illinois University, 153
Western Kentucky University, 186
Western Maryland College, *see*
  McDaniel College
Widener University, 208
Winthrop University, 173
Wireless Networks, 289
Workforce and Human Resource Education
  Program, 225
Wright State University, 239

Y

Young Adult Library Services Association
  (YALSA), 147, 148